CHANT ROYAL

CHANT ROYAL

The Life of King Louis XI of France (1423–1483)

JAMES CLEUGH

DOUBLEDAY & COMPANY, INC., GARDEN CITY, NEW YORK

Library of Congress Catalog Card Number 71–89078
Copyright © 1970 by James Cleugh
All Rights Reserved
Printed in the United States of America
First Edition

The so-called *Chant Royal* form of medieval French poetry was generally considered suitable for heroic themes. In borrowing the title for a prose biography of King Louis XI of France I wished to suggest a view of this king's career less common than that taken by most historians.

J.C.

CONTENTS

ILLUSTRATIONS

(following page 144)

1. Louis XI, King of France
2. Princess Margaret of Scotland, Dauphine of France
3. Charles VII, King of France
4. Agnès Sorel
5. Henry VI, King of England
6. Margaret of Anjou, Queen of England

(following page 168)

7. Duke Charles the Bold of Burgundy
8. Margaret of York, Duchess of Burgundy, wife of Charles the Bold
9. Jacques Coeur
10. Manor of Plessis
11. Castle of Méhun
12. Philippe de Commines
13. King Edward IV of England

CHANT ROYAL

CHAPTER I

The Court of Charles VII
(1423–1439)

✣✣✣ At the hour of siesta in the afternoon of July 3, 1423, the bells of the old town of Bourges in the very center of France suddenly started to ring wildly. Somnolent citizens stirred uneasily on their couches, then sat up in alarm. Was it the English or the Burgundians or the Paris traitors this time? The gunners, archers and musketeers posted along the walls stared out in all directions over the marshes sloping down from the hillock on which the city stood. But they could see no sign of approaching troops, neither banners nor lances. Soon they began to detect rhythms of gaiety rather than panic in the reckless chiming. In the previously silent streets people came running from the churches, at first singly, then increasingly in groups. They were waving their arms, cheering and laughing. For once then, the news must be good, not bad. Within the next few minutes everyone in Bourges knew that the queen they loved, the gentle, pious Marie of Anjou, had been delivered of a son.

Her husband Charles, a pale, knock-kneed youth of twenty, considered as weak mentally as physically, was known only as the "king of Bourges," since he was still uncrowned as king of France. He had retired to that capital of the duchy of Berry after the death of his imbecile father, King Charles VI, in October 1422. The southern provinces for the most part acknowledged the young man as Charles VII. But Paris and the north had long submitted to the duke of Bedford, acting for the infant king, Henry VI of England, son of Catherine, daughter of Charles VI, by King Henry V of England and France, who had himself died two months before his helpless rival, Charles VI.

Charles VII remained on good terms with the duke, who was on the whole a firm and just administrator of the half-conquered country. The "king of Bourges" had in fact neither the money nor the prestige to oppose the English government, which had behind it the powerful duke of Burgundy, Philip the Good, then aged twenty-seven, a publicly calm, privately somewhat tempestuous personality. Charles's authority had been ruined through the murder by his adherents, in his presence though probably not by his wish, of Philip's decidedly objectionable father, Duke John the Fearless, in 1419. This affair caused Philip to prefer the soldierly Henry V to what both men considered the degenerate dynasty of King Charles VI, to take charge of France.

But Charles VII, unlike his idiot father, was not wholly a fool. His weakness of body and mind did not affect a genuine patriotism which looked beyond military exploits for its expression. His cowardice in youth became courage in middle age. Above all, throughout his life, an unpretentious sociability enabled him to secure the loyalty, to an extraordinary degree, of several far abler and stronger gentlemen at his court, and even of citizens who seldom met him. At this period he and his "most gentle" queen, Marie, no beauty, but in every other respect a model wife, were delightful people to be with, so long as bold action was not required of them.

At Bourges they lived in an extension of the Cathedral of St. Étienne, then as now one of the most important Gothic churches in France. It had splendid stained-glass windows, but the matrimonial bedchamber was not very well furnished. The tapestries of the former kings of France still remained in Paris. Some rather dilapidated textiles covered the walls and furniture. These figured cloths were held by Charles on loan from his cousin the duke of Orléans, a prisoner of war in England since the fatal battle of Agincourt in 1415, where the heavily armored French cavalry had been slaughtered in thousands by the fast-shooting archers and agile swordsmen of the English, far outnumbered as the invaders were.

As for Charles and Queen Marie, they were not much better off than Duke Charles of Orléans. For the wretched condition of France as a whole had begun under the demented Charles VI. On November 23, 1407, at the orders of John the Fearless, the cynically ambitious duke of Burgundy, whose surviving portraits leave no doubt of his vulgarly aggressive character, some young men assassinated in a Paris street his cousin Louis, the king's brother and at that time duke of Orléans. Louis and John, Philip's father, had long been competing for the French throne, which Charles VI was obviously not fit to occupy. The murder of the Valois prince gave the signal for civil war between the supporters of Burgundy and Orléans. The latter duchy headed a coalition of Gascony, Languedoc and Armagnac. But this conflict produced no large-scale battles, merely a series of indecisive skirmishes and raids.

The Paris Council, which adhered to the Orléans faction, decided to banish Queen Isabeau, wife of Charles VI, who had been the mistress of the murdered Louis. For since his death she had not only been practicing fornication to an inordinate degree but also political treachery. She found as many lovers among the Burgundians as among the citizens of her other favorite province, Armagnac. The queen, then a year or two short of thirty, and a resplendent, able and utterly unscrupulous nymphomaniac, next coolly called in her late lover's murderer, the unconscionable John the Fearless, and surrendered Paris to him. Her sixteen-year-old son, the dauphin Charles, had to run for his life, escaping at the last moment, on May 29, 1418, to Bourges. There he eventually set up a court, as regent for his father, in opposition to Isabeau.

But she and John, both typical adventurers of the forceful, glittering type, contrived to be popular with the volatile Parisians. They persuaded the citizens that the English, who already held half the country after their victory at Agincourt, would be their best allies against the feeble posterity of Charles VI. The islanders duly took over the capital and added Rouen, the chief city of Normandy, to their booty. In these circumstances the dauphin's advisers recommmended a truce. He and John swore peace on a bridge over the Seine, some miles southeast of Paris, on July 11, 1419. Then the dauphin's party, evidently with revised intentions, proposed a fresh interview. It took place on September 10, at the bridge of Montereau, further up the river. As the two groups faced each other one of Charles's escorts, alleged by some chroniclers to have been a certain Tanneguy de Chastel, suddenly swung up a battle-ax and cut down the duke, who was instantly dispatched by the rest of the Valois party.

This faithless act of brutish violence did not do them much good. The imperturbable Queen Isabeau transferred her important affections to the dead man's son and successor Philip, then aged twenty-three, who never refused the chance of an additional mistress. She disinherited young Charles and appointed King Henry V of England, the victor at Agincourt, regent for Charles VI. It was agreed that the English monarch's eldest son, not yet born, should accede as legitimate heir to the French throne. The dauphin could make no headway against the combined English and Burgundians. His troops were defeated again and again. At last, in 1421, by which time the future King Henry VI of England had come into existence, the despised and rejected young pretender to the French crown settled at Bourges. In 1422, six months before his father died on October 22 in that year and four months before the death of Henry V, the dauphin Charles married Princess Marie of Anjou. Some people thought such a lunatic as Charles VI could not have generated so serious and well-meaning a youth as the unfortunate "king of Bourges." They convinced him for a while that his real parent must have been one of Isabeau's innumerable lovers.

Such was the position when a first son was born to Charles VII, as the southern provinces called their crownless king, and Queen Marie in July 1423. The Anglo-Burgundians tried to seize the infant after again defeating Charles at Cravant, about a hundred miles southeast of Paris, in that same year. But their troops were thrown back from the very walls of Bourges. It was the loyalists' first victory. Charles never forgot it. Both he and his children were forever after grateful to the city.

The little boy had been baptized Louis, at the request of the pious queen, in memory of the canonized king of France, Louis IX (1214–1270), heroic crusader, tallest warrior of his day, a deeply religious and chaste ascetic among his mainly all-too-human knights and absolutely sure of himself without being in the least conceited. He even possessed a somewhat grim sense of humor. But his endless devotion to masses, priests and sermons, coupled with the hair shirts he inflicted on his friends, wore out most of his courtiers. Louis XI could not live up to this ancestral standard as either dauphin or king. Perhaps no one born in the fifteenth century could do so. But in some respects, in the plainness of his dress, for instance, so conspicuous at a period of sartorial extravagance, in his iron will and ease of manner toward social inferiors, he came near it.

For most of the life of Louis the great ducal house of Burgundy overshadowed French history. It was unique among the duchies of France in holding not only its compact state in the west, bordered by Champagne, Lorraine, Franche-Comté and Nivernais, and running as far south as Lyons, but also territory in the north, Flanders, what is now Belgium and parts of Holland. Burgundian wealth arose largely from the manufacturing and trading centers in this area, though Burgundy itself had always been agriculturally rich. In these circumstances Burgundian civilization, more stable than that of the rest of France for most of the fifteenth century, may be thought, apart from people like John the Fearless, to have eclipsed French in general cultivation and outward splendor. In any case Burgundian prosperity and prestige, especially under Philip the Good (1396–1467), influenced all Europe north of the Alps. Philip, a tall, handsome man of distinguished presence, had a positively Italian love of luxury and pomp, literature and scholarship, commerce and industry. He patronized such eminent men of letters as Georges Chastelain, poet and historian, the memorialist Olivier de la Marche, champion of Burgundian feudal glories against all comers, and Antoine de la Salle, author of one of the most famous satires in French, *Les Quinze Joyes de Mariage*, supposed also to have been concerned with equally popular collection of tales of life at Philip's court, the *Cent Nouvelles Nouvelles*, and certainly responsible for *Petit Jehan de Saintré*, a highly entertaining account of education and manners in his time.

In the very year, 1423, of the birth of the future Louis XI, Duke Philip gave his sister Anne in marriage to the duke of Bedford and proceeded to throw in his lot with the English for twelve years. This official alliance brought Charles into greater danger than ever. Bourges was no longer considered safe for Louis, whom the two dukes already wanted to kidnap. The boy therefore spent his childhood in the loyal provinces of Berry and Touraine, while his parents, almost as if they were on the run from Anglo-Burgundian aggression, traveled from one fortified city in southern France to another.

Under such conditions the child never had a chance, during this crucial period of a developing mentality, to get to know and feel affection for either father or mother. Brought up by substitutes who seem to have been simple yokels, he felt much less like a prince than a peasant. By the time he was admitted to the poverty-stricken Valois court he had, fortunately enough in the circumstances, come to despise ceremony and fine clothes. He actually looked, with his usually uncouth, sullen expression and clumsy movements, like a somewhat overworked farmer's boy. But at seven he already showed signs of a stouter physique than his fragile father's. At this date he had acquired a governess, a woman of good family, one Madame de la Trémoille. This lady, however, while deafening everyone with her protestations of austere virtue and piety, turned out to be in reality a harlot and dissembler. Louis, though precocious, was not yet quite old enough to have derived his later misogynism from these revelations. He probably disliked Mme de la Trémoille, in the usual manner of strong-minded children of his age, about as much as he objected to the severity of a tutor, Jean Majoris, who appeared in the household at approximately the same time. Majoris, nevertheless, appears to have been a perfectly straightforward character, a true scholar and a man of integrity. Yet Louis, whose respect for culture took a considerable time to develop, is again unlikely to have been any more influenced, at his age, by his male than by his female mentor.

The question of his marriage, as was usual in that age where children of exalted birth were concerned, had long since been raised. In 1428 King James I of Scotland replied favorably to Charles's inquiry as to the availability of James's eldest daughter Margaret. It was a natural choice in view of the long history of Scottish hostility to England at this date. James had been captured by the English but well treated by Henry V. By 1424 he was back in Scotland with an English wife and a respect for English administration. But he had made no attempt to withdraw Charles's Scottish bodyguard and it was obvious that most of the nobility of Scotland detested their sovereign's Anglophile ideas. In fact, they murdered him nine years later.

It could not be helped that James I was nearly as poor as Charles, the French pretender, and his cousin and brother-in-law René of Anjou. Nothing better could be expected in the state of France just then. But at least a Scottish connection could be trusted to constitute a nuisance, if nothing more, to the most deadly enemies of Charles, the English. The vagrant Valois court remained almost literally beggared. The "king of Bourges" sold his jewelry and sent his old doublets to be patched. Certain tradesmen refused him credit. The queen's wardrobe contained hardly any linen.

Negotiations with James began. But it was clear that they were going to take time. In Scotland opposition to the match obtained support from Margaret's own brother and a number of other lords who feared that English objections might lead to a renewal of the wars that had ended disastrously for the Scots at the battle of Homildon Hill in 1402. Revenge for this defeat might be in the air at Edinburgh. But for the moment the earls were working underground to that end and could hope for no substantial aid from a foreign monarch still uncrowned, living on the edge of destitution and in any case, so far as anyone could see at present, the very reverse of a gallant warrior, however agreeable his manners might be.

For the English in France were already besieging Orléans and repulsing all French attempts to relieve the town. Then, early in 1429, a strange dark-haired young woman in male dress which suited her robust build and confident smile, was brought before the desperately weary French king, whose natural charm had by this time almost vanished under the incessant pressure of his frustrations. Disappointment had turned his formerly mobile features into a set, pallid mask. His face expressed nothing but boredom, hardened by suspicion, as the girl told him she was from Lorraine and had been repeatedly commanded by God, as she watched her sheep, to free France from the "Goddams," as the invaders were generally called from their favorite oath. Charles had heard this sort of talk before, though never from a nineteen-year-old peasant, male or female. It had always previously turned out to be hopelessly unpractical. He could only temporize, as formerly, by appointing a commission to inquire into the antecedents of "Jeanne d'Arc," as his visitor named herself, thereby admitting her sex and adding to the king's inclination to dismiss her out of hand.

But nothing, either socially or theologically, could be proved against

Jeanne. She was authenticated as a respectable farmer's daughter, appropriately enough employed to keep flocks from straying, and an orthodox Catholic who could not possibly be suspected of heresy or fraud in her detailed account of the "heavenly voices" she had heard in the Lorraine pastures. At last she was allowed to go to Tours for consultation with the military staff. No one in France at that time was in a position to deny absolutely that an honest woman might receive personal messages from the Creator. It remained to be seen whether she could impress professional soldiers. She did so. They presented her with full armor, a banner and every facility to raise a force for the relief of Orléans.

In May she entered the town, not without some fighting, and held it successfully. By July she had persuaded the still dubious Charles to be crowned legitimate king of France at Reims. Bedford withdrew from Paris. But the king still would not advance on the capital. He wished first to detach Philip of Burgundy from the foreigners. At last, on August 28, an armistice was signed with the Burgundians. "Joan the Witch," as the English called her, assaulted Paris. But when an arrow from the walls hit her in the thigh and she was dragged, protesting loudly, from the open ground, her forces retired. Unable to ride and surrounded by respectful, middle-aged captains who advised her to take a few weeks' rest and return to the charge at the head of an army inspired by her recovery, she bowed eventually to their experience of so many campaigns and allowed herself to be carried to Charles's court. In October she felt well enough to take part in some further active service, but with only partial success.

After going into winter quarters she took the field again in May 1430, making for Compiègne on the road to Paris. Joan entered the former town unopposed. But there were two hostile camps in the neighborhood, that of the Burgundians, whose truce with the French had long since expired, and, close by, that of the English. Joan led a sortie against the Burgundians. But her men were driven back and she was captured in a desperate endeavor to cover their retreat. Jean de Luxembourg, the Burgundian commander, was persuaded by the duke of Bedford, who was determined to destroy this "saint" in the ranks of his enemies, to sell her to the English. Charles made no attempt to help her. The tragic sequel is well known. The Maid was burned alive, ostensibly for heresy, in the market square at Rouen on May 30, 1431. The future Louis XI, then eight years old, was probably, but not certainly, incapable of judging the cowardly conduct of his father in not even trying to rescue the prisoner to whom he owed his crown, however much of a farce the ceremony at Reims might have been. Charles's character strengthened to some extent during the next two decades, and by 1456 he had made amends to the memory of Joan of Arc. But Louis never really respected him. It would be too much to say that the king's deplorable behavior between 1425 and 1431 caused the dauphin, as he grew up, to despise his unstable parent. The two men were just mentally incompatible. The final break between them did not occur for another twenty years. But it had been inevitable from the start.

It is interesting to find that according to a German chronicler the boy had seen Joan of Arc at Loches in Touraine, where she had come to visit the seven-year-old heir to the French throne. She bent over him, the story goes, in her usual intent manner, studying the child's pale, serious features and unwinking, gray-green stare. "You will be a great king, Louis," she is said to have told him. "But not till you are near thirty. Your father will last that time." The forecast was out by over ten years, a period which was to be one of furious impatience for the dauphin. But if the tale is true the little prince must have been agreeably impressed by the Maid's informal use of his Christian name, as was her habit even in speaking to Charles himself, whom she often called "Charlot," perhaps with some good-natured contempt for that young man's cautious irresolution in her presence. Louis may well have remembered Joan, in afterlife, as the one woman he could ever bring himself to admire wholeheartedly.

Meanwhile the boy's education, largely theological, but also historical, proceeded mainly in Touraine. In addition, he learned Latin, how to deal with official correspondence and how to handle weapons. Of these various disciplines he enjoyed chiefly the history of France and the writing of dispatches. Both were to absorb him to the very end of his life, not without profit to the development of civilization. He himself made a decisive contribution to the rescue of French culture from the disastrous mirage of medieval chivalry. His two thousand surviving letters are models of lucidity and point in an era of cumbersome baroque in prose except for the works of the great Philippe de Commines, his intimate friend. Philippe's literary genius is unquestionable. He wrote like Thucydides in an age which preferred Ammianus Marcellinus. But it is probably true that his judgment, in his anxiety to represent Louis as a prodigy of diplomatic skill, was sometimes seriously at fault.

The years of anarchy and civil war in central France, while the English still held on to the north of the country, were scarcely interrupted by the death of the duke of Bedford in 1435 and the Treaty of Arras between Charles VII and Philip of Burgundy, which was concluded in the same year, rendering the duchy practically independent of the kingdom of France. Partly as a result of these conditions the dauphin was transferred from Loches to Amboise, further up the Loire, between Tours and Blois, in 1433. At Amboise he joined his mother, Marie of Anjou, whom he had previously so seldom seen. The castle, pleasantly situated in that glorious landscape, had a terrace on which he could play tennis or practice archery in the intervals of contemplating an extensive view over the picturesque valley, with its broad and fast river flowing at the foot of two great towers which lent his new home the aspect of a fortress. Time passed agreeably there under the contrasted stimulations of lessons and sport. The prince's exceptional energy rose rapidly to meet them. Unlike the majority of aristocratic youths of the day he never discovered the least interest in romantic dreams of chivalrous combat and amorous passion, both of them governed by rules of extreme intricacy and very little practical importance. Louis had no objection to rules now. In fact, he rather liked them. He was a ready learner. But he wished what he learned to enable him to restore and raise to solid power, at the earliest possible opportunity, the distracted realms he would one day inherit. Business matters, therefore, commerce and industry, and above all politics, interested him far more than the glittering panoplies of either war or love, as these phenomena were understood by the European nobles of the fifteenth century.

He was growing fast and already felt fiercely impatient to play his part in public affairs. But he heard little of them. Queen Marie took small interest in news which was always bad. At any rate she remained either incapable of or averse to explaining matters of high policy to a boy of twelve except in the most general terms. All the same, important things were happening on the chessboard of the Continent. He plagued his tutors for details of them.

But no one seemed to know exactly how things were going. Charles, enigmatic as ever, came rather more often to Amboise. He was closeted for hours with his steward, with Queen Marie or with Jean Majoris. In due course the royal household began to eat better, to wear slightly grander clothes and smile more often. Certainly no one could suppose, on looking out from the castle terrace, that the country was anything but prosperous. Shipping crowded the Loire, sailing down from Orléans to Tours and back again. Majoris told Louis that some of the larger vessels went as far as Nantes in Brittany and even out into the Atlantic. But they had to be armed. The Bretons, according to Monsieur Jean, were a lawless sort of people, much given to piracy, and the English still worse, capable of kidnaping even kings like James I of Scotland on the high seas.

But the people of Touraine, the tutor went on confidently, had nothing to fear so long as they stayed where they were, exploiting their rich forests, vineyards and meadows, and not attempting to travel into the turbulent and treacherous north. He instructed the dauphin, who listened with strained attention, in the meaning of economic self-sufficiency, the only effective guarantee of any community against the greed and violence of its neighbors. The boy was shown a map of France, on which his father's domains seemed to reach from Poitou, south of Brittany in the west, to Languedoc and Dauphiné, south of Burgundy, in the southeast. But Gascony and Bordeaux in the southwest, he was told, were unreliable, full of Goddams.

In 1434 Charles's advisers suggested that the time might be ripe, now that he had a well-grown and promising heir, to test the loyalty of his official subjects. The king, for a start, took Louis with him to Tours, where the young prince made such a good impression that it was decided to leave him there for a while. Presents of clothes and jewels for the boy fairly rained in from the warmhearted citizens, whose natural generosity and optimism had been immensely stimulated by the prospect of at last having a king with some common sense and energy. For another two years, until he was fourteen, his education went on at Tours, where Jean Majoris now called his pupil's attention explicitly to the teachings of a more eminent scholar, the philanthropic moralist Jean Gerson, a former chancellor of the University of Paris who had died in 1429. These maxims had always inspired Jean's own theories of education, and their influence still eclipsed that of any other French cleric of this period.

Majoris now considered the boy capable of absorbing, in particular, Gerson's eloquent insistence upon humility and self-sacrifice, upon both the letter and the spirit of true Christianity, coupled with the shrewd observation that these virtues never failed to pay off eventually in practical affairs. Louis seemed to take this point with remarkable readiness. In fact, he had frequent occasions in later life, when he saw arrogant and selfish princes go down to ruin, to remember how often his old tutor had been right.

At Tours the dauphin, poring over illuminated manuscripts of past ages, which his father, who knew little about such things, had given him at the prompting of people who did know something of them, found his previous impression of the importance of historical study confirmed in a very special way. He came to the conclusion that similar situations occurred repeatedly in the course of public events, forming, therefore, a most useful series of precedents for a future ruler of men. All one had to do was to allow, in calculating personal action, for certain social changes, the substitution, for instance, of relatively small units of political power and a unified religion for the vast monolith, with its hundreds of faiths and nations, of the ancient Roman Empire.

He read, spoke and wrote Latin and Italian with ease. His command of his native tongue was extensive and precise, often tending, in the typical French style, to irony. At fourteen his naturally intense curiosity and highly developed sense of vocation had led him to learn so much from records on paper and the conversation of his older contemporaries that he felt these sources had little more to teach him. He was wrong, of course. Actual independent dealings with life were to instruct him far more deeply and widely in the vagaries of human nature. He came to know more about it than most people, even other kings and other men of genius like Philippe de Commines. But at any rate by the time that his marriage was definitely decided upon in the spring of 1436, the prince considered, with much justification, that his childhood had ended.

Charles had already noticed in Louis signs of that kind of stubbornness in a boy on the threshold of puberty which is often softened by feminine influence. That girls bored the robust young student of history was obvious enough, but it was inconceivable for an heir to the French throne not to marry. Whatever his disposition might be it was his irrevocable duty to propagate his line, and the sooner the better. In 1435 the king was suddenly jerked into action on this matter by the news that certain English lords were after Margaret of Scotland as a politically desirable bride for the fifteen-year-old King Henry VI of England. This union would be a step up in the world for her impoverished father James I, a monarch uneasy among dangerously contending nobles. He liked the English well enough and appreciated his wife Jane Beaufort, a daughter of the earl of Somerset. But personal inclination was one thing, patriotism another. A political union of hereditary foes was the last project either he or the majority of his subjects could agree to. He now rapidly came to terms with Charles.

Princess Margaret, aged twelve, arrived at La Rochelle on April 17, 1436, after a prolonged voyage of three weeks due to the need to avoid English corsairs, who were at their old game of recklessly kidnaping royal personages between wind and water. Her escort persuaded the sentimentally rapturous local authorities that she needed a rest after all these excitements. The royal family of France remained tactfully invisible for the time being. Margaret was quartered in a monastery near the city, with her numerous attendants, for another three weeks. Then she proceeded slowly as far as Poitiers, some eighty miles to the northwest, reaching the town on May 20. The streets were festively decorated, the crowds gay. Arches of flowers and garlands strung between the houses provided a setting for formal singing and dancing.

Charles, who was busy elsewhere, kept up a cordial correspondence with the Scottish visitors. But he told them quite bluntly that he simply couldn't afford to keep the whole two thousand of them in his kingdom indefinitely. In these circumstances most of the Scots gradually re-embarked for less ecstatic scenes in their relatively gloomy native land.

At Poitiers two highly born French ladies taught little Margaret the etiquette and language of the French court. The marriage, it was announced, would take place at Tours on June 25. The delay had been due to the need for ecclesiastical dispensation, required in view of the extreme youth of both parties. The princess was affectionately greeted by the sweet-natured Queen Marie at the Tours court on the twenty-fourth. It was the first occasion for official rejoicing that the royal household had experienced since Charles VII became king. But, as compared with other such contemporary celebrations, it didn't amount to much. No expensive jousting was organized, merely a rather modest banquet. The tapestries of the duke of Orléans were again hauled out to cover the naked walls of the castle at Montilz-les-Tours. The loyal city of Chinon on the other side of the Loire, about thirty miles to the southwest, supplied silver plate for the table.

Now at last young Louis, skinny, sharp-nosed and perfectly self-possessed, entered the castle hall from below stairs. He knew well enough what was expected of him. The children kissed and played together in the presence of the gorgeously arrayed adults of the court, who stood around the walls against the faded, here and there threadbare textiles of Charles d'Orléans. Margaret looked charming, like most well-bred girls of twelve. One delighted onlooker compared her little face with a "star." But others whispered that she was evidently not going to set the Loire on fire. The best thing about her rather doll-like countenance was a certain suggestion, not uncommon among schoolgirls, of intellectual leanings. The prince probably did not even notice it. If he did, his mood of dutiful dedication to a burdensome but inevitable task would certainly not have changed. Girls were all alike to him, whatever their characters, earnest or frivolous. Unfortunately, the maintenance of the Valois dynasty required him to undertake physical intimacy with at least one of them. But fortunately psychological conjunction for this purpose would be quite unnecessary. So all this distasteful prancing in the castle hall was merely a prelude, never to be repeated, he hoped, to quite a simple matter, a good deal easier, he had been given to understand, than fencing or tennis.

He noted with carefully veiled contempt the little Scotch girl's awkwardness in her great crimson mantle and how she kept touching her coronet to make sure it did not fall off. He himself, he knew, presented a much more grown-up figure. A long, heavy nose, irregular but mobile features and bony legs rather enhanced than otherwise his mature appearance. So, too, did the keen and haughty glances he flashed around at the attentive spectators. So did the brisk yet controlled movements he owed to his sedulous athletic training. The velvet doublet he wore, embroidered in gold, and the great sword, a gift from James I, on the hilt of which he took care to rest his left hand continuously, were not in the least inferior to those of the French and Scottish noblemen present, among whom he recognized his uncle Charles, count of Anjou and Maine, the count of Vendôme and the earl of Orkney, ambassador to the French court.

Their self-consciously theatrical bearing and ostentatious attire contrasted with the long, soberly colored robes of the stately ecclesiastics and lawyers, from the archbishop of Reims and the chancellor downward. The French secular peers, all clean-shaven on account of the lately introduced shape of their helmets' chinpieces, had much bigger sleeves, some almost touching the floor, to their slashed and padded doublets than the bearded Scottish lords. Fantastically long, pointed shoes called attention to their tight, groin-length hose. The ladies grouped around Queen Marie sported extraordinarily elaborate linen headgear, with wings like a huge bird's, which were always getting in one another's way. But they showed so little hair that its color could rarely be identified. Against the florid, complex design of the wall tapestries these motionless but occasionally murmuring figures of the social elite of France beheld with mixed feelings their future rulers, neither of them appealing much to contemporary taste in budding royalties, going through the motions of a decorous ballet, in which they had each been coached beforehand.

Charles arrived next day, in time for the wedding. He had little fault to find with his new daughter-in-law. She was pretty enough and lively enough, he supposed, to attract a boyish husband. It remained to be seen whether she would be prolific. As for the dauphin, his father for the first time began to admire his high, arched brows, typically a thinker's, his piercing, resolute glance and firmly set chin. Also, the boy looked as if he knew what he was doing, which Charles himself seldom did, even on this important occasion. The monarch, in fact, had not bothered to change his gray riding suit for the ceremony. He tramped up the nave in his great boots and jingling spurs, to the great scandal of the archbishop and his subordinate clergy, while the Scottish lords ground their teeth, interpreting this carelessness as a studied insult to their poor but proud nation.

Nothing, however, could have been further from the king's thoughts at that moment. He was really glad of the marriage, which would be a definite counterbalance, he believed, to the permanent English danger.

But no one ever understood what Charles VII might be thinking, if anything. His misfortunes had given his lean, pallid features an expression, in almost all circumstances, as of a not very intelligent man faced with a problem he was determined neither to try to understand nor to allow anyone else to imagine he was going to tackle. His court painter, Jean Fouquet, the supreme French artist of the fifteenth century, rendered this look precisely in oils a few years later. No one could be sure, in the cathedral of Tours on that morning at the end of June 1436, whether the king approved, was indifferent to, or was irritated by the union of his first-born with Princess Margaret of Scotland. The politely closed, bloodless countenance showed no emotion of any kind. Actually, he felt pretty sure that, his country being in the state it was, he could have done no better for Louis.

He dismissed the last of the bride's Scottish escort rather summarily, with comparatively few presents. Arrangements were made for the future queen to be turned into a Frenchwoman with the least possible delay, under the tutelage of his own wife, the tactful, devout and unassuming Marie of Anjou. The court doctors, despite the dispensation, advised against immediate physical consummation of the marriage, in view of the immaturity of both partners. It was felt that their health and consequently that of any offspring they might have would be undesirably affected by sexual congress until at least two more years had passed. Louis could not have cared less. He was not much attracted by what he had seen of Margaret and was burning to achieve manhood by embarking in political rather than erotic activities. He was delighted when his father proposed, as before, that they should set out together, leaving the princess to complete her education, on a long tour of the kingdom, taking in at least Auvergne, Clermont-Ferrand, Lyons and Languedoc.

But the social relations between Charles and his dauphin, comparative strangers, neither of whom yet knew quite what to make of the other, were not then close enough to allow this business trip to assume the character of a family picnic. The king remained a bit nervous of his son, whose surprisingly ripe intelligence, coupled with a certain secretiveness and severity of temper, were daily confirmed by his tutors. Louis on his side had already begun to be more repelled than seduced by his father's too easy good nature and also to scorn so indolent a monarch, incapable, apparently, of thinking for himself. Charles saw that, as usual, he was not making much of an impression on a potentially important personage. He decided that it would be best for the forthcoming journey to proceed on parallel rather than on interweaving lines, which might produce friction.

Accordingly, he gave Louis a household of his own, to ride separately from his own party and sleep in different accommodations. The prince's new retinue included a "governor," the Comte de la Marche, not of course the verbose Burgundian chronicler of that name, but a guardian rather too pious for the boy's liking, together with the faithful and discreet Jean Majoris, a confessor, a chaplain and a private physician. There were also a Master of the Horse, a treasurer and a secretary. The dauphin threw himself with zest into the company of these people, all much older than himself and only too anxious to instruct and serve him. He found them on the whole more frank and energetic than his father's closest councilors, men like Charles of Anjou, the Constable Arthur de Richemont, brother of the equivocal Jean V, duke of Brittany, the celebrated and successful soldier Jean count of Dunois, affectionately known as the Bastard of Orléans, an old comrade-in-arms of Joan of Arc, and a considerably younger officer, Pierre de Brézé, able, honorable and discreet as well as handsome and gay. These advisers all had a good influence on their weak sovereign, keeping him up to the mark in his genuine but too easily disconcerted patriotism. Louis's group, equally set on saving France from the English but favoring a bolder policy, since they saw that this was what their young chief wanted, formed, at first unconsciously, a sort of opposition to the royal government.

As the tour proceeded the prince found himself most interested in the great cloth-manufacturing city of Lyons. He could already see that trade was more important to the welfare of a nation than pikes and lances, and a merchant like Jacques Coeur, Master of the Mint and minister of finance to Charles VII, and interested in exploiting the values of all the material products of the earth, a mightier force for the consolidation of society than any theologian. Coeur, son of a Bourges furrier, had already set up at Damascus an agency for selling Levantine goods to France. In 1436, still only in his late thirties, he was reforming French coinage, which had been much debased during the last three reigns. But far more astonishing political and diplomatic triumphs were to come, as well as conviction on a false charge of murder and an honorable death in the service of Pope Calixtus III. It will be necessary to refer later to this truly remarkable benefactor of France and of humanity. For the present he may merely be noted as having attracted the dauphin's attention as a more intriguing figure— both literally and metaphorically—than any of the flamboyant soldiers of the day, even Joan of Arc's veterans, who might have been expected to elicit the admiration of a usually stern-faced boy of fourteen.

The Lyons textile magnates, for all their commercial aptitude and the wealth it brought them, were not destined for such heights of glory as Jacques Coeur. But their generosity and princely style of living, which secured devotion from their associates and employees, turned the mind of Louis, who cared nothing for luxury himself, to a recognition of what a reputation for magnanimity might do for an ambitious ruler, as it had done, he knew from his reading of contemporary history, for many Italian lords, in particular, who could command respect for little else. He began to act, at once, in strong contrast with his father's enforced parsimony. He gave his confessor a lavishly equipped traveling chapel and his Master of the Horse everything needed for the escort of a powerful prince.

The dauphin had been reminded of Italian civilization, at this date ahead of French, quite recently. After the reconciliation by the Treaty of Arras between France and Burgundy in 1435, Charles, though humiliated by the loss of the revenues of all the towns on the river Somme demanded by Philip as the price of leaving him alone, had felt able to concentrate more intensely on getting rid of the English, his most menacing and obstinate foe. But for this purpose he required a new alliance to reinforce that of the dubiously reliable James I of Scotland. The French king obtained this theoretical support by betrothing his two-year-old daughter Yolande to the prince of Piedmont, later to be Duke Amadeus IX of Savoy, just before starting the royal tour in August 1436. The duchy of Savoy exercised considerable influence over the richest cities of northern Italy, Genoa, Milan and Venice, as well as in Rome, where the reigning Duke Amadeus VIII was eventually, in 1439, elected pope, in spite of being a layman, with the title of Felix V, as a rival to the deposed Eugenius IV. But the connection never did the anxious king of France any good worth mentioning.

In the country between Clermont-Ferrand and Lyons both father and son had been much depressed by the devastation inflicted on a beautiful and various landscape by the roving bands of freebooters, brigands under the command of mercenary captains who sold their services to anyone and cared for nothing but pillage and massacre. Great cities like Lyons managed to keep these savages at bay by taking advantage of the quarrels that continually broke out between the rival groups and paying one gang to slaughter another. But the villages were helpless against them. Time after time the two separate parties of king and dauphin rode past blackened ruins, stripped corpses and emaciated beggars who had once been members of a prosperous farming community.

When the travelers turned south into Dauphiné, the province Louis knew would be his personal possession as soon as he came of age, they found economic conditions no better. The merchants of Grenoble met their sovereign and particularly his heir with lavish presents, on their knees. But they pulled long faces when they described the outlook for the administrative reforms the dauphin assured them he was determined to inaugurate. It was here for the first time that the tight-lipped boy, who had nevertheless by this time assumed, apparently with ease, the gracious manner of a ruling monarch, heard himself called in public by the ancient title borne by adult heirs of the kings of France. It had originally been a proper name of the counts of Vienne, Albon, Valence and Grenoble. The last count of the family sold his lands to King Charles V of France in 1349. Thereafter the senior Valois prince was automatically invested with the style of "Dauphin" or count of Vienne and officially in charge of the county or province, the "Dauphiné," lying between Provence and Savoy in southeastern France.

Louis and his father, now greeted almost as if they were twin kings of the country, crossed the Rhone into Languedoc, which they saw at its best, so far as weather was concerned, in the spring of 1437. But at Montpellier, in April, they heard alarming news of the depredations of bandits in central France, serious enough to require military action, and turned north sooner than they had planned. A certain Rodrigo de Villandrando, who had become a kind of legend in Languedoc during the previous year, for his daring, cruelty and sexual insatiability, was said to be ravaging the district of Berry in the neighborhood of Bourges and approaching Touraine, which Charles preferred to all his other provinces and where the queen and Princess Margaret were living. Louis, investigating, with his usual impulsive energy, this news in person, saw the women of Languedoc cross themselves at the name of Villandrando and shudder as if they already smelled the odor of burned flesh and anticipated the agonizing horrors of violation and sudden death.

The king, panic-stricken but roused at last to decisive action, galloped north, outridden at every stage by his exhilarated son, for once intent on blood and the shock of arms rather than details of government and commerce. For he heard on the way that Villandrando had got in touch with rebellious nobles and was aiming at no less a feat than the deposition of the unsatisfactory monarch and his replacement in due course by the brigand himself. It would not be the first time in that period of European history that a reckless military terrorist had fought his way to a throne.

The next news, however, brought the royal relief forces some encouragement. A copy of correspondence between Queen Marie and the ferocious mercenary reached Charles. In reply to a dignified remonstrance by the lady the rascal had coolly written: "For the honor and reverence I bear to Madame la Dauphine and my Lord the

Dauphin, at whose service I shall ever remain, I agree to Your Majesty's request." This changed tone meant, of course, that he intended to incite Louis himself against a king generally believed to be responsible, by his criminal negligence, for the miseries of France. Villandrando in fact withdrew from the neighborhood of Touraine as Charles and the dauphin advanced. The freebooter's four thousand undisciplined ruffians were actually at one time quite close to the royal troops marching up from the southeast. But no engagement resulted. It was obviously Villandrando's policy to wait until either Louis or the discontented peers gave him some sign of practical support before he risked a pitched battle with forces superior to his own in both numbers and obedience to their officers.

The prince and his friends had naturally been disappointed by the flight of an insolent revolutionary, more treacherous and bloody-minded than any devil. Yet at the same time they could not help being conscious of the dissatisfaction with the king expressed in much more respectable places, actually among men of rank encircling the very center of Charles's power in the north. The royalist spies ex-aggerated this feeling, which was in fact already in decline as the monarch's new energy made itself felt. In council it was resolved, after the receipt of news that Villandrando had taken himself off to Germany for the time being, to give any possible hard core of mal-contents something to do by attacking the English on the central Loire, to the east of Orléans.

The Comte de la Marche, a useful soldier, took the town of Charny, northwest of Auxerre. The place turned out to have been defended by Burgundian troops, whom it was considered important to detach from the English. The prudent French commander therefore offered his prisoners their lives if they would enter the royal service. Then Louis in person led the storming of an "eagle's nest" of a fortress overlooking the river. It was his first military action and completely successful. But the impetuous fifteen-year-old victor did not imitate his merciful "governor." All the English prisoners were hanged, all the Burgundians beheaded. This precocious ferocity, which he never showed in later life, was probably due to the dauphin's passionate resentment in being kept so long out of real warfare, which he was convinced represented the only chance of freeing his country. Charles was prob-ably shocked. But he could see that it would be serviceable for the English to recognize his son if not himself as a relentless opponent. After this impressive lesson given by the prince not only to the invaders but to all France, the campaign was adequately concluded by the Comte de la Marche with his usual discretion.

There can be no doubt that on this one occasion Louis fell victim to an excitement, a kind of frenzy, that no one was ever to observe in him again. In subsequent years the disappointments and treacheries, the terrifying ordeals and long-deferred triumphs that came his way never either broke his courage and faith in himself or carried him to extremes of vainglory. At most he would change color, compress his thin lips or grin. But his first battle and personal victory, at an age when most boys, of comparable rank even in the fifteenth century, would be still under tutelage, drove him into a storm of exultation which exploded in pitiless violence. The captives taken at the fort were executed after a magnificent banquet at which all his officers received splendid gifts. He spurred back into his father's presence at Gien, further down the river, spared the nervous Charles no detail of what had taken place and, most significant and uncharacteristic of all these doings on his part, demanded to see Margaret at once. With his blood still boiling in the intoxication of military glory he had determined that the second great experience of adolescent life, a first act of copulation, should follow immediately upon a first massacre of his enemies.

No one, not even the court doctors, dreamed of opposing the will of the still beardless hero. The awed little Scottish princess, scarcely thirteen, did her best to please the king and queen by submitting to the necessary physical conjunction, as essential a duty, she was informed, as the worship of God. But the child, by nature oversensitive and in any case no actress, displeased Louis by her awkward flinchings and ill-disguised sobs. He was also disgusted, it seems, by the constitutional sourness of her breath. Margaret, in fact, was not at all the sort of girl, either physically or mentally, to take premature defloration in her stride. She collapsed for some time after this operation. The prince shrugged his shoulders, telling himself that he had done, against his will, what his parents wished, for the sake of France. It was not his fault if the chosen bride turned out to be too feeble to breed kings. Then he dismissed the matter from his mind and despite his father's protests dashed off on another warlike expedition, against the English.

For Charles VII had been more than shocked by the events of the last few weeks. He determined not to let the newly revealed forcefulness of his heir get too far out of hand. The boy had by now achieved a general and increasing popularity among all Frenchmen which threatened to supplant that of his parent, never very warm or steady so far, except among the peasants for whom he had done so much. But they hardly counted against the bellicose peerage, members of which appeared to be slipping away, day after day, to join Louis. The only way to counter this dangerous situation would be for the king himself to stand forth, sword in hand, as the champion of his people, and score a decisive success against the Goddams before his son did.

The moment looked favorable for such an enterprise. Most people were utterly sick of the English, who had produced no outstanding leader since the death of the duke of Bedford in 1435 and apparently could not make up their minds, with their own king, Henry VI, a devout, muddleheaded, innocent lad, only two years older than Louis, what policy to follow in France. Paris itself, so unreliable in the past, took the initiative in offering Charles funds. Other towns followed suit. The king was encouraged to take command of his forces in person and advance on the capital. His party, after all, despite the rising prestige of reforming groups sympathetic with the dauphin, still represented the majority of solid, conservative opinion in France, favorable to the maintenance of the *status quo*, a tradition involving personal loyalty to the monarch whatever his shortcomings might be. In these circumstances the king now felt strong enough to dismiss his loudly protesting son "for a rest" at Bray-sur-Seine while his newly invigorated parent took the road for Montereau, a key point held by the English some fifty miles southeast of Paris.

Politically and intellectually the prince's attitude in more or less veiled opposition to his father remained a lonely one. His supporters, for the most part, merely wished to increase the power of the nobility against a weak sovereign. Louis could already see that this policy would be no good to France, which needed, not a quarrelsome collection of dukes and counts at the head of affairs but, to put it bluntly, a strong dictator, to wit, himself. He felt a fish out of water among the extravagantly clothed, affectedly ceremonious courtiers of Charles VII. Their fantastic frivolities repelled him as much as the obverse of such moods, a morbid obsession, equally prevalent, with the symbols of death, the grinning skeletons and hanged or prostrate corpses that in fact prefigured the inevitable end of so much gaiety and luxury.

He took no interest in either representations of this *danse macabre* or the agonized farewells of dying poets to the amorous revels of youth. The pictured allegories of mortality were all over the place in his day, painted on walls, sculptured in relief or imbued with spectral motion on tapestries stirred by mysterious gusts in the drafty castles and monasteries. The grim and ghastly humor of these scenes did not appeal to him either. A serious and energetic boy, very conscious of the stern work of political reconstruction that lay before him, he considered jeers at the discomfiture of silly rich people unworthy of a boldly progressive spirit. The pathos of their condition, sometimes remarkably vivid in the woodcuts which have survived of the dance of death, did not touch him. He had no trace of the cruelty of adolescence. His execution of helpless prisoners of war had been purely a matter of policy, carried out, it is true, in a great state of youthful excitement, yet not enjoyed vindictively or for its own sake. Such things had to be if France was not to go down into utter anarchy. It was as foolish to lament their necessity as to weep for, let alone mock, beautiful young women or gallant knights swept prematurely into eternity. It must be admitted that Louis, throughout his life, remained, in his uncompromising realism, a bit of a Philistine. But this failing actually promoted, instead of impeding, his practical success.

The arts of his time and place, especially distinguished in the masterpieces of manuscript illumination, left him cold in spite of their elegant naturalism. He preferred old-fashioned fortresses to the new palaces. He could work at his papers anywhere, in pleasant comfort or in an utter lack of it. So long as the parchments were ranged in due order, reasonably intelligible and within reach of his hand, he did not care whether they were exquisitely or clumsily produced. The man who, it is hardly too much to say, enabled the French Renaissance of the sixteenth century to rival that of Italy in his own age by rendering his country more peaceful and prosperous than it had been for hundreds of years, respected artists and intellectuals far less than he did bankers, farmers and huntsmen. For the latter three groups at least shared, in their degrees, his predilection for arduous and prosaic, if repeatedly ingenious and stimulating, toil, the only reliable source of lasting wealth.

Without it, in the dauphin's view, long before he became a king, life on this earth could be nothing but a gamble which seldom came off and was therefore unacceptable by anyone out of the nursery of the mind. He did continue the Valois tradition of helping men who added to the national prestige by their visible and tangible works. After his accession he recognized with affectionate though not continuous respect the genius of Philippe de Commines, a historian in a class by himself at that period. Commines became almost his only true friend. But the prince could not be bothered with the minutiae of style, a point sufficiently proved by his always careless dress and contempt for other splendors, such as contemporary court ladies and even *courtisanes*, as top-ranking harlots were just beginning to be called, could supply. His unquestionable literary ability was much more intuitive than cultivated. He never spoke or wrote obscurely or even at length. But this faculty, most unusual for his time, was due to a rational and orderly rather than an adventurous intelligence.

At Montereau King Charles, while his son meditated sullenly at Bray-sur-Seine, stupefied his officers by performing prodigies of activity during the six weeks' siege. He actually imitated Louis by leading the assault on the town, fording the moat sword in hand and climbing a ladder to the walls. This dazzling change from nervous irresolution to reckless gallantry could only have been motivated by the monarch's long-delayed recognition that he must play the man or submit to violent deposition. After the enemy had been cleared from the streets on October 10, 1437, Charles sent for the prince to storm the citadel of Montereau itself. The gesture, perhaps not so generous as it seems, may have been chiefly meant to show the boy what his long-inactive father had so gloriously done. The king ostentatiously adopted a somewhat tactlessly protective attitude to his heir, who responded in his turn by an unexpected suggestion to his parent that the cornered English garrison should be allowed to retreat. "They are only acting under orders," he is said to have remarked, "which they do not really want to obey." But he had no objection to the French-speaking prisoners being hanged as traitors.

The boy was evidently beginning to form a policy. No doubt he had received information that the English were tiring of the war and that the Burgundians and their adherents would prove decidedly more implacable foes of the French sovereign. Paris, in fact, had got rid of the occupying English troops a year earlier, not long after Bedford's death, by merely rioting against them. The University, moreover, long in the pay of Burgundy and Henry VI, offered Charles unopposed entry into the city. The luxury-loving Duke Philip the Good was himself said to favor peace. But so far Charles had always feared to trust his person to municipal councilors with so long a record of treason. Now he accepted, cantering over the Saint-Denis bridge a month after the capture of Montereau.

Louis had never yet visited the capital, though he knew it was the biggest city in France. He had read of its past with veneration. But that day its ruins horrified him to actual tears. The English had razed the walls and gates. Houses great and small lay in tumbled heaps of stone. But the Cathedral of Notre Dame still contained the dazzling tombs and gilded statues of his ancestors. The prince for the first time realized in a flash of certainty, as though these monuments were addressing him audibly, that no one but himself could and would restore his fallen and outraged country to its former pinnacle of glory. This idea absorbed him throughout the vociferous congratulations of the citizens, the processions and the pageants they staged to welcome a king who seemed to have come back to life and a grim young dauphin who appeared perfectly capable of keeping him there against whatever violence his enemies might contrive. Few could believe the evidence of his boyish figure. The sternly set features above it, so different from those of his vaguely smiling father, were much more credible in their reminder of the fierce maturity he had shown in the action above Charny earlier in the year.

The streets of Paris had been dressed for the royal arrival till they looked like tunnels of embroidered silks and velvets, covering the often damaged house fronts with all the colors of the rainbow. Underfoot, leafy branches and flowers strewed the rubble of the roadway. Garlands had been strung across it from chimneys and windows to symbolize a unified loyalty. Fountains of wine and milk, free for all, spurted in the squares. Street altars, stages for open air tableaux, strolling musicians, dancers, storytellers and hawkers provided an air of carnival that did not exclude a suggestion of solemn dedication.

Eight hundred archers preceded the solitary figure of the king. The prince, wearing armor chased in gold, followed at a distance. Then came plumed and glittering military officers, clattering on horseback, with richly but soberly gowned councilors, canopied magistrates and great merchants pacing behind them. The Church and the University authorities assembled opposite Notre Dame, where the two royal visitors and their personal escorts dismounted to hear a sermon from the Public Orator. Then they entered the cathedral to the strains of a *Te Deum.*

For the next three weeks, while ordinary citizens reveled till dawn, interminable religious and civil deputations waited upon Charles to beg him to settle in their city, now unquestionably the capital of his kingdom. He answered them politely, but in his usual reserved style, promising nothing definite. Louis proved no more accommodating. Neither father nor son would ever forget the dark municipal history of recent years, the abject submission of Paris to the English usurpers and their Burgundian allies, the resistance of the University and the Church to Joan of Arc, culminating in their condemnation of her as a heretic and her consequent abandonment to execution by foreigners.

At last the king announced that military necessity required his presence at Montargis in Loiret, between Orléans and Auxerre. The place, held by the English, was being blockaded by his forces. But actually he and Louis went by way of Orléans to Tours, where Queen Marie and Princess Margaret welcomed them with festivities for once free, apparently, from disagreeable undertones. Charles had never looked better. Conscious of increasing political power after the recent French victories, he dispensed on all sides the characteristic easy charm of the Valois, which every member of that family, even his imbecile father, even his normally inscrutable son, could turn on at will. The dauphin himself, if not quite so jolly, remained calm and courteous with everyone, even his young wife.

But in Paris the councilors, half-ruined by their lavish entertainment of the monarch, cursed, as no tangible concessions came from that quarter to justify their gamble. Penury set in with an exceptionally severe winter. Prices soared. The shivering, hungry populace changed its mind about the royal family, considering it personally responsible for their new misfortunes. Nor did conditions in the provinces improve as the new year of 1438 went on. Everyone was demanding money, the king most of all, and none seemed to be forthcoming. Louis, seeing that his parent was slipping back into his old petulance and refusal to face facts, let alone deal with them, began traveling about the kingdom, especially the west, which he had not hitherto visited, to investigate the situation for himself.

He found it really desperate, needing radical reform unless foreigners were again to take over and swallow up the sources of national prosperity. They were still all over the place, corrupting true patriotism everywhere. He decided that they would have to be driven out as a whole. It was not much good taking an occasional fortress. But such massive measures could not be undertaken without funds and effective alliances which simply did not exist in present circumstances. They would have to be created, and by himself alone. Louis was now discounting his father altogether as a force in politics. Charles was wasting his time all through 1438, in the prince's opinion, by mere endeavors to bolster up the failing despotism of the throne through a whittling away of papal claims to exercise jurisdiction in France. This policy, argued before an assembly of clergy at Bourges that year, derived from a concept of Roman law termed "pragmatic sanction" in the codes of the emperors Theodosius and Justinian in the fifth and sixth centuries. It had been intended originally to regulate the government of reconquered territory by defining the constitutional position of the individual rulers controlling regions formerly administered by the old empire. Charles VII was now invoking it in the interests of providing his personal authority with a legal basis recognizable as internationally valid. But such pretentious claims, putting the cart of theory before the horse of reality, did not appeal to the dauphin's practical common sense. He began to act, discreetly but firmly, on different lines, independent of the airy disputes at Bourges and therefore basically in opposition to the royal prerogative. Such was the origin of a process of self-assertion that was to culminate in actual armed revolt.

CHAPTER II

Rebellion and Reconciliation
(1439–1440)

⚜⚜⚜ The prince's first surviving letters date from the period 1438–1439. The second of them may be regarded as highly typical in its mixture of benevolent but resolute authority, expressed with a kind of affectionate arrogance, precise, categorical, fairly polite, with an undercurrent of irony. It is clear that the writer was both determined to be obeyed and convinced that every service, even to a personage fully entitled to demand it, deserves adequate reward. The communication in question is addressed to an accountant of Louis's household, and reads:

> My dear fellow (*mon compère*), I appeal to and beg of you, relying upon your desire to be of service to me in all things (*sur tout le plaisir que faire me voulez*) to be so good as to deliver the sum of ten crowns to my crossbowman Piectre, that he may get away (*se délivrer*) from Tours and betake himself to my presence (*s'en venir devant moi*). Let there be no mistake in this matter and I promise you I shall remember it and return the favor. So God be with you, my dear fellow.

The writer was not yet sixteen. But he already had a formidable, not to say ferocious, military record behind him. Twenty-five years later he was writing on far more weighty subjects in exactly the same style.

At the beginning of 1439 the king and the dauphin traveled south together once more. They went, as before, ostensibly as partners in government, to see what could be done for the important industrial city of Limoges or, if it were not so distressed as reported, to see what could be done to it in the way of taxation for war. But the son's estrangement from his father had by now grown very marked. It was due to something more than boyish impatience with elderly indolence. The contempt of a mind exceptionally capable of seeing the main point in desperately complicated situations was hardening, morally as well as intellectually outraged by Charles's neglect, a supine attitude consequent upon sheer cerebral incompetence, of what was undoubtedly his plain duty. Louis could hardly bear to be in his parent's presence by this time. The king for his part grew more and more weary of so surly a companion, whose suggestions for action he could barely understand and whose feverish rage of patriotism got on his nerves. In these circumstances, though the two proceeded simultaneously, they kept at a distance from each other and rarely met, just as on their journey eastward in 1436.

Charles really hated these tours of inspection. He felt bound as a king and a Valois to undertake them. But they did nothing but present him with economic problems quite beyond his comprehension. He tended to behave with timid constraint under his son's irritated stares, wondering at the boy's enthusiasm for and prompt decisions about the troubles of manufacturers and merchants.

Prince Louis, meanwhile, rode in great style, accompanied by hawks, hounds and even a lioness, to which pet he was childishly devoted. When the animal perished in an accident he wept for the second time in his life. From Limoges, which the travelers found almost depopulated, the party trotted on majestically southeast, as far as the boundary of Languedoc. There emissaries from that province recited to their sovereign so complex a tale of administrative and financial woes that he realized they could only be dealt with by the prolonged residence on the spot of himself or a deputy fully invested with the royal authority. Louis was the obvious choice for such a post, desirable not only because he had more common sense than his father but also because trouble would certainly arise in other parts of the kingdom if the monarch should be absent for more than a few weeks in Languedoc.

The king therefore appointed the sixteen-year-old dauphin lieutenant general of that province, with the powers of a viceroy, supported by a council of prelates and technical experts. Then Charles, hugely relieved after his temporary stupefaction, dashed off headlong to Lyons, where he expected less ominous entertainment. He did not believe that, as one or two of his oldest courtiers hinted, the only too able and resolute young lieutenant general might use his new appointment to shake the already tottering throne of France.

However that might be, no one could deny that the boy flung himself into his bewildering assignment with the greatest enthusiasm. Languedoc, almost a quarter of the whole kingdom and including the great cities of Toulouse, Carcassonne, Beaucaire and Béziers, had been prosperous until the accession of the mad King Charles VI. But then its extraordinary fertility and wealth attracted the masterless brigands of that dismal age. Their merciless depredations were followed by seasons of storm, drought, plague and floods. Still the wretched inhabitants were obliged to pay out blackmail and ransoms to the freebooters or see their houses set on fire and their relatives and friends, seized as hostages by the bandits, dragged to execution in the open street. Under such conditions the formerly jovial and generous natives of the region developed a cynically selfish mentality, rivaling the robbers themselves in their deadly quarrels. Even the clergy wrangled and swindled. The potentially richest area in all France fell into total disorganization.

The prince found himself confronted on every side by pillage, pestilence, catastrophes of nature and personal feuds among leading churchmen and nobles. Rodrigo de Villandrando was back from Germany and ravaging the province in every direction. To the west, in Guienne, the English were methodically plundering and massacring the peasantry. One might as well be in the middle of a civil war. Yet, again, nothing could be done to stem the tide of violence unless funds were subscribed for the purpose. The young lieutenant general forced the desperate local authorities to admit this incontrovertible point and screwed everything possible out of them. At the same time he traveled about, listened to an endless variety of grievances and insisted on the production of evidence before his own eyes. For, serious as the position undoubtedly was, those who merely wailed of ruin without tangible proof of it made matters look worse while astutely feathering their own nests in the process.

Louis saw at once that only money would stop the rot. To dash about with the inadequate troops at his disposal would merely inflame the situation and might result in absolute disaster if he were surrounded and captured or killed in some unforeseeable hazard of battle. But reliable forces sufficient to impose his decisions proved hard to come by. They would cost far more in pay than he could see any prospect of raising. It was easy to set one band of marauders against another. But they would act only in opposition to law and order, never in defense of the legally established government. The dauphin bought off some of them and hanged others whenever he could catch them red-handed.

Previous princes in France had never troubled to acquire any real contact with their subjects. But Louis had been educated not only by books and tutors but also, owing to his parents' almost continuous absences, by playmates of his own age who ran wild in the fields and farms of Touraine and rarely met anyone else who could read and write. This rough school taught him to start, in considering every problem of conduct, not from abstract principles, but from the concrete personalities that faced him. He had long learned how to talk easily and unaffectedly to simple and humble men. For his violently authoritarian and implacable temperament did not include the least particle of vanity. So he never felt that he must insist on his superior social position or alternatively attempt to conceal it. No fifteenth-century ruler was ever so truly fraternal in his consultations with lords, business-men or laborers as Louis. Yet the adamantine severity of his decisions, once taken, could hardly be matched in that perilous age, when swiftly varying circumstances obliged most repsonsible people to change their minds more often than they would have wished.

At Albi and Toulouse he dictated a rain of demands for funds and persuaded the citizens by his confidence and vigor that they were gambling on a certainty. They found that he really was using their money to get rid of the plague of freebooters. He showed them documentary proof of how carefully he was supervising the expenditure, checking every disbursement himself and noting with his own hand the unexceptionable reasons for allowing it. Everyone could see, more-over, that he spent scarcely anything on his own requirements, which were practically limited to the maintenance of hawks and hounds. His larger outgoings included, as well as propitiations of powerful persons, good or bad, by various concessions or gifts, an unusually generous payment of his office staff and mobile representatives. He had long since discovered that no one, courtier, citizen or priest, not to mention common or uncommon thieves, ever refuses any form of gratuity of the right amount, namely, one proportionate to the re-cipient's estimate of his own importance. That figure was the first one to be worked out. Consequently, Louis always preferred service by obscure individuals. They cost him less and generally did what he wanted just as well as the more eminent. Why, he used to ask with his usual crafty expression, so like a Touraine farmer's, when his advisers raised their eyebrows at names like Bachelier and Durant, pay for a fellow's ancestors in addition to the man himself? This was an idea that occurred to very few magnates in France at the time.

In a few weeks the dauphin's popularity rose to considerable heights in stricken Languedoc. He seemed to be the only authority one could trust throughout the region. The inhabitants were also greatly struck by his dauntless and high-handed way with pompous scoundrels who thought themselves perfectly safe. A free-lance captain, for instance, one Symon de Dampont, imprisoned a citizen of Cepet, Paul de Roset, and released him on payment of a ransom of two hundred crowns down and a written promise, signed and witnessed by a notary, to pay another two hundred within a certain time. When this transaction was brought to the prince's notice he not only declared the duly authenticated document held by Symon de Dampont to be null and void but also ordered the freebooter to repay the ransom already received or else submit to the confiscation of his ill-gotten estate.

Both Rodrigo de Villandrando and the Bastard of Bourbon, the two most powerful brigand chiefs, had fought well against the English when there was no regular French army to do so. Louis perceived that it might be tactless as well as hazardous to proceed against them by force. He also reflected that he might himself wish to use them one day to expel the foreigners in Guienne, at present acting in support of them. So he simply bribed Villandrando, the Bastard and one or two other bandits of about the same strength, to keep away from Languedoc. But he made it a condition of these lavish payments, in each case, that the recipients should on frequent occasions hang some of the more reckless offenders in their gangs, pointing out that this sort of discipline would improve their prospects as a force in the inevitably forthcoming war against the English, as well as gaining them valuable support among local citizens who did not happen to earn their living by casual robbery. This was the sort of language that Rodrigo and his rivals understood. They took the bribes, reveled in hanging some of their private enemies and left Languedoc.

Again, two real aristocrats, the rich landowners Mathieu de Foix and Count Jean IV d'Armagnac, were just then fighting each other to the death in a feud as disastrous to the province as an invasion by aliens. The mother of the ferocious young Jean IV, Marguérite, Countess of Comminges, had already been twice widowed. Yet at fifty-six she married her cousin, the handsome Mathieu de Foix, aged thirty-four, gaily debonair but with no more principles than a wolf and bankrupt into the bargain. The moment Mathieu came into possession of his elderly wife's property he shut her up in a castle elsewhere and began to enjoy a glorious life of hunting and debauchery on her extensive estate. Jean IV considered that as a loving son he had more right than a cruel husband to these pleasures. So with thundering hoofs and blaring trumpets he burst in upon his cynical relative, who responded in kind. The woods and fields of the Countess de Comminges resounded to the clash of steel and the crackle of burning farmsteads. The war spread into neighboring districts. No local lord or prelate had the courage to interfere. But the dauphin coolly ordered both Mathieu and Jean to appear before their sovereign prince and explain what they thought they were doing. To everyone's amazement this summons was obeyed. Probably both the young men were intrigued by what they had heard of Louis's personality, so different from their own, as much as by any sentiment of feudal loyalty. The businesslike lieutenant general came straight to the point. The sword and the torch, he observed in a perfectly neutral tone, had not so far succeeded in deciding the issue, whatever it might be, between the equally gallant contestants, who would obviously soon both be ruined by such tedious hacking and hewing to no purpose. Surely they were each in need of a rest by this time? What about signing a provisional truce, as had been the habit of kings for centuries? They could always start again after a breather, during which his lawyers would try to find an honorable solution to the dispute.

Once more Louis, by his well-tried expedient of talking the language of other people, however uncongenial they might be to his own out-look, succeeded in restoring peace to a distracted community. Mathieu and Jean agreed to a temporary armistice. In fact, as the prince had seen the moment he laid eyes on them, they were both dog-tired but had not been able, by their own proud code, to think of an excuse for shaking hands.

By this time, young as he was, he had perceived clearly what was the matter with France. The root of the evil lay in aristocratic arrogance and greed, failings from which he did not suffer himself and was there-fore able to observe coolly. Nothing could stop them, in the structure of society at that time and place, from repeatedly breaking out into ruinous violence unless some person intervened who was believed to represent directly the will of heaven. In the Christian past saints and kings with the necessary intelligence and force of character had checked, over and over again, the barbarous strains in human nature. Louis was no saint. But everyone knew that if he outlived his weak father he would one day receive the sacred oil that confers the aura of divinity upon a monarch. His unattractive and unfashionable physique therefore made no difference to the awe his presence imposed upon lords and even prelates. Moreover, the citizens of Languedoc found that his directions were based upon uncompromising common sense rather than the moral rhetoric which so often does duty for statesmanship and which had long ceased to impress them. In these circumstances the dauphin's reputation for working economic miracles grew steadily. The hitherto terrorized magistrates of the towns began to pass sentences, behind the shield of his prestige, upon the more or less disguised bandits who were fleecing them, whether these happened to be scions of a noble house like the Bastard of Bourbon or mere baseborn ad-venturers like Rodrigo de Villandrando.

Louis soon realized, in the course of his investigations into the activities of these formidable personalities, that they were acquiring a political background. Their close relations with the English in Guienne and Gascony were by no means to be ascribed solely to sympathy with fellow bandits. The warmongers of London were plotting to raise rebellion throughout southern France in support of an English invasion to retrieve the whole country, from most of which they had been driven out. But Henry VI, much against his personal will, that of a pacific student of theology only two years older than the dauphin, remained officially the king of France according to the treaty signed at Paris in the days of Henry V, the victor of Agincourt.

Sure enough, in July 1439 an English army disembarked at Bordeaux. Peace negotiations between Charles VII and Henry VI had been in progress. But the war party in England, headed by the duke of York, was determined to avenge its defeats on the Seine and Marne by seizing, to begin with, the southwest of France. For some time Louis had been keeping an eye on this quarter, Guienne and Gascony, where the foreigners had always been strong. But he had not been able to get Charles, who considered the north more important, to do anything about it. He now sent an urgent dispatch to his father, but again without result.

Action, however, had to be taken at once if the English and their French collaborators in the Bordelais area were not to come flowing into Languedoc and upset once more its still only feebly recovering economy, which he himself, almost alone, had so strenuously labored to revive. The young lieutenant general galloped into Toulouse, ordered the Garonne frontier to be strengthened and proclaimed mobilization throughout the province. His fiery energy put heart, at last, into the assemblies he addressed in the capital, at Albi and at Castres. He told them precisely what funds would be required to meet the new menace and how they would be expended on the payment of troops, the paving of highways, the establishment of strong points and the refortification and provisioning of towns and castles. All these plans were laid down in detail and put into operation with a new zest which had not been seen in Languedoc for generations.

The two most powerful magnates in the district, the Comte de Foix and the Sire D'Albret, were put in charge of the reserves called upon to defend the region. These measures seem to have intimidated the English, who had probably not anticipated that the prince would be able to rally the disaffected and impoverished southerners. At any rate the invaders made no attempt to move eastward. Louis was on the point of marching into Guienne and Gascony himself at the head of a now united Languedoc peerage when, to his fury, he received a command from the king to return to Tours at once. A mere six months had gone by since he had parted from his father. But the time was long enough to have involved that unhappy monarch in further desperate difficulties. They had resulted from a crisis the consideration of which may be postponed while the nature of French society at this epoch is

examined in rather more depth than was thought requisite in the last
chapter, together with the dauphin's own peculiar position among the
ideas and outstanding personalities of his youth.

Few modern historians have had much use for the European aristocracy of the fifteenth century. But a counsel for the defense might
argue that by then they had been deprived, in France at least, of much
of their property, which had vanished into the hands of the trading
classes, the lawyers and the formerly tenant farmers. In fact the French
nobility as a whole at this period possessed neither the physical resources, the money nor the brains to contest the social rise of groups
that outranked them in all three respects but had no idea who was
whose grandfather. The embittered lords accordingly took refuge in
mere dreams of grandeur. Their education had well qualified them to
do so. They had been bred as much on the fantasies of epic poets and
tales of knights errant among sorcerers and giants, as on flowery
sermons, mostly descriptions of heaven and hell. When they turned, as
did many of the courtiers of Charles VII, to the briefer, more sophisticated imageries of ballads and sonnets on the inexhaustible theme of
generally unhappy love, they actually felt happier than when concerned
with more majestic subjects. The worlds of politics and war, where their
ancestors had won such glory, now baffled the posterity of St. Louis
and Gaston de Foix with a seething arena of upstart faces and base
tactics. In such an atmosphere the rules of chivalry were mocked or
defied and the rattle of coins meant far more than the clash of shield
and lance. The men who bore names made illustrious in the past
found it difficult to breathe an air that still reeked with the disgrace
of Agincourt and the burnt bones of Joan of Arc.

But there was one sphere, as old as war itself, in which regulations
of a complexity delightful to any student of the *Song of Roland* and
the *Roman de la Rose* had long since been drawn up. The sonorous
lines of early French poetry dealt with many an unjustly accused or
betrayed hero, from Charlemagne to King Arthur, and a little later
many an impeccably chaste heroine, from Blanchefleur to Nicolette,
who rescues or consoles a prince in trouble. It was easy for a disgruntled peer of France, in the first half of the century at least, to
identify himself with such male figures and to build up any good-looking
young duchess or countess into an earthly Madonna. If he could not
find such company where he actually lived, he zestfully invented it.
One had only to keep strictly to as fanciful and intricate a ceremonial
as possible and strike legendary attitudes. No matter if the magnanimous
adventures contemplated could never be carried out. The important
thing, the only resource which would keep one's personal dignity
intact, was to conceive one's actions on the basis of a meticulous code

of honor, in the techniques of love as in those of the tournament. Let the plebeians laugh or demand to know what the point was. They would never understand the mystical answer to their rude inquiries.

First of all, one had to look different. In the old days, when no one questioned the mental, moral and material superiority of a chevalier, the owners of wide estates dressed very little better than their retainers. But by Joan of Arc's time, when Prince Louis was six, the subsequently murderous sadist Gilles de Rais, a wealthy nobleman who greatly admired her and fought at her side, dyed his beard blue. Other courtiers of the period went in for equally surrealist outfits, which they themselves called, with benign self-mockery, *costumes de folie*. These aristocrats were often in a position on their own account or through globe-trotting relatives to get hold of exotic, usually Oriental textiles and ornaments, such as their crusading ancestors had occasionally brought home. But now they regularly appeared at court smothered in pearls, precious metals, the gaudier sort of jewels, shoulder knots and feathers.

All these elaborate adornments, however, meant something, could convey to the initiated a state of mind, for instance menace, obsequiousness or indifference. They were a kind of silent poetry. This idea was also developed by the actual embroidering in pearls, on sleeve or cloak or skirt, of staves of music and their accompanying verses, both usually such as a grave churchman would approve. But the private conduct of the wearer, as opposed to the proclamations of his dress, was very seldom edifying. The permanent conflict between pride and the humbler instincts of humanity was resolved at this period and for long afterwards, and not only in the politer social circles, by a conspicuous outer display of piety covering the grossest appetites. François Rabelais in the next century was certainly not the first French satirist to exploit the humor of this situation.

The alleged sexual orgies of Charles VII and his cronies have never been described by anyone who took part in them. The stories are mere gossip of the kind frequent in all the chronicles of past centuries. It is clear, however, that Charles himself, despite his poor health, was much given to eroticism, especially as he grew older. The king is supposed to have inherited these habits both from his demented father, Charles VI, and his scandalously dissolute mother, Isabeau of Bavaria, to whom the Church, when she died in 1435, refused funeral honors as if she had been a mere savage. It would have been strange in these circumstances, if her presumed son Charles, whoever his real father may have been, had turned out anything but a weak debauchee. Such he certainly was at the beginning and end of his career, but less certainly in his middle years, after 1440, when he had prudent and energetic advisers like Jacques Coeur, the Constable Arthur de Richemont and the exceptionally honorable soldier Pierre de Brézé. For a while such men, aided by Count Charles of Anjou and Count Jean of Dunois, contrived to render the much tried monarch more of a man than an oversexed puppet. But he relapsed into that condition after his interesting mistress Agnès Sorel had come and gone (1444–1450). The mystery, to a modern mind, of Charles's character, his appalling mental and physical feebleness in early life, his abominable treatment of Joan of Arc, his subsequent courage and industry over some ten years and his final ludicrous and contemptible behavior for another ten years before his death in 1461, can only be explained by reference to the title he bears in French history, "Charles the Well Served."

He was unquestionably given sound counsel after the English authority in France had declined owing to the fumbling of the respectable young king Henry VI, who had some degree in him of the psychological instability of his grandfather, Charles VI. In other words the judgment declared about another Charles, the second of that name to occupy the British throne, can be reversed in the case of the French Charles VII, who said many foolish things and seems to have done quite a number of wise ones. The anecdote of Charles Stuart is well known. He was confronted one day, in mixed company, with the malicious epitaph:

> Here lies our sovereign lord the King
> whose word no man relies on.
> He never said a foolish thing
> and never did a wise one.

The monarch only chuckled. "Quite so, ladies and gentlemen," he remarked. "My sayings are my own, my acts are my Ministers."

But there was about Charles VII, as about Charles II of Britain, something which rendered him popular in spite of his deplorable lapses. Not only the less sophisticated of his subjects but also relatively clever and serious persons could not help liking him. Perhaps his basic simplicity and good nature, though these qualities often made him cowardly, appealed to most people. His repeatedly awkward and reserved demeanor was excused in view of his political misfortunes. His sexual laxity counted for little in that realistic age; his willingness to listen to reason, for much. Nor was he in himself wholly a fool. He did see, though never so clearly as his son did in maturity, that the heyday of feudalism was over. He also recognized that assemblies of lawyers, merchants and farmers, though their theoretical importance was growing year by year, could never by themselves, any more than assemblies of dukes and counts, wield with success the authoritative administration required by a potentially great kingdom. Its power must come, he could only suppose, with the prestige of a throne occupied by the representatives of an ancient dynasty. He did his best to arrange matters in this way. But a stronger man might well have failed in the conditions of his time. Two great foreign nations, England and Burgundy—for the great duchy had long been independent of its titular king in all but name—were trying to crush and partition ravaged and impoverished France between them.

The other outlying duchies, Brittany, Normandy, Alençon, Lorraine and Bourbonnais, the county of Armagnac and of course Guienne and Gascony, packed with Englishmen and brigands, were hostile to Paris. The capital itself, at first ecstatically friendly in its new emancipation from the English, then sullenly uncooperative when it saw that the king had not come to give but to borrow, could not be trusted. At last even his own son, destined long afterwards to render France truly independent of the rest of Europe, as he could not, began to work against him. It was, in 1440, too much. Meanwhile many ladies were available and he was not yet sixty. What was the good of racking his brains when such ministers as de Brézé and the ingenious financier Jacques Coeur could do it for him? Gradually the bored monarch withdrew from politics and gave himself up, as he had in his teens and twenties, to the society of young women. Whether or not he knew what a ridiculous figure he cut among them, he knew that he was still the king and that they had to do, by immemorial custom, whatever he told them.

Meanwhile the incorrigible nobles, as a whole, went on with their grotesque dreams of conquest in the field against anyone, even their anointed sovereign. They deepened their studies of elaborate camouflage for coarse erotic debauchery and their manias for the now merely apparent perils of jousting and the chase. These amusements had once been cultivated, with some reason, as training for war. But they had long since been staged with a view to pageantry rather than risk to life and limb. A few bruises were the most that the participants had to fear during their formal encounters in the lists or with the tusks of a wild boar already half incapacitated by the teeth of hounds or the spears thrown by cautious retainers on foot. Hunting, like all the aristocratic diversions of the age, had grown largely symbolic. The pursuit of harmless deer, for instance, typified that of an ideal, aesthetic or moral, originally remote but gradually assuming a more definite character if one took a little trouble over it. Gaston IV, for example, hereditary Count of Foix and devoted to Charles VII, declared that the tracking and slaughter of game in the shape of forest animals and birds allowed perishable mortals an enjoyable road to the achievement of that sanctified immortality of virtue which would be the lot of the good huntsman after death. As he galloped along, with every bodily sense and faculty of judgment on the alert, and exalted by a fervor akin to that of prayer, he could easily suppose himself in a state of eternal bliss.

Each variety of quarry, moreover, represented a different sort of ethical quality. The stronger and fiercer brutes exemplified courage and determination. The more elusively fugitive creatures supplied models of sagacity and resourcefulness. The many breeds of hounds and falcons employed also showed traits to be found in admirable human beings. Their almost miraculous scouting intuitions resembled those of statesmen or administrators. Their splendid audacity in action, coupled with a tenacity that took no account of danger, inspired every ambitious lord or lordling in France. Any landowner who rode out into the woods and fields to take his pleasure was familiar with the species illustrated and exhaustively, sometimes absurdly, annotated in the medieval bestiaries, which included numbers of quadrupeds and bipeds not native to Europe, in addition to nonexistent monsters. Some of the richest noblemen possessed African, Persian or Indian leopards which they trained like hawks, transporting them to the copses in low carts without sides. There the big cats sat hooded and chained till a hare or buck was sighted, usually at a distance of about two hundred yards. Then the leopard, the fastest of all animals, was released and streaked after the prey. Not only the thrill of watching a feat that not even a mounted man could emulate, but also an awareness of the extraordinary features attributed by the ancient zoologists to the miscellaneous objects of their study, lent a subtle and far-ranging excitement, amounting to fanaticism, to the preoccupations of a fifteenth-century hunter. Louis, from youth to age, remained intensely dedicated to this complex and absorbing pastime.

As for tournaments, by this time they had come to be more like ballets than battles. Lance and sword were blunted, the mace or ax lightened in weight. Only certain portions of an adversary's body could be aimed at. In any case the combatants were so heavily armored and padded that little damage could be inflicted. Prizes were not awarded for the power of a blow or thrust but for the elegance and dexterity with which it was delivered. The knight was applauded much more as a master of movement than as a pile of huge muscles. The disciplined grace of a dancer rather than the stunning impetus of a reckless giant would bring the elderly warriors who judged the contest to their feet with flashing eyes and a ringing "Ha!" of appreciation.

For the social leaders of that age longed to be thought supercivilized as compared with their grandparents. Ostentatious ceremony was considered to be the hallmark of such heights of refinement. Bedrooms, however, and the massacres of real war saw little of this pose. There the exquisite mask dropped and the blind ferocity of instinct took command until sheer exhaustion set in.

Nevertheless, the art of military action, if not of amorous encounters, was changing fast. Jousting would never have been allowed to become so relatively frivolous if battles were still being won by cavalry charges. The English archers on foot at Crécy, Poitiers and Agincourt had destroyed the mounted French lancers. Nimble, lightly clad swordsmen, on the same field, had proved more than a match in hand-to-hand fighting for opponents rendered unwieldy, if they advanced as lines of infantry, by ponderous body-armor and offensive weapons too long and heavy to handle effectively.

Italian artillery was only just beginning to be useful north of the Alps. But any experienced soldier could see that before long it would be as deadly to horsemen as the longbow. The picturesque tradition of galloping squadrons, paramount over so many centuries on battlefields throughout the world, was dying very hard, all the same. So it became natural for it to be given expression more and more as a sport, both in tournaments and in ordinary hunting, than as a truly profitable martial exercise. The mounted man retained his prestige over the gunners and marksmen with musket and rifle who really decided victories during the next five hundred years, right down to modern times, when airborne divisions are sometimes officially called "cavalry." But the riding soldier was to act, from the early fifteenth century onward, rather in the pursuit of a defeated enemy already decimated by long-range weapons than as a rank-breaking shock trooper thrown against the bristling pikes of an earthbound peasant infantry, when he was often made to look ridiculous.

For these reasons the professional soldier trained to the saddle was inclined to evade regular engagements during the fifteenth century. He preferred to roam about in unattached bands, plundering unarmed civilians. Such was the origin of the "freebooters" whom Louis, both as dauphin and as king, was to find such a nuisance. Twenty years before Louis's birth the poet Eustache Deschamps (d. 1406) had exclaimed: "The corn, the blood and the bones of innocent countrymen make up the riches of this earth, of which these wolves take toll. The land cries to heaven for vengeance, demanding *malheur à la seigneurie!* (Down with the lords!)," i.e. the mercenaries who pretended to be chevaliers, since they could afford horses.

Some really had such a rank, being ruined landowners who had taken to the highways, and very many more "lords" could not be simply described as brigands. They really did in certain cases advance the cause of French civilization, largely for the reason that they did not have to work for a living and were not therefore tempted to be greedy and opportunist. The Valois dynasty started the habit of protecting writers, architects, painters, sculptors and musicians. By the end of the fourteenth century translations into French of the Bible and the works of Aristotle, Ovid, Seneca and Petrarch were available. Charles VII himself, though no intellectual, so innocent, in fact, of these matters that he once asked a doctor if writing poetry gave people headaches, encouraged Alain Chartier (1390–c. 1440). This author, responsible for the extraordinarily powerful poem *La Belle Dame Sans Merci*, which so impressed John Keats, championed the rural laborers of France against both their secular landlords and the sometimes equally oppressive clergy who exploited them. This attitude pleased Charles, a firm upholder of the throne in opposition to the excessive rights often claimed by both noblemen and the Church. The monarch was perhaps less gratified by the fierce diatribe mounted against his debauched courtiers by Chartier, but all the same, the poet remained in the royal service until his death.

His great poem is only the most striking illustration of the general feeling about women prevalent among educated men in the fifteenth century. These critics recognized the civilizing influence of feminine refinement and sensitivity on the coarser type of male. Yet at the same time they considered characteristically female the vices of hypocrisy and cruelty that so often drove gallant and honest knights to a melancholy extinction of all that had made their lives worth living. Chartier's hero in *La Belle Dame Sans Merci* "rose unhappily from the banquet and departed weeping. His heart almost burst, as if he were near to death. He called for death to come to him fast, before his senses left him and cut short the remainder of his anguished days. What then became of him I know not, not whither he went. But his lady soon forgot him in the merriment of the dance. I have heard that after roaming awhile with wildly disheveled hair he fell at last into such sadness that very wrath did kill him."

The extravagant cults of medieval chivalry, started by the Arab-influenced troubadours of the twelfth century, had culminated in the production of a race of young noblewomen tempted by the almost divine powers attributed to them to go in for a positively murderous coquetry. Furious masculine satirists retaliated by obscene slanders. Sometimes the knights themselves, driven beyond endurance, exposed their heartless mistresses to public shame from which recovery proved impossible. Antonine de la Salle (d. 1462) relates a story of this kind about a lover who had detected his lady in a flagrant affair with a baseborn cleric. "Thereupon he seized her by the headdress and raised his hand to box her ears. But suddenly he refrained, remembering the great delights he had known with her, for which he himself could be blamed. Weeping, as though aswoon with sorrow, he flung her to a bench, whence she did not dare to move. His eye fell upon a blue sash that she wore, all tricked out with gold. He tore it from her waist, crying: 'How now, lady? Thou hast heart to wear this sash of blue, a color that stands for loyalty? And yet thou art the most disloyal of all ladies that I know. Thou shalt not wear it any longer.' With that he folded the scarf and hid it in his bosom."

The last sentence is significant. The deceived lover could not bear to throw this adornment of his still secretly adored mistress out of the window or onto the floor, but placed it against his heart, beneath his doublet. Fifteenth-century literature is full of such pathetic evidence of the abject subordination of generous men to cheating women. Only rarely did an aggrieved lover, in France, stab his delinquent beloved fatally, as often happened at the same period in Italy and Spain. In general an aristocrat of the court of Charles VII would not even seriously beat, but only curse, a woman of his own rank who had played him false. In his self-conscious pride as the possessor of exquisite manners he would leave that sort of crude vengeance to foreigners. Or else, like Alain Chartier's hero, he would simply leave the traitress forever and fall into utter despair, being unable to get her out of his mind.

In real life, of course, the sex war remained mostly at the level of camouflage and verbiage. Not many wellborn young women were coquettes or actually dissipated. At the wilder revels in castles they mostly kept to the walls and watched the expensive harlots of both sexes. Few ladies of good family were easily shocked, however much time they spent at their devotions. But just as in modern times this tolerance did not of itself mean that they were ready for any seducer. Their dignity was encouraged on all but the most intimate occasions by the lords who actually or potentially loved them. But their activities, unless they belonged to one of the many ruling dynasties in France at this time, remained for the most part purely social. Isabel, duchess of Burgundy, and the maid of honor Agnès Sorel, mistress of Charles VII for a few years, did rather more than play at politics. But on the whole, women at fifteenth-century French courts affected practical erotics less than education, both in the sense of bringing up children and in that of inoculating their lovers, husbands and brothers with the gentler virtues. The day of the brilliant courtesan of humble birth had not yet dawned in French high society.

The satires against women at this period, incidentally, do not much resemble the savage invectives of the kind in earlier centuries, inspired by the Christian doctrine of the sin of Eve. Charles's writers tend more to reproach ladies for not living up to the new humanist idea of individual liberty. Females accorded such deference themselves, these more courteous censors seem to imply, should not invade to such an extent the territory of ideal masculine freedom from tyranny. In other words, they must not flirt, lead a man on till he is distracted by frustration and then snatch away the prize they impudently dangle before him. Such conduct, it was suggested, takes improper advantage of the respect for feminine beauty and charm which had by now reached heights a sensible gentleman would judge to be inordinate if women did not play the game. Were they not, after all, the weaker sex and so ordained by God? Coquetry in these circumstances amounted to something very like blasphemy. It is to be feared, however, that a good proportion of young ladies in the higher income groups laughed at these pleas. For the very men who wrote them fell victims again and again to the irresistible fascination of the frivolous beings they attacked, lamenting in vain such setbacks to the pride of scholars and moralists formerly in the van of the intellectual progress of mankind.

Such, more or less, may have been the sexual conventions at the court of Charles VII, a certainly beloved but far from wholly admirable sovereign. His popularity did not arise only from the ease with which he could be influenced by stronger characters and intelligences. He was, after all, half a priest, an intermediary, owing to the sacred oil with which he had been anointed, between humanity and a heaven conceived as both concretely existent and unquestionably all-powerful. Charles even looked more like a canon than a king, some of his more or less good-natured contemporaries asserted. Portraits of him in fact confirm this view. Actual prelates, since they were inclined to use their God-given authority, as a general rule, for the benefit of their own profession rather than for those of laymen, were feared rather than loved by other Frenchmen. The king, though he had to be wary of the Church, could in theory divide his beneficence equally between ecclesiastics and the untonsured, from secular lords to lawyers, traders and agriculturalists, not to speak of the above-mentioned artists, the latter being often intellectually more than a match for less imaginative citizens, so that their advice could be used on occasion in fields other than their own specialties.

It was also the case at the time of the birth of Louis that the English wars of the previous century had reduced the kingdom and its rulers, including Charles, to such a miserable condition of poverty and political embarrassment that the official, divinely appointed representative of the state, however silly in some respects he might be considered, automatically attracted the sympathy of thoughtful patriots, especially

if he were known to be a semi-invalid. Louis XI also suffered from ill
health for most of his life. But he was never even an intermittent
psychopath like his two predecessors. On the contrary, he knew what
he was talking about when he so often said, with the sly grin so
characteristic of him in maturity: "*J suis France!*" It was not an
arrogant boast like that of Louis XIV declaring "*L'État c'est moi,*"
or the less securely based adoption of the phrase by Charles de Gaulle.
It was the exultant recognition, which had no need to be rhetorical,
that he alone, in both a practical and a mystical sense, incarnated the
fate of his country. For good or evil his personal acts set the national
spirit in motion. It was as if he were, for all his shortcomings, an
indisputable god on earth, to be hated perhaps by some, rightly or
wrongly, but to be disobeyed only at the risk of an ultimate ruin of
the rebel which, when it came, seemed to be caused as much by the
inexorable trend of history as by the monarch's will.

Ironically enough the strong son of Charles VII, though superior
in so many aspects to his shaky father, never achieved the latter's
popularity. Charles was generally loved for his all-too-human failings.
Louis was generally suspected, if at the same time respected, for
apparently not having any. He had inherited a slightly offbeat version
of his predecessor's charm but nothing of that sovereign's diffidence.
When the implacable schemer who occupied the throne of France from
1461 to 1483 and at last gave his kingdom a unity, power and security it
had never known before was succeeded by the flashy young imbecile
Charles VIII most Frenchmen actually heaved a sigh of relief. But the
eighth Charles, if he had not received so well-organized a state from
his father and then died at twenty-eight, would obviously have thrown
France back into the bloodbath and destitution the country had
suffered before Louis acceded, a king considered by only too many of
his most powerful subjects far too familiar with money-grubbing merchants and landless proletarians.

Yet, however fond of more or less obscure businessmen Louis might
be, it never occurred to him any more than it did to his parent to
govern under their advice or even that of their legal counselors. In
other words the official French parliament, the States-General, might
never have existed, except as reluctant bankers, for Charles. When he
did, in lucid intervals, think of administration, he turned it over to his
individual favorites. Louis eventually proved more tactful. He was a
pretty good lawyer himself and knew how to put a case that could only
be countered by what he reserved the right to call treason. He did not
interfere with the actual machinery of legislation. But he enforced, as a
sacrosanct monarch, the ends to which he wished it to work, quite
irrespective of any moral views against them which might have been

advanced but of course never were. This procedure, to a modern mind, does not commend itself as an honorable way to national prosperity. But it was effective. Louis found France in political chaos and left it a formidable European state, as much envied as it was feared. Other despots have done the same from that day to this, but always by military violence. Louis understood war well enough. But it was so far from obsessing him that he gave it low marks as a political or even economic expedient and never pursued it wholeheartedly, though he often had to face pretexts for doing so which a twentieth-century liberal statesman would accept without hesitation.

The heir of Charles VII would have sympathized with the retort made by the nineteenth-century German chancellor, Prince Otto von Bismarck, to the inquiry whether he "wanted war." "War? No, I don't want war. I want victory!" Outstanding statesmen of the very first rank long after the time of King Louis XI, Cardinal Richelieu for instance, are found again and again to resemble him in discounting resort to public violence in order to gain their ends.

Charles VII too was essentially a man of peace, though on instinctive rather than rational grounds. Yet, surrounded by restless devotees of battle, he was now, in the autumn of 1439, facing a fresh crisis in his attempts to govern his country. It was one, actually, for which he could hardly be blamed. On the contrary, he had reached the eminently sensible decision, partly in consequence of what he heard about his son's doings in Languedoc, to forbid his feudal nobles to raise their own troops. He meant to substitute for these eternally quarrelsome, quasi-independent units an army owing allegiance only to himself. Nothing could be more desirable if France were not to be overrun by dozens of petty tyrants each plotting his own advantage and by no means averse to summoning foreigners to his assistance. But the privilege now to be abolished had been permitted by law for centuries. Its cancellation roused a majority of the senior aristocracy to passionate resentment, maintained especially by the bold and popular dukes of Bourbon, Brittany and Alençon. The king felt that he needed the dauphin's already proved diplomatic skill, courage and realism to enable headway to be made against these formidable opponents, who were supported both by the framework of existing legislation and the conventional loyalty of their hordes of retainers.

But Louis, exasperated by his father's interference with the work of reorganization in the south, felt more than half inclined to join the dukes. He listened sullenly to Bourbon's veiled suggestions of seizing the person of Charles and transferring the allegiance of the peerage to his heir, the youthful redeemer of Languedoc himself. But the prince refused to commit his personal power to the machinations of the rebellious nobles. All the same, the king found his attitude to them oversympathetic. Charles, who had no idea of the principles of diplomacy, had expected out-and-out cooperation from the dauphin. He now feared that this only too astute and none too affectionate son might really oppose him. In a panic he issued a royal decree establishing a standing army, to be stationed on the frontiers and paid by the treasury, in replacement of the feudal bands. The lords did not feel in a position, as yet, to counter this decisive step by declaring war on their anointed sovereign. He had the businessmen and the lawyers of the country behind him. The dukes could only call on the freebooters and the English to support a cause that would have scandalized all Europe and inevitably led to treachery in their own ranks, corrupted from the start by brigands and foreigners who cared nothing, as the nobles in general, to do them justice, did, for the constitutional security of France.

That security was in fact being threatened, just then, in a quarter nearer to the throne than Languedoc. Poitou, to the southwest of Touraine, had fallen into an anarchy exceeding that so recently characteristic of the Midi. The royal officers were being beaten up, robbed and even ejected from the province. Some of them, in consequence of this treatment, had joined the local bandits in plundering and murdering rich and poor alike. It seemed only a question of time before this region too, like Guienne and Gascony, would be taken over by the English and launched against the rest of the kingdom by the duke of York's party. On December 12, 1439, a month after the edict setting up a standing army, Charles sent his wonderworking son, with dictatorial powers, to restore order in Poitou. The worried monarch hoped by this measure to kill two birds with one stone by also removing his potentially dangerous offspring from the influence of the dukes.

It was a hope that turned out to be half forlorn. Louis, now an expert at bringing people to their senses, had actually less difficulty in this area than he had experienced in Languedoc. In a very few weeks Poitou, under his magic wand, which was really no more than the application of reason, backed by merciless severity, to the excesses of a lapsed civilization, had regained its self-respect. The king was delighted. He publicly congratulated the prince, who replied with dutiful deference. Father and son appeared at last to be running in harness together.

But this, in fact, was far from being the case. The dauphin's temperamental incompatibility with his intermittently unstable and foolish parent had hardened from dislike to hatred, whatever he might consider it desirable to say at one critical juncture after another. What Charles did not know was that he had been in touch with the dukes all the time of his operations in Poitou, notably with the half-crazy Jean II, Duke of Alençon, his godfather, whom he met at Niort, in the south of the province, in February 1440. On that occasion Louis had felt free, or been irritated enough, to tell his incalculable senior that he detested and despised Charles VII. Alençon excitedly advised the already soured young man to assert himself against a parent who did nothing but prevent him, out of sheer jealousy, from achieving still further glorious work for France, and saving the realm from collapse under the reckless antics of a sovereign unfit for anything but listening to flattery.

One result of this conversation was the prince's dismissal of his honest and reasonable "governor," the Comte de la Marche, whom he told that he meant to have his own way in future. The count could do no less, eventually, but repeat this defiant statement to the king. Charles, in great alarm, saw that his deposition might be imminent. Hit in this highly vulnerable spot of his sensitivity—he would have forgiven Louis anything but treason—the embittered monarch acted, for once, with uncompromising determination. He warned every town in France which he could trust that his son was indulging in treasonable talk. He summoned the young duke of Bourbon, whom he feared and respected more than the other lords, to his presence. The duke, a handsome and urbane character, of course reassured him. Nevertheless Charles, to make assurance doubly sure, led his new standing army into Poitou, obviously against his own son.

The loyal Constable of France, Arthur de Richemont, an excellent soldier, anticipated little difficulty in the campaign, on which he accompanied the king. Both men had information, in fact, that the dukes would not act in a military sense. Louis perhaps, led on by the incorrigible mischief-maker Alençon, who had persuaded even Joan of Arc to tolerate him socially, believed that they would. They could count on Dunois, the gallant Bastard of Orléans, who had shared with Joan her victories over the English and after her death fought them to a standstill in the north. Duke Charles de Bourbon, a conqueror of ladies rather than of armed hosts, but a clever negotiator, had told the dauphin that he would look after the political side. In 1435 he had brought the important Treaty of Arras between Charles and Philip of Burgundy, which so discomfited the English, to a successful conclusion. But the Duke considered that he had been inadequately rewarded for this service by the king. In revenge he proposed in due course to proclaim Prince Louis regent of France with a program for the reduction of taxation by disbanding the expensive new army and returning to the old decentralized system of levies financed by the great landowners.

Charles's propaganda, on the other hand, as he marched into Poitou, represented his son as a headstrong child misled by treasonable villains into an absurd bid for the throne, which would only be supported by irresponsible adventurers, backed, if at all, by the universally hated freebooters. As he spoke openly, with all the prestige of a dynasty and on frankly patriotic lines, addressed to the whole country, while the dukes worked mostly underground in much more equivocal terms, the consensus of the towns seemed to be with him. His troops, moreover, proud of their new discipline and status, devoted to their gifted commander Richemont and bursting to inaugurate a triumphant career by hunting down the wretched rabble of bandits known to be already ruining a rich province, could not have been in better heart. They might be sorry for the young dauphin, who had hitherto stood conspicuously for law and order, though by no means a romantic figure in the view of an average fifteenth-century soldier. But if he had chosen to conspire against his own sacrosanct father he must take the consequences. In such a mood the orderly ranks of the royal punitive expedition crossed the river Sèvre and descended into the allegedly rebellious district. It was not long before the van reported the glitter of lance points on the horizon.

Richemont, as he had expected, decisively defeated this first opposition and proceeded methodically to send the rest packing. He was looking for the prince. But Louis had already been persuaded by the discreet Bourbon to retreat southeast, as far as the almost inaccessible mountains of Auvergne, where more reliable forces had secretly been assembled to carry on the revolt. The rebels thought at first of rousing Languedoc, which greatly admired its former lieutenant general, to join them. A meeting was called at Lyons to discuss this proposal. But meanwhile, in their rear, more and more castles were surrendering to the royal troops. The experienced Dunois saw no point in further resistance. He left the camp of the insurgents. Other nobles followed him. Charles grew more and more confident. He turned down an offer of mediation from Philip of Burgundy and coldly announced the terms upon which he would cease hostilities. The revolutionary lords must demobilize their ranks, swear allegiance to their rightful sovereign and deliver up to him the son they had so unwisely advised. A long list of the fortresses and persons to be similarly restored to the crown followed.

The king's summons read, in part: "Let them [the rebel peers] return to the King my lord the Dauphin his son, prepared to render to the King due obedience, counseling him so to do, and if he will not—which God forbid—let them by no means advise, favor or encourage him in such a course, or receive or keep him in their towns and fortresses against the will of the King his father."

The pedantic legal language of this official document cannot disguise

Charles's intense anxiety, so strangely compounded of political panic and paternal solicitude, one as real as the other.

The dauphin responded, on behalf of himself and his friends, with all his old diplomatic skill. He wrote that his group still regarded Charles as their legitimate monarch, that they were prepared to lay down their arms and accept his own return to the king's court. But first, he added emphatically, his father must undertake to cease his "pitiless oppression of the people" and renounce custody of the persons he was pleased to call "evil counselors," since the heir to the throne, "the chief of us all," would never agree to such a betrayal of his "faithful servants."

He went on in his usual smooth style: "The said Lord Dauphin asks the King to permit him to continue in his good grace and favor, as hath ever been his chief desire. Further, he asks the King not to bear him ill will for past events, but to pardon him for them and forget them." A petition was appended for written indemnities covering any act by his confederates that might have displeased the sovereign. Lastly, "In order that the said Lord Dauphin may maintain his estate, may the King be pleased to grant him possession of the Province of Dauphiné, since it appears to him unjust that the Province hath been so far withheld from him, though past Dauphins received it before they arrived at the present Dauphin's age." The region in question, between Provence and Savoy, had been sold, as already stated, by its last independent proprietor to King Charles V of France in 1349 and by him bestowed upon his eldest son. Consequently, Louis had a legal claim to its possession.

But the writer coolly added that as the revenues of Dauphiné would not suffice to uphold the dignity of a prince, the king should make further provision for this object by appointing his son governor of either Guienne, Gascony, Languedoc or the Île de France. The first two of these provinces, in the southwest, were hotbeds of English intrigue. The last comprised central France with Paris. This virtual partitioning of the kingdom could easily be interpreted by Charles as implying intentions of either dealing with the English or seizing the royal government itself. Naturally enough, he temporized, replying courteously but firmly that "when the Lord Dauphin presents himself at court with due humility the King will treat him as his son and provide for his estate as well as for that of Madame La Dauphine in such manner as shall content him. The other requests made in his letter, touching the associates of the Lord Dauphin, will be met to his satisfaction when he appears before the King."

Louis returned stubbornly to the charge. He demanded either national war against the English, with himself, the "redeemer of the

French people," as commander-in-chief, or else a consideration of his case by the States-General of the kingdom, before which assembly the duke of Burgundy would be prepared to give evidence. This arrogant retort, amounting to an accusation of his father of incapacity in his high office, could only force Charles to further military action. In June Richemont attacked and took all but one of the prince's last castles. The rebel troops melted away. Finally Bourbon himself refused further collaboration in the revolt. Philip of Burgundy declared publicly that he would never help a son to make war on his own parent. There was nothing for it, in these circumstances, but to submit.

The dauphin, inwardly fuming but for the moment taciturn, set out with the duke of Bourbon and some other noblemen to meet Charles at Cusset, just north of Vichy, in the Bourbonnais itself. But before they reached the town a royal rider met them with the information that the king would receive no one but his son and the duke. Louis cursed his father outright and swore he would never see him again. But Bourbon, pointing out that Richemont's vanguard lay across their only line of retreat, persuaded the infuriated young man to proceed.

At Cusset the prince and the duke knelt at the king's feet, begging his pardon. Charles dismissed his son immediately, telling him he was welcome, though he had been long on the road. For this very reason, the monarch added with a certain malice, the boy needed rest and would be received the next day. After the dauphin had gone, in silence but with set teeth, his father turned to Bourbon, a man he knew to be his enemy but no fool, and gave him a long lecture. It was couched, however, in comparatively moderate though aggrieved tones.

Both men were admitted to the presence of the king and his council on the following day. Charles began the interview by declaring that he was not prepared to pardon the absent noblemen. Louis burst out: "What, sire? You would have me break my pledged word to these gentlemen?" His father for once answered him sternly: "Louis," he said, "all doors are open to you. If they be not wide enough I will make a breach through which you may depart whithersoever you will. You are my son. You may not grant favors to anyone without my permission. If it please you to go then with God's will we shall find some other prince of the blood to do us better service than you have rendered."

This was plain enough speaking, severe, yet not undeserved. King Charles VII, these days, had changed since the time when he had shifted and shuffled over Joan of Arc and finally left her to die a miserable death. No doubt he had learned some wisdom over the years, even how to act on occasion like a man and a ruler. It is possible, however, that his advisers rather than he himself had urged this line of action to tame the obdurate dauphin. Yet Louis, too, had been able to consult experienced and resolute counselors. Now, for the first time, he seemed to be listening to them.

As a result of this audience the suave and supple duke of Bourbon changed sides and swore allegiance to the king. The prince, so far from obtaining possession of rich provinces, found himself reduced for a while to dependence on his cook and his confessor. But this humiliation of course could not last. At the end of July 1440 Charles handed him the government of Dauphiné and a substantial pension. Reconciliation between father and son appeared to be complete. The revolt of the nobility, known to historians as the "Praguerie" because a similar rising had recently taken place at Prague, had failed dismally owing to the unexpected energy of the royal leaders, the realistic attitude of Bourbon and the sudden intimidation of the youthful Louis. Like other strong-minded boys he had found at last that he could not carry all before him by mere bluster. Neither as prince nor as king did he ever forget this lesson. He never again acted on pure impulse, without reflection, though to his life's end he was constantly tempted to take such a risk.

CHAPTER III

Three Campaigns
(1440–1445)

❧❧❧ The discomfited prince, back at Tours, vented some of his ill humor on his wife. Margaret's natural gaiety and intelligence had been only slightly impaired by the temperamental divergences between herself and her husband. His neglect of her had been compensated to some extent by King Charles and Queen Marie, who had both grown very fond of her. But Louis now reproached his dauphine, in hardly veiled language, for barrenness, frivolity, hypochondria, dress mania and extravagance. He even complained, for the first time to her face, of her sour breath. There was certainly no question on his part of any affection for her.

The princess, though still only sixteen, had already developed a personality as marked, in its judicious assessment of invincible circumstance and in its stoical determination not to give way under such pressure, as the mind of Louis himself. Her submissive reception of the prince's rudeness was dictated both by the contemporary conventions governing wifely behavior and by her growing sense of the dignity of her social position. But even so, if she had not been so typically Scottish in the intellectual pride that could not be reduced in private by natural grief and disappointment or in public by oppression at the hands of foreigners, she might well have turned to take vengeance upon her alien consort by resort to adulterous or political intrigue.

She had been prepared to love him in the tranquil fashion which was all that her innately frigid temper would allow, especially when she realized that his own excluded any kind of sexual ardor. But his practically immediate repudiation of her on both physical and mental grounds left her no resource but aestheticism and scholarship. For both practical erotics and practical politics bored the daughter of the highly artistic King James I of Scotland, murdered by rebellious nobles in February 1437, not long after she discovered for certain that her evasive husband despised her.

No examples of Margaret Stuart's verses survive. Louis had them all destroyed after her death. But it is known that she fervently admired Alain Chartier and Charles of Orléans. No doubt she imitated them indefatigably, to the best of her ability, writing of course in French. It is improbable, however, that she attained the heights of lyrical imagination and delicacy of statement which they achieved. But she may have come within measurable distance of her father's *The Kingis Quair*, itself an artificial allegory, a long way after Geoffrey Chaucer. King James is likely to have seen to it that an acquaintance with the Englishman's work formed part of the education of his children.

But Margaret, however inferior her literary effusions may have been compared with the best of her time, never varied, so far as can be ascertained, from a day-to-day conduct which no one but the most hidebound religious fanatic or the most unscrupulously malicious slanderer could condemn. Some priests thought she ought to go more often to confession or to her private oratory. Some rigidly prosaic ladies and gentlemen censured her long hours of study, devoted to prosody rather than to prayers, either alone or in mixed company. Some of her younger maids of honor enjoyed poetry or pretended to. Some male courtiers also shared her tastes. But many people outside her immediate circle contended that such scribbling and abstruse chatter as was indulged in at these parties did not become a royal princess.

On the other hand, few objected, as Louis did, to his wife's costly toilets, delight in dancing and generosity to poor knights who wished to excel in the tournament but could not afford the equipment to do so. The dauphin of course knew as well as anyone that great ladies were expected to dress gorgeously, attend balls till they almost fainted and subscribe heavily to charitable objects, among which the training of future commanders in warfare naturally figured conspicuously. His criticisms of Margaret's expenditure in these generally approved fields, where her ostentation only exceeded that of other noblewomen on account of her exalted rank, arose mainly because she had proved infertile, thus making futile his one original reason for marrying her.

He never forgave her for this shortcoming, one of course quite beyond her own control. He even tried, as will be recorded later, to trump up an excuse for divorcing her on grounds of adultery, since the pretext of barrenness would hardly do after a marriage of less than ten years. But Louis never made personal war on women, much as he disliked the sex as such. He came to regard the dauphine, in the end, with the same sort of smoldering rage he felt in thinking of the dukes

who had let him down. It amounted at times to impulses of murderous
hatred, instantly repressed, whether it was Margaret or one of the
Praguerie peers he had in mind. The perfidious nobles were gentlemen,
after all. And the little Scotch girl, who produced only stanzas, not
children, was of royal birth, for all her stinking breath, pseudo humility,
intellectual affectations and frivolous invalidism. She was his wedded
wife, contracted to his sacred person by the highest ecclesiastical
authority. Violence, even if she betrayed him, would be out of the
question. Nor had any of his spies, as yet, proved her unfaithful.

Louis therefore decided, with characteristic self-control, to endure a
situation as maddeningly obstructive of his desires as the continued
existence of his father. He would of course keep the princess under
constant surveillance by his confidential agents. But meanwhile he
would put her out of his mind so far as possible and turn his restless
energy to more profitable ends. Fortunately, France still had plenty of
enemies to be crushed or circumvented. Charles appeared ready to support a new move against them.

Accordingly, the king and his son in common now proceeded to
undertake campaigns against both the English, who in September
1440 had begun to besiege Harfleur at the mouth of the Seine, and the
Burgundians, who had made Charles uneasy by sending an expedition
to deal, so they said, with certain bandits regrouping in Champagne,
south of the Ardennes, a region which Philip had always coveted in
pursuance of his fixed policy of conjoining his separated dominions
by the provision of a corridor from Luxembourg to Burgundy proper.
The king certainly did not want any such thing, since it would cut him
off from his good friend and brother-in-law, René, in Lorraine and
prohibit access to Franche-Comté on the imperial frontier, a rugged
territory most useful for the defense of France in case of trouble with
Germany or the Swiss. He therefore determined to warn his "good
cousin," by a military gesture, not to be too adventurous.

In January 1441, moving eastward from Tours, he arrested at Bar-
sur-Aube a number of brigand chiefs, including an active promoter of
the late Praguerie, the duke of Bourbon's bastard brother Alexander.
This ingenious ruffian was at once sewn up in a sack and thrown into
the river. The rest were imprisoned. Louis watched the trials impassively. He had now become convinced that his best policy would be
to back his father so long as that incalculable monarch continued to
show any sort of energy.

Further north, at Laon, west of the Ardennes, negotiations were
opened to clear up the difficult situation with Burgundy, still half
committed to the English, despite the Treaty of Arras. Philip was
absent in the north of his dominions and in any case disliked com-

plicated political discussions. He deputed his Duchess Isabel, a mature lady of considerable diplomatic talents, to represent him. Originally a Portuguese princess, charming and shrewd but not beautiful, she enjoyed much respect in England, where she had arranged in the previous year the release of the poet Duke Charles of Orléans from his long captivity. The matter which the duchess was now asked to settle concerned a possible peace treaty with the mild and scholarly King Henry VI, aged twenty, who was known to favor a conclusion of the present hostilities. Louis himself had never ceased to judge this problem the most important one in France, in urgent need of solution, if not by argument then by force of arms.

But in spite of all of Isabel's tact and eloquence the meeting at Laon in April 1441 between French, English and Burgundian politicians came to nothing. Henry could not induce his warlike barons to adopt a more reasonable attitude. All through the spring and summer fighting went on, close to Paris, with varying fortunes. Then at last, in September, the dauphin, after a hard struggle, took Pontoise for his father, who was thus enabled to turn his attention again to the brigands in the east. There he captured the busybody Duke of Alençon and stripped him of all his possessions.

By Easter 1442 father and son were in southern Poitou, on the way to tackle the English of Guienne. On Good Friday morning, which turned out fine after recent storms and heavy rain, the prince, his uncle Count Charles of Anjou and Maine, his chamberlain de Tillay and a gentleman named Louis de Valory embarked in a small boat at the village of Ruffec, adjacent to the swollen river Charente. They were probably performing an act of pilgrimage, but may have been merely relaxing from military duty. In any case they all nearly lost their lives when the wind rose again and the fragile vessel capsized in a millrace. Encumbered by their long gowns, they were already drowning when a providential wave flung them back to their tossing craft and at the same time righted it. All four, after helping each other to strip off their heavy and sodden garments, managed to clamber aboard and steer out of danger to the bank.

The incident throws some light on the dauphin's quite conventional attitude, entirely typical of the period, to Christianity. He regarded the hierarchy of heaven, in particular the Virgin Mary, as existing mainly, like so many feudal suzerains, for the protection of outstanding members of earthly society like himself. Without hesitation, he attributed his escape from drowning to the personal intervention of Our Lady of Béluart, whose neighboring shrine he and his friends may have been intending to visit on this occasion. He therefore lavishly rewarded the fortunate priests who administered the consecrated building.

Throughout his life Louis continued to appeal constantly to the Mother of God or one or other of the saints in paradise for support in his political schemes. He acted in almost exactly the same way as the dukes and counts in his own service when they implored his practical assistance in furthering their own purely mundane ambitions. The only difference was that the prince paid the representatives of his supernatural saviors in hard cash or valuable gifts when his plans came off and begged heaven's forgiveness of his sins if they didn't, while the noblemen who petitioned him could only swear eternal fidelity if their entreaties were granted or at most send him a highly reputed hunter, man or horse, a couple of greyhounds or their best falcon. They would know better than to supply him, as they did others to whom they were indebted, with a pretty and lively page or housemaid, a cask of wine or some exotic dish for his table. It was only toward the end of his life that Louis let it be known that every species of live quadruped or biped, from elks to lapdogs and from eagles to canaries, would be welcomed at his private zoological establishment.

Just now, in the spring of 1442, the dauphin, approaching his nineteenth year, seemed to most of the men who were watching him so closely, to be altering for the better. He had always been brave and resolute in the field. Now he began to be also modest in council, no longer behaving like a headstrong and obstinate boy, too easily exasperated. But in reality he had not changed his mind at all about France or Charles. He was simply biding his time, a procedure which was to govern his actions, to their great advantage, for the rest of his life. He continued his successful military exploits during the next few weeks, advancing deep into Guienne and threatening Gascony. But in the following summer more dramatic events in the north caused the king to send the dauphin, now his best commander, posthaste to Dieppe.

John Talbot, earl of Shrewsbury, was beleaguering that port, held by a French garrison. His forces were strong and it looked as if they might take it in the near future. In 1435 the place had been seized for Charles by the bold pirate Desmarets. He had been using it ever since as a base for attacking English merchant ships and water-borne trade up the Seine as far as Rouen. Eventually Talbot had lost patience with these raids and determined to destroy their source by occuping it himself.

Louis reached Paris, from Guienne, on July 20, 1443. He had to raise funds from the capital to finance the substantial expenditure with which he was faced. He knew it was going to be difficult. The Parlement, in his view and the king's, had always seemed to put the interests of foreign invaders before those of native Frenchmen. The dauphin felt sure that the metropolitan authorities, if left to themselves, would have let the earl of Shrewsbury into Paris, as they had let Duke

John the Fearless of Burgundy occupy the city in 1418. The prince resolved to stand no nonsense of this sort. He took up an attitude, from the start, which can only be described as despotic.

For the first time he was acting, as he would act again and again in the future, like a sovereign whose will was law even when it came into conflict with the proudest and most learned legislative body in France. He put aside with open contempt the Parlement's politely phrased objections, based on existing legal theory and practice, to his peremptory demands. When the august assembly expressed its formal agreement as having been due to "the King's will only," thereby in effect signing the document under protest against arbitrary government, the prince, in a fury, ordered this offensive passage to be expunged from the record. He stood over the lawyers until they had canceled it. Their functions, he told them, were those of registration, not of discussion, of royal decrees. Then he left, with all the money he needed, for Compiègne, riding northeast up the valley of the Somme, followed by his entire force.

The reason for this indirect approach to Dieppe, at so urgent a juncture, was characteristic of the dauphin's careful diplomacy, the obverse of his intolerance of opposition from his own compatriots. The Somme towns of Saint-Quentin, Corbie, Amiens, Abbeville and Ponthieu had been ceded by Charles VII to Philip of Burgundy under the Treaty of Arras, though the king had reserved the right to buy them back for 400,000 crowns whenever he wished. Nevertheless, they were legally, for the moment, Burgundian territory. Louis had never ceased, since his first outright quarrel with his father, to keep in tactful touch with Duke Philip, who might prove a decisive ally in the event of any real chance to depose Charles by force. The dauphin therefore intended to protect his rear, when he assaulted the English blockading Dieppe, by a manifestation of solidarity with both the citizens of the Somme valley and their titular if provisional ruler, the duke.

He received, as he had hoped, a tumultuous welcome from the towns, which regarded him, a successful soldier, rather than the indolent, pleasure-loving Philip, as their best shield against the dangerously advancing English. Nothing could have provided a greater contrast with the smooth but unmistakable hostility of Paris than the cheers and frank exultation of Amiens and Abbeville in particular. He set up his headquarters in the latter city, the nearest to Dieppe, and sent out reconnaissance parties. They reported that there were only about five hundred Frenchmen, under Desmarets, defending the seaport, while the besieging force numbered something like two thousand. The latter depended chiefly for its success on the big wooden fortress of le Pollet outside the walls of the city. From this stronghold firearms of every description, from muskets to cannon, in addition to the equipment of the archers and crossbowmen, commanded territory in all directions.

Shrewsbury himself, incidentally, had long since withdrawn from the operation, "having fared so foul with his men," the *Chronicles of London* remark somewhat cryptically, "that they would no longer abide with him." Probably the choleric old general, who had been called a "mad bull" by the bishop of Beauvais in Joan of Arc's time, had lost the confidence of his troops before Dieppe through being unable to adapt himself to the new tactics of siege warfare, which found machines more effective in reducing fortifications than the old-style massive assaults by ladder, often found to be as wasteful of time as of mens' lives. No doubt so exuberantly bloodthirsty an officer soon wearied of the cautious economy represented by engineering and the mere cutting off of food and water supplies to the garrison.

But whether or not the absence of this fierce veteran encouraged the prince, at dawn on August 11, 1443, he issued his forces, which had been preparing weapons and dispositions all the previous day, just out of range of the fortress guns, with an exceptionally generous ration of wine. At seven o'clock they began to advance under an increasing hail of fire, reinforced by javelins, arrows and crossbows as they drew nearer to the ramparts of the le Pollet building. On Louis's instructions the local peasants drove their carts into the trenches of the first line of defense. His soldiers leaped from the vehicles, cutting down all opposition with sword and ax. Behind them a second wave, with ladders, rushed to assault the walls.

Roars of "For God and the Holy Virgin! St. Denis and St. James!" mingled with the thunder of explosions and the crash of rocks and masonry hurled from the towers and battlements by the defenders, who fought with all the confident obstinacy of troops so often victorious in this part of the country. Then, suddenly, the bells of every church in Dieppe began to ring wildly. Louis, gripping the reins of his plunging charger at the parapet of the trench, glanced in the direction of the town. He saw long lines of men, mostly on foot and carrying battering-rams, issuing from it at several points to converge on the fortress. The powerfully built dockers of Dieppe were coming to his aid.

He rose in his stirrups, flourishing an already bloodstained sword. "On to the walls, men! In the name of the Virgin! *Voilà les Dieppois!*" He flung out his left arm for a moment toward the city. The cheers of the assailants redoubled. Within minutes the onslaught by ladder had begun. Soon the smashing impact of the rams could be heard clearly through the din. Some of the English confronting the dauphin's men as they scrambled up the ladders turned to meet this new attack. But the rest stood their ground stubbornly. Not until midday could the battlements and base-courts be cleared of the enemy, trapped between the prince's storming parties and the Dieppe cavalry pouring through the breaches on the seaward side of the fortress. Then at last the survivors surrendered.

Louis dubbed a number of his officers knights on the spot. He hanged a few Frenchmen wearing the Cross of St. Gerorge in collaboration with the defense. But he spared the lives of the English prisoners who had put up such a stout resistance. Finally he set the fortress on fire, after arranging for its artillery to be handed over to Dieppe. Due religious and civic solemnities welcomed him in the port. But he cut them as short as he decently could. Then he returned in triumph to Paris. He had fully justified his dictatorial treatment of the authorities there, who were obliged to receive him like a conquering hero.

Moving on thence, in this atmosphere of general acclamation, to Tours, he was glad enough to find that his father's congratulations were followed by an almost humble request to teach the obstreperous young Count Jean of Armagnac, whom he knew of old, a further lesson. Jean had apparently won his battle with Mathieu de Foix over the property of Marguerite de Comminges, the former's mother, now dead. At any rate Armagnac was now behaving like a royal despot, levying taxes on the inhabitants of the southwest, calling in the English and actually offering his daughter in marriage to Henry VI.

Louis smiled grimly at this news. He was not in the least afraid of Jean, a mere cavalry leader, who understood nothing of organized war and would be easily dealt with by such a veteran as himself. He saw, too, that if he could go on scoring victories like this, at the king's express command, it would not be long before his father ceased to count altogether in administration of the realm. Then he, Louis, would be in practice king of France and able at last to show the world what he was capable of, an example of prudent autocracy such as Europe had not seen since the age of Charlemagne.

But on entering the count's territory he found that the position was more dangerous than he had supposed. Jean had good, disciplined troops and was showing some capacity in handling them. He also sent a personal message of loyalty to the prince, implying that the obvious plan of action would be for them to join forces and eject the unsatisfactory Charles from a position he had proved himself unfit to hold. The count had mistaken his man in making this proposal. Louis was the last person to brook any rival in his secret designs, least of all so wily a customer as Armagnac, one of the most important nobles in France, now appeared to be from the wording of his dispatch. The dauphin decided characteristically to tackle the problem of Jean's disposal piecemeal.

He began by capturing a town, Rodez, held by one Salazar on behalf of d'Armagnac and persuading its conquered commander to change sides. For the victor's subsequently famous charm of manner, which he could switch on or off at will, was already fully mature at twenty. It added greatly to the prestige of his military prowess, a quality which professional soldiers in opposition were always quick to recognize. So in interviews with defeated antagonists whom he wished to use for his own purposes, as was generally the case, he started with a good deal of advantage. The unpretentious joviality he displayed on these occasions masked to perfection a nature basically harsh and unforgiving. Above all, the apparently reasonable lucidity and often the dry wit of his talk, far from the vague and rhetorical fashion of his day, could captivate even his political enemies, which was more than could be said for even such an alluring personality as that of the duke of Alençon.

The prince employed this technique in Armagnac on one originally hostile officer after another, till Jean found himself almost alone at Île-en-Jourdain, where he had been forced to take refuge from an army which included most of his own former troops. Louis captured the place in the middle of January 1444. He paid no attention to the count's obsequious apologies but simply incarcerated him and his whole family, among them the child destined as a bride for Henry VI, in a castle at Carcassonne. By this bold act he not only terrorized all the provincial gentry, who regarded Jean as their sole protector, but also worried the king himself, who had quite enough powerful aristocrats against him already, without adding Armagnac to their number. Charles thought it would have been more tactful to send this latest rebel peer to Tours under escort, rather than to prison as if he were a common criminal. The strength of feeling in the Countship could be gauged by the fact that after the fall of Île-en-Jourdain the last of Jean's generals, Lescun, continued to hold out at Sévérac till Louis stormed the place at the beginning of March. But Lescun, too, thereafter did whatever the dauphin told him. It should be added of course that lavish bribes played their part in bringing these hard-bitten warriors, who had mostly learned their trade in the rough school of banditry and could hardly tell good manners from bad, to the prince's heel. No man whom Louis wanted for his service could ever complain that he was ill-rewarded.

It was actually at this period that Henry VI, whether or not he had ever heard of Jean and that worthy's daughter, at last made a definite move toward the establishment of peace. René I, hereditary duke of Anjou and Lorraine, count of Provence and Piedmont and titular king of Naples and Sicily, was a good-natured man who preferred painting and poetry to the multifarious duties imposed on him by his high rank and royal connections. He made rather a mess of his political affairs and had fought ineffectively, though bravely, in defense of his Neapolitan dominions against the Aragonese and against Philip in Lorraine. He had already seen the inside of a Burgundian prison. Yet he remained in general very popular and respected. He had attended, for instance, the abortive Council of Tours with the English and Burgundians in 1441. "Le bon roi René," as everyone called him in his lifetime, has retained this somewhat patronizing and ironic title in the works of subsequent historians. He never did anything very brilliant in any sphere. But he lived a long time, pleased a great many people by his harmless personality and exercised a by-no-means-negligible influence, not only cultural and social, upon the events of his age.

René, however, had a daughter, Margaret, who was destined to play a more striking part than he ever did himself in public affairs. In this year, at fourteen, she already displayed a beauty and still more an energy and even severity of temperament that were causing favorable comment in diplomatic circles. In January 1444, before Louis set out from Tours to Armagnac, King Henry VI sent a highly amiable and accomplished ambassador to King Charles VII. The earl of Suffolk, William de la Pole, had fought in all the later campaigns of King Henry V, had been captured by Joan of Arc, ransomed and recalled to England in 1431, where he had acted as host to Duke Charles of Orléans during the latter's long captivity. The two men were almost the same age, Charles being only five years older, and had much in common. William's admiration for his official enemies went so far that he actually wrote his love lyrics in French, while Charles had always greatly enjoyed the more boisterous sides of English life, its athleticism and frank erotic diversions, though they did not affect his delicate verse.

The Francophile earl made first, as the nature of his mission demanded, for Margaret's father, King René, who was in conference with Charles of Orléans at Blois, east of Tours along the Loire. They were soon joined not only by Suffolk, the dean of Chichester and other carefully chosen English envoys, but also by the great Duke Philip of Burgundy himself, who had locked René up in 1431 for disputing the Burgundian claim to Lorraine. The *bon roi*, delighted to hear that Henry proposed to marry his daughter Margaret, escorted the party to King Charles's court at Tours. There a distinguished company awaited them, including René's sister the queen of France, her daughter-in-law Margaret of Scotland, the duke of Brittany and almost all the grandest French lords. Negotiations were prolonged, but in a festive atmosphere enhanced by the bright spring weather.

When Louis returned to Tours in April he found jousting, archery competitions, picnics and dances in full swing. But the political debates ran into certain difficulties. René could not afford so rich a dowry as one king might expect from another. There was no comparison between the wealth of the throne of England and the resources available to the embarrassed duke of Anjou, who drew little or no material profit from his other titles. In these circumstances the English representatives declined resolutely to evacuate the economically important provinces of Normandy and Guienne. The French government had to be content with the compromise of free trade between the two kingdoms and a two years' truce to the fighting. Then at last Margaret of Anjou was formally betrothed to Henry of England in St. Martin's Church at Tours, with the blessing of the papal legate.

The reasons why London approached so poverty-stricken a princess as a bride for the young English king are rather obscure. But it is certain that the political situation, dominated by a resurgent France facing an England with its back to the wall in that part of the Continent, required a royal marriage beween the two countries in accordance with long-established diplomatic tradition, to hold the balance of power. Charles VII had no daughter to dispose of. His eldest girl, Catherine, was already the wife of Philip's son Charles, count of Charolais, and the others were all under ten years old. Nor had the duke of Burgundy any female offspring. Even if he had possessed one of marriageable age, she would hardly have been considered within hail of Henry's rank. But King René, brother-in-law to King Charles VII, had a daughter whose character already appeared, in its direct opposition to Henry's weak and retiring nature, highly desirable as a source of strength to the English crown, since its present wearer showed no signs of being able to resist in his own person only too likely threats or at least undue influence by ambitious aristocrats.

England wanted peace at home in order to recover from recent misfortunes in France and eventually to avenge them. Margaret was Charles's niece. But Anjou and still more Lorraine had long been practically independent of the French ruler and might at some future time be induced to revolt in support of English claims to possess France, if a strong queen of England born in René's territory should ever look forward to the chance of so great an inheritance.

It is probable that these considerations turned the scale in Margaret's favor. Henry had enough material assets to render the somewhat unsatisfactory financial aspect of the proposed union negligible. He did not need money. What he did need in his government's opinion was energy and a backing in France for English interests. Margaret of Anjou certainly had the first quality. She might in due course also provide the second condition. Anyhow, no other continental princess could be found to fill the bill. King Henry's advisers explained to the English Parliament, implacably hostile to everything French, that the girl from Lorraine, a king's daughter, was not really a Frenchwoman like the late "witch" Joan of Arc, though she might speak the same language, if with a slightly different accent from that of the notorious shepherdess. In any case, after all, had not the great hero Henry V, conqueror of France, married Catherine of Valois, sister of Charles VII? These arguments at last overruled popular prejudice in England, which decided to wait the further developments promised.

Meanwhile, in France, the country as a whole gave itself up to the greatest joy it had known for decades or was to know for many future years. Hilarious processions took place in the towns. Gay excursions roamed through the forests and valleys, so long ominous with the menace of ambush, robbery and massacre. Paris, for once, showed as much pleasure in the new situation as Burgundy and even repentant Armagnac.

But the dauphin took little or no part in these celebrations. He had never cared in the slightest for pageantry and for organized amusements. In private he found some of the Burgundians and other foreigners less than happy about the future. For King Charles, at forty, his volatile head turned by all this excitement, seemed to be losing his grip again. He insisted on taking part in the tournaments, though hardly any of the other contestants were over thirty. Moreover, a girl of twenty-two, Agnès Sorel, attached to the service of Isabel of Lorraine, René's wife, had completely bowled over the once more sexually susceptible occupant of the throne of France.

He was fascinated by her wit, her low-cut gowns, the most provocative hitherto seen at any Christian court, and her complete self-possession. She certainly had brains as well as magnificent fair hair and blue eyes. At this date she was probably the mistress of Etienne Chevalier, the king's secretary, who subsequently commissioned Jean Fouquet's portrait of her, his masterpiece, in the guise of a highly sophisticated Virgin Mary, for a diptych at Melun. Another lover was undoubtedly the royal chamberlain Pierre de Brézé, a gallant soldier and able councilor, always absolutely loyal to Charles VII, and perhaps truly in command of the heart of the equivocal Agnès. She might have chosen worse. For this shrewd couple, both relatively honest and reasonable, in their combined influence over the king, rendered his next six years the most prosperous of his reign, thereby confounding the numerous critics of the lady. Louis soon became one of the most censorious.

He saw at once that she was going to be important and began by cultivating her for political reasons. But he found her a match for him intellectually. He soon turned against her, so much so that gossip pretended he had once boxed her lovely ears. It could not have been so. The prince's native caution never allowed him to perpetrate such a breach of manners, even in dealing with individuals he considered much less dangerous than Agnès Sorel. There is no reliable record of his ever having touched anyone, even his wife Margaret, in anger. Yet it was common enough in those days for men and women of all classes to lay hands on people of either sex who irritated them. Nevertheless, Louis certainly came to fear the rising star of Agnès not only because he automatically detested anyone whom Charles favored, but also because, for the first time in his life, he had reluctantly to acknowledge that a woman, if she combined remarkable bodily allurements with exceptional intelligence, ambition and strength of will, might outdo any equally well endowed male in the struggle for political power, which was all the physically insignificant dauphin cared about, since he considered that he alone had the capacity to rule France for its ultimate benefit.

It was no wonder, therefore, that in 1444 Louis, despite his already glorious military and diplomatic reputation, felt about as depressed as he had ever been. He did not believe for a moment that the English were yet done with. Their smiles in council at Tours had made far less impression on him than their calm refusal to see why they should get out of Normandy and Guienne. But, apart from the English, another obstinate sore in the body politic of France which Pierre de Brézé and Agnès Sorel appeared to ignore, worried the dauphin to the point of desperation.

The truce had given the roving mercenaries in every province of the kingdom a leisure which they were bound to misuse. There were between twenty-five and thirty thousand of them, a very miscellaneous lot. Some of their commanders were native aristocrats who had lived by pillage in the name of patriotism. But many were aliens, Spaniards, Italians or Germans who cared nothing for a France too weak to control their depredations. The rank and file could for the most part be described as the scum of Europe, though some, whatever nation they belonged to, might be genuinely dissatisfied with conditions in their own lands. As a whole they constituted a reckless force of greedy and stony-hearted brigands, inaccessible to negotiation, terrorists in the field. To Louis the matter seemed extremely serious. But at first he could not get Charles to listen to him.

Then it looked as if a solution of the problem might be found outside France. The Holy Roman Emperor Frederick III of Habsburg needed mercenaries to keep the Swiss Confederacy out of his allied city of Zurich, the only one of the cantons which admitted his suzerainty. He applied to Philip of Burgundy, who was not interested, and then to Charles VII, who wished to keep on good terms with the empire, since his daughter Radegonde had been betrothed to Frederick's son. It was arranged that Louis should lead the freebooters, who had become known as "flayers" owing to the way they stripped their surroundings bare of every kind of product, against the Swiss cantons on behalf of the emperor.

By July 1444 the dauphin had collected about twenty thousand of these marauders, together with an equal number of their camp followers, at Langres on the upper Marne, some forty miles northeast of Dijon. The men spoke nearly all the dialects of France and most of those of Europe. Spaniards, English, Scots, Bretons, Lombards and Gascons predominated among the foreigners, Brittany and Gascony not being in those days regarded as truly French, any more than Burgundians or Lorrainers, who were conspicuous by their absence, neither of these regions caring much for their eastern neighbors, the German princes of the empire, who occasionally claimed parts of their territory.

This polyglot horde, mainly simple ruffians, but formidable for their numbers, which exceeded those of any professional army then available in the Continent, duly set out, on August 5, for the Swiss border, living of course on the intervening country and committing their usual outrages on the population. Complications arose at once, for their route lay through Burgundian lands. Dijon in particular complained vigorously to the prince of the depredations and atrocities of these invaders of a peaceful area, guaranteed against war like the rest of the duchy and France itself, by the recent truce proclaimed at Tours. Duke Philip begged Louis, in the name of their long-standing friendship, to restrain his men and accompanied this prayer with a substantial bribe in cash. The young commander took the money but did little to earn it. He knew that if he prevented the beatings and tortures inflicted by his mercenaries on the Burgundian peasants to force them to disgorge their savings he would have a mutiny on his hands. Any such conflict would lead to the immediate resumption of the very situation the expedition had been designed to end. It would also disgrace him in the eyes of Frederick, who was already pressing him to hurry.

The huge multitude, more like a hodgepodge of migrating barbarians than an army, moved slowly, at the footpace of its thousands of supernumeraries borne in carts or on muleback and its lumbering baggage wagons and trains of artillery. The procession, moreover, often halted during forays into the surrounding farm lands or owing to riots which continually broke out between different national contingents. Sometimes, again, it settled down to mass orgies with its four thousand turbulent prostitutes. The noise and gaiety of this vast swarm of irresponsible sensualists, who were only on the move because they were being well paid and fed to take part in what most of them regarded as a picnic with no holds barred, deafened and wearied the prince's own escort and staff, perpetually engaged both in keeping the so-called soldiers at least from spreading over the countryside and also in warding off their assaults on the reserves of weapons and ammunition.

Louis decided that the time had come for real military action. Having plenty of siege artillery and materials, he made for the strong fortress of Montbéliard, standing due east of Dijon and just south of Belfort in Franche-Comté, very near the Swiss border. The place commanded the main roads to both Alsace and Basel, which last town itself covered Zurich further east. No point could be better adapted strategically as a base of operations. He detached seven thousand of his best fighting men to take it. On the approach of this overwhelming force the Count of Württemberg, who owned the territory, promised to abandon it for eighteen months on condition that pillage would be prohibited. The dauphin agreed to this stipulation but could not of course guarantee it to the letter. Despite his commands the farmers in the district suffered heavily.

At Montbéliard, which he occupied without difficulty, he found Austrian envoys urging him to assault Basel without further delay and Burgundian representatives who warned him to keep out of Philip's domains in his rear. He agreed with the greatest calmness to both these requests, as if they were self-evident items in his plans. But he had not yet made up his mind about Basel, a great cosmopolitan city still at this time officially independent of both the Swiss Confederation and the Rhine princes. A most important ecclesiastical council, the third of its kind since 1409, had been sitting there ever since 1431. In 1439 it had deposed Pope Eugenius IV in favor of Amadeus VIII, duke of Savoy, who took the title of Felix V. This equivocal situation still existed in 1444, dividing Europe into two camps of opinion, that of Italy and England, favoring Eugenius, growing steadily stronger than that of the rest of Europe, which backed Felix.

In these circumstances it seemed doubtful to Louis whether his cause, that of the emperor, more or less neutral in the religious dispute, would be greatly served by letting loose his violently unscrupulous mercenaries on a venerable city not openly hostile to Frederick and filled with important persons more concerned with intellectual than political issues. But he did go himself, in disguise, to inspect the fortifications of Basel. He found them solid and well manned. Half his escort were shot down with arquebuses from the walls.

The very next day the confederate cantons launched a surprise attack on his vanguard. The Swiss came on with great determination, in good order, and at first drove their less disciplined opponents backward. But before this retreat could become a rout, the main body of mercenaries, far outnumbering their assailants, plunged to the offensive. The battle became a massacre, for the Swiss held their ground to the death, most of them falling in or near a large hospital for lepers called the Saint-Jacques, which was set on fire by the dauphin's cannon. Fifteen hundred of the confederate force of two thousand perished. All the survivors were wounded. But they had extorted a fearful price in casualties from the victors. No less than eight thousand of the mercenaries, contemporary historians report, lay dead under the walls of Basel, which had, however, taken no part in the fighting.

The spirit of the Swiss who had faced invincible odds with such superb valor is illustrated by the story that one of the few renegades, a baron who had joined the freebooters, jeered at a dying halberdier, lying with his weapon lost and an arrow stuck in his ribs under the hoofs of the traitor's horse. "Hallo, boy!" shouted the turncoat rider in his compatriot's vernacular. "We'll be supping on roses tonight!" "Then start with this one!" the mortally wounded soldier growled back. With the last of his strength he picked up a great stone and hurled it full in the horseman's face, cracking his skull. Both men fell dead at the same moment.

Louis was on the whole pleased with the result of the Saint-Jacques encounter. He had not only scored an unquestionable triumph in the field but had also susbtantially reduced the numbers of the "flayers," which was the whole point of the expedition in French eyes. He could boast, moreover, that he had spared the neutral city of Basel, which he could easily have stormed, and had only defended himself against a ferocious attack, which he had not expected so soon, from the other cantons. Also, he had been deeply impressed by the magnificent performance of the Swiss infantry. Using only halberd, pike and sword against firearms and cavalry, each individual on the average must have accounted for four of the enemy before he himself went down. The most experienced of the French officers on the prince's staff agreed with him that they had never seen anything like it before. These reflections led to a decisive change of plan by the invading commander.

It was reinforced by the news, reported by his spies, that all Switzerland was now gathering to repel his ill-famed horde of cruel marauders. The outcome of such a defense, after the scenes at the battle of Saint-Jacques, could not be in doubt. The prince had no intention, after so many victories, of appearing before the world as a defeated general, stained also, perhaps, by the scandal of the utter destruction by his ungovernable rabble of the famous old cities of Basel and Zurich. It would be far better in every way, he saw, to gain a reputation for magnanimity and impartiality.

He therefore withdrew his battered but still formidable host of international adventurers across the frontier into Alsace, at that time German imperial territory, announcing that he would be prepared to act as mediator between his ally Frederick and those he secretly hoped would soon also be his allies, the indomitable Swiss people. At Altkirch on the road to Belfort he told a nervous embassy from Basel, on August 31, 1444, that so far from wishing to attack their city he would be prepared to protect it against all comers if it would definitely repudiate the confederacy and leave the emperor in peace. A treaty of alliance with the city was signed then and there, to the fury of both Frederick and the Alsatians, the former astounded and the latter terrified by the presence of so large and fierce a collection of foreign soldiers on the imperial soil in question.

But the dauphin's own territorial ambitions had now been aroused. He ignored the Alsatian envoys and told the Germans that their emperor, of whose listless incapacity for both war and statesmanship he was well aware, had broken his promise to supply funds and subsistence for the mercenaries he had hired, who had therefore been obliged to live off the country. The prince added haughtily that he had duly gone to Switzerland and chastised the enemies of Frederick, as agreed. Now he was in Alsace to recover lands that had been French from time immemorial and had actually renounced their formal allegiance to the empire. This open threat of force, the German ambassadors immediately perceived, was aimed at the rich city of Strasbourg at the northern corner of their western frontier, only about seventy-five miles north of Altkirch along the border. They retired, much disconcerted, to warn Frederick that the son of Charles VII seemed to be thinking of expanding his control into Germany, with the dreaded Swiss infantry behind him.

In the first week of September a quadruple conference began at Ensisheim, about twenty miles north of Altkirch, attended by German, Swiss and Alsatian representatives in addition to Louis himself. All this time his ravaging hordes were moving steadily toward Strasbourg, taking fortress after fortress. When they reached Marckolsheim, just north of Colmar, he came to assume command of the assault himself, captured this strong-point and went on to Dambach in the Vosges foothills, more than halfway to his ultimate objective.

But here, for the first time in his life, he was seriously wounded by an arrow in the knee, pinning him to his saddle. Unable to ride, he abandoned the siege of Dambach and had himself carried back to Ensisheim. Here an imperial delegation awaited him, hoping for a softening of his attitude to Germany after this personal misfortune. But the stern young commander, lying back pallid and motionless among his pillows, his long nose wrinkling, told the Germans as firmly as ever that he meant to make the Rhine the French frontier. By October 28, still at Ensisheim, he had signed a pact of "firm friendship" with the Swiss confederacy. Physical weakness seemed to have raised his fever of aggression to inordinate heights, nothing less than a climb to the imperial throne on a tide of Swiss halberds.

This gossip threw Charles VII into a panic. Now that his internal administration was going so well under Pierre de Brézé and Agnès Sorel, and France proper was clear of the "flayers," he wanted nothing less than a quarrel with Frederick. His agents in Germany reported that the whole empire was mobilizing behind Strasbourg, which was determined to resist his son to the death. Worst of all, Philip of Burgundy was said to be thinking of changing his mind about Louis and taking a hand in the preparations to stop his unwarranted belligerence from throwing all Europe into a bloodbath.

The prince's wound gave the king a good excuse to recall the dangerous young firebrand to Tours for a rest and more expert treatment than he could expect at Ensisheim. Urgent messages from the French court began to reach the dauphin's bedside. They did not for a moment cause him to alter his intentions. But he decided eventually to force his will upon his father in person, as he had so often done before. He needed more and better troops than his barbarous freebooters for the conquest of the empire and could only get them from France, with Charles's consent. Ordering his forces in Alsace to keep on the defensive for the time being against the mounting hostility of the population and the threats of Philip, he set out for Tours with a small cavalry escort. The country looked extraordinarily prosperous and peaceful compared with the scenes he had so recently witnessed in the northeastern areas. But he had only ridden a few miles when he heard that his father was in the north, at Nancy, King René's capital.

The prince found Charles a much tougher proposition to deal with than he had bargained for. The king appeared well dressed, happy with his recent victories in René's cause and on the surface at least popular. *Le bon roi* and his brother-in-law seemed on positively affectionate terms, for which there was good reason apart from Charles's engineering of the English marriage for Margaret of Anjou. French policy required that the king-duke of Lorraine, now on the upgrade once more after his recent loss of Naples (1442) to Alfonso of Aragon, should be set securely enough in his duchy to defy the claims of the "free" imperial city of Metz, only fifty miles north of Nancy, and the local lords. Charles had managed to get a treaty signed to this effect and had also induced the powerful neighboring bishops of Toul and Verdun to accept French protection. Louis for once had no objection to these feats by his father. Anything which strengthened the approaches to the Rhine had the ambitious dauphin's approval.

But before confiding his grand design to the king of France he had to deal with an unexpected event which rapidly changed the Franco-German situation. The desperate population of Alsace had at last united and dealt the hated mercenaries a mortal blow, ambushing their main body in a deep valley and wiping out the trapped "flayers," who, almost to a man, had characteristically grown careless in their leader's absence. Apparently they had been too drunk to defend themselves effectively. A great deal of booty was taken, which had mostly been Alsatian property. The avengers left nothing behind them but stripped corpses. This example was at once followed everywhere in the province. Detachment after detachment of the foreigners was cut off and slaughtered without mercy, by superior numbers of the native inhabitants. The survivors reached France in chastened mood and isolated groups. The best of them were summarily recruited into Charles's newly reorganized army. The less promising were branded as criminals and exiled from the country.

Louis dealt grimly, day after day, with this setback to his hopes, while the gay court of Nancy reveled around him, led by his rejuvenated father and Agnès Sorel. That coolheaded, realistic beauty had experienced no difficulty, from the first, in ensuring that her tapestries, linen, plate, jewels and table, all gifts from the king, outshone Queen Marie's and those of René's wife, the Duchess Isabel. The trains of Agnès' magnificent gowns became the longest ever seen in France, her bared shoulders and more than half-bared breasts the most imposing in any assembly. The prince loathed the sight of her, less on account of the insult she represented to his mother than because he knew her to be largely responsible for the new confidence and dignity of Charles, whom he found daily less and less approachable.

Many of the same lords and ladies who had been present at the festivities accompanying the betrothal of Margaret of Anjou and Henry VI at Tours in the previous year had come on to Nancy, where the actual wedding was to take place by proxy. The English, headed by the former earl of Suffolk, now a marquis, were there in force, including such veteran opponents of France in the field as the earls of Shrewsbury and Salisbury. There is some reason to believe that the brilliant and agreeable Suffolk's wife, Alice Chaucer, may have been the granddaughter of Geoffrey Chaucer, the first unquestionable genius of English literature. At any rate the company was a highly cultivated one and in the highest spirits as the preliminaries to the marriage of Margaret and Henry drew to a close. King Charles was behaving like a lad half his age. He actually joined once more in the jousting,

wielding lance and sword with the greatest exuberance, to the wonder
of all who had known him in former days. A tremendous lot of
dancing, play acting and ceremonial kissing went on. The costumes
were dazzling, the smiles and laughter continuous.

But the tight-lipped young prince, still lame from his wound, excused himself, without much grace, from taking part in these amusements. He spent most of his time disposing of the ignominious
remnants of his mercenaries, ratifying treaties on behalf of René and
negotiating to extend the power of Charles, which he could hardly
wait to make his own. Then suddenly, on March 19, Princess Radegonde, the king's fourth daughter, betrothed to a son of the emperor,
died at Tours. Her health had always been poor and her end was
not unexpected. But relations with Frederick at once deteriorated. He
and Louis began to exchange bills for the expenses of the Swiss campaign, each proclaiming the other responsible for them. Nor was this
the only addition to the dauphin's diplomatic worries. Philip of Burgundy sent his duchess Isabel to Châlons with a long list of queries
and complaints.

They arose from two main sources. In the first place Louis, in
pursuing his policy of extending his father's domains, had raised the
question of the recovery by Charles of the Somme towns, now that
money was available to buy them back from the duke, as stipulated
by the Treaty of Arras. But these flourishing cities, especially Amiens,
were proving of great advantage to the duchy, as well as constituting
a natural, easily defensible frontier with France. Philip was determined, on one pretext or another, to hold on to them. Second, he had
a more reasonable grievance in calling attention to the behavior of
the dauphin's mercenaries, who had invaded Burgundian territory after
the relief of Dieppe in 1443 and in the following spring and summer
had ravaged the areas of Mâcon, Charolais and Dijon on their way
to the Swiss border. Isabel brought with her incontrovertible proof of
the shameless plundering, torturing and hanging of the rural inhabitants, subjects of neutral Burgundy. Children had been killed,
females of all ages brutally violated.

Why had the prince, known to be a strict disciplinarian in his other
campaigns, permitted this conduct in the lands of a friendly state
if not to intimidate a power which he imagined, and quite rightly,
to stand in the way of his unjustifiable and inordinate ambition? There
was the case of Montbéliard, for instance, in Franche-Comté, a fortress
which had always been protected by Burgundy and was even now
being held by troops under Louis's command, though King Charles
had promised his "cousin" Philip long ago that it would be evacuated

by royal decree. All these matters, the duke intimated, must be discussed, as extremely urgent problems, with Isabel at Châlons.

It was not considered appropriate by either side that she should come with these gloomy questions, involving French delinquency, to the gay cosmopolitan court at Nancy, filled with festal celebrations of a wedding not particularly congenial to Burgundian interests. First Reims and then Châlons were suggested as suitable localities for the necessary conference. The prince, always a stickler for international courtesies, hastened, with his wife and his mother, to meet Isabel at Châlons. That decidedly sharp-set character did not think much of his defense. He denied that he was occupying Montbéliard against the will of the local authorities or that he had any direct control over the garrison. He countered the duchess's demand for financial compensation to repair the damage done by his mercenaries by alleging that they and his own purely French compatriots had first been assailed by Burgundians in the regions mentioned. He asserted that the Bruges magistrates, for example, had exasperated French detestation of Flanders by hanging some sailors from Dieppe who had seized an English vessel in the Flemish port of Sluis. He claimed, in his turn, compensation from Burgundy for these "outrages."

The duchess contemptuously repudiated these charges for what they were, mere evasions of the main issues. She knew she had right on her side and that this smoothly elusive young man also knew it. She appealed at once to Queen Marie, a woman of her own age, who might be presumed experienced enough in the ways of the political world to be fair-minded. But the worthy queen of France was much too frightened of her far more intelligent and strong-willed son to intervene. Isabel then turned to Charles with better success. The king acted, no doubt on the advice of Pierre de Brézé and Agnès Sorel, with all the irrefutable authority of his dynastic position. He peremptorily ordered the abandonment of Montbéliard and the retention by Philip of the Somme towns till further notice. These measures satisfied the Burgundian delegation for the time being. Once more Charles, or rather Pierre and Agnès, had checkmated what might be read as a preliminary move aimed at his deposition. The dauphin could only grind his teeth again, in silence.

As before, he turned with ferocity upon his wife. The unfortunate girl was undoubtedly innocent of even entertaining the idea of adultery. But Louis, determined to get rid, if at all possible, of an incompatible and barren spouse, had been intensifying his surveillance of her private life. His chamberlain, the Breton Jamet de Tillay, a useful soldier who had served the king well in Lorraine and elsewhere, but an adept at telling his social superiors what they wanted to hear, irrespective of its truth, related to the embittered prince a queer story about the young bluestocking of a princess. He said that he and Margaret's steward Regnault de Dresnay were going their usual evening rounds of her apartments when they found her sitting in the firelight, without torches or candles, in the company of a well-known poet, the Sire de Blainville, a bold, handsome fellow, and another gentleman whom they failed to identify in the shadows. De Blainville had his elbow on the couch occupied by Margaret. Jamet of course apologized, if rather grimly, to the princess for his intrusion, due, he said, to his having found the room unlit and unusually quiet. Then he swung around to berate the steward for neglecting his duty to keep the room properly illuminated, especially as the court was in France proper, but in Lorraine, a technically foreign country. Any malefactor or intriguer might have found his way into the quarters, so eccentrically darkened, of Madame la Dauphine. These remarks naturally alarmed Margaret as a veiled reflection upon herself. But fortunately the steward did not venture to defend himself and the intruders left without further comment.

Jamet felt bound to add to his report, which strongly implied that Margaret or her guests had blown out the candles themselves, that neither she nor either of the gentlemen with her seemed at all perturbed when he and Regnault entered her dimly lit apartment. Presumably, he intimated, with a scarcely repressed sneer, modern "intellectuals" thought nothing of such indiscreet behavior. Louis did not respond to this suggestion. He merely stared, with a slight frown, at his bowing chamberlain. But he ordered the man to continue spying upon the princess.

CHAPTER IV

The Final Break
(1445–1446)

❦❦❦ In April, after the excitements of the wedding were over and Margaret of Anjou had left for England, Charles started his usual rounds of his kingdom, rather like a policeman on his beat, to detect possible signs of subversion. In May further disturbing reports reached the prince from Jamet, who saw which way the wind was blowing and sedulously fanned it. The chamberlain called his master's attention to the large sums the princess was spending on athletic young men, not poets this time, but champion jousters. He named one Charles Morillon and an absolutely irresistible lady-killer, Jacques de Lalaing, who bowled over the hearts of duchesses and countesses within doors as easily as he did knights in the tiltyard.

That master of purple prose, Georges Chastelain, calls Jacques, no doubt with some exaggeration, a flawless paragon of chivalry, handsome as Paris, pious as Aeneas, wise as Odysseus and fiery as Hector, rushing from battle to battle but gentle when off the field, a pattern at such times of humility and courtesy. Lalaing's whole life was dedicated to feats of arms. But he never missed mass. His end, typical of one of the last representatives of the feudal period, did not come, as he would have wished, in hand-to-hand combat with sword, mace or lance. A cannon ball discharged from a distant gun by an unseen adversary laid him low. As for his dealings with Margaret and other ladies, not mentioned by the memorialist, Chastelain disposes of these rumors with the calm epitaph:

> Here lies one purer than ivory
> who took chastity as the pillar of his fame.

The well-documented character of King Louis IX of France (1214–1270), known as Saint Louis, proves the existence of such Galahads long before the age of Thomas Malory (d. 1471), the popularizer of the tradition of Arthurian romance. There is no evidence that Lalaing could not have been one of such specimens of virtue. But Chastelain's account of him, written by a contemporary of both his subject and Malory, is a little too wistfully nostalgic for an assumed golden period of Christian nobility and prowess to be entirely credible.

Lalaing was born in Hainaut, now a southern province of Belgium. A subject, therefore, of Duke Philip of Burgundy, he always remained as fully devoted as that magnate to fantastic and useless projects. Oddly enough, Jacques Coeur, who would have been quite at home in twentieth-century Wall Street, so admired the dazzling knight-errant that once, when they met by chance at Montpellier, the normally shrewd millionaire offered to pay all the younger man's future traveling expenses. This apparently reckless proposal was proudly declined by the incorrigibly peripatetic Lalaing. If he had accepted it, the fact would soon have been known all over Europe, much to the advantage of Coeur's moral reputation as a munificent patron. No doubt that possible result would have been present to his mind. Yet a certain impulsive warmth in his character, evident from his whole career, indicates that this calculation need not have been his only motive in putting his wealth at the disposal of a popular athlete, like a modern newspaper proprietor backing a record-breaking yachtsman who used only anachronistic sails instead of up-to-date engines, as Lalaing used skill in the tournament rather than machinery and gunpowder.

Margaret had plenty of excuse, in her husband's chilly attitude to her, for carrying such activities to extremes. Louis was incapable of bullying or even being publicly rude to a woman. But he took every opportunity of removing himself from his wife's presence for prolonged periods, criticizing her personality when he interviewed her in private and when other people were looking on adopting a pose of icy formality as if she, not himself, were the offending party in their association. It was really only Jamet who persecuted her. But she understood perfectly well that he was acting at the prince's orders, and the reason why they had been given.

Nevertheless, in spite of the Breton's allegations that she kept a special treasure chest for subsidies to her favorite performers in the lists and although the jealousies of their unsuccessful rivals spread rumors that she secretly entertained such handsome athletes as Morillon and Jacques de Lalaing in a more familiar fashion, no hard and fast evidence of any such behavior was ever discovered. Her character

as it appears from other sources seems to have been the very reverse
of amorous. She could not help the fact that the elegant contemporary
versifying to which she was addicted dealt almost exclusively with the
subject of *amour*. But the best of it never descended, as that of the
early troubadours so often did, to frank licentiousness. Guilhem IX,
for instance, duke of Aquitaine and count of Poitiers at the turn of
the eleventh and twelfth centuries, repeatedly used four-letter words
in boasting with ludicrous exaggeration of his erotic exploits. The
ballads, however, and other forms of lyric, such as the *chant royal*,
virelai and *rondeau*, popularized by Guillaume de Machaut (1300–
1377), changed the medieval directness of statement about actual copulation to oblique reflections on the thoughts and feelings to which the
prospect or frustration of sexual intercourse might give rise. Machaut's
account of his love affair in old age with Peronelle d'Armentières
shows the utmost delicacy in this connection. He relates, for example,
how at their first interview the young noblewoman's secretary laid a
green leaf upon her mistress's lips, as she lay with her head upon the
poet's knee, and directed Machaut to kiss the leaf in that position.
He timidly bent to do so. The the secretary slyly removed the leaf
and Peronelle exclaimed "very gently":

> *Friend, thou art overbold.*
> *Knowest thou no other games to play?*

This was the sort of poetry that Margaret Stuart enjoyed, lines that
indicated a retreat from rather than an advance upon crude lascivious-
ness. The melancholy of unrequited affection, so characteristic of
early fifteenth-century literary composition, forming an artificial, imaginative parallel to the only too real ruin of French society after the
Hundred Years' War, must also have attracted her on purely personal
grounds, her unhappy marriage to a man constitutionally inaccessible
to the softer emotions of humanity. It is clear enough that only her
intense, inherited preoccupation with the written word, coupled with
a temperament innocently gay rather than adventurous, prevented
the collapse of the princess into either hopeless dejection or unbridled
promiscuity.

There is no evidence that either Margaret Stuart or anyone else
ever wrote a *Chant Royal* about the highly respectable thirteenth-
century King Louis IX of France. His life, unsuccessful in its two
main objectives, the extirpation of prostitutes in Christian Europe and
the recovery of the Holy Sepulcher in Syria, would not have made a
bad subject for this kind of secular hymn. But the life of Louis XI
would make a better one, with its noble plan, its steady upward beat

through one cruel setback after another, its brilliant victories against heavy odds and its final burst of grandiose achievement.

The court of Charles VII, dominated by his virtuous wife, his discreet mistress and his woman-hating son, was not an easy place in which to hunt down adultery. Nevertheless, it was this sin which Margaret's enemies, among whom Louis himself must be counted at this date, wished to prove against her. They began with her unmistakable inclination, typical of the tuberculosis which undoubtedly affected her, to outward displays of animation on festive occasions. Jamet, well aware of the prince's contempt for pageantry of every kind, which he considered an absurd waste of money, insinuated that Margaret was going further than she needed to in this respect. He also professed to wonder why so prim and proper an intellectual as Madame la Dauphine should suddenly reveal such enthusiasm for gentlemen who never opened a manuscript or thought of anything but war and its ceremonious imitations. But this new craze, he added, did not seem to have stopped the princess's habit of sitting up till all hours ostensibly engaged in verse composition with male as well as female friends. He was no doctor himself, the chamberlain went on. But he had sometimes heard medical men say that wives fond of turning night into day, in whatever fashion, often suffered from a sterility which annoyed their husbands.

Louis was moved by this sort of conversation to reprehend Margaret sharply, but no more, for not getting enough sleep and also for perpetually chewing green apples and sipping vinegar, a practice which he understood her maids gossiped about and which he pretended to find disgusting. She protested, rather pathetically and probably with truth, that these forms of nourishment had been recommended to her as specifics for keeping her figure fashionably slim, simply and solely to please him rather than herself. The prince responded only with a haughty grimace to this defense. But Margaret had long recognized that it was no use hoping for any sign of affection from a man forced into marriage with her for political purposes that had not been achieved. The assassination of her father in 1437, as the result of a conspiracy among his nobles, had prevented the payment of her dowry, as well as any useful aid James might otherwise have afforded to Charles VII.

The situation, by this time, had begun to sour the temper of a girl naturally cheerful and attractive, for all her inconvenient aesthetic leanings at a somewhat Philistine court. She would have been happier with a Burgundian lord or one of René's favorites, when no one would have dreamed of censuring her midnight poetry sessions. As it was, she had begun to get sick of running across the bowing and smirking

Jamet at times and places when he would have been better employed in attendance on his master. She knew now, very well, what the chamberlain was up to and let him see pretty clearly that he was not wanted at her elbow or even in her sight. He swore with all the eloquence at his command, which was considerable, that he wished for nothing except to serve her. But she would not mollify her attitude.

De Tillay heard from some of the more irresponsible of her maids that she was actually in the habit of sometimes borrowing money for the benefit of ambitious young squires from her chief female attendant, the forty-five-year-old Mme de Saint-Michel, a strictly pious duenna, and even from the groom attached to the household, a respectable character named Gervais. The chamberlain felt himself entitled to adopt the airs of a condescending, jovially blunt and boisterous soldier in conversing with the princess's maids of honor. Mme de Saint-Michel did not like this behavior. That was perhaps one of the reasons why the Breton reported her to Louis as overindulgent to Margaret's extravagance.

One evening, when the venerable matron was proceeding, with her usual solemnity, through a room full of the younger women who served the dauphine, Jamet happened to be lounging there. He called out impudently: "And where are you off to, old girl?" ("*Où allez vous, la vieilee?*") The lady was in fact on her way to vespers in the princess's oratory. She retorted with unconcealed hostility: "Not to see you, impious one!" He only laughed at her, while the junior maids bent their heads to hide their smiles. It was not an episode of which Mme de Saint-Michel would have dared to complain, the officer being so much more important a personage than herself. But it proves the graver members of Margaret's establishment shared her dislike of the prince's agent and understood his mission.

Louis, for his part, seems to have been rather bewildered and perhaps abashed by the matrimonial position. It was decidely awkward for both parties. He could not honestly suspect Margaret of unchastity and may have been rather ashamed of spying on her. After all, she was not a slippery political customer like Agnès Sorel or Isabel of Burgundy. He knew that she took no interest in anything but fashionable diversions on the one side and her girlish literary romanticism on the other. Yet the reproach of barrenness was a serious matter. Since he felt physically repelled by her he could only take the one decent course open to him in such circumstances by divorcing her. But where was the source for such a scandal? No one who knew Margaret could imagine for a moment that she was sleeping with Morillon or de Blainville, whatever Jamet might insinuate. Firelight conversations and the sharing of a great lady's purse with promising young warriors did not prove adultery. In no other way did Margaret's behavior afford the slightest pretext for censure. If he set in motion the cumbrous machinery of an application to Rome for separation from so attractive a consort, with at least twenty years of childbearing age ahead of her, on the grounds of sterility alone, he would run into prolonged and tedious arguments with the king, the clergy and the council. The more frivolous courtiers would start rumors, to which his frail, prematurely wearied appearance and reserve of manner would lend color, that he was impotent. He, the victor of battle after battle for the last five years, the solver of problem after problem of administration, with a clear plan in his head already for the future security and glory of France! An intolerable situation and worsening day by day!

Louis was just twenty-two. At an age when the majority of young men, particularly those who have, as he had, exercised high responsibility with marked success, feel on top of the world, he had fallen once more into deep depression. He despised his father. He cared little for his sweet, saintly mother. He detested his guiltless, twenty-year-old wife, whom everyone except cynical opportunists like Jamet loved. But the prince would have hated any partner forced upon him by Charles. An ambition which could not have been more inordinate, aimed at nothing less than the throne of an emperor, from which he could dominate the king, consumed him. He felt sure he could fill such a post better than most autocrats of the past. But such dangerous ideas had to be kept utterly secret for the time being. Even if he had been temperamentally capable of trusting anybody, he had no friends to whom he could impart them. Nothing and no one rivaled in his mind the sense of intellectual power, the very essence of his personal being, which drove him on. The pleasures of society, feminine or masculine, were really distasteful to him. The thrills of sport served only as a relaxation from more serious preoccupations. Even command in war now appealed to him less than the intricate practical activities of diplomacy and business. His great misfortune perhaps, though it is doubtful whether he ever recognized it, remained his indifference to all aesthetic interests, in which men like Suffolk, King René and the duke of Orléans found consolation for the frustrations of court life.

Then, quite suddenly, Margaret fell seriously ill. On August 7, 1445, a very hot day, after returning from an excursion to the shrine of Our Lady of the Thorn near Châlons, where the court still was, though almost ready to leave for Tours, she had caught a severe chill through sitting half-undressed in a cool, shadowy apartment of the old Château de Sarry, a dilapidated house of gray stone belonging to the bishop of Châlons, with doors and windows wide open. The drafts had felt so refreshing! But within a few hours she was coughing heavily, in a high fever, and could hardly breathe. The pulmonary congestion was undoubtedly of tubercular origin, as the dauphin's private physician soon recognized. He ordered the patient to be transferred to the cathedral convent, where she could be kept perfectly quiet and warm.

Jamet, however, seized this opportunity to hint that the princess's collapse had been due to nocturnal debauchery. Charles, who was genuinely fond of the girl, asked him what the devil he meant by such a suggestion. The Breton changed his ground adroitly. "Oh, I was only referring to the headaches she complains of, sire. I'm sure they must be caused by all that rhyming in the small hours. I understand it's terribly hard work." The king looked nonplussed. "But my cousin the duke of Orléans says it's the greatest fun in the world." Jamet bowed. "Then I must be wrong, sire. I am only a poor soldier and don't know anything about maladies not caused by wounds. I apologize to Your Grace, to the duke and to this most unhappy lady, whom God preserve from her unfortunate sickness." Charles shrugged his lean shoulders. "It's a good thing you don't make such mistakes in the field, my friend. I must give you some more fighting to do that will keep you from loosening that long tongue of yours. You talk too much these days, Jamet."

He seemed to make light of the matter. But the rumors of impropriety, if nothing worse, in the boudoir of Madame la Dauphine gained ground. Neither the king nor the queen nor Louis himself came to visit the invalid, ostensibly on the doctor's orders. Nor did anyone even write her a letter. She had, of course, some of her closest attendants already at her bedside. But these young women, thrilled at the slanders that were being whispered elsewhere, passed them on to her, coupled with pious exhortations to forgive the original calumniator, whom they maliciously named. The unhappy girl, in despair, called God to witness that she was utterly innocent of even thinking of adultery.

"Ah, Jamet, Jamet," she exclaimed bitterly. "Now your evil plans have succeeded. If I die it will be owing to you and the pretty things you have said of me that had no substance in fact."

Her cough grew steadily worse. Reports from the convent alarmed Pierre de Brézé, Charles's most honorable and sensible counselor. He defied the general sentiment by going to see for himself how the patient was. He found her almost speechless, dreadfully agitated by the court gossip, which he did not believe for a moment. "This lady's sorrow and anger," he told everyone he met on his return, "are pitiful to behold."

Whether he actually taxed de Tillay with her murder in the words: "Ah, false and wicked villain, it is you have killed her!" is not certain. But the phrase undoubtedly represents his view of this favorite officer of both Charles VII and the dauphin.

Mme de Saint-Michel, her senior official companion, normally a charitable matron, tortured the sick princess by telling her that if she didn't pardon the unconscionable Jamet, whom the speaker, incidentally, herself detested for his "impiety" and "frivolity," then God would never forgive so gross a sin. Margaret, driven temporarily out of her mind by this cruel threat of eternal punishment, cried out in a kind of ironic desperation: "Oh, I pardon him, ay, and the whole world too!" It is clear that she meant nothing of the kind, but only wanted to get rid of her foolish, if well intentioned, persecutor, who no doubt felt that she was saving her beloved mistress from damnation. Only one of the doctors present, Guillaume Lhotier, had the courage to request all the ladies-in-waiting to leave the room. Whether or not he told them they were a set of importunate busybodies, he sternly told Jamet himself, who had the nerve to visit the convent and express a hypocritical sympathy, that such a rain of inquisitions from these women was breaking down the sufferer's resistance to her illness. *On lui rompt la tête de tant de questions!* (All those questions are driving her crazy!) he informed the poker-faced chamberlain.

A younger maid of honor than Mme de Saint-Michel, one Mme Aqueville, aged twenty-five, heard the princess murmur that if she had not considered it her duty (*si ce n'était sa foi*) she would now wish she had never come to France. Worse was in store. The doomed girl's last words were caught by Jean Boutet, one of the dauphin's valets. He was listening, like all the rest of the group in the bedchamber, for a possible confession of adultery and explicit forgiveness of Jamet, in order that so important a member of the royal family could go straight to heaven. "Fie upon the life of this world," Boutet heard her whisper. "Speak not of it, for it wearies me beyond anything."

Soon afterward, between ten and eleven in the evening, the doctors pronounced Margaret's life extinct. It was August 16, 1445. Twenty-four hours later King Charles, Queen Marie, who was pregnant, and the prince all left Châlons without waiting to attend the funeral. One of the ambassadors who saw them off recorded that he noticed Louis weeping. It is true that in the highly impressionable fifteenth century even strong-minded men wept more easily than they do now. Louis seems generally to have been an exception to this rule. But the prudent husband may well have felt he ought to pretend a sorrow

he did not feel. An inquiry into Jamet's conduct was afterward held
by the king's household. It dragged on for a whole year. But in spite
of much evidence hostile to the astute Breton he managed to talk
himself out of retribution. He remained in the royal service, though
never again at court.

Margaret might have died young in any case. The immediate cause
of her death had undoubtedly been her own indiscretion in tearing
off half her clothes after getting very hot. It is certain that her constitution was consumptive. Unquestionably too she had been overworking
her verses and in long abstruse discussion about literature when she
ought to have been in bed. Yet it is equally incontrovertible that
Jamet's mischievous persecutions, probably much exceeding what Louis
had ordered, hastened her end before her twenty-second birthday.

He must therefore be exonerated of contriving as some historians
have asserted, the murder of Margaret of Scotland. She died owing to
circumstances beyond his control, her tubercular condition, her youthful recklessness in ignoring it, the inefficiency of fifteenth-century
medicine and her sensitivity to the savage bigotry and credulity of
persons who should have been the first to protect and reassure her
in the misery of her predicament. A mentality more open to com-
passion than the dauphin's and less rigorously concerned with his
personal dignity, which could not endure the prevalence of rumors
in which he only half believed, would at least not have dissuaded him
from visiting the invalid. Yet the convention of previous generations
by which an ideal consort's reputation must be above suspicion still
prevailed in his day. At the court of Duke Louis I of Orléans (1372–
1407) Guillaume de Machaut was asked by a lady whether a gentleman would prefer his beloved to be unjustly spoken of, though he
knew her to be chaste, or praised for a chastity he knew she did not
possess. The poet answered: "I should prefer to hear her well spoken of
even if I knew her to be wicked."

All the same, the prince's absence, even the absence of the good-
natured king and the kindly Marie, did not kill Margaret. All three
no doubt feared infection. But they were also restrained by the
fashion just mentioned, a sort of protocol, from communing or showing
public sympathy with a member of their family who had fallen,
however innocently, under a heavy cloud of mistrust in so essential
a sphere of her being as the sexual. Jamet had done his work in
what he conceived to be his master's best interests only too well.
The load he laid upon Margaret, starting in his fertile imagination,
had turned as if by magic into a real and fatally crushing burden.

Prince Louis, freed by this tragic event from one of the most pressing
of his vexations, turned again, with all his former zest and impatience,

to investigate and manipulate to his own advantage the intrigues that surrounded his father. In these preoccupations he had a dangerous opponent, more difficult to deal with than that scrupulous upholder of the royal prerogative Pierre de Brézé. The calm enchantress Agnès Sorel confronted the dauphin's fierce dreams with her soaring and swelling forehead, made even more conspicuous by the concealment of the hair, smothered by the extravagant headdress of the day, her high-set, delicate ears, pointed like those of a faun, and her plucked eyebrows over coolly prominent pupils impossible to read. The scandalously revealed globes of breasts, rising far apart, almost under the armpits, dominated an exceptionally slender waist and protuberant abdomen. These beauties, all exuberantly admired by the modish sexuality of the period, harbored, he knew, an intelligence as keen and imperturbable as that of the duchess of Burgundy and much harder to counteract. For from the French point of view the duchess was a foreign enemy. The Dame de Beauté was purely French and the king of France her obsequious slave.

The prince determined to leave Agnès out of his calculations and resort to sheer force. But he felt it would be fatal to the outcome of this plan if he himself appeared in the guise of an open rebel against his father, as when the Praguerie of 1440 had been crushed so easily. He required a bold and devoted subordinate who would take the blame if things went wrong. A certain Antoine de Chabannes, comte de Dammartin, a mercenary commander who had backed him in the previous abortive revolt and thereafter been with him in Switzerland, seemed to Louis to fill the bill. He suggested to Chabannes that it would be possible to surprise Charles's Scottish bodyguard at the castle of Razilly, near Tours, where the court then was, if necessary kill Pierre de Brézé, seize the king's person and take over the government.

The experienced soldier, who had actually commanded for Louis at the battle of Saint-Jacques the year before, shook his head over this wild scheme. "Easier said than done," he commented dryly. The question was discussed between the two friends for a long time, on the prince's side with eager confidence and embittered determination, on the mercenary's with professional caution. The count's detailed arguments, based more upon military than political considerations, prevailed in the end over a mind always accessible to practical reasoning. The dauphin agreed to think again. But Chabannes had been alarmed by this conversation. He had his own career to make sure of and the country at present seemed to be prospering in the hands of prudent administrators. There appeared no prospect in these conditions of a successful revolution against Charles's nominal control.

The count thought it might be as well, before his excitable young comrade in arms embarked on some other mad enterprise with a less discreet adviser than his recent confidant, to drop a hint of the project to the monarch himself.

Meanwhile he found to his mingled indignation and triumph that Louis had already played into his hands by approaching some of the officers of the guard, with a view to sounding their loyalty. Their evidence and that of Chabannes himself was heard on September 27, 1446, by the king's command, before the chancellor. There was no reason to doubt the testimony offered. Charles summoned his son to a personal interview and confronted him with these witnesses. The dauphin took up a haughty attitude, coolly putting the blame for the plot squarely on the shoulders of Chabannes. It was a characteristic example of the young man's quick thinking, whether or not he had suspected, before this meeting, what its subject would be. He might have guessed that the guard officers would talk. But probably he believed that they would have little to go on. He was already an expert at disguising, if he thought fit, the true object of any feelers he might put out in conversing with his inferiors, especially the compatriots of his late wife, whom he lumped together with her as a set of unpractical aesthetes, though he also found their manners detestable. It is very doubtful, though, that it ever occurred to him, before he came face to face with Chabannes, that his old friend had betrayed him.

The count of Dammartin of course hotly denied the charge the prince, with an air of cold contempt, brought against him. "You lie, monsieur," Louis retorted, as calmly as before. The count laid his hand on his sword-hilt. "By God, my lord," he cried, in a passion of resentment. "Were you not the king's son I should know how to answer so foul a slander with this weapon, mine against your own!" Charles, outraged, started up from his throne. "Silence!" he thundered. "Louis, I banish you from this kingdom for four months. You will remain in Dauphiné to await my pleasure."

The prince is unlikely to have felt anything but relief and even pleasure at this sentence. His father might quite conceivably, under pressure from Agnès Sorel and de Brézé, have ended by locking him up. Exile to the province of Dauphiné, which he knew so well, would at least provide him with an uninterrupted base from which to renew further machinations against the unworthy king who was keeping him off the throne of France. Privately he resolved, as he told friends at a much later date, that he would not stay there until his parent recalled him or took some other even more undesirable step. He would stay there until the man died or fell a victim to some future revolution which the prince would certainly encourage and might actually inaugurate, from a distance.

For the time being, with unimpaired dignity, he swept off his hat, which he alone could wear in the royal presence, and declared between his teeth: "By this head, now uncovered, I swear to enact vengeance on those who now drive me from my country." Then he stalked out of the audience chamber without another word. He was obviously thinking not only of Chabannes but also of the men, and the woman, he considered responsible for Charles's severity. It would in fact have been much more in accordance with the king's character and real affection for his unresponsive son if the monarch had simply reasoned with him in private, warned him against any further reckless talk, which ill-disposed persons might interpret as treason, and then forgiven him.

The enmity between Agnès and Louis, both genuine patriots, but the lady confident of molding Charles into a "great" king in the sense of making him the mouthpiece of her own proved political ability, and the dauphin absolutely convinced that his father was hopelessly intractable, renders it highly probable that the Dame de Beauté had resolved to get Louis out of her way by working on the king's irritation with his son's constant opposition to the throne as represented by her domination of the infatuated monarch.

The situation resembled only superficially that between Joan of Arc and Charles, a sovereign both betrayed and betraying, sixteen years earlier. Joan had also been certain, as energetic young women so often are, that she could reform the negative weakness of his character into a positive strength inspired by her own, despite the opposition of more cynical or at least more realistic males like Philip of Burgundy and the archbishop of Reims. They understood, as Louis did in 1445, that Charles would never act decisively unless influenced by political talents at any rate equal to their own. The brave, simple, chaste idealist Joan could not be compared in this respect with Agnès Sorel and her wily lovers. Louis himself had all the qualifications required to save the country. But he could not exercise them in a kingdom now contented under the rule of the de Brézé group. The desperate France of 1429 had remained beyond rousing by the subtlest statecraft. Only the belief that the virgin from Lorraine incarnated the will of heaven brought the distraught and prostrate realm to its feet. Even then it was not "Charlot" or actually Joan herself but skillful and devoted soldiers like Dunois who consolidated her preliminary victories.

Louis was recognized by Charles's most levelheaded advisers as an equally able military commander, but on the wrong side. He might be as capable as Jean de Dunois of expelling the English. But since it appeared that he would not do so until he had deposed the king, the existing government's conveniently pliant figurehead, with a royal prestige and popularity naturally superior to his son's, the dauphin might just as well be a rebel, the rival of his own father, in the struggle for control of the realm, which at the moment remained quite satisfied with its new prosperity. For these reasons it is likely that Agnès and Pierre played a part in the ultimate revelation by Antoine de Chabannes of the prince's rash conspiracy.

A banishment to Dauphiné as the penalty of this ill-conceived scheme could not after all be considered an unduly severe sentence. The province had been assigned to the eldest sons of the kings of France ever since 1364. In the case of Louis the element of compulsion by the sovereign to administer it in quasi-independence of the crown gave this step the character of a punishment expressing the royal displeasure with the conduct of the heir to the kingdom. The command might be thought morally unjust but in law no one could find fault with it. The king's right to do what he liked, even with his own son, in the name of orderly government, could not be questioned.

The power of Agnès Sorel in the public affairs of France was also greatly reinforced at this time by her close friendship with Charles's minister of finance, Jacques Coeur, who kept a statue of her in his office at Bourges. In 1445 he was a man of fifty, son of a wealthy furrier of that city, who had not bothered to have him educated in anything but bookkeeping and salesmanship. But Jacques, precociously daring and imaginative by nature, had applied these qualities to his trade so conspicuously that in Joan of Arc's time, when he was thirty-four, he had been found guilty of debasing the coinage in company with a Norman named Ravant le Danois, deported from his province by the English and given control of the mint by Charles.

But the king was then so short of money and supplies of all kinds, as well as of docile businessmen, most of whom resented his necessary if heavy taxation and considered him an untrustworthy debtor, that the monarch soon found it expedient to annul the sentence passed on the highly ingenious Coeur, who repaid this service by acting as the royal broker with prodigious success. By 1432 he was at Damascus in Syria, buying and transporting to France the wares of the Levant and dealing with Genoese, Venetian, Florentine and Castilian merchants. Shipwrecked and robbed in Corsica, he returned to Paris with empty pockets but still full of far-reaching ideas. By 1435 he had supplanted his old partner Ravant at the Bourges mint. He was soon transferred to the capital in a similar capacity, on the principle, perhaps, of setting a thief to catch a thief. From both cities he effectively reformed the coinage he had debased in 1429. In 1438 he obtained the appointment of finance minister and in 1441 was ennobled. In 1444 he presided in Languedoc over that region's new parliament. By 1445 he and Etienne Chevalier stood at the controls of French policy both at home and abroad, with irons in every fire.

Through Chevalier he met and probably entered into an intimate relationship with Agnès Sorel, already Etienne's mistress. As the first in time of French captains of industry and international bankers he was destined at this stage to go on from strength to strength till the death of Agnès, absurdly laid to his charge in 1450, brought him down. Yet he ended his life in 1456 as a valued admiral and commercial agent in the papal service.

There is no evidence of any close association, either as friends or enemies, between the quinquagenarian Jacques Coeur and the prince, less than half the financier's age. Both men had exceptional talents for organization. Both understood to the full the value of money. But there the similarities ended. The daring but never reckless trader, with gold and silver in his blood, widely traveled, an expert in every market that his ships could reach, cared for nothing but to make fortune after fortune, not in order to gain political power, but simply because all other occupations bored him.

Like the champion jousters of his day or a modern Olympic athlete, Jacques Coeur, with his unfailing good humor and adroit tact, delighted his social and cultural superiors by never pretending to be their equal as he steadily climbed, after only one brief check, to the bridge of the ship of France. He may have recognized the dauphin's gift for administration and appreciated the prince's cultivation of the middle classes of society. But the jovial, cosmopolitan Coeur could not have seen in the ugly, sullen young aristocrat, with a grievance against the crown he was heir to, an ally who would be any use at all, but rather a nuisance, to the continued rise of the industrialist.

In short, from the finance minister's point of view, Louis, who no doubt respected him, sat on the wrong side of the fence. In the eyes of the dauphin, on the other hand, Coeur could only be regarded as the latest of Agnès's lovers and therefore a man to be avoided like the plague. If she had never existed, if the great merchant had been twenty years younger and the prince already a king, the two men together might have made France a world power capable of withstanding every shock that the next five centuries were to bring. But such speculations are of course only of interest as illustrations of the curiously contrasted yet potentially correspondent characters of the furrier's son and the greatest of the Valois princes. It is improbable, however, that any direct communication, except in the way of ordinary courtesy, ever took place between temperaments compatible in nothing but an equal absorption, for quite different reasons, in the architecture of economics.

In any case the king's resolve to act with unmistakable rigor rather than indulgence in the matter of the disclosures by the count of Dammartin involved consequences wholly unanticipated by either the monarch or his grimly insubordinate offspring.

It is easy to represent the dauphin's conduct at this period, when he was twenty-two, in a sinister light. France was being well governed by Charles's ministers. The army had been reorganized on a national basis. It was maintaining a firm front against both internal sedition by the nobles and external pressure from abroad. The English had been temporarily neutralized by the marriage of Margaret of Anjou to Henry VI. Philip of Burgundy also seemed satisfied at present with the existing situation, though he was not one of those relatively susceptible personages who had undergone the rickety spell of Charles VII. The emperor Frederick, aged thirty, could not be taken seriously in either military or diplomatic terms. His ambition was only being expressed, just then, by regular proclamations, in typically Teutonic style, that Austria was destined to rule the world (Austriae Est Im- perare Orbi Universo).

The initial Latin letters of this boast had been deliberately chosen as the five vowels, in alphabetical order, also in German (Alles Erdreich Ist Österreich Unterthan), conceived as regulating the struc- ture of all European languages. By a quaint conceit Frederick was fond of inscribing them on the title pages of the manuscripts he col- lected and on other articles he treasured. Personally, he was good- looking, dignified and cultivated. But even if he had possessed more solid qualities the feudal princes he nominally controlled could no more agree among themselves than so many tribesmen. In French and Burgundian eyes he remained a decorative but distinctly unreliable puppet, to be manipulated if possible, but scarcely to be feared by more civilized and coherent communities than those east of the Rhine.

Into this comparatively stable position of power politics Louis in- troduced a jarring note by his implacable though not openly declared enmity to his father. This feeling, beneath its intellectual justification, that is, the impatience of a superior mind with an inferior one, had an even deeper foundation. Modern psychology has traced this in- vincible and widespread tendency in young men of talent and energy to an irrational source, the sexual jealousy of brutes. Adolescent bulls of every species inevitably challenge the aging patriarch of the herd for the command of females. Accordingly, by way of evolution, the legendary Greek king Oedipus could not help killing his father and thus giving rise to one of the most powerful symbolic myths that has ever guided poetic and philosophic meditation.

Religious sentiment less freethinking than that of classical Greece, where the almighty Zeus, in common with the other Olympian gods, is repeatedly plastered with the mud of rascality, set itself in vain to counter this ineradicable trait of male human nature. Jews and Christians eventually drove it underground without otherwise weakening it. After the unquestioning submission of the Hebrews to a fierce Jehovah came the successful substitution by the early Christian theologians of a mystical Trinity, blending the mild and merciful figures of Christ and the Virgin Mary with the originally stern and single supernatural ruler and judge of all mankind. The more or less veiled protests of the humanists in the late fifteenth century, followed by the Reformation, took the form of objecting to the tyranny and fraud undoubtedly exercised by certain popes, prelates and even anointed kings supposed to incarnate the will of heaven. Then the way was opened to a more reasonable understanding of the essential impulse of humanity to resort to divine aid for recovery from a predicament felt to be otherwise hardly bearable by a majority of thinking men.

Louis belonged to a place and a time still barely touched by the crises in religious speculation which only came to a head in his later years and then chiefly in Italy. Nor was he in the least given by nature, as already suggested, to such reflections. It never occurred to him or to any of his contemporaries that he was suffering from a complex today called Oedipean. The phenomenon had long been known, but only in its outward manifestations. It was as common in the comedies of Plautus as in the tragedies of Sophocles, in the dynastic as in the domestic conflicts where people took sides with father or son according to their personal circumstances and affections, without recognizing the root of such quarrels in the subconsciousness of all masculine individuals. The dauphin would have retorted to any talk about the inarticulate depths of his being that he was only too conscious, on perfectly practical and defensible grounds, of his hatred of his father.

Its foundation in the sexual field remains, however, clear enough. One of his many psychological differences from Charles, and the decisive element in the incompatibility of the two mentalities, arose from the prince's innate misogynism, not an unusual accompaniment of the drier type of intellectual brilliance. He was an extraordinary man, in fact, and the king was a very ordinary one, never so happy as when laughing at a party or fondling young women. Louis on the other hand much preferred to these amusements concentration upon difficult problems of politics and economics. These involved measures against persons less capable of comprehending them. But Christian social morality has always, in theory at least, reproved rebellious violence, even if its target is undisguised oppression and even if its perpetrators can be admired for brains and courage. The prince had a very high degree of each of these two qualities. The king had neither, to any extent worth mentioning. When he seemed to show them it was invariably because he had been driven to such action by other people's advice. Charles, however, cannot be charged with exercising tyranny at any time. It was only his cowardice, not his deliberate intention, that allowed his protectress, Joan of Arc, to suffer a cruel and inexcusable death.

A modern critic of the dauphin's behavior at this juncture of his career cannot, therefore, praise him as the humanists, a little later, were to praise Marcus Junius Brutus for murdering Julius Caesar. Nor, however, can Louis be blamed in the twentieth century for relentlessly plotting in the fifteenth the dethronement, never the assassination, of Charles VII, a parent who had neglected him in his childhood, forced him into an unsuitable marriage, used him more like a mercenary than a son and, after the young man had proved his ability in the conduct of public affairs, generally faced his arguments in council with polite evasion if not blank incomprehension.

Study of the prince's life up to this point certainly proves that he was a queer mixture. Otherwise, had he been a steadier, more consistent character, his biographers would be reduced, like Bishop Thomas Basin, to representing him as an unmitigated villain or to declaring him, as did Philippe de Commines, a compendium of all the virtues. Yet the contrasts of color in any plausible portrait of him must be bewildering. Almost invariably prudent in his practical designs, able to support them with apparently cogent logic, he nevertheless at this date revealed a shocking impatience in the basic mood that initiated them. His pride in himself admitted no limits, yet he never even began to be vain. His intelligence immediately recognized, in his own person as in others, the onset of this natural yet so often disastrous failing. He was to see it illustrated, with fatal effect, in the case of his most dangerous antagonist, Duke Charles the Bold of Burgundy, whose fall for this reason made Louis's own triumph as the architect of modern France certain.

The dauphin, then, as he went into exile on the first day of the new year, just after the birth of another son to the king on December 28, 1446, had been behaving, in Christian terms, reprehensibly but not wickedly. He wished his father no real harm, but only relegation to a retirement which that easygoing monarch would unquestionably have enjoyed much more than thundering from a throne at the behest of advisers as effectively patriotic as he was feebly well-meaning. Nor did the then twenty-three-year-old dauphin ever cease to work for this end, the voluntary or involuntary abdication of Charles VII, as the prince himself grew more worldly-wise over the long years in Dauphiné. The banishment, whether he realized it or not, was actually a stroke of luck for him, the first, apart from military successes, that he had ever experienced. For if he had remained in France proper, with unrestricted access to the court, it is highly probable that he would have risked a second gamble for Charles's crown and failed to secure it, with consequences that could only have been personally and nationally calamitous. As it was, he never saw his father again, though the two men kept up a fairly regular correspondence, generally tactful on both sides.

CHAPTER V

A Dauphin's Province
(1447–1456)

❧❧❧ The long journey southeast, in dark, wintry weather, with icy winds, deep mud and flurries of snow rendering the few hours of daylight far from agreeable to the prince's party, did not depress its leader in the least. Now at last, for all practical purposes, he had a kingdom of his own, however small, to play with. Nor, as in his previous travels, would he have to report back to Charles before he had finished the work of reorganization properly. This time he meant to set up a model, smoothly running state. It would have nothing to fear from regions in which he believed himself already popular, Languedoc in the west, across the Rhone, and the Lyons country in the north, beyond the river Isère, on which his future capital, Grenoble, stood. To the east Savoy, with the important duchy of Milan behind it, would also be friendly, he considered. Or if not then he, Louis de Valois, would know the reason why. To the south lay the Mediterranean Sea, firmly secured against pirates or any other naval interference by the great ports of Marseilles and Toulon.

The province, when he reached it, seemed clay for the potter's hand. He found it a sleepy region, governed easily by an honest military veteran, Imbert de Groslée, sire de Gaucourt, not a progressive type, but no troublemaker. The quiet, gray-haired officer did whatever Louis told him. The prince in due course established a parliament at Grenoble, applied the spur to industry, repaired the roads, set up a program of fairs in the more substantial settlements, subsidized agriculture, improved its methods and prevented its excessive exploitation by wealthy individuals by establishing a banking system run largely by Jewish talent, hitherto repressed by the jealous Gentiles, ostensibly on religious grounds but really for fear of their generally superior financial capacity. The dauphin had long since recognized this racial quality and characteristically employed it to the full without the slightest hesitation. The lack of scruple and of magnanimity attributed to Hebrews by the conventional Christians of the day, the peculiar mannerisms which marked their social behavior and the bloodthirsty secret clubs they were supposed to maintain by way of revenge for the persecutions to which they were exposed counted for nothing in his mind compared with their invaluable acumen in money matters, indispensable to a stable government.

In foreign policy he at once decided to encourage the ambition of Savoy. The titular duke, Amadeus VIII, had been elected to the papacy as Felix V in 1439. He was still in Rome, taking no interest in his duchy, in 1447. His weak son Louis, officially in charge of it, actually left everything to his wife Anne, a daughter of the king of Cyprus. The heir to this couple, who eventually, in 1465, succeeded them as Amadeus IX, married in 1452 Yolande, the dauphin's second sister. The first, Catherine, contracted while still a child to the almost equally young count of Charolais, only son of Duke Philip of Burgundy, had died in 1446. Anne of Savoy, a strong but somewhat reckless character, was easily induced by Louis de Valois to plot a partitioning between herself and her new neighbor of the republic which had been proclaimed in Milan on the death of its hated Duke Filippo Maria Visconti in August 1447.

But other people too were aiming at Milan. King Alfonso of Naples had been named by Filippo as his heir. Duke Charles of Orléans claimed the property through his mother Valentina Visconti. Frederick III also demanded consideration of his feudal sovereignty in the region. The Venetians, moreover, hereditary enemies of Milan, were determined to secure this valuable addition to their territory. Finally the great *condottiere* Count Francesco Sforza (b. 1401), a far more formidable candidate than any of the rest except the doge, had recently married Filippo's only daughter and heiress Bianca and was on intimate terms with the Florentine Cosimo de' Medici, the uncrowned king of his city and the shrewdest and richest statesman in Italy. The new republic of Milan sent for Sforza to defend it against the Venetians in particular, who were already invading Lombardy.

Sforza, financially backed in secret by Cosimo, whose policy required friendship between Milan and Florence, though the Tuscan state remained formally allied with Venice, dashed north and inflicted a crushing defeat on the advancing army of the doge. Tangled negotiations began between Francesco, Venice, Cosimo and the king of France, Charles VII having been drawn in by the Florentine to hold down Alfonso by resuscitating, if necessary, the claim of the French king's brother-in-law René to Naples. Cosimo also hoped that Charles would persuade his cousin the duke of Orléans to withdraw his own candidature, which would certainly be opposed by Alfonso.

The dauphin already had a network of spies at the French court. He had instituted this service within a few days after his arrival at Grenoble, when he realized that his brother, the newborn Charles, might well in due course provide a focus for the efforts of the royal councilors and such of the princes as objected to the plans of the legitimate heir to the throne, himself. For this reason Louis had determined to watch developments in that quarter very closely. Accordingly, and also as a general precaution, he had arranged for numerous secret agents to follow the king about. At the same time he embarked upon a diplomatically submissive correspondence with the monarch, discounting by implication the suspicions he knew the latter would entertain of his son's designs.

The prince's information about events in Italy came chiefly from the sources thus established in France, more reliable because more neutral than those maintained by Savoy in the Milanese republic. For Anne's men in general thought more of pleasing their mistress than recognizing political realities. But what the dauphin heard from both directions inspired in him a lifelong admiration for the mingled audacity and discretion, so like his own, of Francesco Sforza. The prince was soon in tactful correspondence with that equivocal personage, who also resembled him in being by no means everyone's favorite. Plain men in north Italy, from Venice and Florence to Milan itself, whether aristocratically or democratically inclined, mostly considered the count no more than a baseborn military adventurer of the old school, which he was. But in addition, as Cosimo knew, Francesco had learned to be a good deal more of a civilized diplomat than most successful mercenaries.

The second corner of Europe to which Louis directed his attention in 1447 was Spain. There his father was supporting Juan II, king of Aragon, a pugnacious, unscrupulous but very able and personally attractive veteran of fifty, in his policy of keeping Don Carlos, his son by his first wife Blanche of Navarre, out of the succession. For Don Carlos cherished liberal ideas. The position resembled in some ways that between Charles and Louis de Valois. For the fathers were both politically conservative and the sons both radical reformers. This circumstance was enough to cause Louis, by the end of 1460, to encourage Carlos, who had the backing of the Aragonese and Catalan masses. The dauphin thought the trend of the times would eventually secure the victory of the young Prince of Aragon, just as he was sure it would secure his own. But he had reckoned without Juan's diplomatic and military capacities, infinitely superior to those of Charles VII, and also without the Spanish national bias in favor of autocracy at the top, actually because of rather than in spite of the ferocious individualism, not to say anarchic spirit, of ordinary citizens, who could not themselves, like colder-blooded Europeans, prevent it from degenerating into chaos.

For Louis never understood the peculiar, half-Moorish mentality of the Iberian peninsula, so different from the rest of Europe. He knew France through and through, from top to bottom. He appreciated clearly the Italian genius, so close to his own, for endless shifts of intrigue. He confidently and accurately wrote off the Germans as politically incapable. He felt that French intelligence could always outwit the bold and jovial but nowadays indolent and blundering English.

But the Spaniards baffled him with their strange mixture of absurdly stubborn pride and apparently irredeemable indifference to commerce, both of which he mistook for the results of stupidity. Juan II, living on into extreme old age and purely physical blindness, but as clear-headed and energetic as ever, defeated him permanently in the end, the only ruler who ever did so. This outcome was probably lucky for France, not a country which has ever been able, despite the successes of Louis XIV and Napoleon, to take a deep hold on Spain, even during the psychological influence of the eighteenth century and the military grip of the early nineteenth.

Nevertheless, the dauphin's most absorbing interests during his banishment to his eponymous province lay in that region itself. His master passion, a fascination with the details of administrative reform based upon principles quite different from those generally accepted in contemporary France, increasingly engrossed him. Dauphiné, where only two big towns, Grenoble and Valence, existed, had hitherto been governed, theoretically, from a distance. But in practice feudal conditions, in other words a near approach to anarchy, however supine in this remote quarter, prevailed. Louis set to work forthwith on a root-and-branch transformation of this scene by withdrawing the most oppressive privileges of secular and ecclesiastical magnates and thus easing the position and the opportunities of the Third Estate of traders and lawyers in the more populous settlements. He never lost sight of this ideal so long as he lived. It was in Dauphiné that for the first time he found himself with a free hand to cultivate it. The motivation was of course by no means philanthropic. He intended to show, not so much the royal clique as the kingdom at large, what he was made of and what a model sovereign he would be one day, and the sooner the better.

This program, congenial to the dauphin's patiently conscientious and industrious temperament, so strangely at odds with the impulsive ardor that underlay it, being the obverse, in fact, of his ticklish fury at any sort of interference, soon produced admirable effects in the province. Customs barriers were lifted. Every natural resource in the soil was fully exploited by intensive farming and mining. Roads were not only put under repair, but wholly new highways appeared. Foreign merchants and artisans, employing unfamiliar methods, were welcomed and exempted from taxation. The commercially gifted and hard-working Jewish communities were protected, in their new banks and other enterprises, from bigotry and malignity. Even intellectuals were catered to by the foundation of a university at Valence on a footing equal to those, so much more ancient, of Orléans, Montpellier and Toulouse.

A typical letter from Louis, dated August 5, 1452, illustrates the prince's handling of the interests of his subjects, in this case inhabitants of the Vienne region, of which he was lord in his capacity of dauphin. It was centered upon Lyons, standing on the east bank of the Rhone.

To the Council and Revenue Officers of Lyons.

Valence, 5 August 1452.

Request for exemption from taxation of the widow and children of Guillaume Moreau, Deputy of Lyons, in consideration of his services and the interest of the Dauphin in his family.

By Command of the Dauphin, Lord of Vienne.

Dearly beloved, we have learned that you have imposed or permitted to be imposed on the widow and children of the late Guillaume Moreau, in his lifetime elected a Deputy of Lyons, the sum of thirty-two Tours livres (*livres tournois*) in respect of contributions to the funds now being raised by Monseigneur [i.e. the dauphin] in relief of the city of Lyons and that in order to obtain payment of the said sum you have caused to be seized and sold in a single day all the family's negotiable assets, an act which seems very harsh (*bien grant rigueur*), considering the services their dead father rendered to you while he was alive, the condition of his said widow and the minority state of her said children, we do not appear to be liable for such contribution. Therefore we, bearing in mind the kindness extended to us by the said Deputy in his lifetime and that the said widow is our personal friend (*commère*) and also that one of her children is our godson and bears our name, do hereby beg you most earnestly for the sake of favor and regard to us to cause the said assets to be restored and to refrain from assessing or imposing taxation upon the family until the children are of age and meanwhile for love of ourselves to recommend them highly in all their

concerns or at any rate be pleased to take no further action in
the matter until the brother of the said widow arrives, which will
be soon. In so doing you will afford us very much pleasure, which
we shall be most ready to reciprocate whenever you require any
service from us. Dearly beloved, may the Lord God hold you in His
keeping. Written at Valence on the fifth day of August.

LOYS.

(Witness) THOREAU.

To our dearly beloved Councilors and Revenue Officers of the city
of Lyons.

Moreau had been twice exempted from taxation, in 1450 and 1451,
in recognition of his work on the organization of relief at Lyons. But
on his death shortly afterwards his heirs had claimed exemption for
the whole year following his decease. This demand had been rejected
by the council in June 1452 and proceedings were instituted to recover
the debt. In December, i.e. about four months after receipt of the
dauphin's letter, the court stopped the case at the pleas of Guillaume
du Bech, Master of the King's Private Purse, and the archdeacon of
Tours, both uncles of the Moreau children. But the magistrates stipulated that sixteen Tours livres, i.e. half the original tax, plus the costs
of the lawsuit, must be paid over.

The dauphin's moderately phrased request to refrain from taxing
the Moreaus had accordingly been only half met. Presumably the
widow's brothers eventually disbursed the sums required. But this
outcome proves that Louis did not invariably have everything all his
own way in Dauphiné. It is probable that in these minor matters he
had no wish to use the authority of a despot.

Another letter of this same year may be quoted as indicative of
the prince's careful pose as a patriot, despite his personal antipathy
to the king. It was written to Charles on October 25 on hearing
that John Talbot, earl of Shrewsbury, had descended on Bordeaux
from the sea on the twenty-first and was rousing Guienne, conquered
by Dunois in the previous year, to revolt against the French crown.

> Most dread lord, I beseech your good grace with all ardor and
> humility. May it please you to know, most dread lord, that I have
> learned of the descent of a great English army on Bordelais and be-
> cause I have been told that previously you were somewhat displeased
> when I did not offer you my services during your conquest of Nor-
> mandy and the said Bordelais, yet I did so through Estissac, Remon
> and Benoist, addressing my gallant cousin Dunois, wretched though
> my condition was. I am sorry with all my heart that this offer did not
> come to your notice and I now send you, most dread lord, my friend

and loyal counselor and chamberlain the Lord of Barry to offer you my services in person and goods if it should be your pleasure to do me this favor in giving me such appointment and employment as the said Lord of Barry, whom may it please you to trust, will further explain to you. I pray to the Blessed Son of God, most dread lord, that He may grant you happy and long life. Written at Vienne the twenty-fifth day of October.

Your very humble and obedient son,

LOYS.

King Charles did not accept this offer. The predominant atmosphere of the royal court remained hostile to Louis despite the latter's humble tone in official correspondence with it for the last five years. He had previously been recognized by the present conservative and successful government as a dangerous if covert enemy of the throne. His letter could be construed as a hypocritical cover for the resumption of rebellion on bolder lines than formerly. Once he had obtained the command of substantial military forces in France, they might easily be turned against his father after victories over the English in the field. But in fact certain dramatic developments in the kingdom and elsewhere, which began in 1450, render it unlikely that the dauphin, by his petition of 1452 to Charles, intended the achievement of anything more definite than the temporary appeasement of the monarch and the preservation of the picture of the prince himself as an honest and king-fearing patriot, which he wished to propagate.

In any case the Gascony-Guienne revolt fizzled out after 1453, when Talbot was defeated and killed at the battle of Castillon. But the dauphin, having made his gesture, could not have cared less, just then, how his father got on with the English. The triumphs or failures of the royal generals would hardly count once the prince got into the saddle as king of France himself.

While continuing to complain to his intimates and also to Charles of the injustice of his prolonged exile, he had in reality never been so happy in his life. Good hunting was available, and not only that directed to animals and birds. Ladies could also be pursued with every prospect of success, at any rate those belonging to the squirearchy or to professional circles. For their fathers, husbands and brothers spoke highly of a widower ruler who employed sober jurists and businessmen or at most the lower nobility to assist him instead of the high-spirited aristocrats to whom any other man in his position at that time would have resorted.

Louis is not certainly known to have had any mistresses except during this period in Dauphiné. He may or may not have dealt with

Guyette Durand, the daughter of a Grenoble notary, and Félise Reynard, a squire's widow, mainly to oil the wheels of his administrative
system. But whatever the reason, both these feminine friends presented
him with offspring for whom he was careful to provide. He married the
Grenoble girl, with characteristic discretion, first to one of his secretaries and then, on that gentleman's death, to his equerry d'Archelles.
Félise Reynard, relict of Jean Pic, the late lord of a small estate, Beau-
mont-en-Trèves, bore him two daughters, frankly legitimized by the
grant of generous dowries. Each eventually married well, one of them
actually landing Louis de Bourbon, Admiral of France, and the other
one of the dauphin's chamberlains, the lord of St. Vallier.

There were two chief reasons why the present king's eldest son always
preferred the society and cooperation of the middle classes to the co-
teries of the peerage. In the first place the merchants, farmers and in-
dustrialists obeyed his orders without argument. Second, they resembled
much more closely than the dukes and counts his own real self. They
were autocratic in the sphere to which they applied their activities. But
they were not interested in anything but the steady advancement of
their personal fortunes, to the exclusion of both fun and games and all
dubious adventures that might lead to dangerous violence. The dauphin
had proved himself a soldier equal in courage and capacity to any
knightly commander or even giver and taker of hard knocks. But he
had long detested the uncertainties of battle as compared with the comparatively sure methods of peaceful penetration of the minds of his adversaries and their circumvention by apparently sweet reason.

Nevertheless, he acted in his province like an independent sovereign,
communicating with others, even his father, as such. At the same time
his sovereignty was of a kind then new in France, heralding a different
epoch. He checked decisively, with the prestige of his birth, every sign
of arrogance in the great feudal lords and clerical landowners, gradually
concentrating their former power in his own hands. Simultaneously he
listened with courtesy to humbler persons with more rational ideas of
holding their own in the universal scramble. He paid such men well for
their services once he had recognized that they knew what they were
talking about and did not try to deceive him. But he understood as well
as any sensible citizen that authority of any kind must ultimately rest
upon force.

Louis therefore created a strong standing army with much more success than had attended his parent in the same project. Charles had
indeed seen the need for such an establishment in France. But he could
never control his nobles in the use of troops nominally subject to himself. Backed by the loyal military support the prince had raised for
himself from a middle class which appreciated his favor to themselves

and the orderly government it promoted, Louis dealt decisively with incipient perilous disputes among his aristocrats. He prohibited absolutely the use of arms in the province except for defense against foreign invasion.

Meanwhile he reported to the king, with due documentary evidence, the successful results of his reforms in Dauphiné and wrote that he would like to apply similar treatment to Normandy and Guienne, regions much more exposed to English interference and therefore political agitation than his present responsibility. The army, he pointed out complacently, had already lasted a good deal longer than the four months originally stipulated, to the great benefit of Charles's own position, now free from trouble in that quarter. This communication alarmed its recipient as an obvious demand for extension of the prince's power to districts considerably more susceptible to rebellion against the throne than Dauphiné and also with greater military resources to support such action. The king refused point-blank to grant his son anything of the sort.

It is significant of the young man's growing maturity and cooling temper that he did not argue directly against his father's rather rudely, because nervously, expressed decision. Instead, he went calmly on with his plans for encircling the anxious monarch. "The king is behaving as badly as possible," he would say in private. "But I shall change all that when the time is ripe. I shall get rid of Madame Sorel, who is his evil genius, and bring him back to better ways of thinking. He ought to be planning, for instance, the expulsion of the English from Normandy. But he is wasting his time on such trifles as the recapture of Genoa and the seizure of Piedmont."

Charles on his side had not forgotten the Praguerie. He had reason to fear, from rumors he heard of the conversation of certain of his nobles, that a new outbreak of aristocratic revolt might be imminent, based on indignation with his continued banishment of Prince Louis, who spent half his time representing the iniquity of it to such dukes as Bourbon, Brittany and even Burgundy, and calling for a curb on the undue influence of those upstart counselors Pierre de Brézé and Agnès Sorel.

The king's reaction of creating a corps of "free" archers responsible only to himself roused the wrath of popular song writers. They described this force as a mere band of marauders intent on plundering the goods of helpless citizens. One anonymous bard scribbled:

> Cries the free archer to his host: "I'm here!
> God's death and zounds! I swear I'll kill you!"
> "So please you, sir, keep calm. Our goslings molt, I fear."
> He quietens the lad with some onion soup and a drop of wine,
> heigh-ho.

The next stanza is more malicious.

> The archer goes home and looks for his trollop.
> But the search is long till he finds her in bed with the vicar
> and a drop of cheap wine, heigh-ho!

Others took the theme less lightly.

> The brutes come and gobble the last of our crumbs
> and give us full many a hearty thump.
> So all we can do is to say again and again,
> "I pray you, good sirs, take all that we have."
> I'd willingly give what they want if I had it.
> But alas! All my pence and my goods have gone to supply them.

It is clear that Charles's new corps was not popular. He had been tactless once more, recruiting the ranks from ruffians who owed no allegiance to anyone, since the lords' retainers would only serve their own chief. Foreigners like the brave and faithful Swiss would have been better. But those patriots, in particular, had been so highly praised by Louis and were now such devoted allies of his that the king, out of sheer perversity, would have nothing to do with them. He calculated, quite unreasonably, that once they were in France the prince might well persuade them to bundle him off his throne.

His uneasiness was increased by a farce that took place at the beginning of 1448. A certain Guillaume Mariette, well known to royalist circles as a double agent, produced a letter which he said he had picked up on a road near the Burgundian frontier. It was found to contain, for Philip's information, details of a plot by the dauphin, called in the paper the "Savoyard God," to disgrace de Brézé and his accomplice Agnès Sorel. But the prince was able to prove the document a forgery designed to spread slander about himself, though he would of course have been glad enough, as all his spies knew, to see the persons named dismissed by his father.

Mariette was arrested by the king's officers after this revelation. He escaped, but was recaptured owing to information laid by Jacques Coeur, then about to proceed to the Vatican as French ambassador. Again the ingenious Mariette managed to break jail. He found his way to Dauphiné, where he rather strangely seems to have expected protection by Louis for whom he had worked in the past. Of course the dauphin immediately seized him and put him to the question by torture. The spy insisted that his story was true. He denied that he had acted in collusion with the prince's enemies. Nevertheless, in April he was hanged as a conspirator against Louis. The punishment was probably no more than such an obvious rascal deserved under existing law.

But this affair caused de Brézé also to be accused of treason, a charge he easily refuted by affording the prosecution every opportunity to substantiate it, a task the lawyers found impossible. Agnès too had been mentioned in the indictment, but could not be implicated in any such fantastic scheme as Mariette's alleged letter from Louis to Philip had described. It was obvious from the exchanges in court that neither she nor de Brézé had ever thought of any sort of treason. They were fully exonerated. Even more secure politically than before, they resumed their interrupted plans for the ejection of every English garrison from Normandy, which was later to be Pierre de Brézé's formal sphere of jurisdiction as its seneschal. The prospect of this office, since Louis's application to Charles for it was known, had lent some color at first to the idea that the prince had plotted to evict his rival from power.

In the August of 1449 the king set out, with Dunois and de Brézé, to besiege Rouen. But his son, earlier in the same year, took an important step which further embroiled him with his father. Amadeus VIII of Savoy had now abdicated from the Chair of St. Peter and returned to the hermitage, at Ripaille on the Lake of Geneva, which he had left for Rome ten years before. His heir Louis, as already noted, remained an insignificant ruler. But the energetic Anne, wife of the regent, belonged to a family originally settled at Lusignan in Poitou. For 250 years, ever since the time of the crusader Hugh de Lusignan, her dynasty had held Cyprus against all comers. Anne seems to have recognized a kindred spirit in the dauphin. Up to a point, he returned her respect. He thought she would certainly be able to retain the power of Savoy, whatever happened at Milan, and perhaps extend her existent domains in the empire and Italy. She already held Geneva, Nice and Genoa. The duchy of Savoy, in short, promised to be a most useful ally to the impatient crown prince of France.

Anne and her husband had a daughter named Charlotte, aged eleven. The question of the dynastically necessary second marriage of Louis de Valois had been discussed from time to time in France since the death of his first wife, Margaret of Scotland. Charles VII had suggested, by turns, an English, a Portuguese and a Hungarian princess. But Louis wanted someone nearer home. When he calmly told his father that arrangements for his betrothal to Charlotte of Savoy were well advanced, the king was furious and peremptorily recalled him, for the first time, to Tours. This command disposed of the dauphin's complaints that he was being kept out of metropolitan France far longer than had been stipulated. But matters had gone too far now for a reconciliation. Louis had already resolved to work against his father as if he were a foreign sovereign, without putting himself into Charles's hands even by a formal visit.

He replied to the indignant monarch's summons by a cool exposition of the facts of a situation in which the king of France had snubbed his son's legitimate aspirations to take charge of the most potentially subversive of French provinces, Normandy, given the post to a royal favorite and unjustifiably attacked the prince's good friends, the rulers of Savoy, by sending troops into their dominions.

Genoa had indeed been a bone of contention between France and Milan for the last seventy years and Charles was really at this time taking advantage of the Milanese republic's fear of Sforza's menacing advance to reassert French claims to the port. As for Piedmont, the region centered upon Turin, it had never been French, having been administered by the house of Savoy ever since the eleventh century. In these circumstance Louis could afford to censure his parent's military adventures against the duchy. He himself also took a great interest in it but, characteristically enough, not in its conquest. His aim was to render it an indissoluble ally through his marriage to Charlotte and thus to ensure respect for his power in both Milan, which he foresaw would soon fall to Sforza, and in Florence, where the count's rich friend Cosimo unobtrusively held the reins of government. The prince, in these circumstances, looked forward to the erection of an irresistible trinity composed of Francesco's prowess in arms, the Medici banks and his own well-proved managerial capacity.

Another wealthy ruler, Duke Philip of Burgundy, with whom Louis had not always seen eye to eye in the past, had been impressed by the younger man's admirable government of Dauphiné, which the duke, as a shrewd statesman himself, was well qualified to appreciate. He went so far as to remark that it was time Charles retired to a hermitage like the ex-pope Amadeus VIII. If Philip had Agnès in mind he knew what he was talking about. For his own innumerable mistresses had never been allowed to dictate politics to him. But actually he and Louis had little in common but good business heads, the duke being devoted to art, literature and the grandiose ideals of chivalry as well as to young women. Nevertheless, each saw that the other might be very useful to his own ambitions, once the present dodderer on the throne of France was out of the way. Philip could see himself keeping both England and Germany in their places if he could get on the right side of the next French king. The prince knew that his own progress to the royal crown would be much easier if he had Burgundian as well as Savoyard strength behind him.

Rouen fell to Dunois that autumn, followed by Harfleur on the first day of the new year. Then Agnès Sorel, far gone in pregnancy, arrived

in the rear of his army at her manor of Mesnil near the great Bene-
dictine abbey of Jumièges some seventeen miles west of Rouen. She
told Charles, who had by that time rejoined his commanders in the
Norman field, that he should beware of a conspiracy of nobles against
him, organized by his son in Dauphiné. The news may have been true
enough. But the king, in the best of tempers after the triumph of his
troops over the English, merely laughed at his mistress's anxiety. He
was soon to weep, though not at any outbreak of rebellion.

The admirable Agnès, who had always hitherto enjoyed perfect
health, died of a miscarriage early in February 1450, at the age of
twenty-eight. Imperturbable in death as in life, she made an exemplary
end, leaving the enormous bequest of sixty thousand crowns to Charles,
confessing her sins and receiving the sacraments with the utmost dignity and grace. The news caused a tremendous sensation throughout
France. Every foreign ambassador at the court reported it at length,
speculated about the inevitable rumors of poison and considered probable political repercussions through the shock to King Charles VII.
There were certainly people who hated Agnès Sorel, as always happens
in the case of a woman more beautiful and intelligent than the average.
But on the whole she had been popular, even with the Church, which
owed much to her generosity. Sensible men of the world appreciated
her good manners and wide range of information. Honest and patriotic
statesmen approved her politics, directed steadily to the economic self-
sufficiency of the kingdom and the reduction of English influence. Nor
could anyone, friend or enemy, deny that in the six years of her domination of the king he had changed his behavior from that of a timid,
irresolute figurehead, shifting his opinions from one hour to the next,
into something like an ostentatious determination to be revered and
to rule. It was almost as if a retiring type of canon had been replaced
by a gallant soldier.

Her taste for luxury and display, her profusion of jewels, silks and
furs, her bare shoulders and breasts, were only censured by such stern
moralists as the verbose Flemish poet and chronicler George Chastelain
(1404–1474), a sworn foe of France, which he considered barbarous in
comparison with Burgundy. He complained with disgust that when he
first met Agnès at a court assembly he could see her nipples. As for the
trains of her gowns, he continued, their cost could have fitted out a
troop of horse or equipped a hospital, expenses which would have done
her wretched country a lot more good than her diamonds and other
Oriental fripperies.

On the other hand, another Burgundian chronicler who had no love
for French society, Olivier de la Marche (1426–1502), regularly praised
the good sense as well as the good looks of the Dame de Beauté. Her

worst traducers, like the historian Thomas Basin (1412–1491), bishop of Lisieux in Normandy, sat nearer home. It was thought by some amateur detectives that strait-laced persons of this sort, even Louis himself, who was known to have long found her antipathetic in every way, might have had a hand in Agnès' death. Why should a woman who had already borne three healthy children without ill effects to herself, suddenly succumb in giving birth to another? But the prince, at any rate, soon after his banishment to Dauphiné, proved what any impartial survey of his career makes clear to posterity, namely, that he never even attempted to assassinate anybody. The case of Guillaume Mariette mentioned above testifies that the dauphin, by executing the fellow, meant to dissociate himself entirely from an agent whose activities appeared to suggest a resort to political murder, a design wholly out of character with his former master's proud and ultra-cautious nature, devious as it certainly was.

Charles had a magnificent tomb of black marble, three feet high, erected in memory of Agnès Sorel at the Jumièges abbey and a still more sumptuous mausoleum at the Loches church near Tours. The abbey monument displayed a statue of the deceased, clothed in white draperies, kneeling and offering her heart to the Virgin. The Latin inscription called her, with a tender sentimentality expressive of the stricken monarch's genuine misery in his bereavement, a "gentle, guileless dove" (*mitis simplexque columba*). Charles gave his surname to her daughters Marie, Charlotte and Jeanne. The choice of these baptismal appellations is curious. He called the eldest girl after his own chaste and long-suffering wife, whom Agnès had supplanted, and the second daughter after the child Louis intended to marry against his father's will. The third name, Jeanne, was also that of the king's legitimate daughter, married to Jean II, duke of Bourbon. It can only be conjectured that the monarch wished to compliment his offspring by his mistress by giving them in the cases of Marie and Jeanne truly royal appellations and in the case of Charlotte one which might one day be borne by a queen of France, the birth of Agnès' child having perhaps coincided with the dauphin's first mention to his father of Charlotte of Savoy. But it is impossible to follow with certainty the wanderings of Charles's extraordinarily capricious mind. Neither Queen Marie nor the duchess of Bourbon can have been edified by its tactlessness in this connection. Louis probably only laughed contemptuously at his father's typically idiotic trick of clapping the name of the girl the prince himself meant to marry on one of the royal bastards.

Count Francesco Sforza entered Milan, by right of conquest, early in 1450. This feat altered the balance of power in Italy, throwing Venice and Naples into each other's arms and rendering the Milan-

Florence axis, reinforced by Pope Nicholas V, another of Cosimo's old friends, the weightiest in the peninsula. The Florentine bankers and merchants in France had been multiplying, to the great advantage of financial stability in the kingdom, ever since the combination of Agnès Sorel and Pierre de Brézé in the administrative saddle with the astute veterans Dunois and Richemont in fighting operations, had brought the country a relief, favorable to commerce, from its former strain and confusion. Even before 1450 Cosimo had been assured by the grateful Charles VII that he could count on French support if either Florence or Milan should be attacked from any quarter during a period he left it to his correspondent to define. In reply the canny Florentine had suggested that the agreement should hold until 1453, when he considered that his political position in Italy would be secure.

The king had thus stolen a march on his rebellious son by coming to terms with the Medicean financial empire before Louis could get at it in his own weaker, more remote situation. The prince could only approach Cosimo, whose importance he certainly understood, by way of Savoy and Milan. He was doing his best to attract the expert businessmen of Florence to Dauphiné. But his model little province could not yet be compared, even when the projected alliance with Savoy came to strengthen it, with the might of France proper in European politics. Nevertheless, there was no one in the French kingdom occupying an official post, not even de Brézé, who could rival the dauphin in any conceivable negotiation with the secretive, ingeniously scheming, quietly persistent leader of Florence, only just beginning, as it happened, to be formally recognized as such.

Cosimo was sixty-two, Louis twenty-eight. The former had never, unlike the latter, commanded armies or shown any interest in outdoor pursuits. The banker-statesman was in fact a bit of a coward physically. He was happily married, with a family of promising children and many devoted friends, whose affection he returned sincerely, if without any excessive warmth. But here the differences ended. Both men were among the few in their day to be absolutely convinced that trade alone, to the exclusion of war and even cultural idealism, could consolidate political power, by which, all the same, they were each attracted for quite unselfish, purely patriotic reasons. Neither wished to order the rest of the world about, but simply to ensure that it would not interfere with the peaceful growth and security of their own beloved nations.

Both took to thorny practical problems like ducks to water, were fearfully bored by ceremony and sensual pleasures and yet could exercise irresistible social charm in private when they chose, as occurred much more often than not. Again and again the dry wit of their retorts and comments on such occasions seems interchangeable. It might have been Louis who remarked, as Cosimo did when shown a beautiful landscape by its proprietor: "I prefer a dull view from my own windows to a delightful prospect elsewhere." It might have been Cosimo who said, as did Louis, in discussing an incorrigible political traitor: "I certainly need that fellow's head. But I can do without his body."

Something perhaps in each of these efficient personalities, which never actually either clashed or worked together, corresponded with the mentality of certain Anglo-Saxon nineteenth-century statesmen, popularly known as "empire builders," who remained cynically cool in an arena of hotheaded adversaries while they concentrated undeviatingly on the main chance, the acquisition of material strength through commerce and industry rather then warfare, in order, however, to practice "gunboat diplomacy" in the interests of stable government wherever it was threatened. The morality of such attitudes has recently been questioned. They did undoubtedly lead in the nineteenth as in the fifteenth century to much suffering among the relatively chaotic communities which lost the political games of those times. The anger of intellectuals then suppressed by narrow-minded bureaucrats is comprehensible enough. But it is hard to imagine how the glories of the Renaissance visionaries could have risen so brilliantly on any foundations but those laid by such comparatively insensitive enthusiasts for concrete policy-making as Louis and Cosimo. Nor could the *Pax Britannica* or for that matter the far earlier *Pax Romana* have lasted so long without the frigidly conceived architecture of such manipulators of men as Augustus, Caesar and many of the ministers of Queen Victoria.

One such planner came a heavy cropper in Paris in 1451. Jacques Coeur, already once arrested for fraud and subsequently released and yet so largely responsible for the new prosperity of his country, was accused by a jealous lady, Jeanne de Vendôme, wife of onc François de Montbéron who may have made erotic advances to Agnès Sorel, and by an Italian named Colonna, probably Jeanne's lover, of having poisoned his best customer, Agnès. The charge was utterly absurd. No plausible pretext for it could be adduced. Coeur had nothing to gain and much to lose by the elimination of that remarkable contributor to his wealth and that of France. But the judges appointed to conduct his trial were all his enemies. The unfortunate master builder of profitable contracts was convicted, imprisoned and deprived of his whole colossal collection of assets by the fines imposed upon him, though no one could prove that he had actually murdered the king's mistress. He would certainly have had to lose his exceptionally well balanced mind before dreaming of such a thing.

The poison charge was eventually dropped. Jeanne de Vendôme and Jacopo Colonna were exiled for life from the court. But the prisoner was found guilty of delivering arms to the Saracens, exporting precious metals, winking at the slave trade, pressing respectable citizens into service aboard his galleys, using the royal seal, misrepresenting the king's wishes and pocketing funds legally due to the state. The defense was able to prove in each case that the acts referred to could be justified or at least excused in the circumstances governing their perpetration. The charges amounted to little more than technical violation of the letter of the law. They were punishable, but not by anything like such a savage sentence as was pronounced.

It is impossible to exonerate Charles of this base trick to get possession of a private subject's money, which the monarch presumably required for his forthcoming campaign against the English in Guienne. That region fell to him in 1453 at the battle of Castillon, not far from Bordeaux, capital of the province. But so vindictive an act as the rigged trial of the financier, who would have been quite prepared to lend funds for the Guienne expedition, as he had in the case of Normandy, can only be explained as vengeance for some unforgivable proceeding on the part of so outstanding and hitherto reliable an associate in the government of France. It is not at all unlikely that Coeur had come to distrust the king as a creditor and would not have been sorry to see the dauphin replace him. For the prince's conscientious discharge of all debts, both public and private, and his generosity to all who served him in any way were as well known to his critics as to his friends. It may actually have been discovered that the mighty merchant had offered funds to Louis, either on demand or of his own accord. But this point could not be proved at the trial. Charles remained concerned at this date, like the dauphin himself, to keep the label of treason from being applied to his son's continued absence from the court.

Nevertheless, it is clear that the monarch's character again began to deteriorate after the death of his beloved mistress. His old imbecility showed in the fatuous tomb already described, which he caused to be erected over her grave, with its absurd Latin epitaph comparing that extremely sophisticated and resolute young woman with a dove. This sentimentality also undoubtedly impelled the king to look about for someone to blame for the incredible death of so robust a beauty. The doctors attributed it to dysentery following a difficult birth. But this prosaic explanation their sovereign, like many another grief-stricken lover in similar circumstances, refused to believe. He was ready, in the depth of sorrow afflicting an already unbalanced mind, which only she had been able to steady for a while, to sacrifice any innocent person on suspicion of having murdered Agnès. If such a scapegoat happened to possess a lot of money it would of course have been an additional compensation to the bereaved sufferer.

Louis for his part, no sentimentalist, felt greatly heartened by the demise of this dangerous adversary. It pleased him a good deal more than Charles's decisive victory, scored by his generals the Constable Arthur de Richemont and Louis de Clermont, second son of the duke of Bourbon, over the English at Formigny near Caen in the same year (April 15, 1450). Agnès' death also encouraged the dauphin to proceed further in his negotiations with Anne of Savoy, whose dominions had so recently been attacked in Piedmont by the king of France, on behalf of the claim of his cousin Duke Charles of Orléans to the Visconti inheritance. The prince offered Anne some assistance in her ensuing war with the usurping Francesco Sforza of Milan, who was consolidating his position, not congenial to Savoy, in every direction. The question of a marriage between the widower dauphin and the Savoyard ruler's daughter Charlotte had already been raised, as noted above, in this correspondence. Savoy had no objection to the proposal. Such a union would be a step up in the world for the ducal family.

Louis formally notified his father, without any special emphasis, of this intention. King Charles happened just then to be on fairly good terms with his incalculable son, having blocked, by the trial of Jacques Coeur, what the monarch conceived might have been his heir's latest schemes. A letter was dispatched from Tours to the prince, pointing out that, while it remained necessary for a future wearer of the crown of France to have children, he could hardly expect any from a girl who was still a child herself. The matter was urgent. Why wait so long in these dangerous times? Older princesses like Eleonora of Portugal and the sister of the Hungarian sovereign were available. Charles again requested his heir to return to the court for consultations on this important subject.

But the dauphin had his own reasons for not taking the slightest notice of this demand. Savoy, on the road to Italy, seemed far more interesting to him than London, Lisbon or Budapest. These latter distant cities had nothing to offer the ambition of a future French king determined not only to outshine but if necessary to oust his parent. The son born to that elderly nincompoop at the end of 1446 and also, significantly, called Charles, would soon be old enough to rival his elder brother. It was essential to anticipate a rallying of conservative royalists around this new addition to the Valois dynasty. Moreover Charlotte would shortly be twelve, still considered quite a nubile age in the middle of the fifteenth century. It appeared that she was neither as pretty nor as lively as Margaret of Scotland. But Anne assured Prince Louis of her perfect health and complete indifference to literature.

In these circumstances he hurried on the marriage. The wedding was duly celebrated in March 1451 at the ducal chapel of Chambéry. The impatient bridegroom took care that the French herald sent to delay it should not have access to the court until it was too late. Then, however, with characteristically cynical humor, he invited Charles's envoy to attend the ceremony. The enraged functionary could do no less than obey. He reported to his master that he had seen this outrageous insult to a father and king perpetrated, with immense pomp, under his very eyes, from the moment that the bridal procession left the castle.

Once more the unlucky ruler of France had been tricked by his dauphin. In a passion of wrath King Charles proclaimed that he was about to disinherit a prince whom he accused at last, in so many words, of treason to the crown. This language caused Louis to expect an immediate invasion of his province by the royal arms. He prepared to resist it to the death. But he told everyone, including his "good uncle," Philip of Burgundy, that he counted upon aid from all reasonable men. These, he assumed, would also comprise the dukes of Brittany and Alençon and the count of Armagnac, none of whom in fact had much right to the epithet. The prince even approached Francesco Sforza, Savoy's late enemy, with a surprisingly polite communication, frankly detailing the position between his father and himself. This missive caused the newly appointed Milanese ambassador in Savoy to inform his employer, in reply to a very natural query, that the dauphin of France appeared to be a "restless, innovating sort of fellow."

Louis was actually, in a fashion that remained with him to the end of his life, already in voluminous correspondence with a great many entirely different personalities. Their attitudes toward him varied from downright hostility to irritation. But in every case fear of his audacity and a deep if not always willing respect for his diplomatic powers mingled with these other feelings. His father in particular still hardly knew what to make of him. All the prince's letters were courteously and even affectionately phrased. They presented to the king what seemed to be the most cogent arguments for the recent events in Savoy and the still later military measures taken in Dauphiné to protect the province from attack over its western border. But Charles found most of the considerations advanced by his son very difficult to follow. He decided to persevere in his inexorable mood. He ignored the letters from the dauphin personally and started communicating with the duke of Savoy, also named Louis, the son of old Amadeus VIII, the ex-pope, now dead. The king naturally wished to find out whose side, if anyone's, the lackadaisical Savoyard potentate, or rather his duchess Anne, was really on.

This proved an exhausting task. The duke was every bit as shifty and irresolute a character as the king himself, hated political problems and did not profess to be in the confidence of his son-in-law so far as anything but hunting was concerned. Time went on and on. Charles grew weary of an apparently endless series of cross-purposes and called in counselors of his own court, men of the caliber of Pierre de Brézé, whom he rightly credited with clearer heads than his own. The fortunes of the intellectual and psychological struggle began to change under these new auspices. Louis gradually came to see that the ministers responsible for the present strength and prosperity of France had un-impeachable patriotic grounds for their objections to his behavior, that they had most of the country behind them and could crush him by force if he persisted in his scandalous "treason."

For a while longer the efforts of each antagonist to circumvent the other's presumed intentions continued. Then they degenerated into mutual abuse, each openly condemning the circles of the other as so many incompetent and fraudulent scoundrels. Neither opinion was true. France in general, if not its monarch, was happy enough in these years. Nor were the prince's associates all by any means a pack of rascals. Aristocrats and also the populace of any country at any time are apt to apply this phrase to merchants and lawyers indiscriminately. Louis never chose his associates, like a modern gangster, for exceptional cunning or unscrupulous determination. He knew he had more than enough of such resources of character himself. All he needed in his subordinates was technical dexterity, which is not so often combined with the spirit of a demon as novels designed for the entertainment of less gifted persons have regularly suggested, reaching their climax along this line in the television serial of the present day.

The dauphin, in fact, had no vices and developed none when he became king, despite the lurid pictures drawn of him in both fiction and history for the last five hundred years. His whole moral being was concentrated on the road to his vision of an enriched, contented and impregnable France. He was not diverted for a moment by such illusions of military glory as vitiated the careers of Louis XIV and Napoleon and today reduce the respect which might otherwise be accorded to Charles de Gaulle. Louis, however, may be said, even by his enemies, to have achieved his goal before he died, at the age of just sixty. But in the

1450's it appeared extremely doubtful whether he would ever do so.

He was not popular in France, even in his province of Dauphiné, for which he had already done so much. However highly the important middle classes may have thought of his administrative ability, they were far outnumbered by the conservative masses, the landowning gentry and the clergy, all of which resented his unprecedented taxation, while the nobles, the bishops and the abbots also could not forgive his inroads upon the privileges they and their predecessors had enjoyed for centuries. These innovations and especially, in that ostentatious age, the prince's casual shabbiness, slight figure and detestation of formality, militated in the minds of simpler souls against his clearly proved courage and intelligence. Even artisans, not to speak of more responsible citizens, both lay and ecclesiastical, disliked his insinuating, back-slapping manners, which they thought unworthy of the heir to a great dynasty, more appropriate, with his slyly cast features and disagreeably intent little gray-green eyes, to the rank of a small-scale farmer or shop-keeper.

Everyone knew he was in more or less open rebellion against his father and had therefore broken the Fifth Commandment of the Christian Decalogue. The immense prestige of the monarchy, hardly affected by Charles's earlier weaknesses and greatly enhanced by the prudent government of his advisers during the last few years, as well as by the king's indulgence in not attacking his son directly, presented an invincible opposition to the dauphin's schemes, if indeed they amounted to anything more than disapproval of his parent as a man. But the prince obstinately refused to modify his basic attitude of defiance, even when he saw that he could not turn it into offensive action with any chance of success, but must on the contrary await the inevitable application, sooner or later, of force from the entire country against the far from reliable fortress of his province.

It was in 1453, the year of the fall of Constantinople to the Turks, which hardly affected Louis's plans at that period, that Jacques Coeur, friend of the late Agnès Sorel and at least not hostile to her former deadly enemy Prince Louis, after being practically ruined by his beneficiary Charles and imprisoned for nearly two years, sank into complete obscurity.

But at the end of October 1454 he contrived to escape from his confinement at the castle of Poitiers with the aid of his son Ravant and perhaps the connivance of Pope Nicholas V, who disliked King Charles's revival of the Pragmatic Sanction and appreciated Coeur's more orthodox attitude to the papacy. At any rate the distinguished fugitive sought sanctuary first at one monastery, then at another. Everywhere the priors refused to give him up to the king's agents, probably because they knew he enjoyed the pope's favor. At last he reached the Franciscan convent of Beaucaire on the west bank of the Rhone about twenty miles east of Nîmes, facing René's Provence across the river. Here Coeur's son-in-law the merchant skipper Jean de Villages entered the town by stealth with a band of bold seamen, found the hunted man at mass, fought off his pursuers and conveyed him across the Rhone and then downstream to near Marseilles, whence he proceeded overland, under their protection, to Nice and thereafter by sea to Pisa and Rome.

The fact that Coeur did not cross into Dauphiné at this stage seems to prove that there had never been any close relationship between him and the prince. Louis would normally have been glad enough to protect anyone, even a former lover of Agnès Sorel, persecuted by his father. But in present circumstances, with a newly enriched and aggressive Charles on his western frontier, any such hospitality would almost amount to an act of war against the monarch, ruinous to such sympathy as the dauphin could still command in his country or anywhere else. It is likely that neither he nor the fugitive thought for more than a moment of this expedient. To Coeur the Vatican must have appeared a far safer refuge. To Louis a penniless convict vindictively pursued by the king, however able and energetic the financier's personality might be, would constitute no asset to a policy still determined to avoid the odium of open defiance in arms of his parent and sovereign.

The jovial and learned humanist Pope Nicholas V received Jacques Coeur with honor. Pope Calixtus III, who almost immediately, in March 1455, succeeded Nicholas, put the refugee seaman-financier in charge of a fleet sent to the relief of the island of Rhodes, then under siege by the Turks. But Coeur never reached his destination. He died at another island, Chios, further up the coast of Asia Minor, on November 25, 1456.

Earlier in 1456 the realistic Louis, more capable than most contemporary statesmen of seeing disagreeable circumstances in their true light, heard that the man responsible for his banishment, his one-time friend and present foe, Antoine de Chabannes, count of Dammartin, was advacing into Bourbonnais with a large, well-disciplined army, headed due southeast. That region and all the intervening country, right up to the banks of the Rhone, behind which lay Dauphiné, was quiet. The objective could only be the seizure or execution of the prince himself. He remembered how he had insulted Chabannes and sworn vengeance for his treachery. But this was not the moment to take it, against such overwhelming odds.

With characteristically cool discretion, using quite a plausible pretext, the dauphin informed his father that he was about to accompany the duke of Burgundy on a crusade against the infidels now advancing up the Balkan peninsula toward Budapest and Vienna. Philip was known to have cherished such a project for a long time, following a fashionable preoccupation of most Christian rulers after the capture of Constantinople by the Moslems. The young prince, with a handful of male companions, thereupon, on August 30, 1456, secretly crossed the Isère into Burgundy proper, which extended from that river up to the borders of Champagne in northeastern France.

In Franche-Comté he was entertained for a few days by Louis de Chalon, prince of Orange, the most powerful of the lords in that province. There the traveler was joined by the sire de Blamont, marshal of Burgundy, who escorted him through Lorraine and Luxembourg. The fugitive heard that Charles had ordered his arrest by the French provost-marshal, Tristan l'Hermite, an officer feared by even the first peers of the realm. The Flemish chronicler Georges Chastelain, concerned all his life to exalt Burgundy at the expense of France, reports maliciously that the prince "could only suppose that the king his father was seeking to take his life by having him secretly drowned in a sack," a favorite method of political assassination at this time, as well as of the punishment of rebels taken in the field. It is very doubtful whether Louis supposed anything of the sort. He knew that his father, whatever mistakes that sovereign might commit, would never allow his own son, even if considered guilty of high treason, to be hunted down and slaughtered like a common criminal or brigand chief. At most the monarch might be plotting to bring his heir to Paris for trial, by force if necessary. Success in such an enterprise would be quite enough of a threat to cause the prince to hurry on, while still taking every precaution to guard against ambush on the way.

The party, after safely reaching Namur, rested there for a few days, sending gallopers ahead to give Duke Philip notice of his "nephew's" arrival and the reason for it. But Louis himself remained impatient, hardly pausing in his precipitate flight. He did not care in the least what anyone thought of this tactical retreat. It could easily be represented by his antagonists as panic or cowardice. Actually it was the sheerest necessity if his work for France were not to be cut short by tedious confinement or death in battle or by clandestine murder which could always be put down afterwards to accident or a crime disavowed by the French government. His whole route lay through neutral territory. But its numerous bandits could be bribed at any time to search for and seize him, with or without bloodshed. This possibility grew less as he approached Philip's capital.

The journey northward seems to have lasted about a fortnight, ending at Louvain in the first half of September. Louis was no doubt taking due precautions. But they were certainly exaggerated by chroniclers interested in giving the impression that the prince was so terribly frightened that he hid himself for days on end in order to evade capture. It is probable that once across the Meuse he revealed himself and began to curry favor with the local authorities in his usual insinuating style. They were in general hostile to the king beyond the border and well aware of his relations with his uncompromising son. The lords of this frontier region must also have been flattered to find that the dauphin was seeking refuge with their own duke. All such comings and goings would impose a certain amount of delay. But the prince's party must have ridden hard in the intervals to reach Louvain, about fifteen miles east of Brussels, by mid-September.

There he entered upon an environment very different from any he had hitherto known. The uneasy, beleaguered court of Charles VII prior to 1446 and the atmosphere of earnest endeavor and defiance of the king's wishes which had surrounded a rebellious but soberly industrious ruler in Dauphiné for the next ten years bore no resemblance to life in the wealthy, luxurious, confident and easygoing but definitely old-fashioned duchy of Burgundy.

CHAPTER VI

Exile in Burgundy
(1456–1461)

✣✣✣ Georges Chastelain, charged by Duke Philip the Good to write the history of his reign, describes the Burgundian ruler at this period, when he was sixty years old, as "standing straight as a reed, strongly built about the loins, with powerful arms and shoulders." His hair was very thick, his forehead broad, his glance piercing and haughty under shaggy eyebrows where "the separate hairs bristled like horns when he was angry." Yet on ordinary occasions his features and bearing displayed the calm majesty of an emperor. "From these alone he could be deemed of imperial rank and worthy to crown his physical grace with the highest symbol of sovereignty."

These compliments, suggestive of a minotaur rather than the sage administrator Philip in fact was, may be thought the excessive eulogies of a zealously loyal subject, couched in the martial fifteenth-century style. But foreigners usually agreed. A Spanish grandee remarked that the duke had "great nobility of aspect, much energy and amiability, a tall, elegant figure and the alert courtesy of a paragon of chivalry." His pride and touchiness were certainly extreme, leading him into violent outbursts of rage. Yet Chastelain writes that "one humble word could quieten him." He loved luxury, especially gems, fine horses and weapons, which suited him to perfection. His state entries into cities enraptured the crowds of spectators. He excelled in the organization of such festivities as the tournaments, banquets and other ceremonies held in his presence. Guests were astounded at the splendors of his jewelry, tapestries, plate and money chests, due to an income estimated in 1455 as equal to that of Venice, half that of the pope and four times that of Florence.

The duke's private life presented a similar unlimited zest for enjoyment. Apart from innumerable casual love affairs, at least thirty longer liaisons are known to have existed, producing seventeen acknowledged bastards, the most eminent of whom bore the names of Corneille, Antoine, the latter a Knight of the Golden Fleece, David and Philippe, both of these last being appointed in succession bishops of Utrecht.

In such exhilarating circumstances the Burgundian court deliberately set itself to outdo those of contemporary kings and emperors in every kind of brilliance. The ducal residences were all provided with magnificently furnished public and private reception rooms, bathrooms and outdoor covered galleries with glowing stained-glass windows. The chapels resembled miniature churches and were artistically as superb, on their smaller scale, as the best of the great ecclesiastical buildings of the day. The outstanding quality of the tapestries was always noted by visitors, especially that of the hangings of the Hôtel d'Artois, the official Burgundian palace in Paris, which illustrated the life of the Biblical champion Gideon, patron of the Order of the Golden Fleece founded by Philip on January 10, 1430, the day he married his third wife, Isabella of Portugal, at Bruges. There were twenty-four knights, exclusive of the duke himself, the grand master of the Order. He was bound to consult them before embarking upon war. Their disputes could be settled only in their own courts of justice.

Dijon still preserves specimens of the huge kitchen, with its seven gigantic chimneys, which prepared meals of Gargantuan abundance, multiplicity, variety and refinement to the duke's guests. Such feasts were always enlivened throughout the duchy by periodical spectacles, so as to give the diners time to recover from the vast quantities of food and wine consumed. Pantomimes were then performed with the aid of ingeniously complicated machinery staging sieges and sham fights, acrobats and fabulous monsters. Pies could be large enough to contain a whole orchestra of musicians.

On February 17, 1454, at Lille, Philip had given the most famous of these entertainments, with a live pheasant as the showpiece. It was placed on the main table fully feathered and adorned with a collar of gold and precious stones. Formal speeches were next recited by a giant representing "The Grand Turk" and a statuesque but distressed dame symbolizing "Mother Church." The former uttered threats and the latter entreaties for rescue. Philip proceeded to take a solemn oath to lead a crusade for the delivery of Constantinople, captured by the heathen in the previous year. His son, the count of Charolais, and all the other lords present, in order of rank, deposed similar vows in the name of God, the Virgin and the Pheasant. For the French noun *faisan*, designating this bird, is pronounced in almost the same way as *faisant*, "doing," i.e. executing deeds of valor.

It would be a mistake, however, to suppose that such splendid scenes were always enacted with the solemnity typical of religious ritual. The form in which a pious proclamation was made often exhibited a vein of sly humor as characteristic of medieval knights as their ceremonious gravity. A certain Jean de Beaumont, for instance, swore on one such occasion that he would accompany on the projected crusade only a social superior known to be a generous employer. Thrifty princes, Jean declared, could expect no service from him.

But few chroniclers dwell on the self-mockery sometimes to be detected in these wildly sumptuous pageants. Olivier de la Marche, for example, without the slightest trace of ridicule, lavishes on their almost incredible details, matched only in the extravagant fantasies of Oriental literature, a good many more sheets of his manuscript than he devotes to political and military history combined.

Prince Louis of France, flying for his life to the Low Countries in September 1456, was certainly going to need every particle of his already notable self-control, fortitude and tact to maintain his equanimity in a land which he must have regarded as more than half delirious in its mad dreams of hitherto unimaginable pomp and prodigality, phenomena which he loathed from the very bottom of his prosaic soul. Perhaps the forthcoming trial exceeded in its depressive power any he had yet been obliged to face. But he survived it with an imperturbability as astonishing as the scene itself. After all, he had nowhere else to go.

Philip was in Friesland, the extreme northwest of his dominions, suppressing a local revolt, when the fugitive prince arrived in Brabant. But the duke's son, the count of Charolais, aged twenty-three, met the royal exile in the palace at Brussels to which he had been directed. The count resembled Louis, ten years his senior, in only two respects. Charolais cared little or nothing for women, though he was no homosexual, and he could exercise when he chose a positively hypnotic charm of manner which often won over people who afterwards had reason to regret their pleasure in his company. In other ways the two men had nothing in common except a love of hunting. The count, tall, athletic and rather coarsely handsome, with a slight stoop which enhanced his somewhat menacing appearance, like that of an eagle, excelled at all knightly sports. He delighted, like his father, in feudal pageantry and remained absolutely convinced all his life that the military virtues it represented, flamboyant courage and an unshakable resolution in misfortune, which repeatedly took the form of an absurd obstinacy, were all that mattered in the life of a gentleman. He had been as well educated as the dauphin but preferred, as the latter did not, myth, legend and bellicose epic poetry to the cold facts of history and politics. But the first meeting of these two mighty opposites, who never let each other alone so long as the Burgundian lived, could not have been more auspicious for their future relations. Charolais loved to play the part of a magnanimous host and the prince enjoyed that of a humble suppliant, which suited his love of dissimulation. He was one of the proudest men who ever lived. But he scarcely ever showed this trait openly. At the present crisis in his career, moreover, it would have been madness to do so. The truth of the situation, which he saw as clearly as anyone, would have obliged every tactful diplomat, however secretly determined to end it decisively and triumphantly at the earliest opportunity, to meet the charity of a foreign host with modesty and discretion. Louis reveled in giving false impressions when they were politically desirable. He entered with the utmost relish upon his new character of a harmless victim of injustice.

In fact the contrast in circumstances was glaring. The count's were the brightest possible, those of the dauphin dark and even ominous. The towering, smiling, broad-shouldered, splendidly dressed heir to the great rich duchy of Burgundy, with his shock of luxuriant black hair and glittering blue eyes, confronted, probably at first with carefully concealed contempt, the wheyfaced little French refugee in his stained and tattered riding cloak. But in a very short time all the Burgundian lords and ladies realized that the prince's insignificant physique and diffident manners masked an iron will and an intelligence, to say the least of it, out of the ordinary.

Charolais' mother, the grave, middle-aged Duchess Isabel of Burgundy, no more a beauty than most Portuguese ladies, nevertheless again like most of her countrywomen, disposed of an unpretentious sociability that clothed, like an ample garment, a mind sharper than either her husband's or her son's. Louis, rather like her in these respects, already knew the duchess well. She was accompanied by her namesake Isabel of Bourbon, the young count's second wife. His first, Catherine, the eldest daughter of Charles VII, had died in 1446. Courtesies were extravagant on both sides. The duchess actually went down on her stiff knees before the exiled prince. But such deference was not uncommonly shown in those days by ladies too exalted in rank for anyone to suppose that a posture of this kind indicated anything but Christian humility, like that of kings ceremonially washing the feet of beggars. Louis was not therefore deceived by this pious gesture. He returned it, as was expected of him, by gallantly raising the duchess to her feet, with his hand under her elbow, and leading her to the seat of honor on his right hand. But she duly declined this position as inappropriate to her feminine diffidence. When this comedy of stately etiquette was over the two former antagonists in diplomacy, the dignified and stubborn Isabel and her decidedly slippery younger visitor, got down to business.

But not for long. Isabel smilingly refused to embark on any serious discussion in the absence of her husband, though similar circumstances had not worried her on previous occasions. After a quarter of an hour she rose and carried off the dauphin to apartments in the palace which had been placed at his disposal. Charolais accompanied him and suggested a hunting trip as soon as he felt like it. The prince was only too delighted to agree. For this sport, the only one in which he took an interest, appealed to him far more than the gorgeous amusements of a different sort which surrounded him at the Burgundian court. The jousts and the poetry readings, the dances and the theatrical performances merely bored him, though they were a good deal more magnificent than any in which he had hitherto been more or less compelled to participate.

Meanwhile the duke kept everyone waiting for a declaration of his policy. He found it difficult to make up his mind on the evidence of the letters he had been receiving from Charles, from Blamont and from the prince of Orange. But he decided at last to be hospitable. The king was obviously afraid to bully a man who might prove his only reliable ally, on the terms of the Treaty of Arras, signed twenty years before, if the English should decide to renew the Hundred Years' War. The so-called Wars of the Roses, which had broken out in 1455 between King Henry VI of England and some of his barons, might soon come to an end and release the forces required to avenge the loss of all France except Calais. On the receipt of Charles's last communication, which seemed to leave the duke to please himself, so long as he did not positively adopt the dauphin's cause, Philip rode down to Brussels, arriving on October 15, 1456.

He had replied to the king of France:

> Having heard that my said Lord the Dauphin had requested the Lord of Blamont, my Marshal of Burgundy, to accompany him in his journey to visit me, and that my said Marshal had not dared to refuse this request and was with him, I was much astonished. But since it is so you will understand, most dread lord, that for the honor of yourself, of him and of your noble House it will be only reasonable and in fact my duty to do him all honor, respect and pleasure and I shall listen with a good will to anything it may please him to tell and declare to me, of which matters I shall inform you. For God knoweth that with all my heart I would desire that he should acquit himself toward you as every good son ought to his lord and father.

Louis would have been within his rights as a royal prince to await his host within the palace. But conscious of his status as an exile he asked the duchess and the countess of Charolais, but apparently not the count, who did not get on very well with his father, to come with him to meet Philip in the open air at the gates of the ducal residence. The duke in his turn extended equal courtesy to the son of his cousin and technical superior in feudal law, Charles VII, by appearing, not in the guise of a practically independent ruler with the sword of state borne before him, but merely as a vassal with no such ceremonial equipment. He dismounted and knelt before the dauphin, his "nephew."

Both men were in fact descendants of King Philip VI of Valois (d. 1320) through respectively his grandsons King Charles V (d. 1380) and Duke Philip the Valiant ("Le Hardi") of Burgundy (d. 1404), father of John the Fearless and grandfather of Philip the Good, while Charles V begot Charles VI, father, officially at any rate, of Charles VII.

The prince was only restrained by the duchess from impulsively pulling his sixty-year-old "uncle" to his feet, as he had herself. That had been all very well in the case of a woman. But neither she nor her husband actually regarded Louis as powerful enough in present circumstances to be allowed to play the part of a condescending social superior. It was really for them, they considered, to act in such a way toward him. In their own perfectly justifiable view the heir to the French throne needed their protection from the king's vengeance and could be held as a hostage for any demands they might care to make upon Charles, of whose basic sentimentality they were both well aware. So the duke rose by himself and knelt again before the two men finally embraced.

Thereupon, on the surface, obsequious compliments, flowery protestations of unworthiness and even tears of joy passed between the dauphin and his equivocal hosts. Philip kept up this attitude not only in public but also at a private interview with his guest which followed. He remained careful, however, not to promise any definite line of political action. King Charles, whose troops had already moved into Dauphiné, meeting with no resistance, continued to maintain an ominous silence. The Burgundian spies at his court wrote only vague and contradictory reports to Brussels. One of them related, however, that he had heard the monarch growl contemptuously: "Tell your master that he is entertaining a fox in his chicken run."

Soon Prince Louis was assigned the castle of Genappe, near the capital, for his residence, coupled with a generous pension. Hunting with the count of Charolais and study at the University of Louvain took up most of his time. For recent experience had convinced the somewhat Philistine dauphin that intellectual pursuits, apart from that of history, might be useful to a future sovereign determined eventually to become the most important in Europe. He also found himself, ironically enough, playing the part of mediator in the disputes which constantly arose between the fiery young count and his male parent. Charolais could not stand the duke's favorites, the Croy brothers, and opposed in and out of season the influence they exercised on his father's domestic policy. Louis understood, after all these years of more or less bitter negotiations with his own father, perhaps better than anyone else in Burgundy at any rate just how such arguments should be conducted if the object were to avoid an open break, which might be awkward for his own plan of ensuring a united front behind him in the duchy.

He felt less in his element at the informal parties in Hesdin Castle on the river Canche, not far from Agincourt, in what is now the Pas-de-Calais. Here the more dissipated Burgundian aristocrats, at a safe distance from Brussels, seem to have entertained bevies of half-naked young women with more or less obscene chatter supposed to have originated the notorious *Cent Nouvelles Nouvelles*, facetiously lewd tales of court life absurdly attributed in later times to Louis himself. Responsibility for these *fabliaux*, mostly traditional in plot, has also been ascribed, without much probability, to Antoine de la Salle (1388–1462), who wrote the much more accomplished *Petit Jehan de Saintré* (1456). No doubt the *Nouvelles*, like other anonymous collections of the kind, had no single author. In any case Louis, so far from contributing, himself, to this merrymaking, soon left Hesdin for Genappe, where he could enjoy a quiet life divided between hunting expeditions and his political correspondence.

Yet by the new year of 1457 he had succeeded, as he nearly always did among neutral communities, in making himself respected, if not exactly beloved, in Burgundian court circles. His rank as a royal prince, superior to that even of Philip, gave him a flying start. His obvious prudence and diplomatic experience made up for his lack of the fine presence and boisterous affability so conspicuous in the count at this date and also, as modified by a certain calm majesty on public occasions, in the duke. The brilliant, unscrupulous Croy brothers recognized with some misgiving that they could not dominate this important "foreigner" as they dominated Philip. At the same time they were relieved to find that Louis did not intend, as might have been the case in his position, to take the lead over themselves. His carefully correct, almost humble, attitude seemed to exclude any idea of his possible interference in Burgundian politics.

In these circumstances it appeared perfectly natural that when a daughter was born in February 1457 to Charolais and his wife, the

Countess Isabel, the dauphin should be asked to stand godfather to the baby, which was christened Marie after his own mother. No one present at that ceremony, which Philip testily ignored, as he would have preferred a male infant, could have foreseen that when the child had grown up to be the richest heiress in Christendom the solemn, slightly built and casually attired personage who held her over the font in 1457 would declare implacable war against her.

Perhaps this baptism had caused him to remember that his wife Charlotte, still in Dauphiné, was now sixteen, of an age to give birth herself. She was an insignificant, submissive little creature, with far fewer personal attractions than the late Margaret of Scotland and also with far less interest in dress and amusement, not to mention poetry. But something had to be done about an heir to the Valois line. The prince duly sent for Charlotte and cohabited with her. Luckily, she proved fertile. A son was born on July 15, 1459. But unluckily the baby died four months later. A daughter, however, followed at an interval of two years. This event was not at the time much good to Louis, though a few years later he found young Anne de Valois intelligent and she proved a useful, even wise, regent after his death.

It was clear to Philip that no reconciliation between the king and the prince could be hoped for at present. The duke laid his plans, which probably included a bid for his own occupation of the French throne, accordingly. But he remained on quite amiable terms with the dauphin for the time being. He told Charles VII that he had only received the fugitive in Burgundy out of charity and would never keep him there if he wished to leave. But Philip added, on the other hand, that he could not dream of trying to persuade a thoroughly frightened man to put his head into the French lion's mouth. The king cursed. But that was just what the duke, in pursuance of his new ambitions, wanted him to do.

Louis, for his part, had struck up a close friendship with the energetic young count of Charolais. Although neither of these otherwise distinctly tense personalities had married for love or formed any other deep and lasting association with a female, there is no unmistakable proof of any passionate bond between them which might be qualified as homosexual. Both in fact reserved the only affection they were capable of, one in each case certainly profound, for an idea, in Louis that of a powerful and united France, while the count's vision, noble enough at its best, extended to even wider horizons. He would have liked to rule all Europe in the only way he could imagine would wipe out its endless dissensions, that of replacing them with the generous ideals of ancient chivalry.

He was of course badly mistaken. For it was actually the impracticability of maintaining those ideals that had brought the Continent to its present state of disunion. Louis on his side had already come to the opposite conclusion, that knightly glories must never again govern the thought of Western society if it were not to sink once more, this time without hope of recovery, into the barbarity of the Dark Ages, more notable for horror than for heroism. But the prince, as usual, kept his own counsel on these matters.

The quarrels between the count and his father were usually started, strange to say, by the latter. Philip, formerly so secretive and retiring, had become with advancing age excessively irascible in the day-to-day administration of his duchy, though his foreign policy retained all its old discretion. Once, at Genappe, he threw into the fire some papers his son had brought to him for signature, declaring with fury that they were an attempt to evade his orders. The subject seems to have been a revision of some details of organization in the count's household. They may have included some measure for which the Croy brothers were responsible and which Charolais wished to circumvent. "How dare you disobey me, monsieur?" roared the father, purple in the face, the veins on his neck standing out like cords of an even darker tinge. "Leave the room this instant!" When the young man hesitated, the blood drained from the duke's distorted features, till they showed white as a maniac's. He drew his dagger and flourished it under the count's nose. The duchess, who was present, dragged Charolais out of the chamber and into a smaller adjoining one which gave access to a locked oratory, guarded by a youthful chorister, who had charge of the key.

Philip could be heard bawling murderously in the other room. He seemed to be stumbling about, intent on pursuing his wife and son. Isabel coolly ordered the chorister, whom this scene had reduced to petrified dread, to unlock the door of the oratory. She knew it opened into the dauphin's private quarters. His appalled friend rushed blindly into the prince's study and threw himself in a panic at the feet of the dauphin himself, who was reading quietly at a desk. The duchess had turned to face her armed and maddened husband on the threshold of the antechamber. His roars and her steady retorts came faintly to the ears of the pair in the room beyond, the door of which had been banged behind him by Charolais.

Louis rose at once. Leaving the count on his knees by the desk, he strode through the oratory and joined the duchess, who was retreating toward him before Philip. The old man was still flourishing his dagger and swearing like one of his own troopers. But as soon as he saw the prince he sheathed the weapon and begged his guest's pardon. "I am ashamed that your lordship should be disturbed by these family affairs," he muttered obsequiously, the habits of a lifetime of diplomacy regaining temporary control of his rage. "But I must show my son that he is not to try to deceive me. I am not in my dotage yet." He drew himself up in his characteristically stately fashion. "I can reduce the comte de Charolais to the status of a lackey if I choose. But have no fear. I am no more a murderer than I am a dotard. As for you, madame," he added, turning sternly to the duchess, "you have done yourself no good by this improper intervention." He was still trembling a little, though his skin had recovered its normal coloring. The dauphin knelt. He put his arms around the duke, entreating him, with perhaps genuine tears, to be merciful.

Philip lifted him up and patted his shoulder, but without any change of expression. Then the duke left the room in a silence which could almost be felt. He had his horse saddled and rode out into open country alone.

Chastelain, the loyal historian of the house of Burgundy, records what is supposed to be Philip's own narrative of his adventures. "The days at that season were short and it was already late in the evening when this prince mounted his horse, thinking only of taking to solitude in his fields. Rain was falling fast upon the frozen earth. But he paid no attention to the weather, being absorbed in his private vexation. He crossed the level ground and reached hilly country, where he lost his way. But he counted on his horse's instinct to lead him to Hall. Yet, by the time of darkest night, beast and rider together went astray in a vast, thickly growing and pathless forest. The more he sought a way out the deeper he rode into it. While he thus wandered, with God alone as his protector, those in the palace at Brussels were thrown into the greatest alarm. The dauphin rode out with a few friends to seek the duke. But he could find no trace of his beloved uncle, who was continuing his discomforting journey at random. His horse's hoofs now slipped on the ice that was again hardening the rain-soaked ground as the night frosts chilled it, endangering his life. Uphill and downhill, forward and backward he rode. Never before had he been in such a situation, being constantly thrown and remounting till he hardly knew what he was doing. Thus one of the greatest princes in the world then found himself in a state which would have horrified the humblest of his subjects. He who, the day before, had seen men kneel to him, now knelt himself, perforce, to trees.

"Yet, as an experienced soldier, he did not lose courage. He was starving and shivering with cold . . . but he remained energetic and of good cheer, paying no attention to the torments of his hunger and ignoring the cold and darkness, since he knew that dawn must follow and told himself that the worst of the night would soon be over. In this spirit the lord of so many lands let his horse guide him through the accursed forest, hoping only that somewhere, by the grace of God, he might find some little hut or other in a clearing of the woods. He shouted, thinking someone might hear. But however often he called aloud, no one answered. At one moment he decided to dismount and lead his horse by the bridle. At another he remounted and rode by chance into a stream which he mistook for a road, so that his horse snorted and reared, refusing to go on. He had to take another direction and again rode at hazard. At last he heard a dog bark and realized that a hut must be near. He found it to be a woodman's cabin, where the poor fellow and his lean wife lay fast asleep on a mattress. Such was the wretched accommodation upon which the wealthy duke of Burgundy stumbled, half dead with hunger and cold.

"He shouted and knocked. But it was long before the couple answered, for they were sleeping most soundly. Then when they did awake, they feared to show themselves in case the intruder might be one of a band of brigands, evil livers such as swarmed in that remote part of the country. But the duke continued to summon them, saying, 'I am one who has gone astray throughout this night in the forest and I am dying of cold and distress. I beg you to rise and comfort me, for by so doing you will be long remembered.' Finally the woodman felt pity for the stranger and realized from his accent that he must be a man of worth. Rising and lighting a torch, the peasant opened the door, asking: 'Friend, what wouldst thou? Who pursues thee or leads thee abroad in such weather and at this unseasonable hour?' As he spoke the man stared hard at the traveler, seeing that he held the bridle of a horse which, though foundered, could easily be judged of high quality. The duke replied: 'Friend, you shall learn soon enough how I come to be here. Meanwhile I beg you, for God's sake and for payment too, to be good enough to light a little fire for me. I am soaked through with rain and battered by ill winds and I die of cold.'

"The woodman rekindled his hearth and roused his wife, whereupon the duke exclaimed anxiously: 'I am starving!' Unfortunately there was very little to eat in the cottage. Said the peasant: 'I've only one loaf and some cheese from the monastery, wretched stuff, and just plain water, no ale. If you don't mind that, you are welcome to what we have.' 'Friend, friend,' cried the duke delightedly. 'Go fetch it!' Forthwith a cloth was laid before the fire. The duke ate with a hearty appetite, finding more savor and pleasure in that simple fare than ever in sweetmeats and fat capons. He broke the bread with his own hands, lacking a squire to cut it, and helped himself to the cheese without fearing it might be poisoned . . . his thirst he quenched with sober water instead of heady wine and considered himself very lucky to have been allowed it."

Philip did not reveal himself to the woodman, saying merely that he was a "man of worth" and presenting his awestruck host with a Rhenish gold florin, for which the fellow stammered out that he "had no change" but was told this did not matter. He was requested, however, to go next day to the manor of Hall and inform those in charge there that the expected guest had changed his mind and would be proceeding to Beaumont. No doubt the peasant soon discovered at Hall with whom he had been dealing. The duke in fact rode on afterwards to Beaumont, where he had arranged to meet the eldest Croy brother. Eventually, on the following evening, the truant ruler returned to Brussels.

There Prince Louis managed to calm him to the extent of pardoning his son's "indiscretion" for the time being. But this episode had really frightened the dauphin, as he reflected that if Philip disowned Charolais he might well also disown his guest, the young man's most intimate associate, and send this equally "disobedient" son back to a father who would be capable, not perhaps of stabbing him in his mother's presence, but quite certainly of disgracing him by a public trial for high treason, ending with imprisonment and still more waste of time in the preparation for accession. The affair caused Louis, in his letter to Charles, to redouble his efforts at self-control, clothed in phrases of patient courtesy.

He now knew that "Philip the Good" was not to be trusted in his expert pose of chivalrous host and pacific counselor and that his temper, growing more and more uncertain in the last few months, had reached the point of incalculability and might prove very dangerous at any moment. In other words he recognized the duke as one of those rare though not unheard-of cases of an autocrat benevolent in youth and early middle age but turning basically sour and malicious after fifty, even if under normal conditions the former mask remained sedulously in place. At the present stage, however, the very opposite of a mellowing process had occurred beneath it.

Meanwhile Charles too, his son heard, had again degenerated. He was now said to be as wholly in the power of Antoinette de Villequier, a niece of the dead Agnès Sorel, as he had previously been under the influence of her aunt. Nor was Antoinette alone, the Milanese ambassador reported, in dictating to the king of France. There were half a dozen other good-looking young noblewomen, almost constituting a harem, who went about everywhere with the monarch on his endless travels. He himself cut a ridiculous figure with his long, drooping nose, bent shoulders, diffident movements and bandy legs only half hidden by the floridly ostentatious style of silks and velvets he persisted in wearing. The sovereign, who was fifty-five, already looked an old man, much more worn and pallid than the rubicund Duke Philip, seven years his senior and an indefatigably continuous fornicator for the last four decades, mostly spent by Charles in respectable domesticity.

Between the years 1456 and 1459 Philip had been pretending to sit on the fence in his official policy of holding the balance between the king and the dauphin, each of whom, with equal hypocrisy, took up the attitude of an aggrieved party. Louis certainly and Charles possibly represented himself as such in correspondence with foreign rulers like the duke of Milan and several kings in Spain and Portugal. But in 1459 the sympathies of the duke of Burgundy, or at any rate the line that best suited his secret aims, shifted definitely to the side of his guest, the prince. For in that year Charles sent a numerous delegation of ambassadors to Philip to plead his case, only to be reproached for negotiating an alliance with the hereditary enemy of France, Henry VI of England.

Henry, now thirty-eight, had undergone two long fits of insanity in 1454 and 1455–1456. During each of them his able brother Richard, duke of York, had acted as regent. But in 1455 York had felt it necessary to demand the dismissal from the royal council of some incompetent lords in Henry's service, their party being called Lancastrian because the king was the great-grandson of the duke of Lancaster, known to history as John of Gaunt. Queen Margaret, stern daughter of the mild René of Anjou, resisted the duke of York's demand. He marched on London in arms, defeated Margaret at St. Albans in Hertfordshire on May 22, 1455, and captured the bewildered Henry. The "Wars of the Roses," white for York and red for Lancaster, from the party badges worn by the contestants, had begun.

Peace was patched up for a while. The king resumed his freedom and his sanity. But the queen, who dominated him, remained inexorably hostile to Richard of York, exiled his party and beheaded many of its adherents. Charles VII naturally took the side of his victorious niece. But Philip of Burgundy saw that rebellion was coming, due to Margaret's harsh treatment of her relatively reasonable brother-in-law, Richard of York. The queen's always vigorous personality seemed to be hardening into embittered partisanship as she approached her thirtieth year. It was not so much love for her feeble, if respectable, husband that impelled her as a determination to govern, all by herself, the rich, alien country of England, to which she had come as a pauper fourteen years before. Philip did not care for the prospect of an England united under the most domineering representative of a family traditionally favorable to the Valois and related to them. The duke felt that the house of Anjou might well be capable of forcing France into a combination with the fierce islanders, commercial rivals of Burgundy, against his duchy, even at the price of renewed French subjugation to English lords.

Philip pointed out to Charles VII that both France and Burgundy, having regard to history as well as to geography, were bound to support any movement in England tending to reduce the military power of that vengeful island, which would never forget its claims to rule over them. For this reason Burgundy had favored from the start the rebellious Yorkist faction led by the earls of Salisbury and Warwick under Richard, Henry's brother and the father of a promising young son, Edward, earl of March, aged seventeen. Salisbury and Warwick were the uncle and cousin respectively of Edward. All four of these soldierly characters were more popular, both at home and abroad, than the legitimate king and queen, Henry and Margaret. Trouble was certain to arise in these conditions. Philip welcomed it by encouraging Richard and the earls. But he would really have liked to see both the white and the red rose go down in a sea of blood that would drown the aggressive potential of England for at least a century.

Charles deeply resented Philip's attitude. Hearing that Charolais also opposed it, as he opposed all the duke's policies, while Louis of course upheld it, maintaining his implacable quarrel with his father, the king thought for a while of invading Burgundy by force, reducing the duke to the proper posture of a dependent feudatory and seizing the person of the prince, so perversely insubordinate, not to use a harsher term, to a father's natural authority. But the king's health was now fast deteriorating. He did not feel up to such a great effort, despite his anger with the two culprits and the probability that Charolais would help him. His fury turned to depression. But to Philip's and Louis's annoyance he regained something of his old spirits when the news came that Queen Margaret had utterly routed the Yorkists at the battle of Ludlow in October 1459, sending Salisbury, Warwick and their protégé the earl of March flying in a panic overseas to Calais.

But nothing really went right for Charles at this period. His beloved Antoinette de Villequier abandoned him for the duke of Brittany, an old associate of the dauphin's. She kept the prince well informed of everything that went on at the French court. He begged her for advice. "Most worthy lady," he wrote. "Throw my letters into the fire as soon as you have read them. But tell me, if you can, whether I ought to remain in my present position." He was also anxiously consulting astrologers as to when his nuisance of a father might be expected to die. These activities and the query he had addressed to Antoinette, heartless as they might be considered, were intended above all to ensure that not a moment would be wasted over his accession. He knew that there were powerful forces at work against him in France. He wanted to set out for Reims at least, the traditional city for French coronations, as soon as it was certain that the king could not recover, so as to feel the paternal crown on his head within hours at most of the receipt in Brussels of a definite notification of Charles's demise.

By chance or design one of his letters, dated August 30, 1460, to Madame de Villequier, which might be understood as expressing impatience for the monarch's death, fell into the royal hands. It read, after referring to the information she had passed on to the prince about the situation at court: "I have received similar communications from the Count of Dammartin, whom I pretend to hate. Tell him to go on serving me equally well in the future, writing in the same way as he always used to. I shall think over what he has written and he will soon hear from me in reply."

The king, in a panic, banished Dammartin. But when that worthy swore by all he held holy that he had never written any such treasonable letters to Louis, the distinguished soldier, whose previous and subsequent career proves him to have been always loyal to the throne, whoever might occupy it, was recalled. It looks very much as though the dauphin, who had never forgiven that officer for reporting the conspiracy of 1446 to Charles, simply meant to get the count into trouble and therefore coolly lied about him in the letter to Antoinette. If so, such unscrupulous vindictiveness can only be explained by his real belief that Dammartin was a leading spirit in the French opposition to the impending accession of the writer. In fact Antoine de Chabannes, like Pierre de Brézé, was one of those officers about the court who could be relied on to serve any living, legitimate sovereign of France, with utter devotion, no matter what opinions of the royal character he might hold in private. Louis only came gradually to recognize the worth of such men. When he became king he imprisoned them at first, then, with characteristic realism, released them.

But meanwhile Charles, on the evidence of his son's letter to Antoinette de Villequier, feared the worst, poison or armed rebellion. The unhappy ex-patron of that lady questioned his spies in Burgundy. The dauphin, however, had been far too discreet to allow the slightest leakage of any proof of his actually almost frantic eagerness to take over the kingdom. The French agents in Brussels assured the monarch's councilors that the prince remained innocent of any such feeling.

Nevertheless, menacing shadows continued to gather about the distracted king. Apart from Madame de Villequier, more than one previously trusted courtier abandoned him. A surgeon fled to Valenciennes on the Burgundian frontier, obviously to join Louis, who was already on his way south. In a fright, the doomed sovereign locked up another physician, whom he suspected of administering fatal drugs to him. Charles had by now entered upon such a deplorable psychological and physical state that the royal council felt it their duty to warn the dauphin openly of his father's condition.

"Most dread lord," wrote the signatories of this dispatch, who included Antoine de Chabannes himself, René's brother Count Charles of Anjou and Maine, Tanneguy de Chastel and a future chancellor, Pierre Doriole,

> We recommend ourselves to your good grace with all possible humility. May it please you to know, most dread lord, that the King your father, our lord sovereign, has been suffering for some time from a certain malady. It began with pain in a tooth, which caused a great swelling of the cheek and part of the face. Much pus was discharged, the said tooth was extracted and the trouble was so far cured that, according to the doctors' daily reports to us, there was good hope that within a short time he would completely recover. But this result is taking longer than we thought it would. It seems to us that his weakness rather than his strength is increasing. Consequently we, being desirous of serving and obeying you after he is gone, have decided to write and inform you of the matter, as is only reasonable, in order that in the first place we may be acquainted with your good pleasure. May it please you therefore, most dread lord, to send word and command us of your good pleasures, that we may obey your orders to the best of our ability, if it please our Lord. May He, of His Holy Grace, grant you most fair and long life. Written at Méhun-sur-Évre [Mehun-sur-Yèvre] this seventeenth day of July. Your most humble and obedient servants etc.

Thirteen signatures followed. They are for the most part those of men who remained loyal to Louis on his accession. But one important name, that of Pierre de Brézé, is missing. He was in England with Queen Margaret. The earls of Salisbury and Warwick, with the son of the duke of York, Edward, earl of March, now eighteen, had returned to London in July 1460 and beaten the Lancastrians at the battle of Northampton, where Henry was again captured. But the royalists regrouped in the north. The duke of York, after sending the young earl of March to deal with the west of England, hurried from London to scatter the new Lancastrian army. But at Wakefield in southern Yorkshire on December 30, 1460, Richard was ambushed and killed. His lieutenant Salisbury fell into the hands of the enemy and was barbarously beheaded.

The triumphant queen, sure now that her cause was won, moved directly on the capital. But the wintry weather delayed her. It was not

until February 17, 1461, that she and de Brézé attacked Warwick at
three o'clock in the morning near St. Albans, where in 1455 the earl had
sent her packing and captured her husband for the first time. She now
routed Warwick in his turn and released Henry from his second captivity. It only remained for her to face Edward, now duke of York
since his father's death. A very tall, handsome and jovial youth, the
new duke had already proved his notable military prowess by beating
the Lancastrian earl of Pembroke at Mortimer's Cross in the northwest
of Herefordshire a fortnight before the action at St. Albans.

But the excesses of Margaret's rude mosstroopers during their difficult advance on London had embittered the population of the intervening counties and of the capital itself. The west, south and Midlands
turned Yorkist, cursing the "cruel Frenchwoman" who made war like
a savage, doing nothing to repress the ferocious instincts of the northern
third of the kingdom. De Brézé advised her that she was in no position
to resist Edward and Warwick, the two best English commanders, now
combined with the richest half of the country against her. The largely
disaffected Lancastrian forces began to fall back slowly northward.

The queen and de Brézé, by this time perhaps her lover, had hoped
that their last two victories at Wakefield and St. Albans would lead to
both Yorkist London and English Calais changing hands. But Margaret's
harsh temper and the barbaric spirit of the northern counties that
supported her could not be suppressed by either the levelheaded Frenchman or the horrified Henry. None of the three, for different reasons,
had succeeded in winning the loyalty of the all-important south of the
nation.

By the time the sick King Charles VII had made up his mind to
act on behalf of his fierce niece, Edward of York had been proclaimed
king of England in the capital. Soon afterward, on March 28, 1461,
he and Warwick decisively defeated the Lancastrians, in blinding snow
and sleet, at Towton in the West Riding of Yorkshire. Margaret,
Henry and their little son Edward, Prince of Wales, aged eight, were
on that day in the city of York. As soon as the first fugitives from the
fatal field of Towton straggled into the town the royal party could
only take refuge in Scotland, where Pierre de Brézé eventually joined
them. The state coronation of the victorious young king, who was to
have close and equivocal relations with Louis nearly as long as they
each lived, both dying, at last, in the same year, took place at the end
of June 1461, a month or so before the death of King Charles VII.

The dauphin, on receipt of the Paris Council's letter, had piously
ordered, as was expected of him, masses to be said for his parent's
restoration to health. But he also at once crossed the border into France,
making for Reims. At the same time he notified the duke of Burgundy

that "if you hear he is dead I pray you to take up arms and come to meet us before Reims."

Charles himself knew that he was dying. He took food only from the Comte de Foix, whom he believed to be the one royalist nobleman firmly devoted to his person. But on July 22, 1461, the king succumbed, apparently from lockjaw following infection of a wisdom tooth. He died in the very same castle of Mehun, near Bourges, where he had assumed the royal title in 1422. No official reconciliation with Louis ever took place. The invalid's mental misery unquestionably contributed to his end. He continued to call the prince, almost with his last breath, a "bad son." It seemed that he wished his younger male off-spring Charles, then a boy of fifteen, to succeed him. But at the burial service in Paris the ritual cry "Long live the King!" was answered unanimously by the attendant Council with the words "Long live King Louis!"

The unstable character of Charles VII has to be taken into consid-eration in assessing that of his eldest son. The father's heredity and early environment could hardly have been worse. Born of a madman, Charles VI, and his nymphomaniac of a queen, Isabeau of Bavaria, the boy's inherited mental and moral shortcomings were further shocked, when he was twelve, by news of the disastrous battle of Agincourt (1415). This introduction to court life was soon followed by the deaths of his two elder brothers, Louis, duke of Guienne, and Jean, duke of Touraine, and the imprisonment and escape to Burgundy of his wild mother. She returned in 1418 with the ferocious John the Fearless, duke of Burgundy, to seize Paris and cut down all opposition in a series of appalling massacres.

At sixteen the dauphin, as Charles now was, with a political party of his own, is said to have seen one of his adherents, Tanneguy de Chastel, treacherously bring down a battle-ax on the head of John the Fearless at a so-called peace conference on the fatal bridge of Monte-reau. Whether or not Tanneguy was the actual assassin, the scene of this murderous scuffle, which Charles can hardly either have desired or expected, must have further shaken the already precarious balance of the boy's mind. John's successor, Philip "the Good," could only agree with Queen Isabeau to hand the mastery of France, under the Treaty of Troyes (1420), to King Henry V of England. Young Charles, whose authority had been paralyzed by the murder of John, was formally disinherited at Troyes. He retired to the castle of Mehun-sur-Yèvre, near Bourges, where he was to die nearly forty years later. A few weeks after the sickly lad had dropped into obscurity at Mehun, his hopeless lunatic of a father, Charles VI, who had long been of no account in the world, drifted out of life. The date was October 21, 1422.

The new king, aged nineteen and a mere pretender in English eyes despite the almost simultaneous death of Henry V, showed as little promise as ever of becoming an effective sovereign. He had some support in southern France. But he was ruled by unscrupulous favorites and discredited partisans until these personages were removed by the Constable, Arthur, count of Richemont, brother of the duke of Brittany. But Richemont in his turn was attacked by his own former crony, the adventurer Georges de la Trémouille. Civil war broke out in central France, which was thus exposed to the advance of the English, who held the north. On the appearance of Joan of Arc in 1429, at the start of her ultimately victorious resistance movement, the mind of the twenty-six-year-old king had reached its lowest ebb. He passively allowed himself to be crowned at Reims. But he received with indifference the news of the Maid's capture by the English and took no steps whatever to rescue her from death at the stake as a "witch."

The ensuing period, until signature of the Treaty of Arras in 1435 between France and Burgundy, remained inglorious for the cowardly betrayer of Joan of Arc. He permitted his kingdom to sink into an anarchy which was only restored to some degree of order by individuals other than himself. After the Richemont faction had contrived the assassination of Georges de la Trémouille, a new set of relatively honest and energetic advisers, headed by the Constable once again, by Pierre de Brézé, by Joan's former comrade in arms the successful soldier Jean, count of Dunois, popularly known as the Bastard of Orléans owing to his birth to one of the mistresses of Louis, duke of Orléans, and finally by Charles, count of Anjou, brother of the king's harmless nonentity of a consort, Marie. These men put such heart into the monarch's apparently ingrained timidity and indolence that by 1441, with the dauphin's aid, he had captured Pontoise, a few miles northwest of Paris, leading his troops in person. In the following year he raided the south with some success.

The change is startling. It proves that in this basically weak man of thirty-eight, who had begun life under such wretched, even terrifying, conditions, traits of courage and common sense existed which might be capable, if adequately backed by other people, of redeeming his hitherto deplorable record. But his son Louis, then eighteen, as well as the dukes of Bourbon and Alençon and the count of Armagnac, already felt that they had seen more than enough of him. As early as 1440 they staged the Praguerie revolt. But Charles and his new advisers suppressed this rising, more by tactful concessions than by bloodshed. The government then went on to conclude, in 1444, a truce with England, while the royal army was reorganized. It conquered Normandy at the battle of Formigny in 1450, within sight of the walls of Caen, and Guienne three years later, when the veteran English commander John Talbot, earl of Shrewsbury, was defeated and killed at Castillon, near Bordeaux. These routs of the previously almost invincible English were largely due to the disturbances in their native land, culminating in the Wars of the Roses. But French military recovery under Dunois and his colleagues enabled the contemporary historians of their country to dub their revived king not only Charles the Well Served but also Charles the Victorious. His mistress Agnès Sorel and her lover Pierre de Brézé, as noted above, undoubtedly also played a leading part, as did, too, the mighty financier Jacques Coeur, another of the lady's close associates, in rousing the formerly somnolent sovereign to action.

Louis might then have had reason to modify his rooted antipathy to his father. But although by that time both men were practicing the same policy of preferring middle-class administrators or at most minor gentry to feudal dukes and counts, the dauphin remained implacable. Conscious of an intelligence and strength of will in himself far superior to the monarch's, he still could not trust a man incapable of acting on his own initiative, the only procedure in the prince's view worthy of a king truly devoted to his country's welfare. This faith in an autocracy delegating only executive, never legislative, powers to a subordinate class of business experts can of course only be justified if the autocrat stays genuinely unselfish, entirely impervious to flattery, able to spot a mile off, so to speak, attempts to deceive him and quite unscrupulous himself in deceiving others, not for his own sake, but for the advancement and happiness of his subjects as a whole. The judgment initiating any such schemes must also turn out, whether they succeed or not, to have been as a general rule impeccable.

These requirements have seemed impossibly high to most political philosophers since Plato. They still deny that Louis met them fully, as he himself believed, in his own person. This verdict must be accepted in its strictest form. Both as dauphin and as king this exceptional ruler made a few mistakes in detail, mostly of timing, hardly ever in principle. Sometimes too his reading of human character appears to have been at fault for a while, as in the case of the Croy brothers, whom he at first believed more honest than they were. But he generally retrieved such errors before they could do him much harm. It is in any case often difficult to be sure that so secretive and ingenious a mind really was acting foolishly in allowing such a man as, for instance, his eccentric godfather the duke of Alençon so much rope. But a seventeenth-century English proverb suggests that rope enough may hang a rogue. Louis was just the sort of man to have invented such a saying.

It must be admitted also that his dry temperament caused him to underrate people like King Edward IV of England, who wished to enjoy their own lives while simultaneously imposing an order convenient to themselves on the existence of others. Edward turned out to be not quite such a fool as the Frenchman thought him. For instance, while Louis occasionally relied too rashly upon his easy charm of manner, which cost him no effort, the English king, as if aware of his faults of indolence and self-indulgence, worked hard and successfully to retain the popularity which his natural geniality and good looks brought him. Compared with Louis he became only a spasmodically effective despot. But more important people than the ladies he seduced mourned his relatively early death. Perhaps only Philippe de Commines wept when the sexagenarian maker of modern France closed his eyes for the last time.

But it is one thing to agree that Louis, like all politicians, sometimes took steps which from his own day to the present have looked villainous. It is quite another to affirm, with the manufacturers of romantic fiction from Olivier de la Marche in 1492 to Alfred Neumann in 1926, that as contrasted with Charles VII, his opposite in so many respects, the man who in 1461 became Louis XI must rank as a monster of cruelty, lust and fraud. If he had been any such thing he could never have left France, after ruling the country for twenty-two years, a coherent and universally esteemed, even envied, nation in the present sense of the word. He would have been deposed or murdered long before his natural death in a part of the world with so turbulent a history and so robust a population.

The modern parallel of Francisco Franco of Spain, who has at least led his country, almost ruined in 1936, to relative prosperity in 1969, cannot be pressed. Both men, at bottom realistic administrators, were represented as demons, especially abroad, in their lifetimes. But the enthusiastically revolutionary twentieth century cannot be compared with the fifteenth, when nobody of importance in Europe except Louis himself and possibly Lorenzo de' Medici dreamed of any radical change in political philosophy. It is certainly true that both the Frenchman and the Spaniard considered the promotion of law and order out of chaos worth the price of extreme severity in the suppression of obstinate rebels. But Franco, for reasons more justifiable in Spain than elsewhere, was working against the sociological trend of his times. Louis, for reasons which few could understand in the France of his day, was working for a sociological ideal that was to triumph in the humanism of Rabelais and Montaigne before many more years had passed.

The legend of a "black" Louis, therefore, cannot stand. His inexorable opposition to his father from 1446 to 1461, a period of fifteen years, while the prince remained exiled first in Dauphiné and then in Bur-

gundy, right up to the date of the king's death, did not result from
the dark and merciless passions dear to the compilers of melodrama.
It derived from the sheer incompatibility of two well-marked mentalities, one a powerful, thoroughly idealistic spirit, single-minded but
an adept at extraordinarily complex and obstinate scheming to promote
ends certainly not imaginable so clearly by anyone else at that time
and place, while the other scarcely existed in isolation from its environment, though if the virtues of valor and logical thought were to
be found in its closest associates it could assimilate them for a while.

Both men possessed the Valois charm, simple in Charles, peculiarly
mysterious in his son. Nobody could bring himself to hate the former.
To hate the latter because of what one had heard of him was easy. But
after a few minutes of private talk with Louis it became impossible for
anyone with a quarter of his companion's intelligence to take a personal
dislike to the man. He was very rarely boring or discourteous, as
clever people so often are. One might have the feeling that he was
not to be trusted. But this reaction was so common a sentiment in
fifteenth-century France, among practical men of all classes, that it
made little headway against admiration for the powers of analysis and
succinct expression evident on the other side of the conversation. In
short, the facts of the reign of Louis XI, which began in 1461, illustrate
beyond rational doubt his title, one nevertheless still withheld from him
by the consensus of history, to be called a "great" man, who succeeded
a little one.

Louis XI, King of France. Giraudon, The Mansell Collection

Princess Margaret of Scotland, daughter of James I of Scotland, Dauphine of France. British Museum. Photo by John R. Freeman & Co., Ltd.

Charles VII, King of France. GIRAUDON, THE MANSELL COLLECTION.

Agnes Sorel. Detail of an altar piece by Fouquet. GIRAUDON, THE MANSELL COLLECTION.

Henry VI, King of England. NATIONAL
PORTRAIT GALLERY.

Margaret of Anjou, Queen of England.
British Museum. PHOTO BY JOHN R.
FREEMAN & CO., LTD.

CHAPTER VII

Accession
(1461–1473)

❧❧❧ King Louis XI was not at Notre Dame on the day of his father's funeral service but far to the northeast, at Avesnes, just over the Burgundian frontier on the road to Reims. Grimly jubilant, looking more like a master of deerhounds than a king with his queer little round hat and dust-colored riding cloak, the new sovereign set out through stifling July heat to take charge of a realm with which he meant to astonish the world. Nobody laughed at his typical horseman's figure, the thick-set torso and lean legs, crouching in careless ease on a hack rather worse in build than those of his immediate companions. The unfathomable green stare, great hooked nose and disproportionately heavy chin commanded respect even from the debonair Burgundians, knights of the old school, who accompanied a leader very different from the sort to which they were accustomed. He obviously did not suppose himself to be going on a picnic. But now and again he would turn to one of his escort with a gruff witticism. Then his prematurely aged features—he was still only thirty-eight—changed their habitual expression of sly menace to one of positively innocent amusement, as though nothing could ever be taken seriously in this world. He resembled at such times, though the noblemen present were seldom in a position to make the comparison, a small tradesman enjoying himself late at night in a tavern.

The tidings that his detested father was really dead at last had reached him rather earlier than might have been expected from the astrologers' predictions. Philip had instantly supplied him with bag, baggage and a glittering array of troops. This confident army was described by a contemporary chronicler as "terrible and marvelously great." For the duke imagined that Louis would not now be able to do without him and that all France as well as the wide lands of the duchy of Burgundy would soon be at the feet of the richest and most secure potentate in Europe, Philip the Good himself, who had not won his title without earning an admirable reputation as an arbiter of political disputes as well as of elegance and a prudent yet generous administrator into the bargain.

There were in fact good reasons for the duke's optimism, which he probably did not even share with his duchess. He had been saving up for years in the hope of conducting some such vast enterprise, represented, to those who ventured or were encouraged to inquire about his plans, as a crusade in the East. The available funds and man power had long been abundant. When King Louis was informed of the mighty force assembled by the duke, which might be thought to be advancing upon the royal inheritance, he wrote some characteristically ambiguous lines to Philip, who was then at Lille, conferring with his treasurers and marshals. The brief sentences might be interpreted as either patronizing reassurance to a nervous subordinate or rebuke to the insolence of a potential rival. "My good uncle," he advised his senior vassal. "Have no fear. Thou art with me and I with thee. Am I not already king? There is no cause for alarm."

The duke replied, with equal smoothness, that he was not afraid of anyone, but only anxious to provide against any possible emergency. This covert warning to the monarch that the situation confronting him might not be such plain sailing as it appeared for the moment from the long messages coming in even from such magnates as the duke of Bourbon, failed to please Louis, who knew his man better now than he had five years before. He told the Burgundian courier, one of the Croy brothers, whom he did not like as well as the other, coolly enough, that he was grateful for his "uncle's" solicitude and understood the position, adding dryly, as before: "Since I am, of my own accord, entirely dependent on the duke's good favor he has nothing to worry about." Once more the irony that always seemed to lurk in the king's most bland remarks could hardly have escaped Croy, a subtle diplomat if ever there was one. If at any future time, the implication ran, the ruler of France should decide that Philip's officiously offered services were superfluous in view of the strength of the crown, Burgundian ambitions, if any, must give way to his own. Louis then changed the subject in his usual abrupt manner. This haughtiness convinced Croy of what he already suspected. The new occupant of the French throne was not going to allow anyone on earth to dictate to him. The courier duly reported this impression to his master.

Meanwhile the councilors in Paris, well acquainted with the courteous but sometimes unmistakably acrimonious correspondence of the former

dauphin with the late king's advisers—and enemies—during the last few
years, were also beginning to feel some anxiety about his intentions.
He had already refused to receive a messenger bearing good wishes
from that previously powerful member of the French government and
close friend of Queen Margaret, as he had been of Agnès Sorel, Pierre
de Brézé, then still in Scotland. There was something about the truly
gallant Pierre that appealed intensely to women of strong personality.
They appreciated, no doubt, his absolute reliability and discretion in
addition to his good looks, ready wit and common sense. But these
qualities in him had antagonized rather than attracted Louis since
1444. Throughout his life he invariably discounted both outward advantages and inward virtues in determining his attitude to a prominent
personality if the fellow acted against him politically. Such adversaries
stirred his enmity all the more if their amiable manners and pleasing
presences were accompanied by brains and courage, rendering them
potentially dangerous.

Louis now remembered only too well how de Brézé had in fact
consistently back Charles in every point at issue between father and
son. It was only later that Louis recognized that, with Pierre, loyalty to
the dynasty, whatever he might think of its chief representative, came
before all other considerations. Antoine de Chabannes, Master of the
Royal Household, had a similar record. When he heard of the rebuff to
de Brézé and reflected on the dauphin's threat of vengeance the last
time he had seen him fifteen years ago the soldier-councilor could not
make up his mind whether to run for his life or face it out.

The new monarch himself, in talking to Jean de Croy, produced in
that far from reliable servant of Philip the Good the notion of a
certain anxiety behind the king's apparent nonchalance. Louis made
quite a long speech, most unusual for him in its moralizing vein.

"What a curious world is this," he observed. "One in which God
deals strangely with men, sending them good fortune one day and
bad the next. Thus, one may think oneself the most unhappy of
creatures when on the very verge of prosperity. Yet no sooner does that
success appear firmly established than the wheel changes direction
again. Consider, for example, my own case. Yesterday I thought myself
the poorest of king's sons, continuously afflicted by sorrow and
tribulation from my very childhood. Cast out of my patrimony, deprived of my father's love, a borrower and a beggar, I would not have
possessed an acre of land, a roof over my head or a penny piece, had it
not been for the charity and kindness of my dear uncle, your duke,
who hath kept me at his own expense for five years. Yet now suddenly,
as in a dream, God hath granted me great advancement, making me the

richest and most potent king in Christendom, more so even than my father, feared as he was by all nations."

The speaker could not of course really suppose himself better off than the late Charles, unless he was assuming, out of compliment to Philip, that the latter's wealth could be added to his own. The phrase was probably meant to convey some such belief, thus presenting the king of France to the Burgundian as innocently convinced that the duke would act as his banker for the rest of his life. But in fact there was never anything innocent about Louis. He suspected on principle the motives of absolutely everyone. The grand Philip, affectionately deferential to his royal guest as he had never ceased to be, was no exception. It is quite certain that in the king's secret plans the danger constituted to his realm by the great northern duchy figured permanently and that he intended sooner or later to nullify it.

The sermon to Croy proves that Louis's reading of Aristotle at the University of Louvain had borne fruit. His native facility in literary expression had been much increased by a study of Greek logic and ethics, for which he would have had neither time nor inclination if Charles's threats had not forced him into exile. It is improbable, however, that he made this reflection in conversing with Croy. It would have been out of character, as implying self-criticism. He was capable of regretting mistakes, but incapable of twinges of conscience, even to the mild extent of deploring his lack of formal academic education. As for listening to advice of a nontechnical, abstract kind, i.e. just the sort of homily to which he had just been treating Croy, he would himself have dismissed in less than a minute anyone who dared to lecture him in that way. The concrete counsels of practical merchants, lawyers and financiers, men who were more like Aristotle and Caesar than like Plato and Cicero, were all he would tolerate in serious verbal exchanges.

He was never actually rude. But he could be highly unconventional by the standards of his day and certainly, by modern codes of behavior, excessively dictatorial on public occasions. He interrupted, for instance, no less than three times a speech of welcome delivered on his arrival at Reims by the archbishop, ordering that eloquent prelate, in the curtest language, to be brief. Yet people who rushed to the opposite extreme, making the king laugh at their fussiness in dispensing with ceremony, might be well rewarded. The Marshal of France, for example, Joachim Rouault, when Louis was about to mount his horse, pushed aside the kneeling squire and insisted on fastening the king's spurs to his boots himself. "Out of my way, all of you!" the vigorous old soldier commanded noisily. "This is *my* office!" Louis, the least bustling of men himself, was so amused by the marshal's boyish impetuosity that he named the veteran, on the spot, his "first equerry," an appointment generally reserved for younger officers.

The new sovereign, naturally enough, peremptorily discharged those ministers who had most uncompromisingly served his father. They were all men of high administrative ability, who had really governed the country, and governed it well, on behalf of the foolish, clumsy old mountebank, with his frivolous harem, which Charles had shown himself to be for the last few years. But in this connection Louis at first allowed his resentment at being kept out of the succession for so long to overwhelm his reason. He could not forgive these excellent civil servants for not calling him in earlier to replace so degraded a monarch. Most of them proved later, when he reinstated them, that they would have served the son, as soon as he came to the throne in the normal course of events, as loyally as they had served the father. They had the mentality of bureaucrats rather than feudal retainers. But this constitutional attitude did not gratify, in the circumstances of 1461, the born autocrat who was now to rule France. He felt, on the contrary, that the various members of Charles's cabinet had been enjoying far too much of their own way recently to become, so soon, wholly subservient to his personal will. He replaced many of them, for the time being, by certain Burgundians, including Jean de Croy, whom he made Master of the Household.

At Avesnes, just inside the French frontier, Philip and his suite turned up in black to attend the second funeral service which it was considered proper to hold in that city. But the king himself did not assume mourning until August 3, the day on which this further ceremony, staged really in his own honor, actually took place. The archbishop of Bourges had arrived to preside. Five hundred candles flared around the richly adorned waxen image of Charles of Valois, seventh of the name. His corpse itself already lay, with its ancestors, in the royal chapel of Notre Dame at Paris. Three hundred masses were chanted at Avesnes on this occasion for the repose of the soul of the deceased. One hundred francs were distributed among the poorest citizens of the town.

The duke of Burgundy made the first move on his new chessboard by offering to lend his "nephew" three hundred and fifty thousand crowns. But Louis did not immediately accept this gambit. He countered it, to show his previously denied independence, by coolly dismissing the bulk of Philip's army. He retained only five hundred lances.

The term "lance," literally the main weapon of a fifteenth-century knight, was often also used by contemporary chroniclers to mean not only the chevalier himself but his attendants, also mounted. Such a group, unit or section would never number less than three, or more, according to Olivier de la Marche, than eight at most. It always included at least one archer, at most three and at least one swordsman or squire, at most three, for protection of the knight in hand-to-hand fighting. Sometimes a page or groom was added for primarily non-combatant duties, for instance the care of equipment and horses or liaison with other sections of lances.

Such variations in the strength of a lance make it difficult to estimate the numbers of a force as calculated by lances. The largest number of lances mentioned by the chroniclers is 1200, constituting the bulk of the Burgundian force advancing on Péronne in 1465, specifically stated by Commines to have had "three archers to every man-at-arms," i.e. knight, and so comprising 4800 men in all. The smallest number of lances is noted by Louis himself in a letter of 1478 as "four or five" sent through Savoyard and Milanese territory to reinforce Florence. This would be at most forty individuals, a very small force even for a merely benevolent gesture. But the figure may be either an error in transcription for four or five hundred or else deliberately minimized by the king so as not to cause alarm in the recipient of the letter. Other figures given vary from one hundred to eight hundred lances. They have to be interpreted by considering the general circumstances of the occasion, e.g. that of a compliment, as when Louis presented a former prisoner whom he had made seneschal of Anjou in 1483 with one hundred lances, or a certain military situation, as when Charles the Bold demanded from his parliament funds to pay eight hundred lances to keep Louis at bay in the emergency of 1470.

Most French historians believe that in general the lance comprised no more than six mounted men, including the *coutilier* ("dagger man"), a specialist in giving a fallen adversary the *coup de grâce* ("finishing stroke"). On this interpretation of the lance the force retained by Philip at Louis's orders in 1461 would be about three thousand men.

In other words, they were designated by the king as an escort for the Burgundian peerage accompanying him. The soldiers were not to be employed in the royal service but simply in that of his guests on French soil, as an act of hospitality. He meant by this merely polite acknowl-edgment of the duke's importance to remove from Philip's mind any idea that the present succession would have to be imposed or appear to be imposed upon France by Burgundy. For if Louis should seem to have swept to his throne on a tide of more than this number of Burgundians he would have fallen straight into the duke's pocket and would have been obliged to meet endless trouble from every quarter of French territory.

The king left Avesnes for Reims in such a hurry that his respectable little queen, Charlotte of Savoy, had to borrow horses from the countess of Charolais to follow him. The boisterously ostentatious young count for once attended his father in an outwardly calm mood that masked suppressed excitement. For the prospect of war in France was by no means to be discounted. If it came, no matter who the adversary might be, his old friend Louis himself, a faction of French dukes or a revival of English interference, Charolais intended to take a leading and victorious part in hostilities. There was certainly some tension in the air, though it was hard to define precisely. The duke himself seemed affected by it. For he joined the king, with no less speed, at St. Thierry, just outside Reims, and made sure that the five hundred lances Louis had left him made an imposing array, equipped at all points for instant battle.

But the scene at the gates of Reims proceeded quite smoothly, except for the impatient royal interruptions already noted. The archbishop received them without the slightest sign of vexation and duly handed the keys of the city, with solemn dignity, to his sovereign. The king at once, exercising the tact which never failed him when he thought it advisable, passed these symbols of submission over to his "good uncle," inviting Philip to precede him through the archway into the town. He could afford to be generous. For his spies had better information than those of the count of Charolais and had assured him that for the moment at any rate he had nothing to fear. Everything depended, they had said, on the first impression that he made. It must not be one of bristling force, but of a regal progress accompanied by loyal vassals treated, as the majesty of a confident monarch demanded, like honored guests.

Appareled in red and white satin, his personal colors, and with his horse caparisoned in cloth of gold, he rode in behind the duke under a vast canopy conspicuously illuminated by the scores of torches blazing in the streets. For it was already about seven o'clock in the evening and beginning to grow dark. The citizens packed against the houses, grouped at their windows or clinging to their roofs, cheered tumultuously. Louis knew perfectly well that crowds always do applaud gorgeously arrayed persons of royal rank or high political authority, whatever some of the vociferous onlookers may privately think of the occasion for such displays. He understood that a splendid spectacle, boring to his own prosaic mentality, carries away on a flood of sensuous appreciation all rational assessments of the situation in people less sternly concentrated on the underlying reality than himself. He continued to wonder, while carefully observing the appropriate demeanor of an unquestioned despot, just what proportion of the roars that deafened him might actually be addressed to Philip the Good of Burgundy.

The coronation procedure in the cathedral presented the curious feature of a stripping to the waist of the new king by the peers of the realm, in order that his eyes, mouth, navel, armpits, shoulders and loins might be separately anointed with the sacred oil. The inquisitive stares of both priests and secular magnates noted the disproportion of physique but also the grave bearing, even while half-naked, in the slight, undersized figure of their almost unknown master. His calm, motionless features showed no sign whatever of the malicious tales already current about him, illustrating a supposed arrogance, pigheaded-ness and hypocrisy, coupled with a tendency to vulgar cynicism, amount-ing at times to ruthless cruelty, which is so readily attributed by popular gossip to personages out of the ordinary whose social or political power or position renders them envied and therefore suspected by those unable to penetrate a reserve which may be natural to the individual in question or assumed in self-defense.

But the only stories about Louis which were even half-true referred to his incalculable temper and distaste for chatter and revels. No one could fairly accuse him, at this date, of any kind of debauchery or un-justifiable aggression. Duly documented accounts of his behavior so far proved nothing more reprehensible than a relentless obstinacy where his own dignity was concerned and a sobriety under normal conditions not very congenial to the typical French taste of that or any other period.

A red shirt, followed by appropriately magnificent vestments of a sacerdotal character, then surmounted the rather narrow shoulders of the king. He took his seat with due majesty on the royal throne. The duke of Burgundy set first the cap and then the crown on the wide and high brows which were the best physical features of the new monarch, almost redeeming the small, secretive eyes, pendulous Valois nose and enigmatic lips of the rest of his face. Philip himself thundered, as soon as he had lowered the great golden ornament to its place, "Long live the King!" The cry was at once taken up throughout the cathedral and in the streets outside it. Trumpets blared long and loud, drowning every other sound. The duke was genuinely impressed by the traditional ritual. He loved all ceremonies that looked back to the chivalrous past. But he noted with more mixed feelings the apparently unanimous public rejoicing that ensued. Finally, he reflected with some uneasiness on the oath taken by Louis in resonant tones as the tumult died down. "I swear," he proclaimed, with such clear articulation that everyone in the packed edifice could easily hear him, "to regain all my lands, including those sold, alienated or pledged by my predecessors."

The declaration was nothing out of the ordinary and might be taken to refer to areas left in English hands, like Calais, or under English influence, like Guienne and Gascony in the southwest. But the duchy of Burgundy had also been such a land, given by King Jean II of France, surnamed "the Good," in 1363 to his son Philip, "the Valiant," and ceded by Charles VII to the present duke by certain rather peculiar provisions of the Treaty of Arras in 1435. They made it clear enough that Burgundy was to be held in vassalage to the French crown, but in such a way that for all practical purposes it could be regarded as an independent country, dealing as such with true foreigners like the English and Germans. Philip had taken full advantage of this latitude and did not mean to relinquish it without at least a diplomatic struggle. He was particularly concerned with the wealthy manufacturing towns of the Somme valley—Amiens, Abbeville and others—upon which Charles, too, had laid stress in the treaty. He had insisted on the right being reserved to him to buy them back, as property under direct French control, whenever he chose, at the price of four hundred thousand crowns. The duke knew he had a good bargain in this territory while France remained financially weak. The possession of Picardy, the region in question, enhanced both his income and his glory, besides being of vital strategic importance. He did not want, instead, the purchase money fixed by the treaty. Louis might have intended, by his coronation oath, to notify Philip that the reserved right of repurchase would be enforced as soon as he could raise the necessary funds. He could only raise them, the duke thought, by heavy taxation, which might lead to rebellion. For the moment all seemed well from the Burgundian point of view. All the same, after this public pronouncement, future developments in France would have to be very carefully watched and, if possible, controlled.

The king's contempt for formalities less sacrosanct than a coronation appeared, not for the first time, when he presided over a state banquet that followed the service. Convention required that throughout this immensely long function he should wear the crown he had so recently assumed. He did so at first, but soon found it too large or too heavy for his comfort. Thereupon he casually removed the symbol of sovereignty from his head and laid it on the table at his elbow, where it quite eclipsed the gold plate borrowed from his "good uncle." Everyone stared. But no one alluded, even remotely, to the incident. Some on-lookers may have supposed that a monarch who cared so little for the outward trappings of his dignity would be easy to handle. If so, every single one of them found out their mistake within a few days.

In order to avoid the multiplication of such tedious events as banquets, processions and deputations, Louis took the road for Paris in less than a fortnight, spent mostly on paper work, after the Reims affair. Reaching the capital on the thirty-first of August he once more invited the gratified duke, who had arrived on the previous day, to precede him into a city for which the king, when dauphin, had never much cared. Philip had chosen a residence near the Fish Market. Thereafter, when the volatile Parisians wished to tease the more digni- fied Burgundians, the latter would be told: "You smell of herrings." But no such jesting took place at the official entry of the two potentates, staged with extraordinary solemnity and magnificence.

The duke, in black velvet starred with rubies, rode a white charger. The count of Charolais followed, wearing, as became so fiery a spirit, a crimson robe of the same material. Then mingled ranks of French and Burgundian nobles, dressed in all the colors of the rainbow and splen- didly mounted, preceded the royal guard in full armor, contrasting austerely in their compact, darkly gleaming panoply of war with the gay, almost casual company ahead of them. Trumpeters, heralds, the Marshals of France and Burgundy and their escorts provided further complex visions of gorgeous array and glittering accouterments. Then at last the king himself, all in white, riding a white palfrey caparisoned in the Valois red and white, brought up the rear. A vast blue canopy of satin embroidered with the lilies of France and upheld by six eminent citizens of Paris in violet cloaks swayed majestically above the proudly erect, if slight, figure of the sovereign, who always looked his best on horseback.

When the procession reached the St. Lazare hospital a herald pre- sented to Louis five beautiful young women, probably top-ranking courtesans, whose steeds and garments were decorated in such a way as to indicate the letters P, A, R, I, S, spelling PARIS or alternatively *Paix, Amour, Raison, Joie* and *Sûreté.* At the St. Denis Gate a silver ship adorned with the armorial bearings of the city had been set up. It was big enough to contain the figures of persons typifying the three estates of the realm—clergy, nobility and minor gentry. Behind this vessel fountains spouted wine and milk. Next, the ranks halted to contemplate stages upon which clowns and jugglers performed or lightly clad girls danced. Some were disguised as sirens or females from hitherto uncivilized lands, the *belles sauvages* who had figured at the court entertainments of Charles VII. Others disported themselves naked in pools, as "nymphs."

At Trinity hospital the very different scene of a Passion play, culmi- nating in a tableau of the Crucifixion of Christ between the two thieves, was acted. At other points along the route military sham fights were staged, including what could be taken for the capture of the fort of le Pollet outside Dieppe by the present king as dauphin in 1443, with realistic depictions of the English garrison having their throats cut as the French stormed in. Knightly jousts and the various open-air diversions of the populace, from fireworks to the release of thousands of little birds to fly over the procession, held it up again and again.

This highly varied program of welcome lasted nearly all day, until at six o'clock in the evening the weary king reached Notre Dame to take another oath of devotion to his country, in his case completely unnecessary, since this idea had inspired him, to the exclusion of all others, ever since he could think coherently. But this traditional ceremony could not be evaded by a monarch determined to start his reign under the best possible auspices. Scarcely able to stand after all the theatrical demonstrations he had been obliged to witness, he mumbled through his part in the cathedral service in such evident fatigue that it could be construed as positive vexation by those nearest him. The genially urbane attitude of the stalwart duke of Burgundy, a much older man, who had enjoyed every minute of the day and continued to do so at this late hour, strongly contrasted with that of the king and was noticed with appreciation or anxiety according to the varying views of its observers. Some of them would not have minded Philip the Good, who looked so much more regal than Louis, as a ruler. But most of the Frenchmen present wished their legitimate sovereign would at least pretend to respect the symbolism of pageantry.

It was the one mask, however, which he could never assume. He had learned from history that the obvious and easy road to the popularity of a dictator, the obsequious acceptance of all the hollow formalities considered essential to the performance of his exalted office, did not necessarily lead to the achievement of a power that would last. It was the unspectacular and lonely study of dispatches, the penetration of alien minds, the steady concentration of his own upon a definite aim and the courage to act without hesitation on his own initiative, that would ensure success in his only objective, the rise of France to the condition of an impregnable and expanding fortress. In diplomacy and the day-to-day management of business he generally used unconventionally casual methods, often the jocularity of an exceptionally cunning peasant. But in matters of simple finance, the provision of funds for war or the imposition of taxation for commercial or industrial schemes, he could come down with all the thunder of royal prerogative upon objections, especially on the Paris parliament, which he regularly reminded of its constitutional subordination to his own will. Such were the only occasions upon which he tolerated the solemnity of court procedure.

A grand supper party, still more ostentatious than that of Reims, followed the Notre Dame ceremony. Philip's gold plate once more gleamed on the king's table. But Louis, with the elderly dukes of

Burgundy and Orléans on his right and left respectively, did not, this time, remove his crown. He was very fond of the ultra-sophisticated Charles of Orléans, perhaps a little afraid of his influence at the English court, where this almost eighteenth-century character, during his captivity, had been much cultivated. The king, therefore, on this occasion, made a tremendous effort to rise to it. Dancing in fancy dress ensued until midnight. Fortunately no one expected him, by this time, to participate in this masquerade. Half-dead with fatigue and boredom, but outwardly unperturbed, he made his escape after the final tableau, to sink into profound slumber, probably the deepest he had ever known, at his palace of Les Tourelles.

Next day he plunged thankfully into state business, refusing all invitations to gatherings where Philip was only too pleased to deputize for him. But he soon saw that it would be inadvisable to allow the duke too much of the limelight. In order to readjust the balance he visited a few trusted friends. He avoided, however, the Burgundians, except the bold count of Charolais, to whom he paid notable attention. This was less because he appreciated a strong personality than because he knew the man to be on bad terms with his father the duke and that he might therefore possibly prove a useful piece on the French side of the border if Philip the Good should presume too much on his social popularity, entirely due to his excellent sense of the stage. No one could play the jovial hero better than this widely experienced diplomat, at the center of events ever since the murder of John the Fearless in 1419 and never known thereafter to lose his temper except within the family circle. Only his close relatives understood, though Louis guessed, how dangerous he could be if he got the chance of promoting his territorial ambitions or crushing his son and heir's occasional reckless insolence.

But the Burgundian ruler gave the king of France no excuse for quarreling with him, though Louis's attitude to him gradually cooled during these September days. The new monarch received with calm condescension the citizens of Philip's rebellious town of Liége. He expressed open disapproval of Burgundian negotiations with their old allies, the English, now for the most part obedient to Edward IV, who was taking a terrible revenge on the Lancastrian lords for their victories in the winter of 1460–1461. Louis also seemed deliberately and with some success to be competing with his "uncle's" jocose flattery of the Parisians, even to the extent of visiting brothels with a certain young rake, a Burgundian named Guillaume de Bische, quite a new departure for the reputedly misogynist king. The cautious duke, in these circumstances, began to wonder whether his intrusive policy in Paris would ever pay off. By degrees he came to the conclusion that his best plan would be to return to Burgundy and await a more favorable opportunity than the present of intervening in French affairs. Louis's public speeches, declaring continually how much he owed to his former host, could be largely discounted by the opinions on Burgundian questions he uttered with equal frankness.

In other words, the game of chess started by Philip on the death of Charles VII had reached a locked position, where neither side could see a definite advantage unless a daring risk were taken. The odds were perhaps very slightly in favor of Louis. After all, he was a king and young enough to look far ahead, whereas the other, a mere duke, if the equivalent of most reigning despots in resources both financial and intellectual, was wearying of a life already long by fifteenth-century standards. He had in any case never been so exclusively devoted to political intrigue, expert as he might be in such maneuvers, as his "nephew." He also cultivated quite different interests, such as fun and games, splendid pageantry, women, art, literature, education and the ancient rites of chivalry. He now found himself wishing, like many another veteran of public activities, to return to these mainly aesthetic pleasures. In this same year of 1461 he left Paris, before September was over, for his own dominions. But his leave-taking of Louis could not have been more effusive on both sides.

The king was by then engaged in reviewing and confirming the privileges of the Paris guilds, from notaries to costermongers, being well aware of their importance to his own growing popularity. He was also subscribing officially to the funds and powers of various ecclesiastical charities and of monasteries, these too being institutions which a fifteenth-century king would only neglect at his peril. It does not appear that Louis's religious feelings went very deep. They were more like an ancient Roman consul's or augur's than those of a truly devout Christian. He was far from questioning the supernatural government of the world. But he seems to have regarded the Virgin, in whom he was especially interested, more as the head of a promising investment agency than as a divine figure. She was expected to provide a reasonable return on deposits rather than spiritual refreshment.

Nor did King Louis care particularly for the work of reorganizing the Paris trades and professions. He considered the lively inhabitants of the capital to be chiefly idlers, gossips and selfish money-grubbers, typical townsmen in short. He much preferred to deal with peasants and country gentlemen, keen on their rural pursuits of farming, estate management and sport, not afraid of plain speaking and with less time for social assemblies and dissipation than the lords and burgesses of the big cities. He never forgot, all the same, that metropolitan civil servants, businessmen and lawyers constituted the solid bedrock of any powerful state. He had long since found that wherever one looked, at home or abroad, such men could work creatively against the inevitable intrigues of the great nobles and prelates, more bent on destroying their personal adversaries than on building up a systematic administration. It was for this reason, among others, that he sympathized with the sturdily democratic spirit of the northern Walloon and Flemish centers, Liége in particular, witnessed for centuries in their endless rising against their bishops.

He knew and loved the varying landscape and peoples of provincial France, from Normandy to Languedoc, the robust highlanders of Auvergne, the cheerfully noisy Gascons and above all the loyal, industrious men of the middle regions—Berry, Orléans and Touraine. This last area, with its capital at Tours, was where he had been brought up and where his father had so regularly held court. He felt a special affection for its scenery and population, its atmosphere of security as compared with the chaos that had afflicted so much of his kingdom in recent years. It was to Tours, accordingly, that he now went, in the last week of September 1461, to renew his acquaintance with what he called the French *chose publique*, that is, the middle and lower rather than the upper classes.

There were few important lords in Touraine. But elsewhere the dukes and counts, now that the English had retreated to fight among themselves, were reassuming their old arrogance. The highest in rank, mostly of royal blood, ruled their possessions like independent princes and were perpetually quarreling with one another. They held between them three-quarters of the country. The king intended to put an end to this dangerous situation, which almost invited foreign interference. But French history had repeatedly proved that it was impossible to unite these petty tyrants under one patriotic banner. An entirely new method, hitherto unheard of on any large scale in Europe north of the Alps, gradually formed in Louis's realistic mind. It was the idea, in embryo, of majority rule. Educated but landless men, professionals in their various fields of law, government, commerce, industry and finance, outnumbered the estate owners and could, if it came to a struggle, outwit them. But this massive body of brainworkers must have a single leader of unquestionable authority. It could only be the king. One after another, with the weight of a newly self-conscious middle class behind his throne, put there by his own efforts, he must tackle and neutralize the richest of the aristocrats surrounding him.

The lands of Philip encircled France, except where Champagne met Lorraine, and south of Lyons, from north to east. His wealth lay less in his original domain of Burgundy, running from Dijon to Lyons, than in Flanders, Brussels and Bruges. He spoke Flemish fluently and often seemed more like a Dutchman or an Englishman than a native

Burgundian in the strict sense of the term. Louis knew that one of his aims had always been to add the regions of Champagne and Lorraine to his dominions, thereby joining their northern and southern bases, at present separated. Since the English had left, the duke had not dared to declare war on France for this purpose. Yet obviously, so the king believed, this project remained obstinately at the back of his mind.

The next most Anglophile of the dukes was Francis of Brittany, always reluctant in his homage to the French throne, not being a prince of the blood, like the rest, but a mere neighbor, forced into vassalage on geographical grounds. Louis, on the principle known to modern politicians as "kicking upstairs" an inconvenient colleague, proceeded peremptorily to reduce Francis' opportunities to make trouble by appointing him lord lieutenant for the king in the northwest. By a similar maneuver the sovereign's teen-age brother Charles, old enough now to be a focus of opposition on the part of disgruntled lords, was discouraged from cherishing any subversive ideas by the grant of the duchy of Berry, a province with a long tradition of loyalty, dating from the choice of its capital, Bourges, by Charles VII as his favorite residence.

King René I of Naples and Sicily, duke of Anjou, Lorraine and Bar, count of Provence and of Piedmont, required no such treatment. His succession to the duchy of Lorraine in 1430 had been disputed for the next seven years by Philip of Burgundy, who had actually imprisoned him on two occasions. But the marriage of René's eldest son Jean, duke of Calabria, to Marie de Bourbon, Philip's niece, reconciled the two princes for the time being. The marriage of the Lorrainer's younger daughter Margaret, a fiercely resolute young woman, to King Henry VI of England in 1445 and that of his sister Marie at a much earlier date, 1413, to Charles VII, were followed by close association with Charles in his successful campaigns in Normandy against the English and thereafter by the failure of Duke Jean of Calabria, René's heir, to enforce by arms, against Aragonese troops, the Lorrainer's claim to Naples. Le bon roi René then virtually retired from public affairs to devote himself to the study and practice of painting and literature.

In 1461, at the age of fifty-two, he was presiding over brilliant courts at Angers in Anjou or Nancy in Lorraine and only attending ceremonial functions in Paris or at Tours. Louis saw no reason to do anything about this peaceful, elderly dilettante, his mother's brother, except to cement their friendly relations by the addition of the countship of Beaufort near Angers to René's already numerous titles, those of Sicily and Naples, where Catalan and Aragonese adventurers held the real power, being almost wholly nominal.

King Louis did, however, further favor his quinquagenarian uncle, a royal but in his foreign affairs unlucky and not at all wealthy vassal, by a subsidy of thirty thousand francs down and the betrothal of the newborn Anne de France to René's grandson Nicolas, aged thirteen. This arrangement, owing to later political developments, did not last long. But for the time being French concessions in this direction ensured loyalty in the western regions of Lorraine and Provence.

The only too talkative duke of Alençon, about the same age as René, had stood godfather to Louis. Once an Anglophile, for which sin he had been imprisoned by Charles VII in 1456, he was liberated by the new king on his accession, in acknowledgment of the duke's support during the Praguerie rebellion of 1440. Louis now gave Alençon back his confiscated lands, hoping thus to secure the future loyalty of this socially fascinating but in fact utterly unreliable nobleman. As for the potentially turbulent and very rich Jean, count of Armagnac, the king as dauphin had himself locked the count up in 1443 for resisting the expedition Louis had led against certain notorious brigands in his countship. But now Jean found himself, like the duke of Alençon, released from his confinement and once more in possession of his property. Louis had always known him to be a wily fellow and admired his diplomatic wrigglings nearly twenty years before. Such men were not too common in the south. Armagnac, once in the royal bag, might well prove useful in the coming years.

Thus the king astutely curbed some of his ominously fractious aristocrats and pardoned others in order to attach them, if that were not too much to ask, to his service or at least to neutrality in any future struggle with similar figures. But he outlawed Pierre de Brézé, who seems to have had all the virtues a monarch might wish for in a confidential executive. Apparently he felt that Pierre would be capable in his blind loyalty to the memory of Charles VII of rousing all that sovereign's equally pigheaded servants against a successor notoriously prejudiced, to the point of outright hostility, against him. The present king knew quite well that some of them actually suspected him of poisoning his father, a crime for which there is absolutely no evidence.

The question of the disposal of Antoine de Chabannes, on the other hand, who had caused Louis's long exile as dauphin, could be settled without suggesting unjustifiable malice. Chabannes, formerly Master of the Royal Household, had eventually decided to disappear. The arrest of both these gentlemen, the king proclaimed, would be lavishly rewarded by himself. For the time being, no one could find Antoine, who had fled in disguise. But Pierre de Brézé, more courageous and honorable, returned from Scotland of his own accord to give himself up. He was imprisoned at Loches for a short time and then characteristically released by his new master, who found his bearing in these hard conditions more congenial than he had expected.

That equally gallant but decidedly more equivocal figure, the count of Charolais, Philip's heir and Louis's old friend, nearly as much at odds with the duke his father by this time as the king had been with his own parent, came to see the new monarch at Tours, probably just because Philip had preferred to withdraw to Brussels. The king received Charolais with exceptional attentions and a bewildering series of hunting expeditions. These excursions were in fact the only pleasures the two men found in each other's company. The count, a born gambler with men's lives, his own included, cared nothing for the problems of administration and diplomacy. He enjoyed the pursuit of animals and birds merely as the next best thing to the pursuit of armies. Louis, on the other hand, detested having to allow for the deadly hazards of warfare in plans laid for a purpose invariably constructive. He could fight as well as the next man, as he had shown often enough. But he infinitely preferred to the chaos of any battlefield the orderly deployment of documents in the silence and solitude of his study. As for hunting, the tracking of the quarry and the creation of favorable conditions for cutting off its escape interested him more than the actual slaughter of it, just as he would rather force into a corner than destroy a human antagonist.

The king, in his correspondence and conversations with Charolais at this date, reverted to his previous policy of playing off that reckless young firebrand against his scheming old father in Brussels by promising the count the government of Normandy. Promises cost nothing and everyone understood that in the politics of a transitional period they must be provisional, depending upon changes in the situation which could not always be foreseen. Louis himself was displaying the same restless, headstrong activity that had marked his career as dauphin. Now that he was king of France such industry in consolidating his power by distributing territorial grants and matrimonial alliances became more successful. It made him respected but also feared. There were, in addition, some grumbles about his austerity in slashing public and even his own domestic expenditure. He had, for instance, reduced the pensions and privileges of his father's former servants and had also whittled down the financial concessions the late king had made to the universities and certain ecclesiastical dignitaries and bodies. But no one dared to complain openly about this severity in accounting for disbursements, so much at variance with the traditional generosity and even more or less harmless ostentation of the French monarchy.

His indefatigable inquiries into the state of the nation caused him to take the risk, one day in 1463, of going into Guienne, still a hotbed, though now not a very dangerous one, of English intrigue. Some of these foreigners caught sight of him and a few companions in a small boat on the Gironde, pursued them in a larger, armed vessel and actually fired on them. It would of course have been a great feat to capture the king of France and hold him for ransom. But the Englishmen patrolling the river were most probably mere brigands. Official England, with the Wars of the Roses still raging, was in no position to provoke further trouble with a so recently victorious enemy. The king's oarsmen rowed frantically west, toward Bordeaux, against the wind which was slowing down the progress of the sailing craft behind them. At a bend in the banks the French boat was driven ashore till it was hidden by the reeds and remained there for some hours, until the lugger gave up the chase. When the tide turned the little wherry floated off without difficulty and did not sight the bandits again.

On the monarch's return to Tours he found Italian ambassadors awaiting him. They came from Venice, Genoa and Florence. The latter city was then ruled for all practical purposes by the elderly Cosimo de' Medici, who had for years been promoting the fortunes of Francesco Sforza, the usurping duke of Milan, arguably controlling the strongest community in Italy. But his nearest neighbors, Genoa and Venice, wanted French help to keep him below their own military level. Duke Charles of Orléans, as noted above, had a claim to the Milanese duchy through his mother, Valentina Visconti, and would now have been supported by the Genoese and Venetians. Nevertheless Louis, fond though he was of Charles, felt more inclined to back the big battalions of the old *condottiere* Francesco. The king rejected the arguments of the maritime republics, while he cordially received the Florentine envoys and also the resident Milanese ambassador. But at this time he only extended such vague promises to them as he had to Charolais. The duke of Milan might die soon and so might Cosimo. No one could then tell precisely what kind of circumstances would arise.

A more urgent question, relating to England, now came rather suddenly to the front. King Edward IV of York had been proclaimed the sovereign of that country on March 4, 1461. He was now defeating rebels against his authority in the north. Margaret of Anjou was persistently calling for the rescue of her unwar-like husband, Henry VI, by then an almost helpless fugitive, with her, in Scotland, toward which Edward's forces were slowly but surely making their way. Louis agreed to intervene on condition that, if a French expedition were successful in saving Henry, the English crown, whoever might then wear it, would surrender Calais. He must have known that there would be very little chance of this concession of so important a foothold in France by the government of either a Lancastrian or a Yorkist. It is likely that Louis was simply playing for time at this stage of his correspondence with Margaret. But a plan for a French invasion of England was drawn up. Charolais would command the venture, Pierre de Brézé would prepare for its reception in the island and Philip would supply transportation and finance. So the old duke said. But he had always been Anglophile at heart and took the same view of promises in an emergency as did his "nephew." Meanwhile the latter, in the hope of embarrassing Edward, forbade all French and Burgundian trade with England.

Margaret visited France and interviewed Louis, who gave her a small force to take back with her to Scotland, under Pierre de Brézé. The Frenchmen fought well for her against Edward in the north of England. But at last he proved too strong to be beaten. Pierre returned to France.

The position continued to bristle with difficulties. French policy under Charles VII had naturally been pro-Lancastrian owing to the marriage of Margaret of Anjou to Henry VI. But that extremely able, peremptory and excitable queen was disliked as a "proud Frenchwoman" by her English subjects and also by Philip, who had never been able to get on with her family, hostile of course to his designs on Lorraine. Nor did Louis care at all for Margaret. He considered that passionate, imperious women had no business to meddle in politics. He had enjoyed negotiating with the calmly shrewd Duchesss Isabel of Burgundy. But the tear away daughter of the easygoing King René was another matter altogether. Nevertheless, he could not ignore the national sentiment of France, firmly on the side of her nonentity of a husband. He saw that Margaret, however carefully one handled her, was going to be a nuisance in international relations. But he really feared her less at this date than he feared Edward.

That remarkable young sovereign, six feet three inches in height, brown haired, disconcertingly handsome and genial, by unpredictable turns gay reveler and terrifying warrior, with smashing victories and pitiless executions already behind him, had retaliated with much vigor and some humor to the French king's prohibition of the import of English cloth and yarn. In September 1462 King Edward's troops raided Brittany and English ships threatened the coasts of Normandy and Guienne, from either of which localities the French invasion he had got wind of might be expected to start. He sent word to Louis, however, that there would be no need for such an expedition, since he himself would soon be crossing in the opposite direction to save King Louis the trouble and take his country off his hands. The recipient of this note smiled grimly, rather admiring the courage and gaiety of his twenty-one-year-old rival, which resembled those of the count of Charolais. He retorted to the Englishman, with heavy irony, that Edward could be assured of a warm welcome from the king of France if he could overcome the obstacles to his proposed voyage.

But Edward did not find it any more convenient than did Louis to go to sea just yet. Both rulers had trouble at home, the former being still busy in the obstinate north of his kingdom and at odds, like the French monarch, with some of his chief ministers, the stern earl of Warwick for one. In the end it was Margaret of Anjou who landed, not in France but in Philip's dominions, at Sluis near Bruges, on the border between western Flanders and Zeeland. She came, however, almost alone, with her little son and half a dozen female attendants, all practically destitute. But de Brézé now, at the king's request, met Margaret at Sluis and got the half-starved and soaked little party something to eat and a change of clothing. But he could do little more in the absence of instructions from Philip, who was at Boulogne on a pilgrimage. Eventually the queen caught up with the ailing and embarrassed duke, who had no wish for any such personal meeting. But with his usual courtesy he presented her with two thousand crowns and an escort, with Louis's consent, to her father's court of Angers.

Queen Margaret had come at an awkward moment for Philip, who was trying with some difficulty to negotiate a truce between the kings of England and France. They were not yet at war but definitely quarreling. The archbishop of York was conferring with the duke's ministers at Brussels. But Louis kept aloof in Paris. He would have nothing to do with any Englishman after enduring Edward's insults. In fact, by this time the French monarch was planning a campaign against Philip himself. Its object was, as he had implicitly if not explicitly sworn at his coronation, to regain the towns on the Somme ceded to Burgundy by the Treaty of Arras in 1435. The king began by offering the duke 200,000 crowns as an advance on the total price of 400,000 agreed by the treaty for the return of these former French possessions. The money was duly handed over to Philip's emissaries at Abbeville. Thence, at last, Louis went on to Hesdin, where the duke received him with characteristic tact and hospitality.

People noticed with astonishment how insignificant the "nephew," ill-dressed and ill-mounted, looked beside his always stately and magnificent "uncle." But the best informed of the crowds in the streets of the little town replied contemptuously to these criticisms. "Our King," they declared emphatically, "does not need to wear jewels and velvet. He has millions of crowns in his pocket, while the duke has only a few hundred thousands. And King Louis spends most of his wealth on us, the plain citizens of France. Philip spends his on dress and women."

This view received some support when an embassy from the king of Aragon, who was beginning to be important to both England and

France, rode up to Hesdin Castle. The Spanish knights were followed closely by envoys from the king of Denmark and even some Englishmen from London. They all wanted to see Louis, not Philip. But the duke took care to present himself to them first, in all his splendor, before introducing them to his shabby guest, whose dignity, however, proved a match for the Burgundian's. The French monarch assured the ambassadors, with calm condescension, that he regarded Philip as a "father." He praised the Latin of the English bishop and protested that he wished the gallant Edward well, calling him *"un gentil prince,"* and asking how best he could serve him.

The Londoners, astounded at this display of smooth diplomacy where they had expected at best hardly veiled enmity, received the impression that the queer little king of France, with his ambiguous smile, polished phrases and deliberately coarse, old-fashioned clothing, did not mean a word he said and never would. They reported to Edward that he was very dangerous and must be closely watched. For they could see, also, that he had far more power, by now, in this part of Europe than its own duke, since he was buying back so coolly from the Burgundian a region, Picardy, of especially famous soldiers, whose prowess the English had learned to their cost not so very long ago.

At Amiens the king's entry proved a triumph. The whole town had been illuminated in his honor. He and Queen Charlotte were greeted by an actor playing the part of Jonah, stepping out of the jaws of a huge effigy of a whale, as though to suggest a resurrection of the municipality through Louis's beneficent visit. He could not help turning to the Milanese ambassador in his suite. "Do you not agree," he asked the Italian, with his peculiar caustic twinkle, that might have so many different meanings, "that this city alone is worth more than the four hundred thousand crowns I have paid the duke of Burgundy for all Picardy?" The words appeared to be a harmless jest. But they were meant to notify Milan that its potential ally, France under Louis XI, could be of overwhelming importance.

Nor was Italy, as the Spanish embassy had proved, the only country where the king, ever since the beginning of 1462, had been trying to extend his influence. He had a claim to the throne of Aragon in Spain through his mother, Marie of Anjou, the granddaughter of one of its earlier occupants, Juan I. The present ruler, Juan II, an able and energetic sovereign, was fighting Enrique IV, king of Castile, popularly known, on account of his inability to consummate his two marriages, as "the Impotent," and certainly as weak and vacillating in character as his namesake Henry of Lancaster. Louis made Juan pay for French help and the abdication of French pretenses to the possession of Aragon by forcing him to yield Roussillon, just northeast of the Pyrenees and bordering upon Gascony, to the crown of France. But at the same time Edward of England, through the earl of Warwick, was pressing Juan to create a diversion against France if Louis made a determined attempt to come to the aid of Henry, still a nervous prisoner of the government of King James III of Scotland, then a boy of eleven.

"I have heard," Louis had written from Bordeaux, as early as April 1462, to his representative in the south, Count Gaston IV of Foix, "that King Edward and the Earl of Warwick are in communication with the King of Aragon, telling him that Warwick will come to his rescue. I think that if you showed the King of Aragon the letters that Edward and Warwick write to me, jeering at the King of Aragon, he would willingly join me against the English. But you should sound him carefully to see if he means business and would like to see me before Warwick sets out."

The French monarch promised Gaston the kingdom of Navarre if all went well. A defensive alliance between France and Aragon was arranged, Louis guaranteeing to support Juan in Catalonia till he had subdued the rebels there, whereupon the former sovereign meant to take over the province himself, though naturally he did not confide this plan to the Aragonese. Don Carlos had died in 1461, supposed to have been poisoned by his stepmother Juana, Juan's second wife. She still lived at Barcelona, but was hated by the Catalans both for this alleged crime and for her personal arrogance. In these circumstances, favorable to Louis's designs, he met Juan near Sauveterre on the Béarnais frontier and proposed to the by no means wealthy Aragonese sovereign that if either king demanded troops from the other he must pay for their maintenance so long as he needed them. The Spaniard was ready to agree to anything that ensured his victory over Catalonia. But Louis foresaw that in that event Juan would not be able to pay his French ally except by mortgaging the province to the crown of France.

At Bayonne on May 9 the price of 300,000 crowns was agreed, to be secured by the pledging to France of the Catalan ports of Perpignan and Collioure on the Gulf of Lions. On the surrender of Barcelona, moreover, the French king would receive the adjoining provinces of Roussillon and Cerdagne, to be held by him until the whole cost of his previous military assistance had been paid over to him. It was no wonder that the unfortunate Juan remarked on his return from Bayonne that "once you begin to negotiate with that fellow you are lost." It looked as though Louis were going to keep his word, given to Don Carlos in the previous year. He is supposed to have said to that on the whole amiable and cultivated young man: "I shall expel your father out of all his dominions, till he will not have a single plot of land left to bury himself in." This vindictive boast, couched in the rhetoric congenial to the Spanish temperament, is one the Frenchman would have liked to address to his own parent if there had been any hope of its fulfillment in the latter's lifetime. But this time, for once, the cunning schemer had overreached himself. He was going to regret, in due course, what seemed at the time such a triumphant bargain.

Juan had no alternative but to accept these browbeating terms, since he had been unable to get anything but promises out of Edward, who was in no position yet to undertake serious responsibilities abroad. Meanwhile the unpopular queen of Aragon, Juana, fled north, from Barcelona to Gerona, hotly pursued by the Catalan revolutionaries. Juan invaded the province, but could make little headway till in July Gaston burst into Roussillon from the northeast, capturing two small towns while most of the Catalan forces lay entrenched before Gerona. The count, an excellent strategist, then left isolated the strong port of Perpignan while he turned to a methodical conquest of the rest of Roussillon. Next, he relieved Gerona and rescued Queen Juana. The Catalans, as they have done throughout their history, fought heroically. But they were outnumbered and outgeneraled by the French. When Louis then ordered the siege of Barcelona, where numbers counted for less, the city was so gallantly defended that it was able to call for help on Enrique IV of Castile, Juan's rival, whom the rebels accepted as their king, rather than knuckle under to the French and Aragonese.

Gaston and Juan abandoned the siege, withdrawing first northward and finally across the river Segre into Aragon itself. In December an armistice was signed between the combatants, accepting the situation in Catalonia, where Louis's frank imperialism had failed to break the spirit of a region with an astonishing record, to this day, of resistance to domination by others, even by adjacent Spanish territory. But Roussillon and Cerdagne, more permeated at this date by French civilization, proved less difficult. Jacques d'Armagnac, now duke of Nemours, stormed Perpignan for Louis on January 7, 1463. But, even so, conquest of the whole county was delayed until June.

Both Enrique and Juan proceeded to make advances to the French king. The Castilian suggested that he and Louis between them should seize Aragon and then tempt Catalonia with the offer of a king and queen, Charles, duke of Berry, and the Infanta Isabella, both of famous royal blood. But Louis had already experienced quite enough of war in Spain, a country always most formidable on the defensive. He stuck to his alliance with Juan, personally the stronger of the two Spanish kings. But at the same time he wished to prevent the wealthier Castilian from turning against French interests by embracing Edward. For this purpose, at the end of April 1463, he met the "impotent" Enrique on French soil at Uturbie, counting on an easier diplomatic victory over that dull-witted sovereign than he could expect in the case of the far abler Juan, whom he still did not wish to antagonize.

The Castilian, escorted by a bodyguard of three hundred sumptuously adorned and armed Moorish horsemen, in addition to all his nobles, crossed the river Bidassoa in great splendor. The party was borne on ships with gilded sails. The Spaniards wore jewels even in their boots. This ostentation made a bad impression on the French, who were now beginning to imitate their outwardly casual monarch in setting little store by display. French irony and Spanish pride, born to misunderstand each other, came into play. The recently victorious soldiers of France smiled superciliously at the self-conscious swagger of the foreign grandees who had done so little of the really hard fighting in Catalonia. But the Castilians knew themselves to be the only nation in Europe that had fought a war of nearly eight hundred years, only now beginning to succeed, against the fiercest heathens in the world. More terrible even than Turks and Saracens in their obdurate fanaticism, the Moors were constantly reinforced from Africa, while the diminishing ranks of Christendom's defenders in Spain hewed their way forward step by step, unsupported by the remainder of the West. The men with Enrique therefore considered themselves, not unreasonably, heroic champions of the Cross in comparison with the money-grubbing merchants from the other side of the Pyrenees, so disgracefully defeated in their feeble attempts, 250 years earlier, to recover the Holy Sepulcher.

Under these conditions Louis, who now had experience of three sorts of Spaniards, Castilians, Aragonese and Catalans, came to prefer the latter for several reasons. In the first place the country was governed, like certain Flemish territories, by hardheaded businessmen who could see reason, rather than by romantic and overbearing aristocrats. In other words, Catalonia would not mind a king so long as he behaved himself, but would not tolerate a tyrant. Second, Catalans were tremendous fighters once they could be persuaded, even by a foreigner, that their national existence was being threatened. Third, the capital, Barcelona, already richer than Marseilles or Toulon, could soon be made, with its long maritime perspectives to the Levant, into the most valuable ally that could be conceived to the rising economic strength of France. Louis decided to play this big fish against its mainland enemies to the west for all he was worth.

At the beginning of August 1463 he received a Catalan embassy near Chartres with every sign of affection, refusing to let the envoys kiss his hands but embracing their leaders himself on the cheeks, while declaring that his grandmother Yolande, mother of King René and Queen Marie of France, had been half a Catalan, though it would have been more correct to describe her as Aragonese. The ambassadors

CAROLVS I, PHILIPPI BONI F. COMES XXXI,
HOLLANDIÆ ET VNITI A PATRE BELGII HÆRES,
AVDAX AB ARMORVM STVDIO APPELLATVS.
EX ISABELLA BORBONIA EI NATA MARIA.
BELLI ARDORE POTITVS ANTE NANCEIVM
CECIDIT Æ MccccLxxvII. ÆTATIS XLV.

Duke Charles the Bold of Burgundy.
THE ROYAL LIBRARY, WINDSOR.

Margaret of York, Duchess of Burgundy,
wife of Charles the Bold. GIRAUDON,
THE MANSELL COLLECTION.

Jacques Coeur. GIRAUDON, THE MAN-
SELL COLLECTION.

Manor of Plessis. GIRAUDON, THE MAN-
SELL COLLECTION.

Castle of Méhun. GIRAUDON, THE MAN-
SELL COLLECTION.

Philippe de Commines. GIRAUDON, THE
MANSELL COLLECTION.

King Edward IV of England. ROYAL
LIBRARY, WINDSOR. Copyright reserved.

were enchanted with his promises to back them through thick and thin. But their gratitude was considerably damped when they discovered that he had been spreading rumors that they had come to Chartres to offer him their submission to the French crown. It was the sort of tale that could easily be afterwards represented, as it was, as having originated with a mere compliment, the wish that such splendid fellows could be persuaded to become Frenchmen. All the same, the touchy Catalans were alarmed. When Louis rushed off to Picardy they followed him.

Negotiations dragged on for months, while the king of France kept both Catalonia and the kings of Aragon and Castile guessing. He wanted, as usual, to gain his ends without war. At last the Catalans, tired of waiting, rashly elected the Constable of Portugal, Dom Pedro, a learned philosopher and poet, but no soldier, to be their king. He told Louis that he would leave France in undisputed possession of Roussillon and Cerdagne in return for help in dethroning Juan of Aragon. But Louis, confident that he could retain these provinces without Pedro's support and still cherishing a healthy respect for the sly veteran of camps and council chambers, Juan, declined to abandon his old friend. In fact, the latter not only defeated Pedro again and again in the field but came to terms with Castile, Naples, Milan and Genoa, as well as securing Louis's financial support. Pedro, who should never have left his library, died utterly discomfited, at the age of only thirty-four, on June 29, 1464.

Louis still would not give up hope of securing Catalonia for himself. But other matters, really more important than this project, had already begun to claim his attention in France. Meanwhile Juan, now physically blind but as indomitable and tricky as ever in his late sixties, fought the French commanders, including so good a soldier as René's son Duke Jean of Calabria, to a standstill. Burgundy and England, as well as Naples and Milan, saw that the winds of fate were blowing against France in this region and shrewdly favored the bold and brainy Aragonese king. By 1469 he had married his son Ferdinand to Isabella of Castile, thus laying the foundations of unity in Spain and inaugurating its golden age. In the autumn of 1471 Jean of Calabria died of apoplexy. In 1472 Juan entered Barcelona, in 1473 he took Perpignan and the war finally ended with a treaty favorable to the Spaniard, though it confirmed the French-Aragonese alliance.

Louis had cut a rather poor figure in this Spanish adventure as compared with his heroic opposite number Juan. The dream of a seizure by France of Catalonia, mostly for the sake of Barcelona, had really collapsed when the French monarch tried to be too clever in his dealings with the patriotic and levelheaded Catalans by attempting to trap them into a false position of submission to himself. By the time he had realized that Juan was a match for him both on the field and off, the situation could not be retrieved. For developments in Louis's own kingdom, beginning in 1463, distracted him from turning his whole energy to a contest upon which the warlike Aragonese could concentrate powers hardly inferior to those of the basically peaceful Frenchman in the most dangerous areas of political intrigue and violence.

CHAPTER VIII

The League of Public Weal
(1463–1465)

At the end of October 1462 Queen Margaret, after an abortive attack on Calais, an unsatisfactory interview with Louis at Chinon and her correct guess that Philip was more likely to help Edward than her husband, dashed back, in a fury of desperate courage, with Brézé, to confront the Yorkists once more in Northumberland. She dragged with her, from Edinburgh, the unfortunate Henry, who only wanted to be left alone with his voluminous manuscripts on theological topics and his drafts of educational projects. But Warwick drove both wife and husband back to Scotland again. No one wanted an English king restored with the aid of mixed forces of French and Scottish troops.

In January 1463 King Louis appointed Antoine de Croy, of whose persistent double-dealing he was not yet aware, to negotiate with the English. But Edward refused to allow the talks to begin in case they endangered his position in Spain, which depended on his continuing hostility to French schemes in both Aragon and Castile. Louis, on the other hand, content for the time being with his command of Roussillon and Cerdagne, a broad Pyrenean valley to the southwest of the former province, wished at all costs to prevent the English from interfering, on behalf of Juan, with the *status quo*. For this reason he regarded as essential a truce to the present mutual hostility of France and Yorkist England.

Philip, equally intent upon currying favor with Edward at the expense of Margaret, whom he hoped he could persuade Louis to drop, offered to mediate between Paris and London. The French king saw no objection. A Burgundian embassy crossed to the island in April. It returned in May with a promise from the king of England to send representatives to Saint-Omer in Artois, between Calais and Boulogne, to discuss all outstanding questions. But the fulfillment of this promise had to be postponed for a number of complex reasons.

Louis, while the Burgundians were talking in London, had contrived to interview Enrique the Impotent of Castile, thus defeating Edward's attempts to keep them apart. The French monarch, posing as arbitrator between the two Spanish kings, induced Juan to take no further steps toward an English alliance, much to Edward's annoyance. The Englishman turned to Milan and Naples, offering the Garter to both Francesco Sforza and Ferdinand of Aragon, a bastard cousin of Juan and just then making good his claim to the Neapolitan throne against that of René. Sforza would not accept the honor for fear of offending his now powerful friend the king of France. Ferdinand temporized until the summer of 1464, when he took the Order, believing, or so he told Louis, that the French and the English were now reconciled. It seemed to be so, officially. But both kings were in fact too busy with other matters at that time to come to a formal agreement.

In these decidedly trying circumstances Louis, unlike the only too casual Edward, spent day after day and half the night in arduous toil. He rose early, prayed and attended mass, then passed straight from his chapel to his study, where he sat at work until midday. After dining he rode or walked for an hour or two, then returned to his administrative labors or received visitors. When evening fell he ate a frugal supper and thereafter went back to his papers and secretaries till far into the night. He issued, throughout his life, thousands of decrees, ranging from important to quite trivial subjects. At least 2000 letters dictated by him survive. He only rarely wrote in his own hand, but made sure that every sentence was correctly transcribed in the lucid style for which he was famous. He employed no ministers, simple personal staff, military officers and, like the editors of modern newspapers, local correspondents. Most of these were ordinary merchants, reporting on the conditions of trade and industry throughout the kingdom. But very many of such agents were political spies, acting under various covers, including all sorts of pseudo commercial, professional and often laborer disguises, as for instance domestic servants or gamekeepers taking presents of live animals or birds, such as greyhounds and falcons, to persons of rank. But the primary and most common duty, apart from espionage, of all these more or less secret representatives was to raise money for the royal exchequer. Reconstruction of a country half-ruined by a hundred years of uninterrupted war constituted the king's main task. The reorganization could only be enforced by a well-paid and privileged standing army, such as his father had in vain tried to introduce, the fifteenth-century forerunner of a devoted and ruthless police. Their methods were taken for granted, like those of any other soldiers, in the circumstances of late medieval society. It would not be the brutality of such an executive branch but its failure to prevent disorder that would cause a ruler trouble. During the first years of the reign of Louis XI he kept this multitude at a figure of about twelve thousand.

Unlike modern police states, however, with the exception of that established in Russia by ideological revolution, the France of this period concentrated its disciplines on the wealthier classes, chiefly the nobility and episcopate, not the ordinary citizens. The burgesses could get as rich as they pleased, provided they contributed regularly to the king's treasury. For the typical interests of a merchant or lawyer were always best cultivated by peaceful even if by occasionally fraudulent means, whereas a duke or count would be mainly concerned to extend his territory, being thus constantly tempted, owing to the tradition of centuries, to do so by armed raids on adjacent provinces. This sort of behavior always carried the risk of setting the whole realm ablaze again.

Louis meant, above all, to stop these practices for good, such prohibition being the essential preliminary to the erection of a unified state, of which there were no examples on a large scale in the Europe of his day. His success in achieving this feat renders him a figure of decisive historical significance. For on the whole he managed to hammer the unfamiliar concept of a compact nation into the minds of his subjects and by analogy to draw attention to its advantages elsewhere. However much Italy, Spain and Germany for long repudiated the French pattern and however often France itself after Louis's time fell into anarchy, foreigners as well as Frenchmen, and particularly his old enemies the English, remained permanently conscious of the ideal which he bequeathed to them of cohesive patriotism over a vast area theoretically controlled by one man. Till then this nation had only been prominent in such past empires as the ancient Roman. Louis probably looked forward to a time when he could exclaim, like King Henri IV at the battle of Ivry in 1590 between the Catholics and Protestants of France, "No Frenchman is my foe!" But conditions in the 1460's certainly did not permit the formulation of any such principle.

The king's letters are even better evidence for his character than the generally judicious, always eloquent but sometimes inaccurate memoirs of the great Franco-Flemish historian Philippe de Commines. The moods of Louis's vivid correspondence vary from ironic or facetious to intensely earnest and even menacing. An occasional pun makes its appearance, as when he calls the Burgundian herald named *Toison d'Or* ("Golden Fleece") *Trahison d'Or* ("Golden Treachery"). Yet actually, for matters of great moment, he preferred oral to written

instructions and emissaries of humble rank rather than socially important figures. He would make sure that the former learned their lessons
by heart from himself. They usually did so with ease, like most relatively
illiterate people, without necessarily or even often understanding what
was meant. He would then give them a single scrap of paper briefly
authorizing them in general terms to act in the king's name. This
procedure precluded the existence of documentary testimony to any
specific mission. Louis could therefore at a later date either ratify or
decline responsibility for it, just as circumstances might suggest. But
he could also easily find out whether or not his message had been
delivered word-perfect. If it had not been so transmitted, punishment
was instant and severe, involving the loss of both liberty and property.
On the other hand, those who obeyed him to the letter were generously
rewarded in private, even if in public he might pretend not to know
them. His spies included the most apparently innocent servants, from
kennelmen and foresters to one of his kitchen staff coming to fetch
a cook or housekeeper promised to him.

The provincial towns, Lyons in particular, owed his decrees everything. They had to pay him for their international fairs, their right to
impose road tolls and their status as a municipality. But their subsequent
profits usually exceeded the price disbursed in such taxation. The king
often, moreover, ennobled the local magistrates, as soon as he had
tested their complete loyalty to his sometimes complex and seemingly
risky requirements. The administrators so promoted then of course became liable for certain dues to the crown. But they invariably considered
their social elevation, with its accompanying enhanced respect and
privileges, well worth the ensuing expense. Louis did sometimes make
mistakes, during these years, in his judgment of the moral qualities of
persons he employed or condemned. Pierre de Brézé, for instance,
was a paragon of fidelity in any post he occupied, Antoine de Croy a
villain. But the king never failed to learn from such experiences. He
was a very difficult man to deceive in middle life and old age. His
exceptionally acute intelligence inclined him to elaborate planning in
business. Yet he acted, when it came to the point, as a rule upon
impulse, a remarkable instinct for the best way in or out, rather than
on logic. He would cut his losses at once, pitiless to himself as to others,
if a scheme looked like it was going wrong.

He did so even in the ultimately abortive Spanish enterprise, where
the ruling factor, the prize of the great rich port of Barcelona, had a
special reference to his design for extending the already lucrative French
trade eastward. Aggression upon foreign territory, ever since the erection
of the ancient Roman Republic and its expansion northward to Gaul,
westward to Spain and eastward to Asia Minor, as well as southward to

North Africa, leading finally to the *Pax Romana,* has regularly been excused as a necessary defense of commerce with states less well organized for that purpose. Markets on alien soil which are constantly attacked by local inhabitants either incapable of understanding that such opposition endangers their future prosperity or too mutually quarrelsome or proudly insular to undertake a reasonable mercantile system for dealing with originally peaceful invaders, can only, this argument runs, expect military intrusion as a preliminary to settlement under more civilized conditions.

Spain in Louis's time, however, bore little resemblance, except psychologically, to the Hispania of the ancient Romans. Moorish civilization had intervened. But Castile and Aragon, now that the Moors had been driven far to the south of the peninsula, were developing progressive, rather than barbarous, kingdoms. Aragon in particular affected France through its long-standing struggle, dating from the thirteenth century, with the house of Anjou for possession of Naples and Sicily. The Aragonese King Pedro III began the contest by coming to the rescue of the revolt in 1282, known as the Sicilian Vespers, against the tyranny of Charles of Anjou. But 1438 his descendant René had inherited the Angevin claim to Sicily and was fighting the Aragonese in both that island and Naples itself. By 1442 he had failed to establish himself and was back in Provence.

In 1443 Pope Eugenius IV declared Alfonso the Magnanimous of Aragon king of both Naples and Sicily. But both Florence and Milan grew more and more hostile to the growing power of the Spaniards in southern Italy. Both cities encouraged René to return to the charge. He did so, but soon lost heart among the confusing intrigues of Francesco Sforza, Cosimo de' Medici and Venice. He was getting old, fat and self-indulgent. The death of his much-loved wife Isabel in 1453 increased his depression. When he remarried he chose a plain, no-nonsense Breton girl of nineteen, Jeanne de Laval, who kept him at home. His son by his first wife, Duke Jean of Calabria, a good but unlucky soldier, took up the Angevin cause, backed by Charles VII.

In 1458 Alfonso died, leaving Naples to his illegitimate son Ferdinand, generally known as Don Ferrante, and Sicily, Sardinia and Aragon to a brother, who became the extremely able and resolute King Juan II. Ferrante continued to keep Duke Jean out of Naples and even besieged him in Genoa, which had been supporting him, under Charles's directions, with ships and other supplies. Just before the death of Charles in 1461 an attempt by René to relieve the city failed dismally. By August 1462 Jean had been heavily defeated by the Spaniards at Troia in northwestern Apulia and the hopes of the house of Anjou in this direction fell to their lowest ebb.

Louis at this juncture perceived with his usual realism that there remained no prospect of success, or point either, in tackling Ferrante in Italy. But he also saw that René's claim could be used in aiming at Barcelona, the official property of Juan II. The subtle French king gradually maneuvered the Catalans, when they ejected Juan and turned to the well-meaning but incompetent Dom Pedro of Portugal, into offering the throne of Aragon to René.

The struggle for Catalonia between Louis, Aragon and Castile lasted for ten years after 1463. It might have ended in the Frenchman's favor relatively soon if his base at home had not been undermined. But immediately after his coronation he had concentrated on changing all the arrangements made by his father. He began with a substantial lightening of the taxation Charles VII had imposed on the lower-income groups in order to avoid dangerous resistance to such measures by his nobility. But this experiment by his son half-ruined the royal exchequer. Within three years Louis was obliged to return to the old system, a step which naturally incensed the masses he had previously relieved of it.

Charles had also allowed the clergy a lot of latitude. Louis, a lover of saints rather than bishops, curtailed the privileges of the latter. His abrogation of the Pragmatic Sanction as early as 1461 re-established papal supremacy in France on the secret condition tht Pope Pius II would refrain from opposing the king's schemes in Italy, especially in Naples on behalf of his uncle René's claims to that city. This kind of bargaining with the Holy See went on for most of Louis's life and bewildered the French prelates, who could never make out what their spiritual head in the Vatican was up to.

Nor was the University of Paris, which had appointed priests to benefices in Charles's time, now permitted to do so. The king rebuked the lordly directors of that revered institution, it appears, in terms scarcely less coarse than the language used by rebellious students in 1968. "You lead wicked lives with big fat harlots," he is alleged to have told them. "Get out! I can't bear to look at you! You're not worth my attention!" This outburst is quite likely to have really taken place when the sovereign, like a nineteenth-century schoolmaster dissatisfied with his prefects or monitors, summoned to his presence a set of exalted persons who were more or less clandestinely disputing his authority. They were near enough in rank to the throne to be addressed in this blunt fashion, by no means unknown in Europe on similar occasions for centuries both before and after this time.

Louis also signaled his displeasure, in perhaps comparable phrases, to secular magnates who offended him by their *costumes de folie*, i.e. mere ostentation in dress, a mode begun in his father's reign. He attacked this feature of aristocratic arrogance less for its own sake, idiotic as he must have thought it, and unworthy of true noblemen, than as a symbol of the growing political and social independence cultivated by the great landowners, an independence that could interfere ominously with his plans for the future constitution of the French state. Duke Francis of Brittany, for instance, had ejected the king's nominees for the bishopric of Rennes and the abbacy of Redon and threatened English intervention if they were restored by force.

In some cases it must be admitted that the king retaliated to such presumption with ill-judged severity. For example, he took away for a while much of the power of such sensible and gallant advisers of his father, now called Charles the Well Served, as Jean, count of Dunois, as well as reducing the influence of the duke of Bourbon and the count of Foix. Moreover the monarch, in his infatuation with Francesco Sforza, whose very dress and mannerisms he imitated, deeply vexed the dukes of Anjou and Orléans by abandoning to the Italian adventurer the two valuable ports of Genoa and Savona, which the troops of Charles VII had conquered. Interested French lords began to talk among themselves of a reprehensible alliance between fox (Louis) and wolf (Francesco) in this connection.

The king's labors to destroy English dictation in Guienne, where he dismissed Duke Jean II of Bourbon on dubiously adequate grounds from the governorship of that province, could be considered more respectable. His dashing about the whole kingdom, from Normandy to Languedoc, in order to raise funds for the recovery of the economically and strategically important Picardy towns in the north could also be excused in principle. But the speed and energy of these proceedings rendered his older subjects, used to the somnolence of the last years of Charles VII, quite giddy, as if they were attending a circus. Yet it was now the equally intent young count of Charolais rather than his sick and senile father Philip who argued most fiercely against the enforcement of the reverse clause of the Treaty of Arras in this matter. In September 1463 Louis contrived, by bribing the Croy brothers with Luxembourg, to obtain the duke's agreement to accept the price of 400,000 crowns for the surrender of Picardy to unconditional control by France. Charolais and Francis of Brittany promptly went into opposition together, with a view to regaining by violence the towns affected by this change of government.

In the autumn of 1464 Philippe de Commines, then aged nineteen, entered the service of the count of Charolais. Early in November the new squire attended the reception by Philip and his son of ambassadors from King Louis. They were led by a prince of the blood, Charles d'Artois, Comte d'Eu, by the chancellor of France, Pierre de

Morvillier, and by Antoine du Bec Crespin, archbishop of Narbonne. Morvillier began with an angry speech in which he accused Charolais of unlawfully seizing and locking up the person of the Bastard of Rubempré, who was in Holland aboard a ship based in Dieppe, simply because the Duchess Isabel had been told in Bruges by one of the count's secretaries and his later memorialist, Olivier de la Marche, that Rubempré was plotting to kidnap her son. The chancellor denied that any such plot existed and demanded the surrender of Olivier to Paris.

Philip, who knew all about the intricacies of feudatory law, replied that Olivier, a subject of the duchy of Burgundy, not of the French crown, could not be extradited on any such charge as had been made against him. If he could be proved to have lied, he would be punished by the duke himself. As for Rubempré, if he in his turn could be proved innocent, he would be at once released and sent back to France.

Morvillier, not being able to contravene this legally justifiable attitude, switched adroitly to another subject of complaint by the king, not unconnected with the first. He knew, he said, and could prove, that Duke Francis of Brittany and the count of Charolais had ceremoniously sworn blood brotherhood, in the presence of Tanneguy de Chastel, nephew of the alleged assassin of John the Fearless. The chancellor strongly condemned, in abusive language, this conduct, which he stigmatized as politically rebellious. Charolais, who was present, continually attempted to interrupt Morvillier in his own defense, but was each time shouted down by the sincerely or affectedly enraged chancellor.

The duke put an end to this improper scene by ordering his son to postpone what he had to say until the next day. The count obeyed, but on that occasion pointedly addressed his father, turning his back with contempt on Morvillier. He admitted his oath of brotherhood with Francis, but swore that it was a private matter, not directed against Louis. Philip summed up the dispute in mild terms, begging the chancellor of France to believe that neither Charolais nor he himself harbored the least ill will against the French crown.

As the embassy was leaving, the count, obviously in a state of suppressed fury, stepped up to the archbishop, who happened to be the last of the envoys to reach the door. "Give my humble respects to the king," the Burgundian hissed between his teeth, "and tell him how eloquently his chancellor has dressed me down. But you can add that before this year is out I'll have my revenge for his insults."

This reckless speech makes it quite clear that Charolais intended to defy in arms his sovereign and former hunting companion. The count proceeded to banish from his dominions, with his father's reluctant consent, Antoine and Jean de Croy, who had persuaded the sick old man to sell the Somme towns to Louis in accordance with the Treaty of Arras. The next step in the conspiracy was the arrival of the aggrieved duke of Bourbon at Philip's court. As the Burgundian ruler was his uncle and in such poor health the visit could be represented as quite natural. But in reality its purpose was to talk Philip into raising an army to prevent, in common, Bourbon claimed, with "all the other princes," any further extension of "disorderly and unjust government" of King Louis.

Such was the origin of what was afterwards called the League of Public Weal. Philip agreed to join it, not supposing for a moment that it would come to violence. The younger conspirators, including Louis of Luxembourg, count of Saint-Pol, and Thibaut of Blamont, Marshal of Burgundy, gathered at the house of the bishop of Cambrai, a bastard of John the Fearless, in that city. It was resolved to outlaw the Croy family, including the young Philip, son of Jean, who fled for his life from the Burgundian court. The old duke's objections to the rising determination of his son's adherents to use force were overruled. The rebel army set out for Paris in battle array, taking the Noyon road through Picardy.

For all the king's tact, ingenuity, intuitive brilliance and determination, serious trouble had broken out in France after 1464, the English menace having declined with Edward's final victory over the Lancastrians at the battle of Hexham in Northumberland on May 15 in that year. Whether the previous conduct of Louis really justified the rebellion of 1465, known as the League of Public (or Common) Weal (*La Ligue du Bien Public*) can only be decided after a study of his autocratic dealings with the papacy and aristocracy.

On his accession in 1461 the Gallican Church, as the French ecclesiastical establishment was called, enjoyed almost complete independence of Rome. The pope was debarred from all such interference in French politics as he exercised, as a rule disastrously, in other countries, above all, of course, in Italy. Most of the pontiffs meant well, on unexceptionable Christian principles, in their constant efforts to keep the peace among their quarrelsome spiritual subjects. But unfortunately, when drastic action had to be taken, their secular ambitions too often played a part. The so-called Pragmatic Sanction, pronounced at Bourges in 1438, constituted the king alone as defender of the faith in France. In practice he shared this responsibility with the universities and the nobility, so that the adoption of the expedient of ecumenical councils declared by the assemblies at Constance and Basel, to limit the hitherto unquestionable authority of the Holy See, pretty nearly abolished papal power in the secular affairs of France when this idea was transferred to that country.

Accordingly, during the reign of Charles VII relations were strained between him and the indignant popes Eugenius IV and Pius II. When Louis became king he indicated, following his general policy of opposing everything his father had ever done, that he desired a reconciliation with Rome. What he secretly wanted, however, was less to embrace the pope than to deprive the French aristocrats of the dominion they exercised, in common with himself, in ecclesiastical matters. Pius, who was no fool, but on the contrary a most civilized and versatile statesman, soon discovered the king's real object. The Holy Father shrewdly foresaw that if Louis had his way there would be for all practical purposes two popes, one still very influential in Italy and another, a despotic layman, in France. The pontiff therefore began to show favor to the French nobles, increasing it when he got wind of the king's intrigues with Francesco of Milan, the greatest danger in Italy to the temporal designs of the papacy.

Pius had a first-rate representative at the French court, Jean Jouffroy, bishop of Arras and a subject of the duke of Burgundy. The bishop easily persuaded Louis to annul the Pragmatic Sanction, a step which fell in with the royal determination to keep the peers in their places. Jouffroy promised the monarch that a papal legate would be appointed to superintend the collation of French benefices under advice from the throne, without costing France a single penny. King Louis and Pope Pius exchanged fulsome compliments on the conclusion of this arrangement. The former kissed the letter in which the latter ratified the bargain. The sexagenarian pontiff is said to have wept with joy, calling his correspondent a new Constantine the Great and comparing him with such past upholders of the supremacy of the Vatican as the emperors Theodosius and Charlemagne. The French Parlement, however, refused to register the royal edict. The king could not have cared less. He knew that his power now exceeded that of his Paris legislators.

But in Italy, Rome and France were on different sides in the conflicting claims of the houses of Anjou and Aragon to the crown of Naples, the French king backing the eldest son of King René, Jean, duke of Calabria, and Pius the *de facto* ruler of the kingdom, the Spaniard Ferdinand, Don Ferrante, one of those disconcerting Renaissance princes who appear charming and reasonable at one moment and bloodthirsty frauds at another. The pope would not listen to the French ambassadors in this matter. Louis, in one of his rare outbursts of rage, threatened the Holy Father with an ecumenical council and swore that Jouffroy's promise had been broken. French money, the king fulminated, was being used in Rome against the duke of Calabria. Then, with equal suddenness, he changed his tone completely, bestowing the French duchy of Valentinois (afterwards occupied by Cesare Borgia) upon the papacy and offering one of his bastard daughters in marriage to Pius's so-called nephew, also probably a bastard.

The pontiff accepted these gifts. But he continued to authorize his legate to appoint whom he chose to French benefices, whether Louis liked it or not. Such was the situation in 1462. It culminated in threats to excommunicate the recalcitrant parliament of Paris.

The king's chief opponent in this connection, siding with the Parlement, the Anglophile duke of Brittany, Francis II, remained as concerned to defend his caste as his sovereign was to attack it. Both men pretended to be dealing primarily with religious issues. But their real quarrel lay in the sphere of domestic politics. The king again employed startling tactics, this time to bewilder the duke. He unexpectedly announced himself to be in favor of the restoration of the Pragmatic Sanction, actually with the support of the bishop of Arras, who had been disappointed by Pius in the expectation of patronage of a plurality of French benefices. In 1463 and the following year Louis decreed, by stages, the renewal of the Gallican ordinances and finally, in fact, that of the Sanction itself. He also defiantly continued his friendly correspondence with Milan. On the other hand, he discreetly withdrew his aid to the duke of Calabria, whose chances of success in his claim to the throne of Naples now seemed to be nil, Ferdinand having by this time firmly established his authority in the kingdom by military victories.

Then, in 1464, Pius II suddenly died. The next pope, Paul II, a Venetian, had fewer brains than Pius but equal pertinacity. Italy split into two halves, with Rome, Naples and Venice confronting Milan and Florence, each of these last two states being backed by France. Sforza's dynasty seemed secure. But he himself was growing old and feeble, like Philip of Burgundy. In Florence the year 1464 also saw the death of Cosimo de' Medici. But his successor of the same family, Piero, something like Paul II in character and appearance, a handsome, honest, brave but slow-thinking and cautiously acting administrator, was as prepared as Paul to carry on the policy of a more wily predecessor. It was at this juncture that Louis perceived that he had gone too far in antagonizing his aristocracy and clergy. He found himself face to face, in France, with the redoubtable League of Public Weal, a solid phalanx of prelates and feudal landowners, with Philip behind them. He gave in, restoring the rights of investiture to these magnates and making peace with Paul.

As usual, political discontent underlay the religious conflict. All this time the king's unwearying attempts to unify his country by favoring its majorities, in what might arguably be called, in a sense, democratic style, had set most of the upper classes against him. Brittany and Burgundy were their most active and resolute representatives. But Anjou was also furious at the monarch's abandonment of its cause in Italy. Orléans, too, objected strongly to his friendship with its enemy, Duke Francesco Sforza of Milan, who would not allow the French duchy's claim to Asti in Piedmont. Louis was now beginning to think his former idol, the white-haired poet Charles of Orléans, an old fool.

Meanwhile the king's brusque treatment of the brilliant and genuinely Christian Pope Pius II had scandalized the French ecclesiastics, who also resented their compulsory contributions, by royal edict, to the national revenue and the maintenance of order in the cities, a matter which they considered could well be the responsibility of the burgesses their sovereign had pampered for so long. A sizable proportion of plain citizens, moreover, were repelled both by Louis's personal frugality, so unworthy of such a mighty prince, and his endless inroads into their commercial profits. There had already been riots, on the grounds of inordinate taxation, at Reims and Angers. Normandy and Languedoc too, the heaviest sufferers from the Hundred Years' War with the English and the brigandage which accompanied it, complained of unduly oppressive assessments.

The king could have replied that he had found his country in ruins due to foreign occupation, the irresolution of Charles VII and the greedy quarrels and treacheries of the realm's natural defenders, the military aristocracy. He could have pointed out that rehabilitation on the vast scale necessary cost a great deal of money. He might have admitted highhandedness, on occasion, in this desperate situation. But he might also have reminded his critics of repeated concessions to their grievances.

Yet, in the opinion of the clergy, the secular lords and even the municipal councils, nothing could excuse the picking of their pockets by the crown. They were not in a position, as Louis was, to realize the urgency of the need for funds nor to calculate how much hard cash would be required to set France on its feet again, and bring the land out of the social chaos and injustice of the Middle Ages. All the pride and pugnacity also characteristic of former centuries rose to humble the shabbily dressed, only too industrious and supiciously articulate "tyrant" of a people that had once been known as the Franks, i.e. "freemen."

Nevertheless, it was not the king's after all infrequent bursts of impulsive severity or his sudden, disconcerting changes of front that the League was determined to prevent. It was his steady transfer of power, under himself, from the bishops, the nobles and the professional legislators to the traders, to men, for instance, like the late Jacques Coeur, who actually kept the kingdom from succumbing to famine, banditry and massacre. The autocrat so wrathfully reprehended by the Church, the peerage and the parliament, hitherto the real rulers of France, was in fact clearly enough a champion of the common man. But this attitude, thoroughly expressive as it was of Christian charity, could scarcely be recognized by most wealthy Frenchmen of the mid-fifteenth century as in itself, without qualification a virtue.

Francis II of Brittany, a luxury-loving young voluptuary, had annoyed Louis, who did not care for this sort of duke in any case, not only by making difficulties about formal allegiance to his sovereign but also for secretly trying to convert the count of Charolais, whom the king did like at this period, to the idea of an Anglo-Burgundian-Breton alliance against France. Louis admired the count's frank courage and strong will. He had little or nothing of the duke's slippery character. But for that very reason he was more to be feared than Francis, a man who could be described, more justly than the English man of letters Joseph Addison (1672–1719), in Alexander Pope's famous line, as "willing to wound, and yet afraid to strike" (*Prologue to the Satires*, par. 12, l. 10).

It was the monarch's business to detect such intrigues through his ubiquitous agents. The Breton had, furthermore, insolently ordered the bishop of Nantes, on the boundary between Brittany and Poitou, to do him temporal homage. When the prelate, standing on his spiritual dignity, declined to become the duke's feudatory in this manner, Francis coolly seized his estates. The affronted ecclesiastic fled to Angers, further east up the Loire and out of Breton jurisdiction, appealing to the king to bring his rascally oppressor to reason.

Louis, rather alarmed at the reports he heard of a conspiracy between Brittany and Charolais, since he knew that all Burgundians, high and low, were always ready to seek the good graces of England, mainly for commercial reasons these days, decided to steal a march on the two young noblemen. He had no really imperative grounds for taking the field against them in arms. As usual, he tried the diplomatic line first. He talked loudly of bringing in the unscrupulous islanders to "lay low" the presumptuous lords, his own vassals, rumored to be defying the throne of France. Brittany he felt he could deal with if it came to a trial of strength. But Burgundy was a stiffer proposition at present and the English, who now seemed to be struggling out of their dynastic troubles, could be still more formidable enemies, since they continued persistently to claim the French crown.

Francis immediately glossed the royal declaration with a statement that Louis was about to surrender Normandy and Guienne to Edward as the price of English help in reducing the peerage of France to the condition of serfs. After publicly refuting this insinuation, which was in fact quite unfounded, the king, in December 1464, took a characteristically bold step, designed to rally all reasonable Frenchmen behind him. He summoned the estates of Tours and all the princes of the Valois blood, including King René and the dukes of Orléans and Bourbon, to judge the case in his presence. He defended himself in person, using all the arguments which had been indicated in the preceding pages. But he also tactfully asserted that he regarded the aristocracy as the pillars of his realm. He even referred to Francis as a gallant man of honor who had fallen into the hands of ignorant or malicious counselors. He declared that he wished the duke of Brittany no harm, but only better discrimination.

Francis had not turned up at the meeting. When the king asked where he was, Charles of Orléans rose to offer excuses for the Breton's absence which Louis considered disingenuous. He sharply rebuked the old poet, who died a fortnight later, aged seventy-four. He may or may not have perished partly as a result of the recently hostile attitude of his sovereign, who had once so respected him.

The monarch's speech was well received. But some of those present, whom the king had advised to go and remonstrate with the duke of Brittany, simply joined him. Bourbon came to an understanding, by no means favorable to King Louis, with Charolais. Even the monarch's younger brother, Charles of France, duke of Berry, aged eighteen, good-natured but weak-willed and muddleheaded, disappeared into Brittany. The purpose of this trip became clear when the discontented nobles elected him nominal head of their group. It was announced that Prince Charles's policy would involve suppression of a great part of the subsidies at present imposed by his brother on the great landowners and also actually suspension of all taxation for the time being. The duke of Bourbon would command military operations if they became necessary. The money already collected by the royal fiscal authorities but not yet delivered to the treasury would be diverted to the payment of Bourbon's troops.

After publication of the prince's program Burgundy mobilized. Antoine de Chabannes, count of Dammartin, seized Bourges and raised troops on the crown appanage of Berry. The king immediately fortified Paris, sending Charles de Melun and Bishop Jean Balue of Évrex to see to it. Louis also ordered Maine to oppose Brittany and Berry, while he himself attacked the duchy of Bourbon before tackling Burgundy. By May 1465 he had conquered the Bourbon territory, adding Auvergne and Berry before the end of the month. Guienne and Languedoc remained loyal under the count of Foix. But the dukes of Nemours and Alençon, with Dunois and Jean of Calabria, declared against the crown. By the time the king had dealt with them it was too late to reach the Burgundian frontier. He had to make for Paris. Meanwhile he appointed Galeazzo Maria Sforza, heir to the duchy of Milan, who had sent him reinforcements, lieutenant of Lyons and Dauphiné.

But some weeks before these events the monarch, beside himself with fury at the base betrayal by those who had cheered him so heartily at Tours, publicly denounced the rebels by name. He had also been embittered by the unexpected attitude of the count of Charolais and especially scandalized by the designation of the idiotic Charles as practically regent of France. He prophesied that the folly of the confederates would bring upon them the shame of causing the English to take advantage of it by descending once more upon his beloved country and reducing it, with pillage, destruction and butchery, to the piteous predicament of a hundred years ago, while these ineffectual traitors fought among themselves. But he added that he, the king, would prevent this atrocious sequel by offering pardon to all who would withdraw from his childish brother's conspiracy within a month of that date, which was March 16, 1465.

Louis never gave way to blind rage for more than an hour or two. His innate diplomatic dexterity would always quickly resume charge of his actions, if not of his sedulously concealed feelings. But his proclaimed magnanimity, as he probably foresaw, had no effect on the rebellious lords. Only the municipalities and René of Anjou then declared their unswerving loyalty to his person. The others gave no sign of having even heard him. They rejected René's cautious overtures out of hand.

By now it was really the Burgundians, not the Bretons, who stood behind this uncompromising front. Perhaps the volatile Francis had been truly touched, for the moment, by the king's flattering references to him. But Philip and Charolais were for once agreed in their deep resentment over the loss of their main recruiting ground in Picardy. They attributed this disaster to a trick played on the elderly duke by Jean and Antoine de Croy, who had persuaded him that Louis would grant the revenues of the formally transferred town to the duchy. No doubt the brothers had put some such idea into his mind. The duke was now paying the penalty for excessive addiction to sexual intercourse with an endless procession of mistresses. No doubt this obsession was a matter of principle with him, as everything else in his character seems to have been. Such traits included his cultivation of reactionary but in his case effective politics and ideas of administration, as well as his wrathful persecution of a son who appeared never to have heard of paternal authority, and finally the series of manias for pageantry, crusading plans, the Order of the Golden Fleece, which he established, and the knightly code in general.

For Philip was the very reverse of a debauchee except in the erotic line. In sedulous imitation of the heroes of ancient epic he never drank to the point of loss of personal dignity or allowed his women the slightest influence over his public life or indeed to take up more of his private time than his powerful but rapidly satisfied sexual appetite demanded. Like Napoleon he was liable to call for a female friend at any moment and dismiss her half an hour later. In warfare he was considered by his contemporaries quite dangerously merciful, forbidding all useless slaughter and destruction after a victory, just as the laws of chivalry in single combats prohibited the killing of or even, as in modern boxing, the continued assault on an adversary rendered helpless in the duel.

The duke's steep decline in health at sixty-nine, like that of Charles VII before him, at an age something short of sixty, cannot, however, be attributed to corrupt heredity and a poor constitution. His physical energy, like that of his father John the Fearless, remained exceptional for most of his life. But on this very account it wore him out, at his desk and in councils and campaigns as in repetitive bouts of copulation, by his middle sixties. After discovering the treachery of the Croys he wearily left to his only too strenuous son the future conduct of the difficult situation that had arisen on the proclamation of the League of Public Weal. It was then that the count of Charolais, exuberantly throwing off the leash on which his father had so long held him, joined the duke of Bourbon in organizing preparations for the imminent armed insurrection of the League against the king of France.

The adherence of Burgundy to the princes was a serious matter for Louis. Everyone knew how rich the duchy had long been. Philippe de Commines wrote of this period:

> The subjects of the house of Burgundy then possessed great wealth on account of the long peace they had enjoyed and the generosity (*bonté*) of the prince [i.e. Philip] who controlled them. For he taxed them very lightly. In my opinion his domains at that time could be better described as Promised Lands than those of any other in the world. For they were overflowing with riches and entirely at ease . . . both men and women spent a great deal on superfluous clothing. Their meals and banquets were on a scale and of a prodigality which I have never seen equaled anywhere else. Their bathing parties and other festivities, in which women took part, were attended by great numbers of persons who behaved in disorderly fashion, with little regard to decency . . . in short the subjects of that house, during these years, considered no prince their compeer.

Duke Jean II of Bourbon, a handsome and bold officer, whose eloquent tongue made him a special favorite with ladies, though he was less successful in battle than in diplomacy, set off at once to invade his own titular province, Bourbonnais, by way of Berry. Meanwhile Charolais appeared before Paris. But the capital, he found, had changed its mind about the sovereign who had more than once ridden rough-shod over it. The university, the clerical establishment and the legis-lators in the Parlement had come to recognize in their king, despite his rude language on occasion and restless pursuit of their pockets, a set of brains at least equal to their own. Moreover, Parisians in general were determined never again to undergo the awful experience of oc-cupation by foreign troops. It was in vain that the enterprising count somewhat disingenuously proclaimed that he had not encamped under their walls with a view to making war upon the French throne but only in order to rescue its subjects from the penury to which its money-grubbing policy had degraded them. The walls of Paris retorted to these blandishments with a bristling array of archers and gunners. The count retired out of range to the suburb of St. Denis and called for a conference with Duke Francis of Brittany, who had set up his tents on the other side of the river, at St. Cloud.

Louis, much relieved at the firm attitude of his capital, turned his attention to Bourbon. The king, with the aid of some Milanese de-tachments he had hired, better artillerymen at this date than the French, captured some of the Bourbonnais castles which were being held for the duke. But he realized that the final issue of the war could only be decided in or near Paris. Marching north again, he found Charolais waiting for him at Longjumeau, due south of the capital. The two forces clashed on July 16, 1465, at Montlhéry, a little to the east.

Commines writes: "The King's men were posted at the castle of Montlhéry behind a great hedge and ditch. Beyond them stretched fields of corn, beans and other plants, good agricultural land."

The Burgundians, in high spirits inspired both by liberal supplies of wine and the impetuous confidence of their young commander, charged at once. For the moment they outnumbered the royal vanguard under that experienced and steady fighter Pierre de Brézé, long since recognized by Louis as absolutely loyal to the Valois dynasty whoever represented it. De Brézé let the Burgundian cavalry break the line of its own advancing archers, thereby losing the successful initiative provided by that arm. He continued to retreat until the main body led by the king himself came up with the van. These fresh troops met the recklessly galloping Burgundian horse head-on, in overwhelm-ing force. The broken squadrons wheeled in all directions, making for the cover of the woods on either side of the open fields.

But they were not accompanied by the count, who had ridden far ahead of the rest. As soon as he heard the news of their rout he came thundering back with a few companions. According to Commines, who was present, "the ground was trampled flat where the corn had been standing only half an hour before. The whole field was strewn with dead men and horses." But before Charolais could reach the trees to rally his cavalry his group encountered a detachment of the royal men-at-arms. One of them cut down his squire. Another slashed him in the throat, left bare, Commines reports, by the fall of the chinpiece, which had been too hastily adjusted that morning. Several of the royalists laid hands on the count, one of them calling out: "My lord, you must yield, I know you, don't let yourself be killed!" He had earlier been wounded in the stomach by a sword thrust. But he fought on so fiercely that a giant of a man, named Jean Cadet, son of a Paris physician but on the Burgundian side and mounted on a mighty charger was able to ride into the melee and disperse the assailants. As they withdrew, the little Burgundian party broke away into the forest and reorganized the rest of the count's troops. The hand-to-hand fighting almost ceased for a while, as the guns on each side came into play.

Pierre de Brézé had fallen in the moment of victory, receiving a fatal wound during the first royalist counterattack which had scattered the rebel horsemen. Louis took charge. At the head of his men he drove back an attempt by the rallied Burgundians to reverse the situation. But by now night was falling. Under cover of darkness the king retreated eastward to Corbeil, leaving Charolais, who naturally thought he had won the battle, to bivouac on the field, ready to renew at daybreak the assault on the village of Montlhéry, where he believed Louis to be.

Commines recorded: "Monseigneur de Charolais remained on the ground very joyous, supposing the glory to be all his own. But this belief afterwards cost him very dear. For thenceforward he never took counsel of any man, but acted only on his own judgment. Whereas before that day he had been unserviceable (*très inutile*) in war and took no interest in any military matters, he later changed his mind for the rest of his life."

The great historian, writing long after he had come to despise the count, appears less than accurate about him in this passage as in certain others. For evidence elsewhere concerning the character of Charolais unanimously affirms his delight in the old epics of knightly prowess. It is on record, furthermore, that Duke Philip of Burgundy once restrained his son's savage impetuosity at the storming of a rebellious Flemish city. Moreover, Commines himself maliciously relates how the duke's heir was overthrown in the lists, as a youth in Paris, by a gigantic opponent put up to the job as a joke, so the story goes, by Louis himself. But perhaps this usually careful author's language may be taken in both passages merely to indicate the young count's impatience with the technical side of warfare, not any positive disinclination for its rough-and-tumble aspect.

The battle of Montlhéry had gone on in a most confused fashion for about eight hours, while deserters fled on both sides. After sunset it was hard to guess which army could fairly claim to have gained the victory. In the light of the bonfires burning on the hills overlooking the village the king's scouts could see, only about three bowshots off, the Burgundian men-at-arms sleeping round their convoys. Charolais, weakened by his wounds, but indomitable, had ordered, from his straw mattress, a resumption of the attack at dawn. But Louis considered that he had done enough to show the count that the rebels could expect no easy triumph. The loyal forces were commanded to retreat a few miles to the east and south. They encamped at Corbeil, where the ground appeared more favorable to a defensive encounter.

When day broke they seemed to have vanished. The Burgundians were jubilant, believing that the king had simply run. They sent confident dispatches in this sense to Charles of France, Francis of Brittany and the other insurgent nobles. But Louis at the same time issued his own account of the action, declaring that his old friend the reckless count of Charolais had thrice taken to his heels during the battle and that his losses were far in excess of those of the royal army, which had held its positions until sunset and was now, on the seventeenth, in full marching order on the road to Paris.

The king in fact entered the capital on that day, before Charolais could reach it. The count, furious at having been outwitted in this way, while his own men celebrated their apparent triumph, dashed up to the very walls of the city and tried to rush the gates. But the garrison, inspired by their monarch's presence, flung back the storming parties again and again. All the same, the parliament, which shared to the full Louis's distrust of the incalculable risks of war, pressed the king to negotiate. He was not unwilling to do so, much preferring such maneuvers to the clash of arms, but felt he must have stronger cards to play than his present army, depleted by the casualties and desertions at Montlhéry, could afford him. It was decided eventually to keep the besiegers guessing while he himself went off to raise an adequate relief force in Normandy.

He returned in a remarkably short time with some two thousand men, finding to his further encouragement that meanwhile eight hundred Milanese lances had made their way into the city. He was only just in time, however. Rouen fell to the rebels a few days later, sealing off Normandy from any more royalist recruiting. The opposing armies by then faced each other across the Seine, based on lines extending from Charenton, where Louis set up his headquarters, to the Hôtel de Conflans, where Charolais had recovered sufficiently from his wounds to stagger downstairs to the cellar when a cannon ball flew past his ears as he sat at table.

But artillery fire did very little serious damage to the Burgundians. They soon decided, with characteristic daring, to cross the river on a bridge of boats. But the king, on getting wind of this dangerous plan, fired his tents and withdrew his guns during the night, deliberately making a good deal of noise over this operation. His object, as often in his military tactics, was to suggest to the enemy that he was ready for a conference and at the same time, if necessary, to lead them into a trap. Yet he still could not bring himself to trust the Parisians, for all their obvious determination to defend their city against his antagonists. The garrison might decline to sally when he retreated. Or it might actually attack his rear if the count really crossed the river.

Fortunately Charolais, barely able as yet to stand up, and disappointed both by Brittany's feebleness as a commander and the unexpected hostility of Paris, immediately responded to his adversary's feint of retirement by sending single agents over to the royalist headquarters. They passed the king's spies going the other way. Both sides were getting nervous. One night some unknown citizens treacherously unlocked a gate of the Bastille. Later the Burgundians opened fire in the dark on what they thought was an advancing detachment of the enemy revealed by the flash of a big cannon. But this bristling and apparently moving block turned out to be merely a field of thistles.

At last Louis, sick of the uncertainty, coolly had himself rowed across the Seine and escorted by a few attendants into the opposing camp. Demanding to see the count of Charolais, as soon as he came face to face with his former hunting crony he risked a direct question, with his customary equivocal leer on view. "My friend, will you grant me safe-conduct?" The chivalrous Burgundian could not resist this calm courage. He answered impulsively but in an equally tranquil tone: "Ay, my lord." "I was sure of that," replied the king instantly. "For I know you to be a nobleman of France." This phrase, as so often with Louis, had a double meaning. It not only complimented the count on his knightly honor but also recalled to him his formal status as a vassal of the French crown.

The monarch went on to remind Charolais, as if they had met peacefully, by chance, of the details of their previous intimacy in

the woods and fields of Brabant. The quiet smile never left the
king's prematurely worn features. But the other, frowning, interrupted
him to retort sternly that Burgundy must be guaranteed the possession
of Picardy and the province of Normandy recently conquered by the
League before he would order a cease-fire. Louis continued to smile.
But he shook his close-cropped head quite definitely. "I will make
you Constable of Saint-Pol in the Pas-de-Calais, Charles," he told
the tall, scowling duke. "But your other conditions are out of the
question." The count threw up his chin, giving his senior a grim
glance, enough to show that he would not yield. Then he assumed
a ceremonious posture. Bows were exchanged. The king returned to his
lines, not altogether ill-pleased. He felt now that he could afford to
wait.

In fact, a second meeting at Conflans, on the royal initiative, was
soon arranged. This time Charolais proved more tractable. He laughed
a little at his sovereign's jokes and looked at him with something like
the old affection. No one could hold out for long against the positively
boyish charm Louis could exercise if he cared to do so, which was quite
often, even on the most serious occasions. He was fond of relaxing
tension in this way when tempers were rising. He knew that such
behavior, coming from a feared source, would often restore an adversary's confidence in the good faith of a ruler with a "terrible"
reputation, so described by the Milanese ambassador to his master, for
getting what he wanted.

It was really the Burgundian, with his heavily molded, dark features
and burning eyes, and his mad fury in battle, who better deserved the
Italian's epithet. But now the count actually unbent so far as to go for
a stroll with his unpretentious, if exalted, visitor. As the two former
friends and present enemies, the tall and the short, walked slowly on
together, without the count taking much notice of the way they were
going, since he was doing most of the talking, the king made an
interesting discovery. He gathered from Charolais's not overly discreet
complaints of the situation that the besiegers of Paris were running out
of victuals and funds, with both of which the garrison was amply
supplied, and also that some of the League's noble supporters were
quietly deserting its cause or else doing little but sleep in the camp.

Then suddenly the pair, with its handful of attendants, was challenged
by royalist troops entrenched on the paris road. Louis made himself
known. Weapons were lowered, to the accompaniment of a gruff but
obviously sincere outburst of cheering. The Burgundian leader, an
expert now at military inspections, noted the well-fed appearance and
good humor of the French soldiers. The king called for an escort to
take the count back to Conflans. It was provided at once. This exhibi-

tion of respect for the laws of war, at a juncture when Louis might easily have seized the person of his most dangerous opponent, alone and unprotected at a considerable distance from his camp, caused a good deal of admiring comment in both armies.

Eventually, at the Parisian suburb of Vincennes, in October, a treaty was signed. Charles of France did homage to the king for Normandy, Charolais for Picardy. The count of Saint-Pol, Louis of Luxembourg, who had led the vanguard of the rebel forces, was appointed Constable and took the oath of allegiance to the throne. Dunois and Antoine de Chabannes were reinstated in the royal Service. The Burgundians and Bretons were admitted to Paris, where they could eat their fill, but only after being disarmed and swearing solemnly to behave themselves. The duke of Brittany was allowed to win his case against the bishop of Nantes and to coin his own currency. René's son Jean, duke of Calabria, who was now governing Lorraine on his father's behalf, was relieved of the formality of homage for that duchy. For Louis intended to employ Jean as a commander in Spain against Juan II of Aragon and therefore required the Lorrainer's good will.

On the whole the princes of the blood could feel that they had done better by taking advantage of their sovereign's pacificism than if they had fought him to the end. In that case they would probably, in their disunion, have been defeated and made to suffer the vengeance of a conqueror. Louis was temperamentally averse to aiming at such a result. He knew that the pride and obstinacy of his nobles, since he could hardly exterminate them all, would return to the charge, after discomfiture in the field, so long as he lived. He had already lived long enough, in the midst of turmoil in which no single chief could trust any other, to realize that mercy would be more likely to reduce them to obedience than mere slaughter. He considered himself intellectually superior to any French or Burgundian aristocrat and looked forward to proving it, over however prolonged a period, at conferences rather than in campaigns.

He had perhaps, at the council table of Vincennes, deliberately permitted the first round to go to the princes, forcing them only to make formal declarations of their status as vassals. But he was still not sure of any of them, of the turbulent Charolais least of all. At the monarch's own request he and the count rode back together to Flanders. But both men, as they approached Picardy, remained much more on their guard than they had been on their recent walk from Conflans. Then the king had made airy promises he never intended to keep and the Burgundian had talked, with tempestuous irritation, of his own increasingly perilous embarrassments. Now Louis, though genial, said very little, contrary to his usual custom on a journey. His equally circumspect companion, when they halted for the night, slept in full armor, closely surrounded by his retainers, themselves under vigilant supervision by the royal escort. By the Treaty of Vincennes the province of Picardy had been made a feudal appanage of the crown again. But when the party reached Amiens the king, with superb tact, indicated his wish for the citizens to render homage to Charolais. He did the same in all the other towns of the Somme valley. Clearly, the performance of this polite gesture, which committed him to nothing, had been the main object of his ride north with the count.

He could, after all, be justified in muttering to himself his favorite motto, *sapiens nihil invitus facit*, "The wise man never does anything contrary to his will." The precious League of Public Weal was smashed. It had not been crushed at Montlhéry, but in negotiations at the siege of Paris. The royal army remained very nearly intact and by this time quite devoted to his interests, after the personal audacity and skill he had displayed in the recent battle and the chivalry he had extended at the roadblock before Paris to an equally brave enemy. He remarked to a trusted agent, not wholly in jest, that a rainstorm had rattled the windows of the council chamber at Vincennes while the treaty was being debated. "But do you not remember," he added dryly, with his characteristic sly twinkle, "that as soon as all the papers were signed the wind dropped and the sun shone?"

The secretly complacent monarch watched with grim amusement his nincompoop of a brother, Charles of France, quarreling with the duke of Brittany, as might have been expected, over their respective shares in the royal magnanimity. He saw that Francis would eventually win this dispute and planned, by making certain agreements with him, to recover full possession of Normandy for himself. When the clumsily petulant boy, as his elder brother had guessed he might, turned from Brittany to Burgundy and went off to aid the always difficult citizens of Liége in a revolt they had staged against Philip's authority, the king openly paid a state visit to the Burgundian camp and made much of Charolais, who was in charge of it. A marriage between the count, whose wife Isabelle of Bourbon had died in September, and Louis's legitimate eldest daughter Anne, aged four, was there and then announced. It was perfectly obvious that the ruler of France meant by these proceedings to check any idea of subversion that might remain in the muddled mind of the former nominal head of the defunct League. For the sovereign was closely identifying himself with that very duchy of Burgundy, far more powerful than Prince Charles, which the king intended sooner or later to bring permanently within his direct control. He had already begun this plan by sending secret agents to Liége to encourage the town's hostility to Burgundian rule.

Meanwhile, on November 25, 1465, the young prince, fresh from his diplomatic defeat by Francis, had been seized by certain Normans who complained that he had fallen too far under Breton influence. They carried their prisoner off to Rouen. Louis immediately perceived his opportunity. On the pretext of rescuing his brother he entered Normandy in arms. Within two months, while the duke of Brittany, by agreement with the king, lay low, the latter had resumed his own full authority in the province. He appointed Charles, by way of compensation, governor of Roussillon at the other end of the kingdom. In this remote territory, recently acquired by Louis from the king of Aragon, as mentioned above, the boy would be unlikely, it seemed, to cause any further trouble.

CHAPTER IX

Duke Charles the Bold
(1466–1475)

❧❧❧ The monarch now felt himself secure in the west and center. He turned east, to deal with the practically independent province of Lorraine. The king was relying to a great extent on his Milanese ally. That duchy, now ruled by Galeazzo Maria Sforza whose father Francesco had died on March 8, 1466, had recently developed new methods of warfare. If Louis could take Metz with the latest Italian siege artillery he might even go on to break into the Rhineland, pacifically or otherwise, and establish a fresh front in the Burgundian rear. The count of Charolais, however, might object to this move. The king resolved to ensure, by one means or another, that he did not do so.

In June 1467 Philip's heir was besieging Liége when a dispatch rider arrived at his camp with news of his father's death from apoplexy at the age of seventy-one. The "good" duke had been senile for at least two years, playing with old sword blades and fragments of stained glass in a little room more like a nursery than the bedchamber of a powerful ruler. It was long since his splendid presence, exquisite courtesy and jovial manners, coupled with the most industrious promotion of the interests of his subjects, had earned him the title by which he is known to history. In those days his virtues included a talent for business which enabled him to accumulate an immense fortune and keep most of it out of the grasp of his innumerable mistresses.

A magnificent funeral was staged at Bruges. The fiery new duke, who had already acquired a popular title, that of Charles the Bold, duly attended the ceremony. But he soon rushed back to his lines before Liége. The progress of the investment was being held up by certain administrative difficulties concerned with the privileges claimed by the Flemish cities of Ghent and Malines. Charles was also in the thick of negotiations with London for the hand of King Edward's sister, the beautiful and accomplished Margaret of York. Louis's daughter, the five-year-old Anne, no longer interested him. He had no intention of going under to France through matrimony, but rather to bolster up his duchy by an alliance with France's hereditary foe, England, led by a mighty young warrior like himself. The rumors that Margaret, like her brother, seemed unduly fond of the opposite sex did not worry the far from amorous duke, who was pretty sure he could handle women in their courts of love as well as he could handle men in the field.

Louis naturally resented this scheme. It gave him a good excuse to remind the "Bold" Charles that he was only a duke, not a king. The French monarch, too, sent envoys to Edward, indicating a fellow sovereign's surprise at the Burgundian's presumptuous behavior in this affair. The French ruler was counting on the influence of Edward's cousin, the formidable earl of Warwick, victor in many a battle on land and sea, whom he had recently been strenuously cultivating at Rouen. But Warwick was not now in such high favor, at London and Windsor, as he had been. King Edward had been married since 1464 to Elizabeth Woodville, an irresistible but haughty and ambitious widow some five years older than himself. The eldest daughter of Lord Rivers, who had married the second wife of the late duke of Bedford, Elizabeth had innumerable relatives who were undermining Warwick's policy of friendship with France rather than Burgundy.

Louis offered, as the price of Edward's support against Charles, four thousand marks a year for four years, the re-establishment of free trade between England and Burgundy and, most tempting of all, a papal decision on the question of English claims to Normandy and the region of Aquitaine, i.e. the whole of western France excluding Brittany, that duchy being already strongly pro-English. But Edward's new advisers told him the cunning French king did not mean a word of all this. On July 15, 1467, Charles and England signed a treaty of alliance, the duke's marriage to Margaret of York was arranged, the Burgundian ban on exports to England was lifted and Warwick went off in sullen silence to Yorkshire, while Juan II of Aragon sought English help to enable him to resist Jean of Calabria's campaign in Catalonia on behalf of his father René. All the same, Louis, with his back now to the wall, extorted a six months' truce from Charles.

The king of France had been able to gain the favor of Pope Paul II by agreeing to exclude French clerics from entering upon French benefices unless recommended by the Vatican. He had also been very busy during this period with the further regulation of the national coinage and another great step forward in stable government through a decree, which became law on October 21, 1467, permitting all royal officials to hold their appointments for life. This confident measure proves that the eternally vigilant sovereign felt by this time that he could rely on the best brains and steadiest hearts which had so far rendered him service.

Yet all was still not well with his beloved kingdom. The Bretons were again invading Normandy, no doubt secretly supported by the English. Duke Charles of Burgundy remained inexorably at the gates of Liége, which had been promised assistance by Louis, who felt that he could hardly avoid open war with Burgundy in the near future, since every attempt at diplomacy had failed. He bought more guns from Italy and drew up stern regulations to make his army the best disciplined, and therefore the likeliest to achieve victory, in Europe. The soldiers were never to be billeted on any householder who did not want them. They must pay the market price for everything except straw, wood and accommodation. All of these items, however, were to be supplied only by their host. But he would never be troubled by their presence for more than one night while on the march, except on Sundays and feast days. The men were to go to inns, whenever possible, rather than private houses, and were not to requisition draft animals. All captains of companies must take the following oath: "I swear before God and Our Lady, who will turn all my affairs to nought unless I keep my word, that I will do justice and see it done by all over whom I exercise authority, that I will allow no plundering and will punish all in my charge whom I may find guilty of it, sparing none."

These rules, unprecedented for their day, astonished old-fashioned military men. But commanders all over the Continent soon began to adopt them. For it was found that in war, just as in other games, the tournament and the chase for instance, a loose rein on greed and ferocity paid fewer dividends than a calmly rational approach to the hazards of conflict. The ideals of chivalry, formerly applicable to the upper classes only, were made incumbent upon the ordinary fighting man once the foe was beaten or when he was dealing with helpless civilians, who for the most part were neutral in the squabbles between the opposing forces of their betters. Before Louis's day, battles had repeatedly been lost by knights eager for loot who butchered fugitive infantrymen in a headlong pursuit to the enemy's camp, while their colleagues were being rounded up and slaughtered elsewhere. Such knights themselves were often caught as they returned or were trapped among baggage wagons, women and wine casks.

Louis hated the sounds of clashing blades, whistling arrows and thundering cannon. He knew that they settled nothing and left behind implacable bitterness, the seeds of more useless conflict, as well as impoverishment, famine and the decay of civilized institutions. Yet up to now he had spent almost as much time riding among armed men as poring over documents. He is certain to have hoped that in future men more like himself, cautious and dexterous, even fraudulent if necessary, would come to rule the world. For he clearly thought it better to deceive others for the ultimate good of a peaceful majority of mankind, naturally devoted to the happiness which comes only from commercial prosperity, than simply to cut their throats and take possession of their wealth in a sea of blood. His character would allow him no different solution to the problem of government. The legend of his merciless cruelty is built partly upon a few outstanding cases of the terrible severity with which he punished traitors to his elaborately conceived plans for a just order in France and partly upon the dislike always felt by clever, warmhearted men for an intellectual superior they cannot outwit or confute. Such men interpret a contempt for individuals as a general frigidity excluding even that selfless, abstract dedication to an ideal, for example patriotism, that was the king's deepest instinct.

Louis's greatest misfortune was that he had no aptitude whatever for making any real friends. More than one man and woman fell into lifelong melancholy, which sometimes proved fatal, on hearing of the death of an equally ugly, ingenious and visionary statesman, Louis's later contemporary Lorenzo de' Medici. For Lorenzo could love as well as inspire love. Neither of these capacities were inherent in the character of the French sovereign.

Just before his failure to prevent agreement between Charles of Burgundy and Edward of England, the king of France, in June 1467, had sent two ambassadors, the slippery count of Saint-Pol, Constable of France, and Cardinal Jean Balue, to the duke's camp before Liége. The envoys were charged to beg the Burgundian to be reasonable in the extremely delicate situation confronting France. The prelate, a Poitevin of humble origin but terrifying efficiency in political plotting, had been promoted by Louis to the bishopric of Évreux and by Paul II to a cardinalate for his services in representing to the king the advantages of abandoning the Pragmatic Sanction. Doubtless Paul neither knew nor cared what arguments Balue had used. The pope was concerned solely with the religious issue. But the bishop, a practical French administrator, had long recognized that his career depended on pleasing Louis and knew that the monarch wished above all things to weaken or at least neutralize Charles. The ambassador's task at Liége would therefore be primarily to warn the Burgundian that Rome stood behind Paris and could guarantee that the king would carry out his promises. Balue would not add, naturally, that Louis could as easily quarrel with Paul as conciliate him if the pope proved too generous to Burgundy.

But that contingency was unlikely in view of the sovereign's recent concessions to the Holy See.

Nevertheless Balue, for all his wit, did not succeed in persuading the stubborn duke to leave France a free hand in Brittany in return for the abandonment of French aid to Liége. The discomfited envoys had scarcely departed before Charles delivered an irresistible attack on the fortifications, stormed into the town, razed the walls to the ground and almost ruined the citizens by his extortions.

The July treaty with Edward followed. Louis could only sound Warwick and Margaret of Anjou, who was now back at the court of her father René in Lorraine, on the possibilities of dethroning the nonchalant English ruler. He was already losing his popularity on account of the shameless intrigues of his wife's family. No one seemed to like any of her swarms of relatives and favorites. But Warwick would not commit himself and Margaret could not move without him. Louis was interested to hear that King Edward, in his usual bluff style, had remarked in private that he thought the French king's young brother Charles a perfect fool and Louis himself more than a match for all the lords of his kingdom put together. Yet almost by the same post came news that English money and volunteers were supporting preparations for revolt in Brittany.

Edward and Warwick at last met at Coventry in January 1468. But the earl would not renounce the opposition of his party to the Burgundian marriage. His sovereign, on the other hand, remained intent upon it. The king's object appeared to be a recovery of his personal prestige by a successful invasion of France, backed by the dukes of Burgundy and Brittany. The English masses, burning to avenge their expulsion from the Continent in 1453, could be relied on to supply the necessary funds and soldiers. In February the treaty of the previous year was ratified in Brussels. The king of England received the Golden Fleece from Charles the Bold, and announced openly that he meant to recapture by force the patrimony of his ancestors, won on the fields of Crécy, Poitiers and Agincourt. Louis tried in vain to raise an insurrection in Wales. Margaret of Anjou worked tirelessly to revive Lancastrian sentiment in the northern counties and spurred Warwick to action on the king's brother, the duke of Clarence, the idea being to marry this somewhat unsatisfactory personage, who did not get on with Edward, to Warwick's daughter Isabel.

Margaret of York landed at Sluis on June 25, 1468. Her beauty and gaiety, just like her brother's, made a great impression on everyone, including the not very susceptible bridegroom. In the midst of the ensuing gorgeous wedding festivities Charles the Bold received word that his "good cousin," King Louis, had lost patience at last and was advancing in all the panoply of war upon Brittany. The king's generals took town after town both in that duchy and in Normandy, wherever the garrisons were under Breton control. Nothing could resist the new royal artillery. Francis called desperately on Charles of Burgundy for help. The latter, after a vain protest against the breaking of the truce by France, moved on Péronne in Picardy, near Amiens, apparently with a view to confronting Louis in Brittany itself.

The king, however, was just then not there but at Compiègne, not far from Amiens to the southeast, as Charles may have known. At Péronne Cardinal Balue turned up again. He told the Burgundian that Louis, in conformity with his "friend's" wishes, had already concluded peace with the duke of Brittany, through the good offices of the duke of Berry, i.e. the king's own brother, Charles of France, and the duke of Calabria, René's son and therefore the brother of Margaret of Anjou, Edward's most deadly foe. This news cannot have been very palatable to Charles the Bold. But probably he discounted the truth of it, distrusting the cardinal as a mere agent of Louis, which indeed he was. Nevertheless, Charles received the astute prelate politely, assuring him that he had no quarrel with his sovereign but only desired to assist his sworn allies in Brittany and Normandy.

Then, suddenly, the wind was taken out of his sails by the arrival of a Breton herald with the formal announcement of the treaty mentioned by Balue, which involved renunciation of the alliance of Francis with Burgundy.

Charles realized that the wily French monarch had tricked him by keeping the situation fluid until the abject Breton duke surrendered of his own accord. But the Burgundian, much to his credit, concealed his anger and changed the subject to the question of Liége. He said the town seemed about to rebel again and demanded to know how Louis proposed to act in these circumstances. The matter, he added, could be discussed at Péronne between the king and himself, if the monarch should care to look in on the ducal quarters, where he would be assured of a warm welcome. To show that he meant what he said, Charles then handed the cardinal a safe-conduct for Louis, to be used on such a visit, which might be disputed by honest authorities necessarily kept in ignorance of its true purpose, the maintenance of a secure basis for the prolongation of the truce.

The king of France, having eliminated Brittany from the ranks of his enemies, now felt himself in a much stronger position. With a victorious army behind him, he boldly declared to all and sundry that he favored the claims of Margaret of Anjou and Henry VI to the throne of England, implying, though not of course stating, that he was not in the least afraid of either Edward or his new brother-in-law, the duke of Burgundy.

A few days later he duly thanked the latter for his kind invitation and early in October, accompanied by a small escort of about fifty lances, on this occasion probably some three hundred men, rode across the plain from Compiègne to Péronne, where he submitted his sacred person to the duke. This was a mistake. Louis was gambling on both his own personal powers of fascination, so often tested, and on Charles's old-fashioned notions of chivalrous honor between combatants, especially if one of them were the feudal superior of the other. But the king did not allow for the Burgundian's passionate resolution to preserve freedom of action in his northern dominions. That object was rapidly modernizing his views of permissible diplomacy. It is certain that the duke meant to enforce his sovereign's acquiescence in another rape of Liége. But just how far he intended, at this stage, to go in that direction, remains doubtful.

In any case Charles greeted the royal party, which included the duke of Bourbon and the count of Saint-Pol, with his usual lavish hospitality. But it was a meeting once more, remarks a modern French historian, of fox and wolf. The latter began by apologizing for not being able to offer his guest, in this little provincial town, better accommodations than the comfortable but easily assailable house of the local tax collector. The castle, said Charles, was ruinous and scarcely habitable by such distinguished visitors. But Louis, looking out of the window, noticed, with his first touch of uneasiness, that Burgundian reinforcements seemed to be pouring into Péronne. The old castle, he had also perceived, possessed four strong-looking towers, whatever the foundations might be like. He therefore smilingly replied to the duke, as though expressing a pardonable caprice, that he preferred the more majestic building. The Burgundian agreed with suspicious eagerness, masked as deference. For one of the towers at least, he knew, though this idea had not yet occurred to the monarch, would be as difficult to get out of as to get into.

Then developments began to move faster than either Charles or the king expected. In Liége a fresh rebellion had in fact already broken out. The citizens were waving the white banner of the royalists and cheering for Louis. They had murdered some of the staff of their bishop, a kinsman and personal friend of the duke himself. The latter, beside himself with fury at this sudden outbreak, which he attributed to his guest's underground machinations, accused the king to his face of deliberately deceiving him. Raging like a madman, he declared martial law in Péronne and locked up his sovereign in the castle under a guard which proved inaccessible to bribes.

Louis, like most intellectuals, had underestimated his opponent's recklessness. In something like panic the king realized that his life might be in danger. If he, the cleverest of men, should fall like a fool or a scoundrel to an assassin's dagger, all the careful work of the last seven years would be undone. It was true that he had secretly encouraged the men of Liége to prepare resistance to their overlord. But a revolt at this particular moment was the last thing the monarch wanted. It would be nearly as ruinous to his cause, he believed, once more cursing the detestable violence of people incapable of listening to reason, as his own death. He had read that King Charles the Simple of France had been murdered at Péronne in the tenth century by a Burgundian count in somewhat similar circumstances. Such a crime must not be allowed to happen again. For if it did, the Burgundians, the Bretons and the English would all fall upon his kingdom at once and reduce it for the second time to a smoking, bloodstained wilderness. He tried in vain to get a message through to the exasperated duke. The archers on guard would neither hear what he had to say nor admit a single neutral or friendly human being to his presence.

At last a serious young man, the duke's chamberlain and greatly respected by him, Philippe de Commines (or Commynes, as he always spelled his name), succeeded in appeasing his master's wild resentment to the point of allowing the king a few visitors. They carried back promises from the captive of compensation to Charles for the action taken at Liége, which the monarch declared, probably rightly so far as its timing was concerned, could not be proved his doing. He added that if the duke would allow him to return to Compiègne, where his personal papers were stored, and take the matter up with Liége on the basis they provided, he was sure he could settle the affair to the satisfaction of all concerned. Meanwhile he would order the duke of Bourbon, that duke's brother, the cardinal archbishop of Lyons, who had also accompanied the French escort, and the Constable of France himself, Saint-Pol, to remain at Péronne as hostages during their sovereign's absence. All the visitors were told confidentially that large rewards would be collected by anyone who arranged in any other way the royal prisoner's release. Louis was obviously prepared to make any sacrifice to escape from his disgraceful and perilous confinement.

For some days he heard nothing favorable from Charles or anyone else. The duke of Burgundy continued to pace to and fro in his quarters, grinding his teeth and cursing both those of his councilors who advised that the king should be set at liberty and those who considered that he should be kept under lock and key along with his much more malleable brother, the duke of Berry, sent for to take over business with which his elder could not be trusted. For a while the

Burgundian, if his violent language could be taken literally, even seemed to contemplate not only war to the knife with France but actually the assassination of that country's titular head. These agonies of indecision caused Charles, on the third night of Louis's captivity, to throw himself again and again on his bed, without undressing, and then to leap up, seize his nearest companion by the shoulder and rush the startled man up and down the room while further frantic fulminations issued from his master's lips.

Commines, when it came to his turn to receive these fierce objurgations, did not lose his equanimity. He suggested a number of conditions upon which the duke might reasonably and with honor agree to let the king go. It is probable that the prudent chamberlain had already obtained the prisoner's acceptance of the chief of these terms, which included not only a solemn oath to refrain for the future from intriguing with rebels against Burgundy in Flanders or anywhere else but also compliance with a ducal request of more uncompromising severity. Louis must accompany Charles, Commines calmly suggested, to Liége and supervise the vengeance to be taken, nominally by the outraged bishop, on the town. The chamberlain said he was pretty sure the monarch would make no bones about agreeing to this action, once it was made clear to him that he had no other choice if he were to procure release from the castle.

Charles seemed greatly struck with the idea, which held out prospects of humiliating a man he now detested as a subtle and dishonorable quill driver who had cheated him with fine words instead of meeting him face to face in outright battle, as once at Montlhéry. The duke announced, to the amazement of all his councilors except, perhaps, Commines, who was the shrewdest of them, that he would take these intimidating demands to the prisoner himself.

But in the king's presence rage overwhelmed him again. At first he could hardly speak. Then suddenly the words came roaring from his lips in a terrifying flood. He stormed at his sovereign in the manner of a brutal headmaster trouncing a pupil. When he paused for breath Louis indicated in a tone which could not have been more submissive that he would be ready to do anything his "cousin" wanted. The latter, secretly astonished at this pusillanimity in an adversary he knew to be courageous, gradually calmed down. He produced a document prepared by Commines, embodying the terms proposed in detail. The king signed it immediately, swearing on the Burgundian's most revered treasure, a cross said to have been worn by Charlemagne, that he would comply with every one of the conditions listed in the paper. The date was October 14, 1468.

Still more parchments were presented to him. He scribbed LOYS on them all, even on that which required the suspension for eight years of the right of the Paris Parlement to determine the boundaries of Flanders. He thus rendered that region practically independent for the time specified. He signed amnesties for all the duke's leading allies and subordinates, a further decree exempting all Burgundians from military service in the defense of France, another recognizing the extent of jurisdiction claimed by Charles and his council, and still another acknowledging Burgundy's right to receive homage from certain vassals direct, without the royal assent. Finally he agreed formally to the marriage of the duke to Margaret of York, on the ground that the Burgundian ruler was now almost her equal in rank.

Next day he left with Charles for Liége. Once more the desperately resisting town was taken by assault. The king made no protest while the improvised defenses were battered down and the Burgundian men-at-arms forced the breaches. No quarter was given. For the duke had been enraged by a preliminary success on the part of the besieged, when a bold sally had destroyed a portion of his vanguard and come near to capturing both Louis and himself. But the citizens had neither walls nor fortified gates nor moats nor artillery. They could only fight hand to hand, to the death, or take refuge in the churches. Even there some of the fiercer soldiers followed them.

Charles himself rode into the streets, where a few groups of the inhabitants still maintained the unequal struggle. He compelled the king to ride at his elbow. Occasionally the sovereign was recognized and a defiant shout of "Vive le roi!" would go up from the doomed citizens. Many of them may have thought he was still on their side and had been taken prisoner in the battle. But the grave-faced monarch silenced these loyalists with a gesture.

When it became clear that opposition was practically at an end and the troops began to sack the ecclesiastical buildings, the duke wheeled his horse, drawing Louis after him, and made for the bishop's palace to take some refreshment. But when he reached the gates he still had to cut down, with his own hand, a survivor of the slaughter, on guard at the entrance.

The king had put up with all this merciless violence as if he had been a mere neutral onlooker. At supper he complimented Charles in formal terms on the successful outcome of the assault. He made no reference to the savagery with which the women and children who were left alive after the town had been set on fire were driven out to fend for themselves in what was then heavily wooded country south of the last houses, an area now known as the Belgian Ardennes. Then at last, after a final dispute over some further concessions, eventually withdrawn by the Burgundian, Duke Charles the Bold, sated with his terrible revenge for a fancied betrayal, allowed his humiliated sovereign to leave for Paris.

No one came out of this episode with any credit except the indomitable men of Liége, who had fought to the last in a hopeless position. The duke of Burgundy, in his sane moments a prince of some culture and, unlike his father, austere morality, detesting all forms of debauchery, had managed so far to be almost as popular with his subjects, especially the more martially minded, as Philip had been. But in his ungovernable fury at what he supposed to be cynical double-dealing by Louis he had behaved at Liége with no more restraint than a vindictive brigand.

As for the king, he had deliberately suppressed his native audacity and resourcefulness as soon as he found himself, so to speak, bound hand and foot with an enemy's dagger at his throat. He was the last man in the world to adopt a heroic attitude in such circumstances or even to try to talk himself out of a situation which his clear head told him might at any moment, whatever he did, crush him out of existence. He saw that his life, which he had calmly judged to be more valuable to France than that of anyone else concerned with the country, depended upon utter passivity. He therefore agreed to everything that was demanded of him, the more easily since he was confident of finding excuses to retract such promises later, and shut his eyes to the atrocious treatment of the daring citizens of Liége. He had certainly encouraged them to plot for their freedom. But they had ruined everything by being too precipitate, too sure that he would dash like lightning to their rescue the moment they chose to challenge Charles again.

That had been no part of his plan. It would have involved a continental war on a scale for which he was not yet ready. Burgundy and England in the north, possibly also the empire, with Aragon and Castile in the south, probably to be assisted by Armagnac, would have closed in upon the heart of France. In a struggle of such dimensions the fate of Liége would have assumed no more importance than that of Sarajevo in 1914. Louis's agents in the town had been simply part of a network he wished to establish for a Flemish revolt in the Burgundian rear if the duke should invade France. In October 1468 there was no immediate prospect of such an act.

From the king's point of view the men of Liége had not died in vain. They had rescued him as he would never have rescued them, except as an item in open warfare against Charles. The monarch was now for the first time implacably determined upon the duke's complete destruction as a factor in European politics. The Burgundian had committed high treason in laying hands upon his person. That was unforgivable, a crime that could only be punished by elimination. But

Louis, safe now in Paris, found the position still very dangerous. Edward was aiming at Guienne. Jean V, count of Armagnac, with Castile and Aragon behind him, was getting ready to rouse all southern France against the crown.

A royal army set out immediately, at full speed, for the southwest. Edward was diverted by the false rumor, started by the French king, that the fierce Margaret of Anjou was about to sail from Harfleur with a fleet destined to land invaders in England. Then Louis took over absolute charge of his nuisance of a younger brother, Charles, duke of Berry, titular chief of the late rebellion. He made this basically foolish and timid young man swear on the Holy Cross of St. Laud never to conspire against him again and to give up the idea, with which he had been toying, of marrying Duke Charles's only child Mary, aged eleven, the daughter of his deceased Duchess Isabel of Bourbon and heiress to the still mighty Burgundian power.

In compensation the king presented Berry with the appanage of Guienne, not only the late danger spot but also one as far as possible from the domains of the duke of Burgundy. Armagnac was no longer a threat to the throne's security. But young Charles of Berry was delighted with the honor of being entrusted with the defense of Guienne against Jean and also with his appointment as "first knight" of a new order, that of St. Michael, instituted by his brother as a counterblast to the Burgundian Golden Fleece. The full reconciliation between Louis and "Charles of France," as Berry was usually called, that of the most subtle statesman of his day and one of the most fatuous of royal princes, was eventually ratified at an interview on September 7, 1469. The settlement between them was generally regarded in France as little short of a miracle, certainly an astonishing magnanimity on the part of the sovereign.

But meanwhile he found that Charles the Bold had been moving toward an alliance with the empire, the ultimate objective of the inordinately ambitious duke being obviously, in the French king's view, investment with the imperial dignity itself, a prize of more prestige than of actual material power, the German princes being mostly poor and mutually quarrelsome, much despised by the more cultured Europeans, both French and Burgundian, west of the Rhine. Nevertheless, a Holy Roman emperor, if he chose, with Burgundian wealth to support him, might prove a real peril to the throne of France. Louis watched with uneasiness the three-cornered discussions at Ardres in Artois toward the end of April 1469 between the Austrian Count Sigismund of Tyrol, cousin of Emperor Frederick III, Duke Charles the Bold and the earl of Warwick. The subjects there investigated included the problem of a husband for Mary of Burgundy. The most favored candidate seemed to be the Archduke Maximilian, aged ten, the son of Frederick.

A more immediate danger, however, arose in England. There the duke's brother-in-law Edward IV had fitted out a fleet which was threatening Bordeaux and Bayonne. At the same time he talked openly of supporting a Burgundian bid for the French crown by an English invasion of its kingdom. Coastal raids, involving pillage, destruction and bloodshed, had already begun. But Edward, too, had his troubles. Warwick was now definitely acting against him on behalf of the party determined to get rid of the Woodvilles and their favorites. On July 16, 1469, the earl married his daughter, under the auspices of the archbishop of York, to the duke of Clarence in Calais. It looked as though he were planning to oust Edward in favor of his new son-in-law.

Louis considered Warwick by far the ablest of the chief figures in this situation. If the earl succeeded in expelling the fitfully bellicose Edward from the English throne and thus breaking down the strength of the Anglo-Burgundian alliance, that result would suit the French king's book. But it was hard to make out from the contradictory reports emanating from different parts of England what was really happening there.

Then at last hard news came. The English rebels had surprised Edward at Middleham in Yorkshire, captured the king and taken him to Warwick Castle. Lord Rivers, Elizabeth Woodville's father and many of the queen's faction had been executed. But almost at once London rose against Warwick and enforced the king's release. Again an English invasion of France seemed imminent. Louis hurriedly arranged an alliance with Castile to protect the southern half of his kingdom, for which Edward had always shown a preference, probably because Gascony still remained half English in sentiment. Then the French monarch hastened to meet the earl of Warwick, who had fled to Honfleur. The resourceful English peer, resilient as ever in defeat, declared that there was only one way to hold off the combined forces of Edward and Charles the Bold from their clearly contemplated attack on France. He himself, the earl, must come to an understanding with his old enemy, Margaret of Anjou, marry his youngest daughter Anne to her son and between them, with French help, restore Henry VI to the throne of England by force of arms, whereupon English policy would be reversed and Charles would never dare to assail two kings at once.

Louis was not so sure of the success of this plan. To his mind there were two obstacles to it, the now forty-year-old Margaret's uncompromising character and Henry's weakness. But the main point was to keep

England in a state of turmoil and therefore out of France. By the end of July 1470 he had with much difficulty persuaded the exiled queen to meet at Angers the man who had so steadfastly opposed her cause for the last fifteen years, shed the blood of so many of her subjects and allies in more than one fiercely contested battle and eventually expelled her and her husband from their rightful thrones. The earl immediately fell on his knees before her. At first she cursed him so loudly and bitterly that the king was obliged to exert his full royal authority in order to reduce her to silence while he explained that he would be prepared to pay Anne's dowry so that the Prince of Wales, after marrying her, could afford to maintain the troops necessary to enforce the succession of his parents to the English crown once more. Margaret's father René nervously announced his entire agreement with Louis's views, which had been expressed with the conciseness and tranquillity his "nephew" could always command.

The royal refugee, her sternly furrowed features, once the delight of the Angevin courtiers, set like stone, did not answer for a full quarter of an hour, while the mighty earl still knelt motionless, with bent head, at her feet. Then at last the queen pronounced through clenched teeth the ritual formula of forgiveness. A brief nod indicated that Warwick might rise. But she indignantly refused to allow the proposed marriage of her son and his daughter. Louis needed all his exceptional powers of argument to force her final acquiescence on condition that Prince Edward, then seventeen, acted as regent until he was of age and that thereafter his progeny should take precedence of that of the duke of Clarence and his duchess, Warwick's other daughter Isabel. Nevertheless, Margaret still would not trust either herself or the prince to Warwick and Clarence when this pair landed in Devon, with the Lancastrian earls of Pembroke and Oxford, from French ships in mid-September.

Before the month was over, King Edward, much to the wrath of Charles the Bold, had fled from London to The Hague. Warwick did homage to Henry in October. Charles, to prevent any move by the earl to attack Flanders on the pretext of recapturing the fugitive king, ceremoniously announced his pleasure at the restoration of Henry, his "kinsman," to the English throne. Louis, however, at once seized the opportunity to demand war on Flanders by Warwick, tempting the earl with the offer of Holland and Zeeland if he would align himself with the monarch who had rendered possible the recent triumph of the house of Lancaster. But the prudent English peer replied that the time was not yet ripe in England for military action, especially if the objective were known to be the Low Countries, the London merchants' best customers. He advised testing Charles's attitude to his guest and brother-in-law a little longer. If the duke should switch his power to Edward's side and attempt to finance his return there would be every excuse for an immediate counterstroke by England and France together.

But Louis would not wait. Alarmed by the news that Charles of Burgundy and Edward of England had met at Aire in Artois on January 2, 1471, he declared war on Charles forthwith and launched the Constable of France, Saint-Pol, into the town of Saint-Quentin on the river Aisne, hitherto held by the Burgundians. At the same time a ten years' truce was signed by representatives of the French and English governments, providing for favorable conditions of trade between the two countries. Louis had already staged in London an exhibition, in quite modern style, of French spices, cloth of gold, silks and linens, designed to replace those of Flanders, whence exports to England would now be blocked by his ships.

Meanwhile Charles the Bold, with equal energy, put heart into the discomfited Edward and lent him funds to enable him to reconquer his kingdom. The English monarch, after contact with the impressive personality of his host, had regained all his old courage and diplomatic skill. Though accompanied only by a small force when he landed near Hull in Yorkshire on March 14, his progress proved a triumph. With admirable discretion he at first would not claim his royal rank and professed loyalty to Henry. This modesty, coupled with the splendor of his presence and his easily accessible joviality, renewed his former popularity by leaps and bounds. The northern lords flocked to his standard as he marched south, making straight for London.

Warwick had collected troops to face him. But in the absence of Clarence, who remained inactive in the west, the earl did not venture to risk a pitched battle. When Edward's daily increasing forces reached Leicester, the opposition fell back to Coventry. Then at last the tall, handsome "duke of York" openly proclaimed himself king once more and with a characteristic display of old-fashioned gallantry challenged his "rebellious" peer to meet him in arms. Warwick's only reply to this gesture was to send desperate messages to London and Clarence to hurry to his rescue. But at the beginning of April he heard that the latter had joined Edward at Banbury. The brothers turned north. Edward again vainly called upon the earl to emerge from Coventry and stand the test of battle. But Warwick stayed grimly where he was, watching his chances of success dwindling day by day.

Louis had already, with his usual realism, perceived which way the wind was blowing. Charles, supported by a resuscitated Edward, was going to be too strong for him. He signed a truce with the duke of Burgundy as soon as he heard of Clarence's betrayal of the earl. Meanwhile the Yorkist king, turning his back contemptuously on

Coventry, marched at full speed on the capital. The London merchants, hoping to get their loans to him repaid and their trade with Burgundy resumed under his auspices, opened the gates. Edward entered the city in triumph, condescended to give his hand to the trembling Henry and endured impassively his defeated rival's obsequious embrace. Then he sent the Lancastrian to the Tower and turned to release his own imprisoned wife and children.

Only then did Warwick decide to play his last card and force an issue to the situation by violence. He had often enough seen previous defeats canceled by a sudden overwhelming victory. After a confident address to his troops he gave the word to advance south, dispose of the usurper Edward and rescue the legitimate king of England from his undeserved confinement. None of the intervening counties, from Northampton to Buckinghamshire and Hertfordshire, offered any resistance to his army. But at Barnet, on the border between Hertfordshire and Middlesex, between four and five o'clock on the misty morning of Easter Sunday, his van clashed with King Edward's scouts. The fiercest battle fought in England for a hundred years then began. The sovereign himself led the center of his line on foot, as did also the earl. After nearly four hours of a murderous hand-to-hand struggle Warwick's ranks gradually gave way. He saw that the game was up and called for a horse. But the enemy's cavalry too was now coming into action. The earl had scarcely ridden a mile before he was surrounded and cut down. Edward came up too late to save his life, as the laws of chivalry demanded.

That very evening, as the sun set on the fatal field of Barnet, strewn with over a thousand corpses, Margaret of Anjou and her son Edward landed at Weymouth on the Dorset coast a hundred and twenty miles away. She believed, having counted on Warwick's optimistic dispatches, that her cause was already half won. In fact the Lancastrian defeat at Barnet had been largely due to their center mistaking, in the fog, its victorious right, riding back from pursuit of the Yorkists, for the enemy, and mowing it down with arrows. In the subsequent confusion each side supposed the other to have deserted. Edward's cavalry, aware of the truth, slaughtered both sides indiscriminately.

Margaret, as might have been expected of her dauntless temperament, received the news of Barnet with more anger than discouragement. She moved due north, hoping to rally Wales to her support through the presence of the prince. At Tewkesbury, on the border between Gloucestershire and Worcestershire, she heard that Edward was in pursuit of her and turned to face him. Her old friend the duke of Somerset, who had escaped from Barnet, where he had commanded the Lancastrian center, headed her forces. But his impetuous charge on the right, owing either to treachery or undue caution by his subordinates, was not supported. It was driven back with heavy losses. The Yorkists then broke savagely into the Lancastrian center and almost destroyed it on a bank of the river Severn, within sight of Gloucester, at a place still called Bloody Meadow. The young Prince of Wales, revealing himself and demanding quarter as his companions fell around him, was nevertheless struck down and killed. Somerset was seized in Tewkesbury Abbey and beheaded after summary court-martial. Margaret was captured in an adjacent convent and brought as a prisoner to London. On May 21 Edward returned to the capital. On the twenty-second, Henry was found dead in the Tower. The government declared that he had died of grief at the news of the battle of Tewkesbury. But he had probably been murdered by order of one of Edward's adherents, possibly his brother Duke Richard of Gloucester, afterwards King Richard III. King Edward gave the unhappy, pacific scholar, who had always been quite lost among the unscrupulous men of action who surrounded him, a decent funeral.

The tragic events of the spring and early summer of 1471 had constituted a series of setbacks for the king of France. His enemies Charles the Bold of Burgundy, Edward the Unreliable, as one might venture to call him, of England, and the still more shifty Francis of Brittany, were all jubilant and plotting, at the very least, to clip his wings. He found, for instance, that Francis and the count of Saint-Pol were secretly pressing Charles to allow his daughter Mary to marry the duke of Berry, the king's brother Charles of France, who would then see to it that the lost Somme towns were returned to Burgundy. Louis discovered to his dismay that his trusted counselor Gaston of Foix, who happened to be Francis' brother-in-law, had joined this intrigue. But the king was less surprised to learn that the restless count of Armagnac, always an Anglophile, and married to another of Gaston's sisters, was hand-in-glove with the other conspirators.

Louis set himself resolutely to unravel this tangle. One item in the news from England encouraged him. Edward definitely opposed the project of marrying the duke of Berry to Mary. For a son born to Louis and Queen Charlotte in 1470 was proving a sickly child. If the dauphin died and Charles of France married Mary of Burgundy, England would have to face a powerful continental combination which would effectually block Edward's main design of the resumption of English dominion over western France, from Calais to Gascony. The prospective bridegroom, no hero, weakened at the frown of a more formidable warrior than even Charles the Bold, since Edward now had two more crushing victories to his credit. Would it not be easy for the terrible

English king to snap up young Charles's recently acquired appanage of Guienne, for all that his elder brother, the incalculable Louis, might do?

The king of France in fact was already seizing his opportunity, in these circumstances, to make a friendly approach to London, pointing out that the existence of the Burgundian heiress, who might easily fall into the wrong hands, rendered it all the more necessary for France and England to draw together for their mutual advantage in both trade and the balance of power. In September he managed to extort from Edward a ten months' truce between their respective realms. The fury of Charles the Bold on learning that the English king whose restoration to his throne had been largely financed with Burgundian money had betrayed him with Louis in this way, knew no bounds. The duke went so far as to consider claiming the crown of England himself, through his mother, the Duchess Isabel of Portugal, a descendant of John of Gaunt, duke of Lancaster (1340–1399) and the fourth son of King Edward III of England. John's daughter Philippa had married João I, king of Portugal, the father of Isabel. But this typically ambitious plan had eventually to be abandoned, partly owing to further dramatic developments in France.

The monarch, having made sure of Edward for the time being, turned to collect about his person all those magnates in his kingdom who had any sort of grievance against the duke. The chief of these were René of Anjou and the duke of Bourbon, in addition to the forces nominally controlled by the duke of Berry and Guienne. As soon as Louis felt strong enough to act openly he sent an usher of the Parlement of Paris to cite the mighty ruler of Burgundy to appear before that body and answer certain serious charges of a political nature, amounting to high treason, which had been made against him. At the same time the king took formal possession of a number of the Picardy towns owing feudal allegiance, by his own permission, to the Burgundian.

This audacity discomfited Charles the Bold for a few hours. But he was certainly not going to be bold enough, himself, to yield to the royal mercy, which he knew well enough would be the very reverse of tender. For proved high treason could only mean a death sentence. He defied the usher, who had caught up with him at Ghent in Holland. Next the duke made a sudden rush for the important town of Amiens, to prevent it from seceding to France. But he was too late. The king's troops, under Antoine de Chabannes, once responsible for the exile of Louis in the days of Charles VII but long since restored to favor, were already in the city. The duke encamped outside the heavily defended walls. Meanwhile his other forces, in Burgundy proper, far to the southeast, were defeated by the duke of Bourbon at Macon.

These two checks induced the "so-called duke of Burgundy," as Louis now designated him, to sign an armistice of three months. By July 1471 the king was back in Touraine, well pleased with these first results of his long-term plans to wreak effective vengeance upon his haughty "cousin" for the humiliation of Péronne.

Louis proceeded to offer him Saint-Quentin and Amiens, the two richest of the Somme towns, if he would renounce his intrigues with the dukes of Berry and Brittany and betroth Mary to the infant dauphin, the future King Charles VIII of France. In any case, the monarch added with cool cynicism, it would not be much good now to proceed with the idea of marrying the girl to his young brother Charles, whose health was known, as the winter of 1471 came on, to be rapidly deteriorating. The Burgundian duke at last agreed to extend his truce with Louis to June 15, 1472. But he told the king that the incompatibility of age between Mary, now fourteen, and the baby dauphin, rendered any question of their eventual marriage highly inadvisable, not to say ridiculous. The monarch can hardly have expected any other reply to this proposal, though such unions between mature wives and boyish husbands were not unknown even in the fifteenth century. But Louis was the kind of man who liked to explore all possible avenues. Moreover, he was particularly concerned to flatter Charles at this delicate point in their relations.

For he intended to attack the duke's former ally, Francis of Brittany, before that incorrigibly rebellious lord, whom he had defeated again and again, thought up some other plot against him. Francis, as usual, appealed to Edward of England. But that sovereign, now fearing Charles the Bold and all his works, was falling in with the French king's policy. He sent only a token contingent of archers to Brittany, presumably for old times' sake, or else to indicate his disapproval of Louis's application to James III of Scotland, England's hereditary enemy, for support.

Then, on May 25, Charles, duke of Berry and Guienne, the unsatisfactory brother of King Louis XI, perished at the age of twenty-five. His physique had always been as feeble as his mind and his habitual debauchery had weakened him still further. But his death came so opportunely for Louis that both Francis and the duke of Burgundy accused the king of having hastened it by poison. The charge appears quite unfounded. Not only were both the men who brought it notorious for their reckless talk, but Louis was not that sort of man at all. Whatever his faults might be, he always prided himself on bamboozling rather than secretly exterminating inconvenient persons. Nor had he ever shown any very fierce hostility to his brother, only irritation with his political folly. In fact, since their latest reconciliation he seems to have liked him. For Charles, like all the Valois, possessed the gift of getting on with anyone, even when the conversation took a serious turn, since on such occasions he invariably agreed with what had been said last.

All the same, the king felt considerable relief at the removal of the prince, whose susceptibility to treasonable suggestions had always constituted a danger to the throne. The monarch traveled to Guienne in order to take over and reorganize his brother's property, which had of course been casually neglected by that irresponsible young man. One of Louis's acts in Guienne illustrates vividly his methods of consolidating his power.

The most intelligent of the late Prince Charles's servants, Pierre Doriole, a former faithful steward of Charles VII, had accompanied his subsequent master, the new king's brother, in setting up the League of Public Weal against Louis seven years previously. The sovereign nevertheless now, in 1472, appointed Doriole chancellor of France. For on the one hand he undoubtedly recognized this official's outstanding administrative capacity and steady loyalty to anyone who assumed charge of him, being quite indifferent, like most bureaucrats, to political considerations, while on the other hand Doriole's clear head could be relied on to understand that he existed in the royal favor on sufferance as a proved past traitor, one who might be arrested at any moment on the capital charge of his former treason. The new chancellor was therefore likely to work better for the king of France than many a more technically innocent character. It was in fact Doriole who eventually brought that slippery customer, Cardinal Jean Balue, who had secretly served the duke of Burgundy, to justice. The prelate, who was of a literary as well as of a greedy turn of mind, possessed a fine library. The chancellor, also fond of reading, characteristically appropriated the manuscripts, with Louis's consent, as soon as the Cardinal had been clapped in jail for his double-dealing.

Later on that summer Charles the Bold, without waiting for the end of the three months' truce between France and Burgundy and ostensibly full of righteous wrath at the "murder" of his wretched little namesake, the king's brother, charged down from Amiens toward Compiègne, burning and slaughtering for the first time in his life, except during the rape of Liége, without mercy or discrimination. He hanged or mutilated, by cutting off their hands at the wrists, the defenders of the little town of Nesles, near Beauvais, after storming the former place. This barbarity infuriated Louis, who had merely laughed at the charge of fratricide. The king instructed his commanders to be equally ruthless in Burgundy, as the only way to bring to his senses a once gay and cultivated companion who seemed to have gone mad.

Charles could not take Beauvais. The Constable of France and the bishop were there in force and Louis announced that he was coming shortly from Brittany, where he was trying out his new artillery on Francis's rebellious town of Ancenis. But the Burgundians, fierce as ever, also now had good guns. They breached one of the gates of Beauvais, which caught fire. A furious engagement took place at the spot. The citizens hurled flaming timber in the faces of their assailants, who were at last routed by the veteran Marshal of France, Joachim Rouault, with a sudden incursion of cavalry.

The king congratulated the gallant city. On July 14 he made it a municipality, exempted it from taxation and relieved it from military service for the future. He decreed that on each anniversary of the battle in the gate a solemn ceremony of thanksgiving should be observed. The women of Beauvais, who had stood shoulder to shoulder with their menfolk on the ramparts, were to march in procession immediately after the clergy and ahead of their husbands, sons and brothers. One of these young ladies, Jeanne Laisne, a girl of eighteen, had actually cut down with an ax a Burgundian soldier in the act of planting a flag on the battlements. She sent his body flying head first into the moat and his fluttering emblem after him. For the rest of her life Jeanne was known, from this incident, as La Hachette. Louis saw to it that she married her lover, one Colin Pilon, with a substantial dowry. He loaded the couple with various other marks of esteem. Nor did the delighted monarch stop there. He told the women of Beauvais, who had previously been censured by the local authorities for extravagance in dress, that they could henceforth wear anything they pleased on high days and holidays, irrespective of their social position. For once his notorious misogyny had turned into its opposite.

Duke Charles, repulsed from before Beauvais, marched due west, making for Rouen, which he besieged. But his troops were by this time dispirited and starving, the countryside having been devastated, largely by themselves. The chamberlain Philippe de Commines, disgusted with his master's bloodthirstiness and mismanagement of the expedition, rode off to join Louis. Commines knew the king to be grateful for the attitude the younger man had taken up at Péronne, where he had probably saved the captive sovereign's life. The two men immediately became close friends, the monarch granting his new counselor, most valuable for his brains and integrity, as well as for his intimate knowledge of Charles's affairs, lands and a permanent pension.

Letters from the duke of Brittany to the Burgundian were intercepted by the royalists. The documents proved that the Bretons too were sick of their ally and also of the English, who had broken promise after promise to them. Yet the position still remained obscure. Louis found English troops in Ancenis after he had taken the city. He discovered in September that Edward and Francis had agreed on a fresh project for the invasion of France by way of either Guienne or Normandy. The English ruler had demanded and obtained from his Parliament funds "to set outward a mighty army." Meanwhile, however, King Louis, by mid-October, had induced both Francis and Charles to sign a truce with him. The Bretons were in fact beginning to dread an English descent upon their duchy. Charles for his part, frustrated on all sides in his recent specialty of total war owing to Edward's long delays in coming to his assistance and the defeat of the count of Armagnac by the royal forces, had decide that he must improve his strength by embarking upon certain negotiations.

He began by securing more time for Edward, who was experiencing hostility from James III of Scotland, revolts in Wales and treasonable plots by his brother the duke of Clarence, all secretly supported by Louis, to say nothing of disputes about money with the powerful Hanseatic League, which disposed of ships which the English king needed for his forthcoming invasion of France. The maritime and commercial sway of the League, headed by the Baltic port of Lübeck between Holstein and Mecklenburg, extended from Poland to the Zuider Zee. Even beyond those limits little could be done at sea without Hansa approval. A year's truce between England, Burgundy and France was finally signed in March 1473. Then Charles suddenly turned east to the Holy Roman emperor, Frederick III, whom he almost persuaded to marry the Archduke Maximilian, now aged fourteen, to the sixteen-year-old Mary of Burgundy and crown her father a king. But Frederick, like many people who met Charles at this period, considered him an unreliable character. The emperor did not care for the prospect of a Charles king of Burgundy, though he had no other objection to Maximilian eventually taking possession of Mary's fortune. One night during the somewhat elusive Habsburg's sojourn at Trier on the Moselle, a few miles from the Luxembourg border, for the conference with the duke, his imperial host characteristically slipped away down the river without taking leave of the subsequently infuriated Burgundian. After this display of Teutonic manners the marriage proposal had of course to be dropped.

Charles himself would never have been guilty of such a want of courtesy to a potentate with whom he had no specific quarrel. But nearly all his schemes went wrong on account of two fatal defects in his mentality. His volcanic temper, once aroused, stopped at nothing but an equal violence. On the other hand a tendency to what appears to be the very opposite of savage fury, a romantic dreaming typical of the epics of chivalry he knew almost by heart, an obsession with the Arthurian heroes Sir Lancelot and Sir Gawain, landed him repeatedly in the depths of ruinous fantasy. There he remained wholly out of touch with the realistic spirit so conspicuous in his great rival Louis. Each inevitably misunderstood the other as they grew older. But the king's far superior judgment of human nature was less desiccated by his thirst, at bottom politically motivated, for revenge on the duke than was Charles's reading of his dexterous antagonist by a failure to recognize the monarch's true patriotism, so that the Burgundian too hastily labeled the Frenchman as nothing more than a selfish, deceitful opportunist.

Louis had seen many an old-fashioned feudal ruler discomfited by businessmen not necessarily cleverer than himself, but simply because such conservative noblemen, with their many and varied interests and fancies, could not keep their minds regularly on the dull details of plot and counterplot. Francis of Brittany and Jean of Armagnac were typical recent examples of this weakness, not to mention the late Prince Charles. The king knew the duke of Burgundy, for all his dauntless courage and resourceful spirit in a tight corner, as at this moment of 1473, to be no exception. The man would eventually collapse, so to speak, of his own accord. But so aggressive and able a soldier could not be beaten down in pitched battles, as Montlhéry had proved. He could only be held off by a succession of truces which apparently favored Burgundian ambition but were never of course intended to do so.

Louis and Commines agreed in this view of Charles the Bold. They concluded that the necessary struggle against his persistent challenges could best be maintained, not by thundering cannon and hewing steel, but by letting his forces into ravaged territory, dotted with strong castles and cities which his armies would be obliged to besiege while themselves suffering from shortages of food and accommodations, accompanied by the deterioration and loss of both soldiers and supplies of all kinds. The two fifteenth-century analysts both knew their ancient Roman history. They remembered the "masterly inactivity" of the dictator Quintus Fabius Maximus, which would have saved Italy from Hannibal in the third century B.C. if the Roman had been allowed to continue these tactics by the impatient voters who had elected him. In the France of Louis XI, however, popular discontent had no serious influence on the conduct of military operations. The monarch and his shrewdest adviser watched complacently while Charles the Bold made more and more of a fool of himself over the next few years with unsuccessful adventures across his eastern frontiers, where he hoped to embroil the Austrians, the Swiss and the Lorrainers against the king.

England was a different matter, more dangerous to the safety of

France than the incursions of Burgundian marauders. King Edward IV was gradually getting the better of his domestic opponents and the country as a whole was known to be enthusiastic for the recovery of its former French dominions. Louis calmly prepared to meet this formidable menace by fortifying the anticipated points of overseas attack in Normandy, Poitou and Guienne, equipping a fleet with Hanseatic aid, taxing the provinces and mobilizing man power. Meanwhile he signed anti-Burgundian treaties with the Swiss and the emperor. All these measures tended to make Charles, with whom the French ruler continued to negotiate for a general peace, lose interest in an Anglo-Burgundian invasion of France.

The duke's siege in June 1474 of the impregnable town of Neuss on an island in the Rhine was a characteristically futile episode. The citizens had rebelled against the archbishop of Cologne, Charles's kinsman. The Burgundian resolved to take the place as a step in his infiltration of Germany. He set up his artillery within a bowshot of the walls and his headquarters in a luxurious portable palace close by. His officers, and the whole College of the Golden Fleece, a specifically Burgundian order, were lodged in a neighboring abbey. He dug trenches all round the city, dammed and drained part of the river and started an incessant bombardment of the foe with every engine of war, including a tower on wheels, that had ever been invented. He cut down whole forests to provide ramparts and hutments for his troops. These buildings, traversed by deep-laid lanes, constituted what seemed a permanent settlement, with a market, law courts, tents, pavilions, extensive barracks with vast kitchens, mills, baths, breweries and a gallows. Plenty of women were installed. Weddings and christenings took place. Concerts of choruses to the accompaniment of bagpipes, drums and flutes contributed to the general uproar and bustle. The kings of Denmark and Norway were entertained at Charles's gorgeous, prefabricated court.

But a year went by without any change in the situation. Louis laughed. Commines expressed the opinion, not for the first time, that the duke had gone out of his mind. The pope eventually sent a legate to tell him to stop such useless frivolity. The German princes formed a league to relieve the city. The Burgundian could only acknowledge failure and pack up his splendid equipment. The citizens of Neuss went on calmly, behind their mighty and vigilantly manned fortifications, which did not include accommodation for revels, with their ordinary business.

That summer King Edward IV, as he had so long threatened, disembarked at Calais, the only town still held in France by the English. The recently reorganized French fleet had not been able to intercept his Dutch transports. Louis was reduced to ordering all Picardy to be ravaged in order to confine the invaders to Calais. Farms and castles, as far south as the Somme valley, went up in flames. Edward hesitated to move through the ensuing desert. Brittany had not come to his assistance, as he had been led to expect. Burgundy was heavily engaged with an attack by Frederick on Metz and could spare little support for the English troops. Charles suggested that in these circumstances they should wheel left into his own territory of Flanders and descend on Reims, bypassing devastated Picardy. For at Reims, by ancient tradition, the kings of France had always been crowned. Edward, still described in his official documents, like his ancestors, as king of France, could most appropriately arrange his coronation, as such, in that city. Louis soon heard about this plan and peremptorily warned Reims that if it did not resist the English to the death he would himself raze its walls and buildings to the ground.

Almost at the same time King Edward's herald arrived at the French court. He demanded in pompous language the surrender of France to its "lawful" possessor, who would "deliver" the people from their native "oppressor." The resemblance of these phrases to those which have been increasingly used in the twentieth century to justify warfare of all kinds, from proletarian revolution to the aggrandizement or defense of an empire or an ideology, is most striking. They have rarely, throughout the recorded history of Europe, corresponded with the facts of a political situation. But no more credible excuse for violent aggression has ever been worked out by humanity. The king of France, not in the least deceived or even perturbed by this hackneyed and specious harangue, identical in its principles of argument with that of the Soviet Union to justify its invasion of Czechoslovakia in 1968, smilingly informed the English envoy of a few circumstances he seemed to have forgotten. It was really clear, was it not, that King Edward had been pushed into this hopeless enterprise by a foreign agent, the half-crazy duke of Burgundy, who was now keeping carefully in the background? Was not the English desire for French corn and wine actually responsible for the London Parliament's financial backing of their sovereign in this matter? Was not the herald aware that the extravagant siege of Neuss had bankrupted the duke and that the Holy Roman emperor was determined to suppress him? Finally, could the herald really believe, now that he had met the French "tyrant" in person, that the king of France preferred fire and sword to negotiation or force to reason in raising money to meet his expenses, largely thrust upon him by the reckless behavior of the English and Burgundian governments?

These remarks, uttered without the slightest sign of emotion of any sort, appeared to impress the Englishman. He received, with a gratitude which might be ascribed to a conviction of their truth, the lavish rewards in cash and goods bestowed upon him for his courtesy in listening without protest to the royal statement. At any rate he took his leave noncommittally, not reiterating the haughty summons to yield he had carried from his master.

The herald's report, in itself, might or might not have caused Edward to modify his initially truculent attitude. In any case the pressure of public events came in due course to bring about this result. The young king, still only thirty-three, while Louis was fifty-two, bore some similarity to the French sovereign in certain respects, though in others his mentality remained wholly different. A born charmer and secret autocrat, ambitious and capable up to a point but sporadically lazy and self-indulgent, he never stuck to one line of action for long. He could be ruthless in short bursts of energy but seldom perpetrated unmitigated cruelty. His frank eroticism, good looks, affability and delight in display were counterbalanced by his serious patronage not only of literature and the new art of printing but also by his partiality to the London merchants, whom he favored as much as Louis did those of Lyons and his other centers of industry and commerce.

Edward now took Charles's advice by moving his army northeast, away from the desolation of Picardy. But as he neared the gates of Saint-Quentin, where the duke had assured him he would be welcomed, cannon flashed from the walls and showers of arrows dispersed his vanguard. This hostile reception confirmed the English king's growing distrust of Charles and altered his opinion, if it had ever been sincerely held, of the popularity of Louis. The Frenchman, he saw, would not be so easily disposed of. When the incalculable duke, a day or two later, vanished in the direction of Lorraine and for a while seized Nancy, hanging and drowning his prisoners with the ferocity of a vengeful suzerain, though he was nothing of the kind, Edward realized that he could expect no more reliable support from his wild brother-in-law, more intent upon bullying the weak than attacking the strong. The English ruler thereupon sent a conciliatory message to Louis, who replied in the same sense as he had to the previous herald.

By August 1475 the French and English commissioners had met near Amiens. They reached substantial agreement. The invaders were to be bought off with seventy-two thousand crowns. The dauphin, aged five, and Edward's daughter Elizabeth, aged twelve, were to be betrothed, with Guienne, assumed by a legal fiction to be English, as the bride's dowry. Elaborate arrangements were made to govern trade between the two countries, so as to give more advantage to England in this sphere than had hitherto been acquired. The treaty looked superficially unfavorable to France. But a full-scale English invasion, whether or not backed by Burgundy and Brittany, would have been far worse. The French king explained to his council that his English rival, about whose character and circumstances he was, as usual, accurately informed, could not really be regarded as a warmonger. The monarch in question had already been repulsed in the north and was thoroughly disgusted by the treacherous conduct of his ally Charles. He was not now in a bellicose mood. At the same time a formidable English army stood in France. The country was in no position to conquer it outright. The obvious and most urgent policy was to get rid of it without bloodshed and loss of national territory.

The Constable of France, Louis of Luxembourg, Count of Saint-Pol, had more than once betrayed King Louis and the duke of Burgundy alternately. He now tried, after his recent loyal defense of Saint-Quentin, to climb back on the French bandwagon, a vehicle he judged to have better prospects at present than that of Charles. He sent a gentleman of his household, one de Sainville, with that officer's secretary, to beg an audience of the king. The monarch by this time had full documentary evidence of the Constable's previous dealings with Burgundy and was determined to punish them. But his peculiar sense of humor had been aroused by the visit of Saint-Pol's emissaries. He decided to give an elderly, rather naïve Burgundian prisoner, the lord of Contay, a glimpse of high politics. King Louis told Commines to sit with Contay behind a screen and keep him there while de Sainville and his companion pleaded their master's cause. The visitors, anxious to prove the Constable's devotion to the throne, said that he had previously despatched them to the duke of Burgundy with the object of persuading him to abandon King Edward. But this mission, de Sainville continued facetiously, appeared to be carrying coals to Newcastle, as the islanders' proverb had it. The duke was already cursing his royal brother-in-law up hill and down dale, for expecting his ally to do all the hard work of the invasion.

The count's chief messenger, who could act, gave a magnificent impersonation of Charles the Bold, or "the Terrible," as he was now beginning to be called, stamping to and fro and vowing to get the better of "Blayburgh," his nickname for Edward, referring to the Lancastrian gossip that the sovereign, who could sometimes be coarse in his private conduct, had been fathered by an archer answering to that appellation. King Louis laughed heartily at this performance and asked for more of it. But he bade de Sainville speak louder, as he was a bit deaf and had missed a phrase here and there. Contay, behind the screen, was thunderstruck at the revelation of his duke's change of feeling toward the English and could hardly believe it. After the audience was over he petitioned Louis for release on parole, so that he could travel to Charles's court and see for himself what the position was. The king granted this request immediately. For the whole scene had been staged in order that the influential and unimpeachably honorable old lord of Contay might spread the news that the duke of Burgundy had suddenly turned viciously Anglophobe when Edward had taunted him with supplying false information about the Constable's intention to hold Saint-Quentin.

But Charles, when he heard of the treaty of peace concluded between France and England, changed his mind again. He dashed from Luxembourg to Edward's camp, ready for any humiliation so long as he could keep the essential English army behind him, or preferably in the van of his planned attack on Paris. The king of England received his distinguished visitor at first with marked reserve, then with every sign of annoyance. The duke, he said, had only himself to thank if he had not been allowed a voice in the deliberations at Amiens. Charles retorted with a stormy defense of his necessary absence to suppress invasion and rebellion on his eastern and southern frontiers. Then, with a great effort, hoping to mollify the monarch, he spoke in a lower tone, in English, recalling the valiant deeds of Edward's ancestors among the "false Frenchmen." All was in vain. The big descendant of these heroes did not move a muscle of his still handsome though now rather too fleshy features. Then he signified that the audience was at an end. The duke could only set his teeth and retire, after a first impulse to draw his dagger on this thick-witted lump of a woman-worshiper.

On August 29, 1475, the two kings met in person at Perpigny, a few miles from Amiens, on the bridge of Montereau, where John the Fearless of Burgundy, in 1419, had been assassinated by the partisans of the dauphin of France, afterwards Charles VII. In order to prevent the repetition of any such scene an iron fence had been erected on the bridge with posts only about a foot apart. Louis arrived first, at the head of eight hundred men. He could see the English army, far superior in strength, drawn up in battle array on the other side of the river Somme. When at last Edward approached the central barrier, the French king swept off his flat velvet cap, adorned with jewels and a huge fleur-de-lis, and bowed low. The English sovereign, with an indifference to ceremony as characteristic of him as it was of Louis, returned the salute with a grin and a casual flourish. Then he stepped up to the fence, bent down considerably from his great height and pushed his face between two of the posts, protruding his lips a little, the eyes steady, but with the very slightest suggestion of a twinkle. Louis understood his meaning, rose on tiptoe and kissed the king of England squarely on the mouth.

Subsequent compliments were exchanged in the French language, which Edward spoke well. Then each monarch signed, over a missal with a piece of the "true cross" on the cover, the parchment of the already drafted treaty. The atmosphere lightened as Louis produced a smile for once unmistakably jocular. The Englishman, always ready for a laugh, responded boisterously, especially when his new friend promised him that plenty of fair ladies would be at his disposal in Paris. More serious topics were next discussed, including the problem of Charles's position. Edward's ruddy features assumed a deeper tinge as he remarked with emphasis that if the duke of Burgundy refused to have anything to do with the conclusion of peace such an attitude would certainly not affect his own. But he insisted that the duke of Brittany, a personal friend, should not be punished for his equivocal conduct. Louis agreed. The two sovereigns parted on the best of terms.

A typically frantic despatch from Charles to the king of France, offering to attack Edward on his way back to Calais, was naturally ignored by its recipient. The English troops were not molested by anyone on their return journey. Before the end of September they were all back in London. Margaret of Anjou was released from her captivity at Windsor for a ransom of fifty thousand crowns, paid by Louis. She returned to France in November, a grim ghost of the stubborn fighter she had once been. The almost simultaneous deaths by violence of her gallant teen-age son, her last faithful friend the duke of Somerset, and her ever gentle husband had at last permanently broken the spirit of a woman whose one admirable quality of intrepid resolution, like that of Charles the Bold in his final years, could not save her from ultimate defeat. She would certainly, had she been a man, have died fighting, as the Burgundian did. A harder fate, perhaps, was to spend the embittered six years of life that remained to her in strict retirement near the court of her father, King René.

The duke of Brittany was not only spared recrimination by the king whom he had so often injured but actually, in further compliment to King Edward, appointed lieutenant general of France. There remained the question of the treacherous Constable, whom nobody now wanted. After Louis and the Burgundian ruler had signed in Luxembourg, on September 13, a truce for nine years, Charles broke his word, not for the first time, to the Count of Saint-Pol, who was in his custody. The duke cynically surrendered this prisoner to the French king, who duly had him beheaded in Paris, on December 19, 1475, for high treason.

CHAPTER X

Burgundy in Defeat
(1475–1478)

⚜⚜⚜ Charles the Bold himself was not to last much longer. His betrayal of Saint-Pol, who had sobbed piteously on the scaffold, was generally considered a peculiarly dastardly act. It greatly reduced the duke's popularity and correspondingly increased that of Louis, now thought by most Frenchmen to have God on his side in the struggle against the cruel and perfidious Burgundian. The latter soon gave proof of the deterioration in his character. Bursting into Switzerland after his capture of Nancy at the end of November 1475, he treated the population with excessive brutality. When the town of Grandson at the southwestern end of the Lake of Neuchâtel capitulated to his troops in February 1476 he mutilated and hanged the entire garrison.

Louis was at Lyons with ten thousand men, ready to break his truce with Charles and intervene if called upon. But there was no need for him to do any such thing. All the cantons of the confederacy rose to take vengeance upon the ravisher of Grandson. Columns of pikemen converged from Bern, Solere (Solothurn), Schwyz and Fribourg, charging down the sides of Mount Aubert upon the Burgundians in the pass below, to the war-cry of "Grandson! Grandson!" The leading formations crushed the Duke's left wing before he could bring his cavalry into effective action against them. Then, as he wheeled his guns and the rest of his infantry to support the horsemen, the Swiss center and left caught them laterally in a concerted rush of irresistible impact.

Nothing could stand against the terrible ranks of serried pikes. The Burgundian men-at-arms broke and ran, abandoning their cannon and the camp behind the batteries. Charles saw that it was useless to try to disrupt the bristling Swiss phalanx with his cavalry, which still remained in fair order. He rode off the field with his mounted men, indifferent as he had always been to the loss of mere matériel, which could be replaced, unlike experienced and reliable soldiers, especially those on horseback. For he never ceased to regard, in his old-fashioned way, cavalry as the most effective arm in battle. The dishonor of leaving all his baggage and treasure, including a gold throne, the emblems of the Golden Fleece, the ducal crown and the great pink Sancy diamond, so called from its subsequent purchaser and weighing 133 carats, which he had brought with him as a kind of talisman to enhance the splendor and prospects of his army, counted for little in comparison with the preservation of his beloved knights and his contempt for the accursed cowards of infantrymen who had fled.

The formidable but simple-minded highlanders had no idea what to do with their plunder, gorgeous beyond anything they had ever seen. They took silver and gold for brass, embroidered silks and velvets for homespun and jewels for mere trinkets. They threw away the Sancy diamond, which was afterwards picked up by a priest and sold as a fragment of colored glass to his lord for a florin or two.* What the men of the cantons most appreciated was the huge quantity of steel weapons, firearms and hard cash. Psychologically, their victory simply confirmed what they had known ever since the early fourteenth century. For a hundred and fifty years they had smashed the chivalry of Austria and the lords of their own lowlands in battle after battle. Even when heavily outnumbered, as against the dauphin's mercenaries at Saint-Jacques in 1444, where fifteen hundred of them had killed eight thousand of their assailants before being themselves exterminated, in their rare retreats the enemy had always paid an extravagant price for his advantage. The resultant confident dash of the Swiss pikemen and their indomitable prowess in hand-to-hand fighting had long rendered them the most dreaded opponents of any European forces in warfare. It was only the massed artillery, not the cavalry, of King

---

* The Sancy diamond eventually came into the possession of the French ambassador to Switzerland, Nicolas de Harlay, lord of Sancy. Thence, according to Gordon Brook-Shepherd (*The Last Habsburg*, 1968), it passed to the Medici collection, next to the ducal family of Lorraine and finally to the Habsburgs, when in 1735 the future empress Maria Theresa, daughter of the Emperor Charles VI, who inherited the Habsburg estates and claims on the empire in 1711, married Duke Francis of Lorraine, then also grand duke of Tuscany and afterwards (1745) the Emperor Francis I.

When the emperor of Austria-Hungary, Charles I (1887–1922) renounced his throne in 1921, the diamond in question remained one of the few items of imperial jewelry which escaped theft. But it was not recovered by his widow, the ex-Empress Zita, until after his death.

So far as Prince Paul could discover, the Empress Zita—a difficult personality to approach—still has the diamond. She *may* have sold it. But no reliable person will say.

I don't think myself we need say any more about it here.—J.C.

Francis I of France that ended their military predominance on the blood-drenched field of Marignano, near Milan, forty years later.

But in March 1476 the consequences of the Swiss defeat of Charles the Bold under the very walls of Grandson, the town he had treated with such unjustifiable brutality, proved disastrous for his reputation and power. His enemies everywhere, from Holland, Flanders, Germany and Austria to France and Italy, took heart and conspired against him. They more or less knelt to Louis, whom they rightly considered his most relentless adversary, though the king remained as formally polite to the duke as to everyone else. Louis had good reason for his inscrutable smile in these days. He had seen clearly that he would not have to tax the incomes or sacrifice the lives of many Frenchmen in future, in order to bring down the unconscionable Burgundian who had stood so obstinately in the way of the ascent of France to the economic as well as military leadership of Europe.

Duke Charles himself, however, remained far from discomfited by his misfortunes. It is true that he let his beard grow and seemed enfeebled and feverish to impartial observers who remembered what a giant of energy and intimidation he had once been. The balance of his mind had certainly been disturbed by his frustrations. But this condition merely increased his resolve to re-establish his grandeur. The idea of yielding to the pressure of circumstance never entered his calculations for a moment. Retreating for the time being northeast, he circumvented Lake Neuchâtel, then dug himself in among the hills of the little settlement of Morat, on the lake of that name, very close to the northeastern end of the former, much larger, stretch of water.

He erected palisades to face Bern and Fribourg, ranging his artillery along these defenses so as to be able to decimate a frontal attack coming from those cantons. His cavalry were held in readiness to smash it completely as soon as the guns had done their work. In this commanding position he waited day after day, while the Swiss gathered in the dense woods east of his line. The weather kept fine. But on June 22 the sunshine suddenly dissolved in a blinding rainstorm that was obviously going to last for hours. By noon it had shown no signs of abating. Charles, discounting the possibility of an engagement in such circumstances, withdrew his infantry to rest and eat, leaving only the gunners to hold the palisade.

Thereupon the Swiss, half hidden by the downpour, streamed out of the forest in a direct assault against the fortifications. The Burgundian cannon roared. The racing pikemen dropped in scores. But the survivors dashed on. They rushed the palisade and overwhelmed the artillerymen before a second salvo could be fired. Column after column followed the first waves. The defenders did not run this time. They had been told they would be slaughtered by the cavalry on their own side if they did. But the surprised infantry had leaped from their half-finished meals to rally. They fought desperately against the lunging pikes that gave them no time to form a steady line of battle. Consequently, the Burgundians presented only the resistance of a disorderly mob to the disciplined ranks that incessantly bore down upon them. The whole multitude fled at last, back to their camp and the shore of the lake behind it. Many perished in the actual waters. A third of the twenty thousand soldiers who had held the position died under the long pikes or were drowned. The rest, mostly on the duke's northern wing, escaped, with their leader, in that direction, and then west, making for Franche-Comté.

Charles's feelings at this second decisive rout of his great modern army, reorganized and re-equipped during the last three months and so carefully posted, may be imagined. The disgrace threw him into almost complete despair, causing him to refuse for a while to take any food or wine. For days, finding himself deserted by all his allies and unable to raise any substantial body of fresh troops, now that he had lost the confidence of his best officers, he declined to see anyone or participate to any significant degree in politics.

The young Duke René of Lorraine, son of old René's elder daughter Yolande by a member of a formerly hostile family, Ferry de Vaudemont, was now leading the anti-Burgundian movement in the conquered duchy on behalf of his grandfather, just then, at the age of sixty-seven, in bad odor with Louis on account of some injudicious negotiations with Charles, of whom the unlucky sexagenarian seems to have been very frightened. But the high-spirited René junior, aged twenty-five, detested and despised the brutal despoiler of his country. Determined eventually to eject the Burgundian from Lorraine, he had already fought on the Swiss side at the battle of Morat. He now seized the opportunity of the lull in Charles's activities to make a bid for the occupied capital. In October he recaptured Nancy with the aid of a contingent from Strasbourg and the treachery of the count of Campobasso, an Italian mercenary in the service of the duke of Burgundy and one of those who saw clearly that his master was on the downgrade.

But during this campaign the Burgundian roused himself once more. He made a wild attempt to prevent Savoy, which had hitherto supported him, from going over to Louis. Its Duchess Yolande, the king's able sister, widowed since 1472 and with a character very similar to her brother's in its taste for duplicity, had been constantly in touch with Charles ever since the battle of Grandson. There had been personal interviews at Lausanne in March 1476, at Gex in the following June and soon afterwards at Geneva. The duke wanted desperately to use her cunning brains on his own repeatedly defeated side. If he could do so, it would be almost like recruiting a double of Louis himself. But Yolande had developed a love of Savoy as sincere as her brother's of France. She would not expose her duchy to the king's vengeance by openly throwing in her lot with Charles.

In exasperation he ordered Olivier de la Marche to bring her to heel by force. But the honest and loyal Olivier bungled the job. He managed to get hold of Yolande and imprisoned her. But he allowed her son and heir Philibert, aged thirteen, to escape. The duchess was held at Rouvre Castle near Dijon. But her guards, like so many of Charles's servants at this period, were careless, bribable and inadequate in numbers. She was not on good terms with her brother, on account of her past pro-Burgundian policy. But in this extremity she contrived to communicate with him, begging him to release her from a captivity she feared might end badly for her, since it was impossible to tell what mad violence Charles might commit next.

Louis soon had her out of Rouvre and brought to Tours. He had previously written, with superb tact, in Italian, her adopted language: "My dear sister, I beg you to hasten hither. I forgot to tell you how happy I was to have been of service to you in your escape, so that you might realize how fond I am of you. Your children are very well. I am at your orders and assure you that you will have no great difficulty in recovering Savoy."

At Tours, however, he could not resist a little brotherly sarcasm. He received her with the sardonic greeting: "You are most welcome, Madam Burgundian." She bent her head and answered in a low tone: "I am a true Frenchwoman, sire, and ready to obey your wishes in all things." He could see that she meant what she said, having really no other choice in the new political situation. The brother and sister wasted no time in their reconciliation, which proved permanent. Within a week Yolande was on her way back to Savoy with a strong French escort. She never gave the king any more trouble. By 1478 she was dead.

Meanwhile Charles the Bold, despite his failure to neutralize Savoyard power, had regained much of his old audacity and determination. He resolved to teach René a lesson and advanced on Nancy with every man he could raise, to the number of about ten thousand, mainly mercenaries attracted by offers of lavish pay. This act, under existing law, constituted an attack on one of Louis's feudatories. The previous invasion of Lorraine by the duke of Burgundy had fallen into the same category. But Louis had not then felt strong enough to intervene. Now, after the two terrible defeats inflicted on Charles by the Swiss, the position was different. The king signed a pact with both

René and the confederacy, by which he enabled the former to raise an army double the size of that available to the Burgundian. The latter was advised not to give battle on these unequal terms. But he silenced these counselors with one of the leonine roars for which he had been famous in former years. "Let them all come! If necessary I'll take the field alone!" He was thinking, no doubt, of one of his favorite epics, in which such heroes as Roland or Oliver, emulating Achilles on the plain of Troy or Samson among the Philistines, struck down whole multitudes of the foe all by themselves. But in fact he was playing his last card and must have known it.

The winter of 1476-1477 set in with extraordinary severity. Long before Christmas the roads northward through Franche-Comté and the mountainous Vosges country were blocked with snow. Temperatures fell steadily. But Charles forced his men on, reaching the walls of Nancy some weeks before René arrived to relieve the city. The Burgundian camp in the open suffered far more from the cold than did the enclosed garrison. On Christmas Eve four hundred of the bivouacked troops were frozen to death. Yet in this desperate situation the spirits of the grim duke of Burgundy, always at his best in any kind of active service, rose higher than ever. He encouraged in his old knightly style the officers and men who put up a bold front. He summarily hanged anyone reported to have grumbled. When his scouts brought news that the Swiss mercenaries of the relief force were approaching, he set his batteries to command the only territory through which they could advance.

His trumpets sounded for action before dawn on January 5, 1477. But when the weary soldiers tumbled from their blankets and seized their weapons they could see nothing ahead of them in the freezing murk, scarcely yet lightened from the faint glow to the east. Snow was falling again. But in spite of the wretched visibility the expert Swiss reconnaissance had discovered the guns. The veterans from the Alps, employing their usual tactics, melted away into the woods on either side of the road. Then, as day broke, they unexpectedly attacked Charles's artillery in great force from each flank. Others of René's polyglot horde—Swabians, Alsatians, Lorrainers and Frenchmen in addition to the Swiss pikemen—assaulted the camp from the rear, combining with a sally from the walls of the town.

It was now that for the first time the subsequently famous Cross of Lorraine, with its double horizontal, embroidered at René's orders on standards and pennants, streamed in the increasing light of dawn above the heads of the advancing troops.

The outnumbered and surrounded Burgundians resisted with the courage of despair. Their commander, on a black horse, led charge after charge into the dense ranks of the enemy. He cheered like a conqueror, his sword whirling right and left with the speed and dexterity of a champion of the lists. He seemed invulnerable at first. But soon he was wounded again and again. Half-stunned, reeling in the saddle from loss of blood, he was rushed from the field by a few of his surviving knights. But the little knot of riders was closely pursued and assailed from every direction. The duke's corpse was only discovered some days later, after the utter rout of his inadequate forces. In the midst of a heap of dead men and horses, three cannon-shots' length from the walls of Nancy, it lay face downward, already half-devoured by wolves and stripped by prowling thieves, in an icebound pool. A halberd had split the head in two. A pike had stabbed deep into the loins.

For some time many people, including Louis himself, could not bring themselves to believe in the death of so terrific a hero. He had dominated the imagination of his contemporaries for so long that it seemed impossible he should not have survived even the slaughter of Nancy. But finally no doubt remained that Europe had seen the last of him. The whole political situation changed immediately, much to the advantage of the king of France. He was less prone than any other man of his time to prophesy victory in battle. He did not believe that war, as such, ever settled anything. But no one at the end of 1476 could have failed to see the result of the forthcoming clash under the walls of Nancy. Charles himself, it is highly probable, simply meant to die fighting. He was outnumbered by more than three to one. The bulk of the forces facing him were Swiss, the representatives of a terrible military machine that had twice defeated him decisively in the last few months. To him as to Louis the outcome must have seemed a foregone conclusion.

All the same, though King Louis recognized the Nancy encounter to be the climax of his long struggle with Burgundy, he felt nervous. If Charles lived to fight another day and returned to his intrigues with England, Germany and Italy, the future of France might prove as disastrous as its past. One of the most famous passages in the *Mémoires* of Philippe de Commines describes the monarch's mood as he waited for news at his favorite residence, the strong castle of Plessis-les-Tours in "happy Touraine," overlooking the valleys of the Cher and Loire.

> The King had already organized a courier service in his dominions. . . . he expected confirmation at any moment of the encouraging tidings so far received. . . . Many others were straining their ears to be the first to bring him the latest despatch, for he always rewarded

such messengers generously. M. de Bouchaige and I had been the first to tell him of the battle of Morat. . . . M. du Lude, who lodged at some distance from the castle, was the first to meet the courier bearing letters concerning the above-mentioned battle of Nancy. M. du Lude ordered the rider to hand the papers over to him. The man did not dare to refuse, knowing the confidence the King had in the said lord. M. du Lude came to the castle very early in the morning, when it was scarcely yet light, and knocked loudly at the door of the royal bedchamber. As soon as it was opened he delivered to the King despatches from M. du Craon and others. But none of them contained any definite information about the death of the duke of Burgundy. . . . The King was at first so startled by the glad tidings of this victory that he looked quite blank. . . . then he sent messengers to Tours to show the letters to all the captains and great men there, who were all much delighted. . . . after some talk with the aforesaid gentlemen he heard Mass and next had a table laid in his bedchamber. He invited them all to join him in a meal, his Chancellor and some of the Council being present. They spoke of nothing else but the news from Nancy. I remember well that none of us paid much attention to what we were eating or had any great appetite. Nobody, I am certain, consumed more than half what was on his plate. But whether this was on account of joy or distress I cannot tell. . . . When we rose from table the King took some of the gentlemen aside and promised them certain lands which had belonged to the Duke of Burgundy, if it should turn out that he had been slain. The King then forthwith sent the Bastard of Bourbon, at that time Admiral of France, and myself out of the castle with full authority to take possession of and read all despatches carried by any courier we might meet in order to discover whether the Duke were dead or alive.

Commines and the Bastard were in fact among the most reliable of the personages present at this historic meal. Jean du Lude's main object in life was to obtain special privileges by any means whatever at the court. The marshal Joachim Rouault, a bold and effective but very talkative old soldier, could never speak the truth without distorting it. Dr. Coictier, the suavely cynical court physician, of a type as well known then as today, exercised his profession purely as an industry. The Fleming Olivier le Dain (Flemish for "devil") had begun life as a barber. He was appointed count of Meulan by Louis at about this time, the king being fascinated by the unscrupulous impudence of this early version of a Figaro who, however, made a mess of most of his more important missions by being too sure of himself. His insolent manners generally neutralized any advantage his cunning might otherwise have obtained over less astute minds. Tristan l'Hermite, on the other hand,

the king's master spy and in modern terms police chief, who had once
been employed by Charles VII in detective work on Louis as dauphin,
had the cold intelligence and efficiency of a typical James Bond
villain. Tristan, however, cannot reasonably be accused of anything
more objectionable than inaccessibility to pity in his professional activities. The representation of him by Scott and Hugo as a savage demon
is out of focus.

It was the employment of such men, considered by Louis as
essential in his peculiar position as a monarch uninterested in war for
its own sake and lacking the personality of a noble figurehead, that
helped to blacken his reputation. But the years of his reign were so
critical a period in the history of his country that if he had only
employed such relatively honest servants as Pierre de Brézé, Philippe de
Commines and the Bastard of Bourbon he would soon have been
hustled off his throne by characters scarcely less violently ambitious
than Charles the Bold and very much less puritanical.

The king gave orders to the count of Brienne and the lord of
Craon, noblemen of milder disposition, who represented him in Burgundy, to occupy the duchy at once and hurry on the marriage
arranged between the dead duke's daughter Mary, now aged nineteen,
and Louis's own seven-year-old son the dauphin Charles. The fox,
some Burgundians said, had fatally bitten the lion. But actually both
combatants could reasonably be given either of these nicknames. Charles
the Bold had been nearly as crafty on occasion in his policies as King
Louis, for instance at Péronne and in his negotiations with England and
Germany. Again, the king's courage, in war as in diplomacy, could not
be doubted. Nor did he lack, as Charles often did, the humorous
magnanimity alleged in the fables of Aesop to be characteristic of the
"royal" beast. He wrote ironically, for example, to Brienne and Craon,
who would hardly have been human if they were not fast filling their
pockets from the deceased duke's estate: "I thank you, my lords, for
permitting me the honor of sharing your booty. I have no objection to
your taking half the profits available. But I beg you to use the other
half for repair of the forts on the German frontier. As for the wine,
please keep it for yourselves."

This typical specimen of the sovereign's drier communications also
proves that at this date he was never anyone's dupe, not even that of
the repulsively vulgar Olivier le Dain, whom he ennobled precisely
because the barber would undertake certain imperative tasks that no
gentleman could be asked to descend to. Other Flemings, a race
notoriously obstinate as a rule in their dealings with foreigners, proved
less amenable than Olivier. In order to reduce them, as a nation, to
obedience, Louis had to engage personally in a whole series of cam-

paigns. His main objective was Ghent. For in that city Mary, who was determined to resist his blandishments and to refuse marriage to the sickly little bridegroom proposed for her, had been pleading her cause for all she was worth, since her father's death, to the rest of Europe. Her wealth, in spite of the French depredations which had already begun, could still be regarded as enormous. Money talked. And in Mary's case its voice was rendered more melodious by her youth, her bereavement and above all by the strength of character and intelligence that supported her arguments. Her girlish vivacity merely decorated the surface of a mind that had inherited much of the best in Charles the Bold—his steadiness of purpose, his energy and his indomitable spirit, if far less of his rashness in action. Mary also seems to have shared her father's sexual impassivity. Personable, but no more attractive in face and figure than most girls of her age, Mary did not rely on erotic conquests to hold her own, but on the logic of her position and her ability to define it. In these circumstances Louis found her, from the first, far from easy to deal with.

He began with Dijon in Burgundy proper, after telling the citizens of Lyons, in the first place, that he would respect and protect the rights of Charles's daughter in her inheritance as soon as he had taken formal possession of it as her suzerain. Dijon surrendered to him on February 1, 1477. Next he turned to the Somme towns, capturing Abbeville, Péronne and Saint-Quentin without much difficulty. But further north the opposition stiffened. In March Arras defied him and had to be stormed. The king was wounded during the siege, having come too close to the walls in pursuit of a curiosity which became famous after he had observed in a letter to one Olivier de Coetivy: "I am of the nature of a woman concerning curiosity. When someone tells me something in obscure terms I want to know at once what he is really talking about."

He frankly admitted that he ought to have been more careful at the gates of Arras. But he added a typically humorous comment. "This torn flesh of mine," he told the surgeon, "has really been caused by that malicious chatterbox, the duke of Brittany. For the fellow quite recently called me a coward for being reluctant to engage in war. I just had to prove him wrong." The king was joking in his usual style. But the jest had, as so often, a sting in it. Most of those at his bedside no doubt knew well enough that it was the cautious Breton himself who better deserved to be called coward for his perpetual evasion of demands by Edward IV and Charles the Bold for his personal appearance on their behalf in the field against Louis.

Cambrai, to the southeast of Arras, had formerly been part of the empire. The city gave King Louis no trouble after he had observed jocularly in his address to the garrison: "I see that bird of yours"—he meant the Habsburg eagle—"has come back for the spring!" But at Tournai he had to fight, winning a decisive victory. Then in Hainaut he joined his general, the Comte de Dammartin, Antoine de Chabannes, whose heart he had sworn in 1456 to throw to his hounds, but who was now his trusted friend once more. During a skirmish in this part of the country another old friend, Tanneguy de Chastel, more consistently faithful to Louis than Dammartin, had the king's hand on his shoulder when a cannon ball demolished the nobleman. At Quesnoy the monarch presented his own gold chain to a tremendous fighter, Raoul de Lannoy, previously in the service of Charles the Bold, with the exclamation: "By the resurrection of Christ! (*Pâques-Dieu!*) I must fetter you, my lad, in case I lose such a grand soldier!"

Later in this month of March 1477 the king received ambassadors from Mary's court at Ghent. They were headed by her chancellor, Haguenet, and the lord of Humbercourt, her prime minister. They came in conciliatory mood, which Louis met more than halfway. But to his vexation the envoys, when they returned to Ghent on April 3, were seized by a furious mob, tortured and executed. Mary protested vigorously. But she found that a majority of the citizens was resolutely determined to have no dealings whatever with the king of France. Her countenancing of the recent negotiation with him led to her being held practically a prisoner by the Ghent local authorities. Her action in itself had been reasonable enough in view of the king's late victories. But she was not yet in a position to take so submissive a step without first sounding popular opinion in the matter. The Flemish burghers, those of Ghent in particular, did not intend to allow themselves to be despotically ruled even by the ducal family, as both Charles and Philip in their time had often discovered.

Feelings in the city had also been inflamed by the recent disappearance of the widowed duchess, Mary's stepmother, Margaret of York. She had taken refuge at a secret hiding place in England, whence she was sending frantic appeals to her brother King Edward at Windsor to stop the French monarch from his violent incursions upon her great inheritance. Margaret's rage had been increased by her discovery that Louis himself, in his usual way, had been secretly negotiating with the citizens of Ghent. He had suggested to them that she was planning to remove Mary from their control and use the girl's vast fortune for the aggrandizement of England by marrying her off to Edward's brother, the duke of Clarence, now a widower and conspiring to acquire the English crown for himself. It was not so much that Margaret wished to see her younger brother oust her elder, Edward, from the throne. Probably she did not care which of them occupied it. Her object was rather to erect an invincible Anglo-Burgundian alliance in order to prevent Louis from getting possession of her property by force. This aim would best be achieved by a marriage of Mary to Clarence, Edward being already married and his sons Edward and Richard only seven and four years old respectively.

Louis's excellent intelligence service had informed him correctly of Margaret's schemes. He at once attempted to turn them to his own advantage by revealing them to Ghent in order if possible to draw that important but difficult city to the French side in the struggle for Burgundy. He hinted to the citizens that they would be better off under an indulgent, purely nominal master like himself than if they fell into the hands of greedy and ferocious aliens, those constituting Clarence's faction, if it should succeed in toppling the more cautious Edward from the seat of government in England.

Fortunately for the king of France Mary did not care for what she had heard of Clarence, whom nobody trusted. Moreover Edward himself, already more than dubious of his brother's intentions, naturally opposed the idea of advancing the duke's prospects by marriage to the great heiress. The English king therefore welcomed dispatches from his paymaster Louis indicating that the girl was a "rebellious vassal" of France and would be a most unsuitable bride for an English royal duke commonly supposed in Europe to be plotting to snatch the crown of his country from the head of his elder brother. The recipient of Louis's bounty, which the Frenchman called a "pension" and the Englishman "tribute," replied in almost humble terms to the representations of the king of France. But Edward at the same time felt uneasy at the plan for a French Burgundy. For it might eventually expel England from the last English foothold in France, Calais.

Meanwhile Louis attempted to bring his "vassal" around to his own way of thinking. The barber Olivier le Dain, who still practiced, like many of his trade, as a surgeon, was dispatched to Ghent to press upon Mary the advantages of a marriage to the dauphin. But her Flemish courtiers only laughed at the insinuating little proletarian of a "count of Meulan," who had come originally from the same part of the country as themselves. Louis may have thought that this circumstance would get him a hearing in the city. No doubt Olivier himself swore that it would. But the Fleming's deliberate exaggeration of his native mannerisms had the very opposite effect. His clumsy pretenses of gentility might have deceived Englishmen or Germans. But his compatriots saw through them in a moment, as did Mary herself. When he arrogantly demanded a private interview with her she burst out laughing. "What?" she cried gaily. "Does my cousin the king send me a surgeon because he thinks I am ill? But I can assure him I never felt better in my life!" She dismissed the intruder there and then, with contempt.

The tangle of cross-purposes was at last resolved by the heiress herself. She chose as her husband, with Margaret's consent, the Archduke Maximilian of Austria, son of Emperor Frederick III. The candidature of Maximilian, who was a year or two younger than his prospective bride, had been one of the questions to be discussed at the abortive meeting of Charles the Bold and the eccentric emperor at Trier in 1473, when Frederick, scandalized at Charles's suggestion of a kingly dignity to be conferred upon himself, had rushed off down the river in the middle of the night without taking leave of his guest.

Now the pattern of circumstances had changed in the emperor's favor. Maximilian, though relatively poor, was Mary's superior in rank and likely to succeed in due course to control of the Holy Roman Empire. The overweening ambition of the late duke of Burgundy needed no longer to be feared. His daughter had shown clearly that she preferred a German to a French alliance. The way seemed open to a domination of Europe by a combination of imperial prestige with Burgundian wealth. England had its own domestic troubles and everyone knew that the French king, though strong, would rather negotiate than fight. The generally old-fashioned statesmen of northern Europe could not see that time was on his side. Nor were they yet aware of Maximilian's unstable character.

It was masked under an attractive exterior, coupled with skill in the tournament and an already apparent eagerness for war. His courage could not be doubted and in fact was never called in question. At the same time the decent modesty of his bearing seemed to promise capacity for good government and some degree of reforming zeal, natural to his youth. His basic irresponsibility, which eventually rendered him ridiculous, could not be detected at this early stage of his manhood by his advisers or even by his potential enemies, including King Louis. Finally the archduke and Mary, while they were both children, had contracted an understanding for future marriage and symbolized it by exchanging rings. More serious negotiations for their union were now set on foot.

After the murders of Haguenet and Humbercourt at Ghent in April 1477 the girl was already writing to Maximilian: "Most dear lord and brother, I greet you most cordially. Do not doubt that I shall keep the bond between us as arranged by my father, now in heaven. I shall be a true wife to you, for I have faith in you. The bearer of this letter knows my confined circumstances, though I cannot confide in him. May God grant us our hearts' desire. I beg you not to delay, for your coming will bring help and comfort to my lands. If you do not come they have no other resource. If you forsake me I may be forced to act against my own will."

The last sentence in all probability meant that she might have to submit to the king of France and his dauphin. The archduke, in fact, delayed by his father's insistence on his participation in a campaign against Hungary, eventually set out from Vienna on May 21. But at Cologne another long wait ensued while, according to Commines, who did not like Germans, he needed money from Mary to continue his journey.

Maximilian in later years commissioned the production of an allegorical poem on old-fashioned lines called *The Dangers and Adventures of the Famous Hero and Knight Sir Teuerdank*—the name means "Dearly Bought Reward"—detailing his difficulties on the way to rescue, like a prince in a fairy tale, his future bride from the spell of her incarceration. But such sordid details as financial troubles are not mentioned, naturally, in this highly romanticized version of the expedition of a would-be Siegfried of the fifteenth century to the Burgundian court.

Louis struggled to the last, short of making open war, against the consummation of the marriage in view. In June he sent to London a permanent ambassador, Charles de Martigny, bishop of Elne in Roussillon, to keep watch over French interests in the English capital. They were chiefly concerned with the prevention of English aid to Maximilian's entry upon the Burgundian regions not yet under control from Paris, that is, the territories today known as Belgium and Holland, with the important cities of Bruges, Brussels, Liége and The Hague in addition to Ghent. The prelate selected for this crucial task was gleefully characterized by Louis himself as "a bigger swindler than any Englishman." The bishop started with the considerable advantage that Edward preferred his banker, the king of France, to the archduke. For the future "king of the Romans" and emperor was then so poor that he could not dream of being anyone's moneylender. The economical Flemish merchants even complained that they were obliged to provide him with shirts free of charge. They certainly disliked Maximilian, harmless as he then appeared, simply because he was a foreigner sent to rule over them.

But the king of England, attached though he was, with golden chains, to Louis, definitely shied away from the French monarch's offer to him of the Netherlands, on condition that he would send troops to help France to conquer that region. Edward, so formidable a field commander against his fellow countrymen in earlier days, was now inclined to temporize in politics. His tendencies to luxury and indolence were growing upon him now that he had so large a private income flowing in from the Paris treasury. He proceeded to make counterdemands, which smacked of blackmail, on his "good cousin." England required, he said, the immunity of his sister Margaret's dowry, consisting of the very towns the French were actually besieging at that moment. He conveniently ignored the fact that the dowager duchess of Burgundy was at the same time strenuously backing Mary and Maximilian, who had by this date become Louis's declared enemies. The English sovereign also had the audacity to insist on the French "tribute" to him being made official by law and paid in English money, hard currency marks instead of the cheaper francs. When the bishop of Elne, in his turn, temporized, pointing out the undesirability of such an extra burden on his master's exchequer at a time when it was financing a war on behalf of both countries, Edward coolly signed an agreement with Maximilian to remain neutral in any hostilities between France and the archduke's patrimony of Austria.

The London populace, always resentful of Louis's influence, began to hiss the bishop whenever he appeared in the streets. They assailed his lodgings with yells of "French dogs!" At his banquets toasts were defiantly drunk to the health of the "duke of Burgundy," i.e., Maximilian, actually calling him by the traditional title, normally reserved to France, of "Most Christian King." In these insufferable conditions Charles de Martigny gave in to the extent of promising to submit to his master a draft of King Edward's proposals. The prelate left London for Paris bearing such a document. At first he was refused admission to the royal presence. This notification of Louis's displeasure at the failure of his ambassador's mission was followed, when the military situation in the Netherlands improved from the French point of view, by actual prosecution of the unlucky bishop by the Parlement. He was found guilty of "exceeding instructions." But he was punished only by temporary degradation to a minor post in the chancellery. Soon he was quietly reinstated in his distant bishopric of Elne. It is probable that he and the king acted in collusion throughout this episode. Louis ended the matter in dispute by calmly threatening Edward with a positive suspension rather than an increase and a legal ratification of the "tribute." This menace brought the English monarch to heel as though by magic.

Yet, in spite of all that Louis or indeed Edward himself could do, the fateful marriage of Mary of Burgundy and Maximilian of Austria finally took place in Brussels on August 18, 1477. The brilliant appearance and agreeable manners of the young couple, clearly on the defensive against the devious and implacable king of France, easily won the sympathy of most of the rest of Europe. No one could foresee at that time that the foundations of the Habsburg power, which was to alter the configuration of the Continent in favor of Germany and Spain under the future Emperor Charles V, born in 1500, were being laid with Burgundian money. Louis for his part remained merely concerned to secure as peacefully as possible his legitimate inheritance, consisting of the dominions of his dead vassal Charles the Bold, against encroachment by German princes. He meant in the end to round off his kingdom in the north and east, from Flanders to Franche-Comté and Provence, as a self-contained and impregnable unit.

He felt confident of being able to outwit young Maximilian, whom he rightly regarded as simply another specimen of the outgoing medieval ruler intent only on reviving imperial glories and quite out of touch with the spirit of the new age. Louis had dealt successfully with such people often enough before, in Brittany and Armagnac, in Spain and Italy. He knew also that the stubborn, commercially minded and stormily independent population of the Netherlands would never wholeheartedly support an Austrian archduke wholly incapable of understanding their mentality, which in fact closely resembled the king's own. They had repeatedly rebelled against even a native Burgundian, Philip the Good, who had brought them prosperity and peace by his wise and tolerant administration. Yet they had also regarded him as a despot of unacceptably outmoded views of government, however benevolent in intention. The case had been far worse with his son Charles the Bold, who did not understand traders and decisions reached in committee at all. Beginning in their opinion as at best a flamboyant and resolute saber rattler, he had ended as nothing better than a selfish, brutally cruel and irresponsible tyrant of the old school, a megalomaniac with only personal valor to recommend him. Still less cooperation could be expected by the stiff-necked citizens of Flanders from a foreign prince who happened to have won, as no more than a faint shadow of her father Charles the Bold, the heart of an immature girl, their nominal suzerain, Mary of Burgundy.

But Louis knew the proud and argumentative merchants of the Netherlands too well to gamble on their support of his designs. He respected their courage and their abilities. As usual, however, he distrusted the risks of outright warfare against Maximilian and Mary, especially as they were now formally recognized if not openly aided by the English crown. He negotiated tentatively and tactfully with the archduke, while suppressing in France such Anglophiles as appeared to follow Edward's lead. Only a few days after the marriage the king of France beheaded, on the charge of harboring an English spy, the duke of Nemours, Jacques d'Armagnac, a cousin of the Count Jean V of Armagnac who had in the past given his sovereign so much trouble owing to the English sympathies of that house, which controlled the always restive southwest of France.

On July 31, 1476, Louis had written to the captain of the Bastille in Paris:

> I am sending you the Duke of Nemours in charge of the Lord of St. Pierre with orders to place him in the St. Antoine building. Accordingly, prior to his arrival, you are to seize all such of his people as are in Paris, imprison them in the Bastille and see that they are well chained. . . . you had better be quick about it, for if they hear rumors that their master is coming to Paris they will flee. . . . it seems to me that you have only one thing to do and that is to find out what pledge he has given to the Constable [i.e. Saint-Pol, executed at the end of the previous year] to join him in the plot to make the Duke of Burgundy regent, to have me killed and my Lord the Dauphin captured and so take over the government of the kingdom. Force him to be clear on this point and put him very hard to the question over it [i.e. by torture]. I should be displeased to hear that the irons had been removed from his legs and that he had been allowed interrogation in another chamber, being brought out of his cage [this was a German invention recently adopted in France] for the purpose. Also, I don't want him taken to hear Mass in any building to which women are admitted. . . . Take care that he is kept always in his cage and interrogated there, except when he is put to the question in the other room.

This is the only extant letter in which Louis shows the streak of stern cruelty latent in nearly all the administrators of his age. The king's specific expression of this malevolence reflects the feeling of something like panic which his well-justified suspicions of conspiracy among certain of his nobles to betray him to the Burgundian had aroused in him.

The monarch had previously forgiven Jacques again and again for what might be represented as treasonable activities. But the duke of Nemours was a popular character. His young wife was pregnant at the time of his arrest. Many of his fellow aristocrats considered the sentence of execution unnecessarily severe on a man who had stormed Perpignan in Catalonia for Louis on January 7, 1463. For some years afterwards the king could not always count on the unhesitating assistance of the French nobility in his contest with Maximilian.

Yet by the end of 1477 most of Burgundy had become, for all practical purposes, French. For, as Philippe de Commines wrote, "No one was ever so ready to lend an ear to the people or to inquire personally about so many things as King Louis." His manners in fact were often familiar to a degree which shocked conventional men in

France, though Italians, whom he greatly admired, would have been less surprised at such downright behavior in a prince. The wealthy burghers of Florence, especially the Medici family, had set this example as a counterpoise to their tenure of a power unsubstantiated by royal or ducal prerogative. The Florentines, since they were in the main richer and better educated than the inhabitants of other Italian states, were imitated in their social behavior by their nearest neighbors in the north, Milan, Verona, Padua and Venice. Even Romans and Neapolitans were beginning by this date to be less ceremonious.

The contemporary king of France could sometimes be seen with his hand on the shoulder of a foreign ambassador or arm in arm with one of his own lords, a Guillaume de Bische or a Tanneguy de Chastel. The monarch's love of secrecy was strangely accompanied on occasion by jovial and quite sincere garrulousness. He could use this faculty to lead on a companion to unguarded revelations of private thoughts, as with Charles the Bold on their walk from Conflans. Yet the king's own words could rarely be used against him. For he possessed, except in sudden fits of anger, to a supreme degree the flexibility of mind and the ease of expression which would enable him to give what he had said one day a somewhat different implication and basis on another, varying significantly from what might have been assumed by a previous listener. In this way he would plausibly correct mistakes as soon as he was convinced he had made them, as when he first dismissed, then reinstated, his father's ministers and when he abolished, then revived, the Pragmatic Sanction.

He did admit once that "my tongue hath done me much damage. But at other times," he added slyly, "it may have done me good. At any rate," he went on still more frankly, "it is a fault I must amend." His expert diplomacy had been largely modeled on that of his favorite foreigners, the Italians, particularly the Milanese at this time. The assassination of the far from admirable though dashing Duke Galeazzo Maria Sforza at the end of 1476 would have deeply grieved Louis if the Milanese autocrat, once so respected by the king as to have been appointed by the royal command lieutenant general of Dauphiné, had not quite recently changed his policy to one in support of Burgundian pretensions.

But the French monarch's own special contribution to the art of verbal bargaining, which he often entrusted by word of mouth to quite humble servants, set a precedent that was to be followed all over Europe for centuries. It is true that he was lucky. His most dangerous adversaries, from Agnès Sorel to Charles the Bold, had a habit of dying at crucial moments. Yet the real reason why he quadrupled his father's income was not good fortune but sheer outstanding

business ability. It is possible but not certain that his tireless exploitation
of this gift had rendered him bald at fifty as well as abnormally stout
in middle age and a sufferer from varicose veins in his spindly legs.
He took plenty of exercise all his life in the hunting field. But the
long hours of study and talk far exceeded those he spent in fresh air.

The king's grief at the death from plague of his one-year-old son
François in 1472 had caused him to take a solemn oath, which Commines says he kept, never to have carnal dealings with any woman but
his queen, Charlotte of Savoy, an excellent wife according to the same
historian but physically unattractive. Such pious undertakings were indeed as a rule strictly maintained by Louis, in strong contrast with
the wriggles by which he evaded treaty clauses when it suited him. At
the same time he took good care not to be exploited by the greedier
ecclesiastics of the day, who were often a curse to other sovereigns.
The demands of the men of God were usually for more land. But
Louis, who looked just like one of his own peasants when faced by
such requests, was the last man in the world to give fertile soil away.
He preferred to shell out cash. But he never did so without exhaustive
inquiry into the justification for petitions of this kind. He was also
very likely indeed to have an ulterior motive, such as the increase of
French influence at the Vatican, not necessarily exerted on the incumbent pope. During the reign of Louis XI the cardinals at Rome
grew more and more aware of the rising importance of the French
clergy in the Eternal City, due mainly to the king's judicious munif-
icence.

Though by nature parsimonious, generally shabbily dressed and nau-
seated by splendid, chattering and mixed assemblies, he could sometimes appear in regal magnificence. He would enter provincial towns
with a great, floating plume in his hat, a long, jeweled sword at his
side, a white and red doublet over his armor in the Italian fashion and
a cloak embroidered with a winged stag in gold. At the first meeting
of his newly constituted Order of St. Michael he wore a blue robe
adorned with fleurs-de-lis, a cloak of white silk and a high black cap.
But when hunting he could hardly be distinguished from his companions. Again, at meetings of a politically dangerous character, as at
Picquigny, he would rig out one of his escort, in this instance Philippe
de Commines, exactly like himself, so that a potential assassin might
aim at the wrong man.

He dined in solitary state unless, as often happened, he was too busy
to spare the time. Otherwise the queen, his children and his guests
would sit at a separate high table, waited on by three gentlemen of
his household and seven pages. Ten chamberlains were served at a
second table, eighteen ladies-in-waiting at a third. The remaining mem-

bers of the establishment ate later. They included Olivier le Dain. But the king was always talking to this unpopular character in private and sending him all over the place on embassies abroad and in Flanders, though never again, after the fiasco at Ghent, to see Mary. The barber's Flemish origin, however, was useful on less exalted errands, when he did not have to meet aristocrats, but was simply on the track of suspected traitors or commissioned to restock the royal aviary, Louis being passionately fond of birds, especially magpies, which in their habits might be thought by some humorists to resemble the pilfering messenger himself.

Olivier also sometimes lent the monarch urgently needed sums of money, relatively small of course, which had to be kept secret. No doubt he charged and was paid interest on these loans and knew that the slightest suspicion of boasting about them would cost him his head. The barber-surgeon was certainly no fool and never forgot, as the modern phrase goes, which side his bread was buttered on. Though utterly unprincipled in dealing with everyone except his royal master, he never betrayed Louis, who appreciated the devoted care with which he handled the material tools of his trade, having learned from their use how to be discreet and responsible in other fields. His natural arrogance, however, regularly gave offense to his social superiors. He could never cure this failing. But the king only laughed at it, as if the fellow had been his favorite court jester. The monarch would soon have taken vengeance, as everyone knew, on any attempt to teach him manners.

Only one other man, also a Fleming, was similarly privileged at the French court. This was the grave and scholarly historian Philippe de Commines, a nobleman whom no one could accuse of vulgar conceit, though he too was no more averse than anyone else in his position from taking advantage of it to feather his nest at the expense of other people. Though he had started life as one of the chamberlains of Charles the Bold, and had fought against Louis at the battle of Montlhéry in 1465, he had in 1472 become Louis's greatest friend, dominating all his contemporaries for sheer honesty and capacity in his official work. His portrait in maturity by an unknown artist shows resolute, intellectual features, a frank and calm gaze, general good looks approaching nobility and in short every mark of a deeply civilized temper. It is clear that these two Flemings could not have afforded a greater contrast with each other. That they were the two chief favorites of Louis XI proves both the breadth of his mind and its exclusively practical cast.

The father of Philippe de Commines had been a Knight of the Golden Fleece and sovereign bailiff of Flanders, devoted throughout his life to the service of Philip the Good. But the bailiff's son saw very early that the swaggering, headstrong heir to the duchy of Burgundy would never achieve anything worth-while. Five years after his accession in 1467 the young Commines crossed over from Charles's camp in Normandy to that of the king of France, whose astute and reasonable views of complex situations he had long admired. Louis granted him lands, a pension and a rich wife. Still three years under thirty, the future historian became lord of Argenton, seneschal of Poitou, to which province his wife's family belonged, and captain of Poitiers. The king, at that time not very well off for brainy staff, had first noticed the Burgundian chamberlain's exceptional quality at Péronne in 1468, when it could plausibly be argued that the imprisoned monarch owed his life to the young man's intervention with the raging duke. After 1472 Louis never regretted admitting him to the royal intimacy except on one occasion.

It occurred in the notable year 1477, when the sovereign, perhaps owing to the lucky death of Charles the Bold and the consequently facilitated acquisition by the crown of France of all his property, descended to unwonted recklessness. He plotted to kidnap his goddaughter, Mary of Burgundy, in order to force her to marry the little dauphin, aged seven. The citizens of Arras, who had yet to be convinced, like many other people, that Charles was really dead, asked the French king what he thought he was doing. He at once rode into the town. Heads began to fall. The leaders of an irredentist force of Burgundians which tried to storm the city were captured and hanged. The procurator-general of Arras was brought to the block, together with a captain of the local militia and an archer who had discharged an arrow at the king as he entered the gates.

Next, at Ghent, where Mary was living, a popular revolution broke out. The mob, as stated above, seized and beheaded two of her council who had been to see Louis. The monarch's wrath at this proceeding caused him to start behaving like the late Charles of Burgundy himself. The king stormed Cambrai, had the garrison massacred and the walls razed to the ground. He destroyed crops in Valenciennes and instigated the murder of the president of Burgundy in Dijon. Mercenaries in the royal service began to desert and to operate similar brigandage for their own benefit. It was then too that Louis had Jacques d'Armagnac, duke of Nemours, executed for high treason.

Philippe de Commines, needless to say, had protested against all this violence from its beginning soon after the battle of Nancy. Louis retaliated by banishing the chamberlain to his estate of Argenton in Poitou. But after a few months a certain amount of carefully phrased correspondence began to pass between the imperturbable exile and his master, who had so suddenly thrown his usual caution to the winds. It was probably as a result of hints by the studious lord of Argenton that the king gradually relaxed his ferocious attitude. He started to conciliate Burgundian feeling so far as he considered such measures advisable to check open rebellion. He confirmed a number of provincial privileges and made no great display of military force. But in the wild, mountainous region of Franche-Comté, due south of Lorraine, an ex-freebooter, Guillaume de Vaudrey et Salazar, stormed the only decent castle in the county, routing its loyal garrison in a fierce pitched battle. Nevertheless, a new royalist commander, Charles d'Amboise, soon avenged this defeat. Louis entered Dijon, the nearest big city, in triumph. Despite the recent assassination there, at his orders, of the Burgundian president, the king received an enormous consignment of the town's chief exports, mustard and wine, both as famous then as they are today.

The marriage of Mary of Burgundy and Maximilian disturbed Philippe de Commines, now restored to the king's favor. He foresaw that this union boded ill for his master's schemes. Louis, however, after a few sour grimaces and caustic jeers, decided to ignore the insult to his son. The monarch was at that time busily consolidating his power in Artois, the northwest frontier region of his kingdom, directly facing Flanders, itself centered upon Ghent. He replied calmly to a rather provocative communication from the archduke, complaining of the cynical breaking by the French crown of the truce signed with Charles the Bold nine years before. The king felt safe enough with Swiss mercenaries behind him. Still, he preferred negotiations at this juncture to pike-rattling. Moreover, his health was at last starting to break down under the strain of a task that he sometimes felt would be endless. Burgundians might be half-French. But Flemings, as the Fleming Commines warned him, were another matter. They seemed never to be happy except in revolt. It was at this period that Louis began the habit of isolating himself in his parks, a custom which was to continue to the end of his life, now only six years distant. He also, when he did travel, redoubled his bodyguards and ceased to rely on local entertainment, taking his own accommodations and food with him.

The misgivings of Philippe de Commines came true. Maximilian plunged into Picardy at the head of a mixed army of Flemings and Germans. They took the small town of Condé near Valenciennes. The king himself recaptured the place, proving his personal prowess as an artilleryman by aiming his own cannon. But this exploit was his last on an actual battlefield. He further distinguished his final appearance as a practical commander in hostilities by forbidding his troops to sack Condé. He allowed Maximilian's garrison to retire in good order with its equipment. For his policy was now to lull the energy of his unstable opponent by merely token opposition. Nothing but skirmishing took place in this area between the two forces until in July 1478 a year's armistice was signed at Arras. Both parties gave up the fortresses they had occupied. The mobility of free-ranging nobles and their retainers was prohibited if such groups amounted to more than a dozen knights. On the other hand all merchants were allowed to travel without barriers or hindrance and to provide for their own sufficient escort.

Nothing could indicate more clearly than this last stipulation the change that had come over late fifteenth-century society. It had reached the conviction that only traders, not local aristocrats, could best ensure its prosperity. The king of France shared this feeling to the full. In fact he might almost be said to have initiated it. At any rate he did his best to enforce its recognition on his impulsive, outdated adversary, the ambitious young archduke, who knew a lot more about hunting and military drill than he did about high politics and the ultimately decisive ramifications of commerce.

In April Louis's attention had been distracted by the dramatic attempt in Florence to murder Lorenzo de' Medici, whose younger brother Giuliano was stabbed to death in the cathedral by the Pazzi faction, acting for Pope Sixtus. The uncrowned ruler of the city managed to escape with a slight wound in the throat. That great man, whose growing power had so alarmed the Holy Father, bore a considerable resemblance to the French sovereign. Both men cared little for luxury but possessed restless and imaginative temperaments. Both easily inspired confidence in their diplomacy by turning on overwhelming personal charm whenever they liked. Both could be drily witty without real malice at the expense of an antagonist. Each preferred bribery to the sword and freely gave promises they did not intend to keep, trusting to their intellectual dexterity to extricate themselves from such obligations. Both suffered a good deal from hereditary ill health. Both were born autocrats.

But Lorenzo, not being of royal blood, took care to conceal his despotic impulses. Louis did not mind in the least if his subjects resented the highhandedness which he regarded as his prerogative by birth. But there is no doubt that these two rulers, if they had not been set so geographically far apart, would have contracted a still deeper friendship than that which this limitation largely restricted to the financial field. As neighbors with similarly progressive ideals in political and social thought, determined to be done once for all with medieval feudalism, Lorenzo de' Medici and Louis de Valois, acting together, would probably have blocked for good the reversion to naked autocracy which marked the Counter Reformation movement of the sixteenth century. As just noted, they were each singularly qualified by nature to exercise such dominion but far too levelheaded to adopt it as a principle of government, as did many of the humorless religious fanatics who came after them.

Even so, in the spring of 1478 Lorenzo called on the French king for help against the pope. The regent of Milan, Bona of Savoy, Queen Charlotte's better-looking sister and mother of the ten-year-old new Duke Gian Galeazzo Sforza, supported this plea.

Louis wrote from Arras on May 12 to the signory of Florence, in Italian:

> Most dear and honored friends, we have just learned of the terrible and brutal outrage and opprobrious injury recently perpetrated against both your Lordships and the persons of our most dear and beloved cousins Lorenzo and Giuliano de' Medici and their friends, relatives, servants and supporters by those of the Pazzi Bank, and thus of the death of our said cousin Giuliano de' Medici. By which we have been and still are as distressed as by anything that might have happened to ourselves. Therefore your honor and our own have been equally offended, the Medici being our relatives, friends and allies and we considering the said outrage and the death of our said cousin Giuliano as having the same effect as if it had been committed against ourselves, thus rendering all the said Pazzi guilty of *lèse-majesté*, are by no means disposed to allow their crime to go unpunished but on the contrary desire with all our heart that condign punishment be inflicted as an example to all other men. We have therefore thought it well to send to your Lordships our beloved and faithful counselor and chamberlain, the Lord of Argenton and Seneschal of our Province of Poitou, who is today one of those in our service in whom we have the greatest trust. He will acquaint you at further length of our feelings in this matter and tell you more in regard to it. We beg you to lend all faith and credence to everything he declares to you on our behalf, as much as you would to our own self, since it is in this hope we send him to you, most dear and honored friends, praying that God may guard you in His holy keeping.

The letter, in spite of its conventional phrasing, should not be read as expressing merely official condolence. Louis had been even more frightened than most ruling Italian princes by the half-successful Pazzi conspiracy. He was deeply concerned, as indeed he remained all his life, to nip anything like *lèse-majesté* in the bud, anywhere in Europe, lest it encourage "wicked lords" in his beloved France, a country he honestly believed, by no means absurdly, to be still entirely dependent for its prosperity on his single life. The "more" which Commines was

to tell Lorenzo probably involved proposals for French military assistance to defend Florence against further assaults on its young administrator, whom the king had already recognized as the only European
statesman comparable with himself in patriotic dedication.

The monarch proceeded to suggest an ecumenical council, with the
characteristic remark that he had no objection to an ecclesiastical
schism, since three or four popes would be so much better than one.
He would like such a council, he said, to take place on French soil,
where Italian bitterness of faction would have less influence than at
Constance or Basel. For previous councils of this sort, even in Switzerland, had done little to improve the perennial situation of papal
temporal ambitions. But in the end political events caused both sides
in this controversy to climb down. Sixtus remained in office.

Louis actually, after his reconciliation with the Vatican, did more
or less as he liked in French clerical administration. He required and
obtained unquestioning obedience from the bishops and all the clergy.
Objections from Rome were silenced by the threat of French intervention in Italian politics. The same menace also forced Sixtus to
depose canons and even archbishops suspected of disloyalty to the
king. The so-called "Gallican Liberties" of the crown of France,
which so curbed the power of the papacy in future centuries, date from
this epoch.

Louis returned to Paris in poor health but as energetic as ever.
He persevered in his efforts to please the Holy Father. Yet at the
same time he warned that restless pontiff against secular pretensions
and the financial exactions of his officers both in Italy and above all
in France. In this policy the king was at one with Lorenzo de' Medici
of Florence, of whom the pope had been so inordinately jealous that
he had practically ordered the Florentine leader's assassination. The
conspiracy headed by Sixtus's blackguardly nephew Girolamo came to
nothing owing to the imbecile clumsiness of those who tried to give
it effect. Lorenzo triumphed. But, as the French monarch was glad
to see, he remained emphatically a man of peace, not of war. Louis
backed him steadily, as he had once backed Francesco Sforza, in all
his undertakings, especially those against papal aggression. The Medici
bankers were welcomed more and more generously in France. These
two men, so alike in their physical ugliness, their resolute personal
courage and their clear recognition of the new course of civilization,
came to know and esteem each other quite well, though they never
met in the flesh. It was unfortunate for Europe that their mutual
admiration, cut short by the king's death in 1483, never led to a more
intimate association.

CHAPTER XI

Wheels Within Wheels
(1478–1481)

❦❦❦ Between the high summers of 1478 and 1479 Louis may be said to have been marking time. Not that he was inactive. On the contrary, he remained very busy, playing several fish at once, from Edward and Margaret of York to Maximilian and Mary, from French lords to Flemish merchants, from the Swiss to the Italians and from the Portuguese to the Spaniards. He felt himself to be in his element as he exchanged ambiguous correspondence with all these people, startling them with new schemes for the settlement of Europe, promising this and pointing out objections to that. He did not very much fear any of these groups. They were much less coherent than his own, in spite of the restiveness of his aristocrats since the execution of the duke of Nemours. France alone, he told himself, stood relatively firm in the midst of uncertainty and could afford to wait, while other countries solved their own problems, with luck, in accordance with his always courteously and modestly suggested advice.

He had long recognized that Lorenzo de' Medici of Florence overshadowed every other statesman in Italy for political genius and a reasonable attitude to all the puzzles of government. The king's connection with Milan through his now respectful and loyal sister the astute Duchess Yolande, who ruled the neighboring duchy of Savoy, and his rather fatheaded but pretty and friendly sister-in-law the Duchess Bona, formerly a Savoyard but now of Milan, Queen Charlotte's sister and widow of the late Duke Galeazzo Maria Sforza, enabled Louis to keep a useful road open to Florence, a state he was determined to support through thick and thin against Sixtus, Naples, Venice or anyone else.

To Bona on August 10, 1478, he wrote, from Chartres:

My dear sister, heartiest greetings. I have just received with the greatest pleasure your letter announcing that the visit of my ambassadors [i.e. Philippe de Commines and his party, then in Tuscany] has given good hope and comfort not only to my dear friends the Florentines but also to all their allies and those who wish them well. I wrote at once to our Holy Father the Pope, begging him to be pleased to desist from his enterprise. In order that he and the King Don Ferrante may understand that I do not intend to tolerate their mistaken policy, I have arranged to send four or five lances under the command of M. de Calabre [presumably a son of Duke Jean of Calabria (d. 1471) and brother of the latter's son Nicolas of Anjou (d. 1473)] to bring aid and succor to the said Florentines and the League of Italy [a coalition of some smaller Italian states in the north to resist papal aggression]. I beg you accordingly to arrange to allow them passage through your dominions and see that they are supplied with victuals, for which they will pay, and are well treated by your subjects. I trust you confidently to do this for me. I have also ordered an assembly of the prelates of my kingdom in connection with this matter. [This meeting was to sanction on theological grounds the hostile action now to be taken against the pontiff.] In all things I shall give aid and favor to the said League in order that everyone may realize that I sincerely support it. You would be well advised to inform also Genoa and Savona of my attitude. As soon as I receive the further communication you mention it will be possible for me to do everything necessary. And now *A Dieu,* my dear sister, may He ever guard you in His holy keeping.

On the same day, still from Chartres, he addressed his sister Yolande, who died later in the year: "My dear sister, heartiest greetings. Since I have resolved to give all the aid and favor that I can to my old friends the Florentines, to my cousin Lorenzo de' Medici and all the League of Italy against their enemies, I mean to send thither some five lances and I am very anxious for you to give them passage through your dominions, both this side of the mountains and beyond. I accordingly beg you to advise me immediately of your pleasure in this matter. Dear sister, my beloved, I pray God to guard you ever in His holy keeping."

The small force promised was no doubt meant more as a token of good will or a first contingent than a serious contribution to military operations. In any case by 1480 Sixtus had been repulsed from the north and was in trouble elsewhere, when the Turks raided Otranto. By 1484 he was dead, a failure in both politics and war.

Edward of England, on the contrary, by 1478, was more or less out of the woods at home. His dynastic worries had been ended by the judicial murder of his brother the duke of Clarence on February 18, 1478. England thereafter seemed to be growing somnolent, a condition which Louis hoped to rouse to some participation in his own interests, namely, the prosecution of war with Maximilian or at any rate hostile acts against him. For that young man, in the French king's view, would some time or other have to recognize that the duchy of Burgundy could only be part of his dominions so long as his wife insisted on it. The region was so obviously Franco-Flemish, not Austro-German, psychologically and culturally, that so intelligent a young woman as Mary must in the end turn the archduke's ambitions away from France, preferably east and south, with the ultimate objective, so becoming to a conservative Christian prince and future Holy Roman emperor, of driving the infidels back into Asia.

It had to be admitted that she was not showing much sign of any such change of policy at present. The attitude of the newly wedded pair to the French king had hardened so much that they had actually succeeded in bribing the ungrateful Swiss, who now cared for nothing but money, to come over to their side under a commander, the prince of Orange, who had hitherto supported Louis. This development caused the latter, while carefully maintaining his truce with Maximilian, to redouble his secret applications to Edward for assistance. But the now pacific king of England did not want war with Burgundy. He wanted only the profitable Burgundian market for English goods, closer and closer commercial relations with Flanders, where the population got on well with his own, the English merchants at this period much preferring Flemish mentality to French. For the mixture of rough gaiety with prosaic common sense and a marked intolerance of alien, aristocratic or even regal interference with civil liberties remained common to a latitude that included London, the Low Countries and northwestern France in one climate and racial admixture. On the other hand, the traditional enmity between southern England and the French region centered upon Paris, rooted in history and the temperamental antipathy of Latin and Anglo-Saxon, could not in the fifteenth century be turned into wholehearted cooperation, as Louis wished. Even in modern times such an alliance, when politically enforced, has proved less than satisfactory to both sides.

The French king's ideal therefore, expressed in his persistent attempts to establish an early form of Anglo-French *entente cordiale*, was doomed from the start, highly desirable as it looked on paper. On purely logical and political grounds a firm combination of English and French power, had it proved practicable at this date, would have altered the course of European history, successfully holding a center of reason and devotion to trade and industry against both Mediterranean and Teutonic religious fanaticisms. Louis could only think along these lines, since he was not himself accessible to any passionate racial or sectarian prejudice. Intellectually, his calculations could not be faulted, as Lorenzo de' Medici would have agreed. But in the last resort human action of any decisive consequence is ruled by emotion, not reason. In any case Edward, no intellectual, though sly and obstinate enough, could not see the point. Like most Englishmen of his or any other day he preferred, in his maturity, peace and quiet to a stand on rational principle.

Accordingly, neither the faithful continuance of the French pension that enabled him to live at his ease nor even the offer which Louis made to overlook Margaret's hostility if her brother would come in with him against Burgundy influenced the jovially insular English king. Nor did he seem disappointed at events unfavorable to him in Spain, the future leader of European civilization for over a hundred years, after Louis had been dead for more than a generation. The foundations of that hegemony were already being laid. The French sovereign could not foresee the rise of the great emperor Charles V, grandson of Maximilian and son of a daughter of Isabella of Castile, nor Charles's succession to the inheritance of the Habsburgs. But it was clear to King Louis XI that the indomitable energy of his former antagonist, the blind old King Juan II of Aragon, was leading to Spanish unity. Juan remained officially at war with France until just prior to his death on January 20, 1479. But before then he had transmitted his kingdom to his son Ferdinand, king also of Castile by his marriage to his cousin, the strong Queen Isabella. In October 1478 Louis hastened to make peace with Ferdinand and Isabella by promising to abandon his ally King Alfonso V of Portugal, already defeated in war by those sovereigns. They in their turn, to please the French king, renounced the former alliances of their realm, which had threatened France from the south, with England and Burgundy. Louis now felt secure along his Spanish frontier.

As regards Italy, the great event in the spring of 1478 was the attempted assassination of Lorenzo de' Medici. Philippe de Commines writes:

> A few days after that affair I was ordered by the King to go to Florence. After leaving Burgundy I stayed for two or three days with Madame de Savoye, our King's sister [i.e. Yolande] who made me very welcome. Thence I visited Milan for another two or three days, to request the dispatch of Milanese troops to aid the said Florentines, at that time their allies. They agreed most readily to do so, as much for the King's sake as to do their duty. They sent forthwith three

hundred men-at-arms and further numbers at a later date. As soon as the pope heard of this he excommunicated the Florentines and set his troops in motion, together with reinforcements from the King of Naples. This army, very well equipped and numerous, laid siege to Castellina, near Siena, captured it and also several other strong points. It was very lucky indeed for the said Florentines that they were not wholly destroyed, for they had been long at peace and did not realize their danger. Lorenzo de' Medici, their chief citizen, was young and under the influence of men of the same age. But his personal opinion carried great weight. They had few good commanders and their army was very small. The pope and King Ferrante of Naples were represented in the field by the duke of Urbino, a most prudent man and a good soldier. . . . accordingly they took all the places they besieged, but not so promptly as would be done here. . . .

The historian goes on to compare Italian and French methods of warfare, considering the former better at logistics than the latter but the French superior in tactical operations. He stayed for a whole year in Tuscany, at Florence or elsewhere, and says that he was better treated on the last day than on the first. On his way back through Milan the young Duke Gian Galeazzo did homage to him, as an act of courtesy to Louis, for the duchy of Genoa, thus indicating Bona's solidarity with her brother-in-law. Commines adds a touching tribute to his master's cordiality when the envoy returned: "He confided to me more of his business than he ever had before. I slept in his chamber, though I was unworthy to do so and others had a better title to such an honor. But he was so wise a man that one could not fail to do anything he ordered without offering any opinion of one's own."

Commines, on his return to France in the early summer of 1479, found the king looking older and heard him complain of not feeling too well. All the same, he was showing all his usual energy and shrewdness in the conduct of his affairs. In May his troops took Dôle in Franche-Comté and the authorities at Besançon, the capital, sued for peace. By July this long-unruly province too, highly important as closing the king's eastern frontier, had submitted to the French crown. Louis rode into Dijon in triumph at the end of the month to celebrate this victory.

But only two days previously he had experienced a dangerous military setback. The truce signed with Maximilian in the previous year having expired, much depended on what might occur in Picardy during the next few weeks. The Austrian for the moment controlled Flanders, though his subjects there were by no means unanimous in accepting him as their ruler. He began the new campaign by laying siege to Thérouanne in the Pas-de-Calais. The royal commander in Picardy, the lord of Esquerdes, also spelled des Cordes, moved with a substantial force, which included eight thousand "free archers," to relieve the town. Maximilian at once raised the siege and marched to meet him. Contact ensued at a place called Guinegate, the modern Enguinegatte, near Saint-Omer in northern Artois. The Flemish army, numbering over twenty thousand, also contained a small German contingent and three hundred English men-at-arms, technically volunteers, commanded by Sir Thomas Abingdon, a free-lance captain formerly in the service of Charles the Bold.

The troops under Esquerdes consisted almost wholly of cavalry. His squadrons, which he led in person, defeated those of Maximilian, commanded by one Philippe de Ravestain, and pursued them for about ten miles, as far as Aire on the river Lys. But the Flemish peasant infantry stood firm, encouraged by some two hundred officers accustomed to fighting on foot, as was the habit also of some English gentlemen of this period, for instance in many of the battles of the Wars of the Roses.

Meanwhile the always ill-disciplined French "free archers," mounted on this occasion, took to plundering the Flemish supply train, being cynically joined in their depredations by some of its noncombatant staff. They were soon attacked by the main body of Maximilian's infantry and lost heavily, being eventually put to flight. The archduke thus remained in possession of the field and might consider that he had won a great victory. He could easily have resumed his invasion of Picardy, taken Thérouanne and probably Arras. But his casualties, too, had been considerable. For the time being he did not move.

Louis had not authorized this engagement. He had been hoping that the mere size of his army and its excellent artillery would have intimidated the enemy. His tactics in warfare always concentrated, anyhow, on sieges rather than shocks in open country. He had also believed, with some justice, that he might be able to bribe some of the disaffected Flemish officers. He was therefore much depressed by the news from Guinegate. He even suspected at first that it might be worse than had been reported, to the extent of a total rout of his forces. But when he learned from Esquerdes that the Flemish losses had actually exceeded those of the French, a version of the battle no doubt put forward by that commander in defense of what had really been his failure, due to overconfidence, the king took heart. So far from punishing his general for acting without express orders, he congratulated Esquerdes, who must have been not only a persuasive talker but also, as the sequel proved, a soldier capable of assimilating experience.

Nevertheless Louis sternly warned all his senior commanders against ever in the future risking wild clashes of the character of that at

Guinegate. They were always to decline such confrontations, if offered by the enemy, unless he himself ordered acceptance of them. For he alone was in a position to understand all the circumstances affecting hostilities at any particular juncture. In any case it was a fixed principle with the Italian *condottieri*, for example Francesco Sforza (d. 1466), whom he so admired, to win by trapping a foe into surrender rather than by trying to massacre opposing forces. The result of Guinegate simply confirmed the king's plan to proceed against Maximilian only by maneuvers, sieges and above all diplomatic correspondence aimed at the Austrian's restive subjects instead of their incalculable ruler himself.

Accordingly, after this check Louis decided in the first place to attempt to outflank the archduke by feinting at Ghent and Brussels rather than the territory held by Maximilian between Calais and Lille. By such a move he hoped to draw the enemy after him in what would necessarily be a retreat northward. But first he cautiously initiated further negotiations with the Austrian. Their ultimate object, as so often in the king's strategy, was to solve the great frontier dispute between Burgundy and France by a diplomatic marriage. A daughter named Margaret had been born to Maximilian and Mary on January 10, 1480. The child might in due course be inveigled into marrying the dauphin, by this time nine years old. Meanwhile steps could be taken by agents in the Netherlands to ascertain just how much hold the Austrian interloper had on the population and whether it could have any real objection to future control by a French king with an Austro-Flemish wife, the daughter of the true Burgundian Mary. Such long-term projects were much to the present king's taste, as assuring a firmer foundation for political settlements than the winning or losing, always so hard to foresee, of pitched battles like Montlhéry and Guinegate. In both those engagements, for instance, the alleged winner had lost precious time, while the alleged loser had been freed to triumph elsewhere. At the moment, with the winter of 1479 coming on, a season for negotiation rather than warfare, Louis felt more strongly than ever that delayed action would operate in his favor.

Maximilian and Mary had also produced a son, Philip, on July 22, 1478. The existence of this boy known to history as Philip the Handsome and fated to die at twenty-eight after marrying Juana of Castile, Isabella's daughter, and fathering the Emperor Charles V, does not seem to have entered seriously into Louis's calculations. He had no daughter available for this offspring of an enemy he still probably hoped, at this date, to neutralize or at any rate divert from aggression upon France, if Philip's younger sister could be secured for the dauphin.

The question of the marriage of the dauphin to little Margaret required a favorable consideration by the municipality of Ghent, where her parents lived, somewhat precariously. The king had proposed as early as March 1480 that the terms of betrothal should secure to France the regions of Burgundy proper, with Auxerre, Mâcon and Charolais on its western frontier, while Margaret's dowry should consist of the Artois country, much of which, including the important city of Arras, had recently been conquered by the French sovereign. He did not mention the Picardy towns of the Somme valley, already in his possession.

Ghent approved this settlement in principle and tried to force it, in distinctly intemperate language, on Maximilian and Mary, who both repudiated it. Other large cities in Flanders and Brabant, including Brussels itself, supported Ghent. Discussion grew prolonged. For Mary at least seemed to be entitled under existing law to do what she liked with her inheritance from Charles the Bold and she obviously did not want to pledge it to the French crown. On the other hand her subjects, mostly Francophile after her father's ruin and death, saw no reason why Louis's suggestion should not be accepted.

It was in the midst of this crucial situation that Louis began to undertake a civil task in France which greatly astonished his contemporaries. He had always strongly deprecated the law's delays, largely due to parliamentary interference with the course of justice. One anomaly which he particularly detested was the confusion of various weights and measures in different parts of the kingdom. It scandalously hampered commerce, opening the door to all sorts of frauds, abuses and unnecessary arguments. Accordingly, the king drew up a plan for national unification of the figures involved in trade transactions. Standard weights and measures were all to be clearly registered in a printed book, one of those which had been slowly but steadily replacing manuscripts in France since about 1460. Every local authority in the kingdom was to be supplied with a copy. By this means the monarch intended to stop the notorious legal trickeries arising from the differentiation in question. Unfortunately the pressures of both politics and ill health prevented the complete execution of this project by its initiator. But the mere announcement of it did some good and influenced his successors in the government.

Printing in Europe had been begun as early as 1457 at Mainz in western Germany, promoted by Johann Gutenberg. Though Germans were in general unpopular at this date their skill in nearly all mechanical operations was universally acknowledged except with regard to engines of war, in which domain the Milanese outclassed them. Charles VII had sent one of his medal engravers to Mainz to learn the new art of printing. But when the town fell to an incursion of military marauders in 1462 the French specialist fled to Venice and gave the Italians a lead for a while in this field. Gutenberg's representative, however, Peter Schoeffer, soon reached Paris, where Louis immedately perceived the immense value of printing to administrative efficiency and to his overriding obsession, French prosperity.

In 1471, just after the king had declared war on Charles the Bold, the press established at the Sorbonne* printed works by Sallust and Livy on military affairs, which at once engaged the monarch's attention. The *Chronique Française* followed in 1477, covering the history of France down to the death of Charles VII in 1461. Louis annotated his copy, which still exists, in his own hand. He proceeded to have a French version of Xenophon's texts printed. But he was less pleased by the publication in the new medium of a Burgundian poem celebrating the battle of Guinegate. It appeared toward the end of 1479, by which time political propaganda for all the princes of Europe had begun to pour from the presses in quite modern style.

Communications between states and provinces multiplied, owing to the case, speed and improved legibility with which correspondence could now be issued in several copies at once by the new process. Louis had long since decreed his system of royal couriers, who by this time carried printed documents as well as manuscripts. In 1464 these official messengers had begun wearing, in order to obtain priority on the highways, red breeches and blue tunics like those of nineteenth-century French infantrymen. They rode always at full gallop, changing horses about every twelve miles. They stopped for nothing. They had to keep to a strict timetable, as in a modern railway system, and were provided with passports enabling them to clear foreign frontiers with a minimum of delay. When in 1481 the stages were increased to seven leagues or some twenty miles, the king's dispatch riders set up records which could only be surpassed by deer and greyhounds. The expression "seven-league boots" came into vogue, as in the fairy tale of "Mother Goose," which dates from about that period. At Louis's death two years later no less than 234 of these expert horsemen were tearing about the country on his business. He had at the same time of course continued to employ, for top-secret communications, all sorts of inconspicuous persons, traveling more slowly, who looked like anything but what they were.

Many of the letters carried by both official and unofficial couriers at this time, 1479–1480, were addressed to Edward and also to the French sovereign's own political agents in lands which could still be characterized as Burgundian, dominated by Ghent and Brussels. For the English king's eldest daughter Elizabeth, now aged sixteen, could

* The chief college, founded by Robert de Sorbon in 1256, of the University of Paris.

also be regarded as a prospective bride for the dauphin Charles. Such a union between England and France might be decisive against Burgundy's future as an independent power. At the same time the betrothal, if it could be arranged, would estrange the archduke and Edward, at present, it seemed to Louis, literally "thick as thieves" in their mutual determination to rob him of the domains of his head "vassal," Charles the Bold.

It appeared that Maximilian would like another armistice. But the French king soon discovered that this lull was required by Burgundy to work upon the English monarch to denounce the Perpigny agreement. The loss of his pension, it was hinted, would be made up by Mary if he would send troops to help throw Louis back into Paris. Margaret of York, King Louis found, was the prime mover of these schemes. Implacable as ever, despite his previous offer to protect her patrimony of Flemish towns in any postwar settlement, she had actually already cajoled out of her brother fifteen hundred of his best archers to employ in whatever way she thought fit. It was obvious that these crack troops, with their impeccable discipline and unerring marksmanship, were intended to turn the scale of the next battle in the Low Countries.

The situation grew more and more complex. Plague raged in England all through 1479. Edward and Louis wrangled over Elizabeth's dowry, if she were to marry young Charles. Embassy after embassy traveled to Windsor or London from France, each delegation often contradicting what the previous one had said. Margaret of York raised the question of a possible marriage for another of her brother's five daughters, named Anne, to the baby Philip. She not only managed to get this treaty ratified in Brussels but also committed Edward to a declaration of war on France if King Louis would not agree to arbitration by the English king of the dispute between France and Burgundy.

Louis told Edward point-blank that he would not allow any such thing. Then Maximilian, quite by himself, without a word to Margaret, approached the French monarch with a proposal for a personal meeting between the three rulers of France, Burgundy and England with a view to settling once for all every outstanding question affecting their mutual relations. But Louis by this time had enough of Edward's procrastinations. He said that he did not see what the Englishman had to do with these matters. "Anyhow," he added slyly, "I hear he is about to declare war on Scotland again." He did not add that he himself had fomented the quarrel between the English court and that of James III of Scotland, in order to force England to "mind its own business."

The claims and counterclaims for the possession of Burgundy advanced from Paris and Brussels respectively went on and on, till they began to attract the attention of all Europe. Their ramifications increased more or less secret internal divisions in both France and Flanders. It became impossible to tell clearly who was working for what. Legal arguments and personal prejudices deepened the multifarious rifts on both sides. In some respects the opposed cases appeared plausible and reasonable, in others merely specious, even absurd. Yet neither Louis nor Maximilian, while carefully refraining from violence, would give way in any important direction. The position hardened steadily into a ruinous deadlock.

The king's attention, however, to detail and concern for the strictest discipline, more like that of a junior than a senior commander, continued indefatigably. At the beginning of 1480, on January 12, he wrote to one of his captains:

> Monsieur de Charlus, I have ordered my troops to move into Burgundy on the 15th February. I myself shall be at Auxerre until the conquest of the [Franche-] Comté is completed. Immediately on the receipt of this letter you are to take care to have your men concentrated by that date. Be sure you make no mistake about it, but don't include any horses whatever except those for the wagons, in each of which there are to be four spades, two pickaxes, two hatchets and two entrenching tools. If you fail to obey these orders precisely you may be sure that I shall deal with your company as I did those in Champagne. I shall break up its organization and turn the men into archers,* as I have done elsewhere. You may assume that I myself shall advance as far as possible into Burgundy so as to be able to inspect both your own troops and the rest.
>
> I have also heard that you and certain other captains recruit 5 or 6 men for your own staffs at public expense, which is pure robbery both on your part and theirs. Accordingly, see to it that you take only one man from each settlement of fifty persons or parish. No exceptions to this rule will be permitted. Let there be no mistake in carrying out these orders.

Perhaps it is hardly to be wondered at that in March 1480 the strain on the king's unresting mind came to a head. He collapsed at dinner in a village near Chinon in Touraine, finding himself suddenly unable to speak. Commines writes: "A kind of paralysis came upon him. . . . he was assisted from the table and seated by the fire. The windows were closed. As he seemed to wish to approach them, those present thought it best to restrain him for his own good. . . . he could not speak at all or recognize or remember anyone. . . ."

The archbishop of Vienne, to whom Commines subsequently dedi-

---

* I.e. at this date in France soldiers not in regular service.—J.C.

cated his *Mémoires*, was at that time acting as both chaplain and physician at the court. He was sent for within the hour, ordered a clyster to be applied and had the windows opened again.

"At once the King recovered the ability to utter a few words and some degree of understanding." He took a short ride on horseback, appeared quite sensible and

> made signs to express what he wanted to say. Among other matters he called for the Archdeacon of Tours to come and confess him. He also sent for me. For I was then at Argenton, some ten leagues away. On arrival I found him again at table, accompanied by Master Adam Fumée, formerly physician to the late King Charles and at this period in charge of Petitions. There was also present another doctor, Master Claude. The King understood little of what was said to him. But he did not feel any pain. He ordered me, by a gesture, to spend the night in his bedchamber. For he still could not speak properly. I remained for forty days serving him at table and acting as his valet. I considered this a great honor and was well content with it. At the end of two or three days he began to regain his speech and understanding. He seemed to think that no one interpreted his wishes so well as myself and he therefore desired that I should remain permanently in attendance on him. I was present when he confessed to the said Archdeacon. For otherwise they could not have understood each other. Actually, he had little to say, for he had confessed a few days previously, it being the practice of the Kings of France to confess whenever they touched persons for the King's Evil [scrofula], which he never failed to do once a week. Kings who do not follow this practice are most remiss, for there are always great numbers of such sick persons.
>
> When his health improved slightly he began to ask the names of those persons who had prevented him by force from going to the window and on hearing who they were forthwith expelled them from his household. He deprived some of their posts and never saw them again. Others, like the lords of Segre and Champeroux, he allowed to retain their appointments but nevertheless sent them away. Many were surprised at this capricious behavior, considering it unjust, since they had acted for the best. What they said was true. But the minds of princes differ from those of ordinary men and cannot always be comprehended by those who choose to discuss them. His greatest fear at that time was to lose any proportion of the very great authority that he possessed through being disobeyed in anything whatever.

Commines goes on to point out that the king never forgot how his father had been forced to eat against his will, since he believed that Louis was trying to poison him, and almost immediately afterwards died. The compulsion used in this case on Charles VII by his loyal subjects had ever since been sternly reprehended by his son, who deduced that once such action had been taken, for whatever reason, during the illness of a sovereign, it might well be extended to constraining him in other circumstances on the pretext that his mind was weakening. In the view of King Louis XI, an autocrat by nature as well as on carefully thought-out principle, such a result would be absolutely fatal to good government, since the king alone would be in possession of all the evidence enabling a decision to be reached in any given conditions. To disobey his orders would therefore not only be treason but contrary to common sense.

This concept was of course derived from military practice, where it had so often been proved that disaster followed if subordinate officers thought they knew better than their commander-in-chief and acted accordingly. It was for this reason that the extreme penalty of death had at all times and everywhere been decreed for any such conduct in war. Nor has it ever since, in fact, been possible to regard a kingdom, or any independent state, as in the last resort anything but a unit organized for defense or attack, as circumstances may require, like a professional army. Louis knew as well as any modern statesman that sovereign authority over so complex a corporation as a political entity has to be very largely delegated. But in the fifteenth century it was still practicable for a single, resolute, intelligent and very hard-working man to grasp a situation fully and issue detailed instructions for the handling of it. Louis's very conscientiousness, accordingly, forced him to rule in such a way, which exposed him even in his own day to charges of undue severity in the eyes of people who knew less about the matter at issue than he did.

It is significant in this connection that the modern Belgian historian H. de Man, in writing of Jacques Coeur, calls attention to the king's remark to Philippe de Commines that he had often known courtiers attribute their falls from grace to having served their sovereign "too well." "For in most cases," Louis went on, "the greatest services are requited with the greatest ingratitude. Yet many of those who suffer in this way have only themselves to blame for boasting overmuch of their privileged position and exploiting it against both their master and their own equals in rank."

Again, writes Commines, "the King told me that in his opinion a man desirous of good standing at the court would be better off if his Prince rewarded him richly for a small service, whereby he stood under an obligation to the Prince, than if he placed the latter under a great obligation. For it is more natural in a Prince to be fond of people who are under an obligation to him than of those to whom he is himself obliged."

Whether or not Louis had Jacques Coeur and Charles VII in mind while making these observations to Commines, his attention to detail in ruling so dictatorially may plausibly be argued to have killed him at sixty. But it succeeded in its object of leaving a strong, prosperous nation to posterity. Later rulers with similar ideals and capacities, such as Philip II of Spain and Louis XIV of France, found the task too difficult with the increased populations and responsibilities of Renaissance and baroque Europe. They failed to do what they intended. The theory of absolute personal monarchy became discredited. But the hopes of revolutionary societies crumbled under the dictatorships, masked as democracies, of the twentieth century. In a certain sense Louis XI, for a doomed moment in history, alone upheld the fabric of a reasonably coherent civilization.

The seizure of March 1480 kept him incapable of attending to business, an unprecedented condition in his case, for ten or twelve days. Commines read to him the most important of the dispatches that came in. The king seemed to understand them, insisted on physically handling them, pretended to peruse them and tried to make his wishes known by vague mumbles and gestures of which the gentlemen present could make little. In any case they were afraid to act in the absence of clear instructions. For as Commines observes, somewhat ruefully: "He was a master with whom one had to plow a straight furrow."

At the end of about a fortnight he recovered his ability to gather what went on around him and could utter a complete sentence. Yet he still appeared in a bodily sense very weak and also decidedly nervous about a recurrence of his mental collapse. He knew well enough that he would find it extremely difficult to obey his doctors' advice to take a good long rest. One of his first acts was to order the release of Cardinal Balue, who had been in prison ever since 1468, to the great scandal of the Vatican which had repeatedly urged the king to pardon so able a priest. It is likely that Louis now took this step less to please Sixtus than to recapture the good graces of heaven after its heavy chastisement of him by the recent blow to his intelligence. He may have thought that the cardinal, in gratitude for this concession, might pray for his sovereign's future health and salvation. Surely the petition of so eminent a prelate, so popular in Rome, should be effective? The monarch's native skepticism, as already suggested, did not extend to any doubt of the essential truth of Christianity and the mitigating power of sufficiently solemn supplications to the Supreme Being.

On April 8, 1480, he wrote to François de Genas, the financial secretary for Languedoc, just such an informal letter as one unpretentious civil servant in an hour of leisure might address to an old friend. The king, to tell the truth, though still only fifty-six, was growing bald. But he was less concerned with this deterioration in his appearance than with the increased risk it represented of catching cold.

> I forgot to tell you that I'd like you to get me another hat like the one that the Bishop of Valence, Monsieur Louis de Poitiers, gave me, which he said he had obtained from Rome. It doesn't look to me like beaver, but some other fur. Anyhow, it has a great big thick piece coming down to cover the shoulders, the back and even a bit of one's horse's hindquarters. The front and side brims are also quite high and wide, so that one doesn't need a rain cloak. In warm weather, again, it's as good as a little house. I do beg of you, out of the great desire I know you have to please me, to get hold of such a hat and send it to me as soon as possible, so that I can wear it before the really hot days begin.

This monstrous headgear must have looked very queer, like a sort of shaped and stiffened blanket, on the fragile little monarch. But it is highly improbable that anyone laughed at it, even in the profoundest secrecy. Louis, after all, was generally regarded as a sacred personage, almost an angel, and a very militant one at that, a kind of St. Michael, with an invisible flaming sword in his head instead of in his hand. In any case people of rank, as already noticed in these pages, wore very strange garments in the fifteenth century. On public occasions, especially those of rejoicing, such as dances and tournaments, both lords and ladies appeared in the most complicated and colorful cloaks, bodices, surcoats, sleeves, skirts and shoes, all fantastically cut and adorned, to say nothing of masks, wigs and positive miniature castles or ships of drapery on their heads, so that they resembled glittering, exotic idols rather than human beings. At religious ceremonies the contrast with the plain black or white habits of monks and nuns was of course deliberate, recalling to profane minds the solemnities of heaven.

In one respect certain of the royal advisers, sure that he was dying, dared to attempt a modification of the "straight furrow." They countermanded the collection of some "very burdensome" taxes the king had recently imposed at the suggestion of Esquerdes, now working hard to obliterate what was really the disgrace of Guinegate, though he had managed to persuade Louis that it was nothing of the kind. The general had submitted to the ruler of France a plan for the establishment of a standing army of some ten thousand infantry of the line and twenty-five hundred sappers, together with five hundred men-at-arms to be held at the royal disposition, serving either on foot or mounted, according to circumstances, the whole force to be supported by an abundance of transport and tents at an inclusive maintenance cost of fifteen thousand francs a year. But it is clear from the famous review held at Pont de l'Arche in Normandy on June 15, 1481, that the capital expense of the taxation deplored by the counselors of the throne a year earlier behind the back of the supposedly dying monarch had after all been very largely met.

Meanwhile Sixtus, now freed by the political genius of Lorenzo de' Medici from his fruitless and inglorious war with Florence, decided to do his traditional papal duty by trying to compose what might be considered in Rome equally pointless disputes between other people, to wit, the secular princes of northern Europe who acknowledged his spiritual authority, however much it might be thought by some to have been tarnished by his recent activities. He had been outraged, in particular, by the arrest in 1480, at the instance of the Paris Council, of the bishop of Coutances, an ancient episcopal see in northwestern Normandy. This was a typical example of the confusion in France. The bishop had done nothing worse than practice astrology, a pseudo science highly regarded by many magnates, including Louis himself, in the fifteenth century. But the casting of horoscopes being technically heretical, as impugning divine omnipotence, it sometimes formed a convenient pretext for the seizure of persons suspected of politically subversive operations which could not however be legally proved against them.

In this case suspicion had first fallen upon Jean II, the handsome and adventurous duke of Bourbon, who had married the king's younger sister Jeanne. He may well have been covertly in correspondence with someone at Maximilian's court. To clap so highly distinguished and popular a nobleman in jail was out of the question. But the learned bishop of Coutances, who was so fond of cosmology, happened to be a great friend of Jean's. To proceed against the prelate for heresy would be an indirect warning to the duke, whose brother, the Cardinal Charles de Bourbon, the pope's legate in Paris, may also have been thought to desire concessions advantageous to Burgundy.

Sixtus therefore, on September 4, 1480, sent to France, as at least a temporary successor of Charles of Bourbon, no less a cardinal than the subsequently famous Giuliano della Rovere, the pope's own nephew and a man of war if ever there was one. But at thirty-seven Giuliano, long before he became Pope Julius II in 1503, had proved that he possessed political talents of the highest order in addition to his military prowess. His powerful intellect, accompanied as it was by genial manners and cultivated tastes, made an immediate impression on everyone he met. Louis took to him at once. Charles of Bourbon, inwardly consumed with fear and jealousy, followed him about everywhere, showing him the utmost deference. Olivier le Dain, delighted with the new legate's condescension and easy good nature, took him hunting in the Vincennes woods. For the cardinal had immediately and rightly guessed that this decidedly vulgar and rather repulsive person, generally detested by the king's courtiers, nevertheless exercised much influence on the monarch and could accordingly be of great service to anyone commissioned to arbitrate between him and the archduke.

Della Rovere felt perfectly satisfied with his efforts when he left Paris for Brussels. He saw clearly that Louis was quite sincere in his wish to suspend hostilities, if he could do so without losing face in his relations with the Austrian. But young Maximilian turned out to be a different proposition altogether from his subtle but practically minded antagonist. The adroit, cultured Roman, used to taking long and broad views of any situation and well aware of the changing climate of European civilization, could make little of so stubborn a medievalist as the archduke, still mentally a teen-ager, quite incapable of understanding the issues confronting the world outside his little corner in the northwest of the continent or indeed the mind of anyone not of his own nationality. Maximilian simply would not recognize the pope's right to interfere at all. He refused to discuss the position with the legate in any way. With a discourtesy often characteristic of men who normally stand on great ceremony, he even declined to admit the cardinal to his presence. Giuliano della Rovere shrugged his shoulders, wrote Louis a politely deprecating account of his reception in Brussels and returned to report to Sixtus.

But the king of France begged him to break his journey at Tours, where this urgent but intractable matter was again discussed between two of the most eminent men of their time. In the event it was not until February 3, 1482, that Giuliano reached Rome. The French talks had been perfectly frank on both sides. Louis said he was ready to make every possible concession to meet the pope's wishes and proved his words by calling attention to his release of the traitor Cardinal Jean Balue, imprisoned since 1468 on the evidence of correspondence with Charles the Bold just before the trap laid by the latter for the king at Péronne. Balue, incidentally, had not been incarcerated in a "cage," as so often alleged, but in reasonably comfortable quarters where he worked peacefully for ten hours a day at law and theology and from time to time allotted benefices. He showed no ill effects of this experience when he arrived in Rome to enjoy the patronage of Sixtus. He returned to France after Louis's death in 1483 and died there in 1491 at the age of seventy after a second successful career.

The first career had really been rather interesting. Of relatively humble birth, this tall and stout, eagle-nosed ecclesiastic showed at an early age marked addictions not only to political intrigue but also to women and wine. He rose rapidly to the episcopate and about the year 1466 was recommended by the king, who admired his capabilities, to Pope Paul II for a cardinalate. But this pontiff, though by no means austere in his own private life, did not care for the candidate's morals and declined to make the appointment. Balue did not become a cardinal until the very year of his political disgrace, 1468. He owed his fall to the enemies his unscrupulous ambition had made him and to the risk he took in playing a double game with Charles the Bold and Louis. Others had done the same and got away with it. Nor was it uncommon for French bishops at this date to be sensually inclined. That Balue was no ordinary debauchee is clear from his calm behavior in his confinement and his equally cool resumption of his professional work on his release. On the whole he appears to have been quite a likeable character, a bit too much of a gambler in politics, but at least no hypocrite.

Cardinal Giuliano della Rovere, a much better diplomat than Balue, pressed the king of France to join the pope in a crusade then being prepared against the Turks. Such an enterprise, he urged, would automatically stop the trouble over Burgundy by enlisting the sympathy of Maximilian, also in theory keen on such projects. But Louis, during this talk in August 1481, countered the Roman's pious suggestion by an appeal to common sense. "I will pay down," he said, "two hundred thousand crowns of my own to promote this purpose and my Church will contribute another hundred thousand. But only on condition that all other European sovereigns make a similar effort. England, Germany and Spain, for example, should each pay out two hundred thousand. If any one contributor specified a less amount, all the rest would have to reduce their subsidies to his figure." The cardinal nodded. He saw no objection to the plan. But Louis was pretty sure it would come to nothing. He knew that the old religious zeal for recovery of the Holy Places was dead and that Europeans would now only fight the Turk to defend themselves against invasion, not to conquer him. The king afterwards told the Milanese ambassador in no particular confidence, rather hoping he would pass the opinion on to della Rovere, that in French eyes the pope and the king of Naples were responsible for all the turmoil in Italy and might "sink the ship of St. Peter." He had never really forgiven Sixtus for persecuting by far the ablest man in the peninsula, Louis's admired friend Lorenzo de' Medici.

It is not quite clear why personal relations between Cardinal Giuliano and King Louis began gradually to sharpen during the year 1481. Both men had strong wills and definite ideas about the future they desired for European civilization. Both controlled power at their bases, Paris and Rome respectively, superior to any other, Giuliano having the almost obsequious ear of the pope. Perhaps a clash of some kind was bound to occur. Certainly the cardinal could not have welcomed the monarch's peremptory demand for a "permament legate" in France —"someone like yourself, of course, my dear fellow"—to uphold the spiritual autonomy of the Gallican Church, which Pope Sixtus had only granted with the greatest reluctance. Della Rovere, nothing if not a faithful servant of the Holy See, which he meant to occupy himself one day and with brilliance too, merely said he would find out what could be done to meet the royal wishes. But it is probable that he privately resolved to show Louis that he could not dictate to the Vicar of Christ or indeed to his principal representative, Giuliano della Rovere.

In any case the cardinal took an opportunity which arose in Provence that year to impress the king with his independence, as an Italian prelate owing allegiance only to Sixtus himself, of the French throne. In consequence of the death in July 1480 of old King René, supposedly in charge of that region in the extreme southeastern corner of France, bounded on the north by Dauphiné, on the west by the Rhone and on the east by Liguria, then held by the house of Savoy, much of Provence had fallen into disorder. A certain freebooter, one Jean de Tinteville, was doing more or less as he liked at Avignon, rioting gaily and causing a lot of destruction and injustice. The municipality, on the demand of his creditors, expelled Jean from the city. But he returned with a band of truculent brigands and tried to restore his former reign of terror by force. He failed, was arrested and locked up.

Avignon was a city formally subject to the papacy and governed by a legate. But the citizens were not of course wholly free of French royal jurisdiction, since René and his nephew Count Charles of Anjou and Maine, who succeeded him, had both acknowledged French suzerainty. The count, on his death in 1482, actually bequeathed the territory to Louis. Ever since his coronation, as may now be clear from the preceding pages, it had not only been part of the king's policy but also part of his personal character and convictions to be extremely touchy about his sovereign rights. Giuliano della Rovere made the mistake of taking it upon himself, as the pope's chief representative in France, to punish Jean de Tinteville and his friends with a severity both exceeding that of the citizens themselves and doubtfully within his powers as papal legate. The monarch, in a letter dated September 7, 1481, accused the cardinal of having had Tinteville, a "vassal" of France, tortured in prison and also of hanging and "most dishonorably" drowning in the Rhone several of that gentleman's supporters, also French subjects. The captive, Louis goes on, must be released at once and the cardinal is to retrieve the situation by governing the city without resort to such improper violence as he must know the king would never approve.

It was in vain that della Rovere asserted that Jean had tried to get him assassinated. The prisoner was duly discharged and apparently got off scot-free. It is hard to guess from the evidence available just how guilty he was and of what. He was probably a rascal, if a wellborn one. The case, to Louis's mind, was not one of the culprit's morals but of the assumption of sovereign authority in the kingdom of France by a foreigner. On this account the king proceeded to keep the cardinal in Avignon for most of the autumn of 1481 by the simple expedients of refusing him a safe-conduct and planting the relatives of the Provençal citizens he had put to death to hold every road leading out of the city. These measures were relaxed late in September, on the cardinal's withdrawal of his charges against Tinteville. The future Julius II was too big a man to have been seriously vexed by his failure to ride Louis XI to a Roman destination or to bring peace to Burgundy and France. But he may have been rather shaken by this unusual experience. For he took his time over leaving Avignon and on the journey south to report to Sixtus. His party left the city on November 17 and arrived in Rome on February 3, 1482.

It was in 1481 that old Antoine de Chabannes, count of Dammartin and Grand Master of France, retired from active service. Forty years previously he had been a close friend of Louis as dauphin, yet in 1445 had felt it his duty to betray to Charles VII the prince's conspiracy against the crown. Dammartin had thus been responsible for the younger man's exile from France for twenty years and incurred what seemed for all that time his implacable enmity, expressed in the strongest language. After the coronation of 1461 the king had arrested and imprisoned the unlucky count. But by 1467 he had been fully restored to the royal favor and since then had served Louis as faithfully and efficiently as he had served Charles.

On receipt of the Grand Master's petition for retirement the monarch wrote to him: "Being well aware of the toil and service you have ever put at my disposal and that of my late father, I have resolved to relieve you of active participation in warfare, though I fully understand that there is no one in my kingdom more expert than yourself in military operations and in whose support I have greater confidence if any serious emergency should arise. . . . touching the estate and pension you enjoy from me, I shall never take them from you, but on the contrary shall increase them. I shall never forget, whenever you are spoken of, the great services you have rendered me. . . ."

The case of Antoine de Chabannes is one of the most remarkable instances of the king's forbearance and generosity in the overwhelming majority of matters in which he might have been expected to bear permanent malice. He almost always recognized true integrity even when it had once in the past injured him to the point of furious resentment. Only when he discovered repeated treasonable behavior, as in the conduct of Saint-Pol and the duke of Nemours, could he be utterly ruthless. Chabannes was by no means the only officer or official whom Louis XI came to esteem after disgracing such men, on his accession to the throne, on account of their loyalty to Charles VII.

Meanwhile confusion had been growing worse in the Low Countries and in England. King Edward IV was turning against his headstrong ally in Brussels, whom he accused of conspiring with the Scottish court and secretly negotiating with Louis. Both charges were probably true, up to a point. Maximilian had undoubtedly been most disappointed at receiving no real assistance from England in his determination to resist France and may well have thought it worth-while to sound King James III of Scotland, Edward's enemy, for the same purpose. If so, the Austrian was misinformed. James, in perpetual trouble with his nobles, was in no position to undertake continental adventures and in any case blundered in every political action he engaged in, much preferring the study of music and architecture to the duties of his office. As for the tireless French sovereign, it was he rather than the archduke who kept the Franco-Burgundian debate going. Maximilian would have preferred a decision in the field but knew that without help from abroad he could not make sure of conclusive military victory.

In any case both he and Edward hoped against hope that Louis, who had been deteriorating physically, though not mentally, for a long time, would die soon. Accordingly while the two potentates in Brussels and London bargained in purely hypothetical terms, the king of France pleased these foreigners by undergoing a second, more serious stroke of paralysis in March 1481. As before it deprived him temporarily, but for a longer time, of both speech and memory. He recovered to some extent in due course. But Commines, summoned to the castle of Plessis-les-Tours for consultation with the monarch, noticed that his hearing was affected. Louis indicated that he wished his visitor to stay as long as possible and, as formerly, to sleep in the same room with him, in order that if and when he began to speak and hear properly the two of them might get down to business at any moment. The historian and his sovereign had grown so intimate by this period that a gesture or a grimace could often convey their ideas to each other as well as any words. At last the king seemed to make a complete recovery. Commines, not the doctors, had cured him. He said he felt as though he had awakened from a nightmare populated with phantom calumniators and oppressors. Now he would deal, in his old, resolute style, with real enemies of this sort.

But the king had certainly been frightened by his recent second incapacity, which he felt sure had brought him near to death and heavenly judgment. From this time on, therefore, he began to pay a good deal of attention to the Church, by his usual method of generous gifts, in this case intended to ensure clerical prayers for his salvation. He also, in the secular sphere, advertised himself as an exemplar of Christian virtue by releasing a number of political prisoners. In pursuance, apparently, of this forgiving spirit, but really to strengthen his position against what looked like the beginning of a league between England, Burgundy and Brittany, he dropped his previous assistance to James III and returned to his cultivation of Edward.

James sued for peace almost immediately. But elsewhere progress remained slow. Maximilian, who felt he could not go on alone much longer against the French king, increased his pressure on London, demanding a declaration of war from that quarter if Louis did not withdraw his claims on Burgundy before Easter. Similar requests were despatched from Brussels to Francis of Brittany. But the Austrian, taking a leaf out of his enemy's own book, at the same time maintained his secret correspondence with Louis in person. Taxed by Edward with this underhand behavior, the archduke retorted that Margaret of York had advised it. She may have done so, but certainly not with a view to conciliating Louis, whom she hated, but rather to lulling him into a false sense of security prior to a sudden devastating attack.

The king of England sent encouraging messages, but no more, to his now nearly frantic ally and arranged for Prince Edward of Wales, aged eleven, to marry Princess Anne of Brittany. Maximilian, in despair, prolonged his truce with France for another year. Then the French monarch scored his first success in this labyrinth of cross-purposes by persuading King Edward, who was being harried by the pope to supply troops for the projected crusade against the Turks, to renew the Anglo-French treaty signed in 1477. The unfortunate archduke could hardly believe his ears when he first heard that England had deserted him in this way. In a rage, he threatened Edward with an alliance between Burgundy and Scotland, to which the English king calmly replied that he would do better to sit tight in his present truce and wait for the French monarch's death, which was reported on all sides to be imminent. Then they could all think again, with that formidable piece on the European chessboard out of the way.

But King Louis soon showed himself as dangerously active as ever by setting about the reorganization and rearming of his military machine, the most efficient in Europe. In accordance with the new theories of warfare his soldiers were mostly infantry, some twenty thousand of them, all well and promptly paid, armed with pikes and other hand-to-hand weapons, with many foreign officers, especially Swiss, who led a contingent of six thousand of their countrymen. His other chief instrument, also thoroughly in conformity with the spirit of the times, was the artillery, staffed now by four thousand gunners and sappers. They served very heavy cannon, which he nicknamed the "peers of France." He had disbanded the corps of archers, supposedly crack troops attached only loosely to the rest of the army. For they had proved the very opposite of their English models in their irresponsible lack of discipline, thieving propensities and sometimes downright cowardice, a curious but credible result of the immense prestige they had enjoyed for nearly a century, as imitators of the all-conquering longbowmen of Crécy, Poitiers and Agincourt.

The king's own experience had confirmed the opinion, which had been growing in his mind for a long time, that it was no good relying on any but definitely subordinate commanders and the simple, loyal peasants and citizens who composed the rank and file and thought more of winning victories for France than boasting of their "freedom." He made sure that wherever they went they had effective transport and decent accommodations. On June 15, 1481, a great review of the royal forces was held at Pont de l'Arche in Normandy, where the chief school of military training in the country had been set up. The lord of Esquerdes, now enjoying the king's full confidence, conducted the parade, which was in fact based upon his own recent recommendations. Spectators, who must have included spies from Burgundy, England, Scotland and the empire, as well as more friendly or neutral foreign observers, watched with respect and some astonishment an unusually silent series of movements carried out with impeccable precision to the sound of trumpet calls. There was no fuss or excitement, as there would have been on such occasions in Italy or Spain at this date. The comparatively few squadrons of cavalry drilled as soberly as the pikemen and engineers. The great guns made a particularly striking impression. Weapons and armor, clothing and above all the alert, confident demeanor of the troops, could not have appeared more adequate to their task.

The cost of this demonstration of course ran into millions, raised by ruthless taxation, which had been calculated by the king himself to the last franc. He considered the expenditure essential, not extravagant, for the realization of the great vision of the impregnability of France which he had cherished ever since he first buckled on a sword in earnest at the age of thirteen. Now he was determined that all Europe should understand his position and the reasons for it.

At the end of April 1481, some six weeks before the review at Pont de l'Arche, an important message from Sixtus had reached him at Plessis. It was concerned with the recently developed Turkish menace to Christendom. The heathen had already once raided Italy, capturing the port of Otranto for a while. They were expected to mount a full-scale invasion in the near future. It was the duty, the papal bull continued, of all Christian princes to unite at once to defend their continent against the Moslem hordes advancing from the southeast. The king of France replied that for his part he would like nothing better, as his friends well knew. But if his enemies in the north continued to make war on him in defiance of the pope's announcement, he would not be able to spare any forces to repel infidels still so far from his own kingdom as compared, for instance, with Hungary and the empire.

He then put his case, with all his old lucidity and brevity, to Cardinal Giuliano della Rovere, who had recently returned to France from his abortive visit to Maximilian. In the first place, the king declared, he had signed a peace treaty, the terms of which he had kept to the letter, with King Edward IV of England. But disturbing information continually came to his knowledge that the English were more or less quietly supporting France's enemies in the Netherlands. Therefore France was obliged to hold troops permanently under arms in that direction. Second, it was necessary for the French crown also to maintain a watch on the southwestern frontier, whence persistent reports of hostile movements by the king of Castile had to be borne in mind, though Louis himself did not believe that Ferdinand, who had succeeded the formidable Juan II on the latter's death in 1479, meant France any serious harm. He and his levelheaded, resolute consort Isabella, to whom he owed his Castilian dominions, being an Aragonese himself, had something better to do, namely, the liberation of their country from Moorish influence, than extending their power northward. Still, one never quite knew what Spaniards might be up to, Louis added ruefully, remembering the exploits of Juan II. One had to be careful. Third, and most important of all, Maximilian of Austria, husband of Mary of Burgundy, who supported him, most perversely, through thick and thin, was leading the Low Countries in open rebellion against their lawful suzerain on the French throne. Yet the archduke, in view of the geography of his possessions east of the Rhine, should have been the first to march against the sultan of Turkey. Instead, he was ravaging the north of purely French territory. Let him stop doing that and the king of France would instantly join him in driving back the green banners of Mohammed II.

This speech made a good impression on the cardinal, who thanked the king effusively for his most proper submission to the Holy Father's wishes. But in Rome Maximilian's representatives immediately began to move heaven and earth to proclaim the justice of their cause. Soon afterwards the sultan died. His successor appeared less warlike and rapacious. The crisis in the southeast died down.

In September 1481 Louis experienced a third stroke of apoplexy. Again he lost the power of speech and lay in a coma for two hours. This time his recovery proved less vigorous. But he still kept on the move. For a month or two in the late autumn he hunted with Commines at Argenton. "Next season," he wrote jocularly to a friend, "I shall not be killing boars, but much bigger quarry, the English."

Yet by December 19 he was addressing, rather pathetically, from the neighboring town of Thouars, the prior of Sales: "Master Pierre, my friend, I beg you most earnestly to pray incessantly for me to God and Our Lady of Sales that they may send upon me a quartan fever. For I have a malady which the doctors say can only be cured by such a fever. As soon as I get it I shall let you know at once."

According to the French physician Brachet (1903) the quartan ague was believed by medical men in the fifteenth century to be good for epilepsy. But there is no other evidence that Louis suffered from this disease. He was in such a state, however, that he was liable to clutch at any straw of superstition that might come his way, rather as modern invalids apply to practitioners of more or less unorthodox remedies in their extremity.

As for public affairs, the still very sick monarch remained convinced that Edward's reinforcements to Burgundy constituted the greatest of existing dangers to France. Both of these foreign rulers continued to correspond ambiguously with the French court. But Louis, with some reason, feared the Englishman more than the Austrian. The long tradition of Anglo-French hostility, Edward's former dazzling reputation as a winner of battles, which Maximilian, despite the fiasco of Guinegate, had done nothing to rival, and finally the known restlessness of Flanders under imperial control, contrasting with England's devotion to its affable and pleasure-loving sovereign, all inclined the king of France to be more nervous concerning London than Brussels. But great changes, which could not be foreseen as the year 1481 closed, were to affect the situation decisively during the next few months.

CHAPTER XII

The Spider's Nest
(1482–1483)

❧❧❧ The year 1482 proved to be a bad one for agriculture. Famine threatened. The king of France himself appeared to Commines, who was now, in modern terms, a sort of prime minister without portfolio, "worn to a skeleton." The monarch's quarters at Plessis were kept dimly lit, so that visitors should not be able to note his wasted features. In order to counteract still further all possible impressions of declining health, he gave up wearing coarse gray wool and regularly substituted luxurious, bejeweled silks, brocades and velvets. In his best period a grand presence had seldom been necessary. In those days he had delighted in astonishing important people with the resolute bearing, peremptory decisions and sparkling wit that emanated from his slightly built, insignificantly clothed person.

This kind of humor, arising from perfect self-confidence, came in the eighteenth and nineteenth centuries to be characteristic of certain English worthies of aristocratic birth, or intellectual eminence, or both. Even today in England such roguish affectations can still occasionally be observed among persons of both sexes who bear socially honored names. One often feels, in studying Louis's career, that he resembled in this one respect cultivated Englishmen, particulaly those of a period much later than his own. But this trait in him grew much less evident in the 1480's, when it had been crushed by consciousness of his physical degeneration and the fear of dying before he had finished his work for France, still incomplete under the obstinately prolonged shadow of a man six years dead, Duke Charles the Bold. In these circumstances an outward display of remote, mysterious magnificence replaced the old sharp, plain talk and scornful jests. Ironically enough, this external change contributed to the king's reputation for sinister inaccessibility.

More and more people began to revive Charles's bitter nickname for him, "the universal spider." Only a few of his intimates, Commines and Olivier le Dain for instance, recognized that the real man beneath this masquerade, the underlying pattern of his mind, remained unaltered as he approached his end.

On March 26, 1482, Mary of Burgundy, a passionate addict of the chase, like her father in his youth, was thrown from the saddle while hunting herons near Bruges. The sight of her falcon seizing its prey had caused her to give her mount a delighted slap on the neck. The startled beast, at that moment crossing one of the many ditches of the region, stumbled and staggered. Mary fell violently to the ground, receiving internal injuries which killed her three weeks later, at the age of twenty-five. This event seriously weakened her husband's position as a ruler of the Netherlands, where he had really only been tolerated for his wife's sake. It was in vain that he pointed to his infant heir Philip, half a Fleming, and claimed to be recognized as regent during the child's minority. Many of the cities rejected this argument with contempt. The authority of the archduke's government began to break down in a series of civil disorders.

Louis of course watched this process with great satisfaction. He had always feared Mary's inherited energy and determination, which reminded him of his most implacable enemy in the past, far more than Maximilian's alternate vacillation and violence. The king at once put in a claim for her two-year-old daughter Margaret as a future bride for the dauphin, characteristically ignoring the latter's existing formal betrothal to Princess Elizabeth of England. After all, Mary's slightly older child Philip had already been earmarked for Edward's daughter Anne and the English king could think himself lucky to have even one foot in the important Burgundian camp. To have another in France would be more than he could reasonably expect now that there was every prospect of the long-delayed reunion of Burgundy with France taking place.

The weary French sovereign, in his intimidating stronghold at Plessis, was by this time only capable of lucid thought at intervals. The neighboring city of Tours, with its notable population of businessmen, remained all his life the place he loved best. But he preferred to live outside its walls in the pleasant but strongly fortified manor house called by contemporary chroniclers sometimes Les Montils ("Hillocks") and sometimes Plessis. This building, originally a hunting lodge, was situated in an extensive park forming an undulating section of the Loire and Cher valleys. The climate, generally mild and sunny, permitted most of the countryside to be covered with flowers half the year round. The king had bought the manor in 1463, soon after his accession, from his chamberlain Audoin Touchard, lord of Maillé. But during the next six difficult years, those of the League of Public Weal revolt and the first stages of the long conflict with Charles the Bold, Louis spent very little time at this new royal residence.

It was not until 1469, the year in which he finally decided upon relentless if often veiled hostility to Charles, who had so humiliated him at Péronne in the previous autumn, that the king determined to make Plessis-les-Montils his headquarters, the "nest" in which the "spider," according to his enemies, lay in wait for his victims.

Considerable works to this end were set on foot. They comprised roads to give easy access and fortifications to render seizure of the castle, as it could now fairly be described, troublesome in time of danger. The place became almost a fifteenth-century Versailles, though no hint of frivolity was allowed in the architecture or its inhabitants. In 1473 a freestone wall about eighteen feet high was erected all around the precincts. In 1478 the chapel, dedicated to St. Martin, the patron saint of Tours, was furnished with paintings and sculpture. It was also adorned with scrolls bearing the pious inscription *Misericordias tuas Domine in aeternum cantabo* ("Lord, I shall forever sing thy mercies"). This phrase reappeared, with remarkable insistence, on the walls of all the chief apartments.

By 1479 the architectural effect had come to be quite imposing, much larger than it is today, and gaily inviting with its many-colored bricks. From the first floor a splendid view could be obtained right across the varied landscape as far as the spires of Tours on the horizon. The traveler from that direction first reached a drawbridge leading to a wide courtyard irregularly surrounded by the quarters of the subalterns of the Royal Scottish Guard, some two hundred archers more trusted by the king than any Frenchmen. Commanded by a captain and two lieutenants, they wore tartan uniforms of red, green and white, embroidered in gold and crossed over the chest by a diagonal sash. The helmets carried high, nodding plumes of the same colors. A tower stood at the center of the court. At the back it was closed by the chapel.

All round the base-court a second square enclosure, protected by an exterior moat fifteen feet deep, could only be reached by a postern gate or sally port, provided with a drawbridge and set between two round turrets surmounted by spires. Beyond it stretched the accomodations for the monarch's personal staff, a wing with rectangular, barred windows and served by two staircases. A passage led from one end of it to a second chapel, dedicated to St. Matthew, and behind this building to a third, St. John's, which had a gallery on the first floor and a slender spire adorned with a cross at the apex. The king's private apartments, adjacent to this chapel, occupied the main wing of the castle, overlooking the base-court to the east and the park to the west. A well-proportioned wooden gallery with a row of brightly hued stained-glass windows led from the chapel to an octagonal tower counterbalancing the chapel architecturally and containing a fine spiral staircase.

The rectangular windows of the ground floor buildings overlooking the base-court were separated by stone statuettes. The first floor carried three spacious semicircular dormer windows, elaborately framed and bearing pediments in the antique style. The park side had eight similar windows under a gracefully sloping roof with tall chimneys. The wing confronting that of the staff quarters with a lower elevation of a single story ended at the octagonal tower and comprised the domestic offices, stables, kitchens, cellars, water pump and tank supplied from a spring communicating with the river Cher through pipes of lead or reinforced earthenware. Vaulted underground dungeons were also constructed here and elsewhere throughout the edifice. A well and trough stood in the courtyard. The main wing overlooked extensive gardens to the west, where fruit and vegetables were cultivated. Many smaller buildings clustered at intervals around the high exterior wall. Farther off, farmsteads dotted the meadows in the direction of Tours.

Northward lay the park, big enough for the hunting of hares and rabbits with greyhounds. The latter were Louis's favorite animals, especially the white or red varieties from Lombardy. But he also collected mastiffs from that region, and even lapdogs. These last miniature creatures slept on cushions in his bedroom and were given such pet names as "Dearest," "Paris" and "Artus," i.e. "King Arthur." They were provided with jeweled collars and fed on goats' flesh. If they fell ill, prayers were offered to St. Hubert, patron of the chase, for their recovery. If they ran away, all the boys of the locality were rounded up to look for them.

Birds also, as already mentioned, were much beloved by King Louis. Many flew about his rooms in perfect freedom, to the discomfort of certain serious ambassadors and the amusement of the more sophisticated. But other feathered bipeds were caged in four large aviaries, occupied by partridges, quails, sea gulls and white peacocks, mingled with canaries, goldfinches, linnets, chaffinches, barn owls, crows, herons, pigeons, turtledoves and geese, in addition to sparrow hawks, gerfalcons and other such predatory breeds. Magpies, of course, were ubiquitous. Great care was taken of all these winged favorites by a specially trained staff, which fed them on the best juniper berries. Some of the most tuneful songbirds were kept in round cages at the monarch's bedside.

He slept in a very large apartment, capacious enough for the entertainment of a numerous company to dinner. But for most of the day he would crouch at the enormous chimney piece, poker in hand, being highly susceptible to drafts and chills, against which he had the galleries carefully protected by linen curtains and the sitting rooms furnished with cushioned benches and armchairs, backed by tapestries. A portable clock struck the precious hours left to the extremely busy and mortally sick sovereign. A few pictures and a sideboard completed the indoor amenities.

The royal wardrobe hung in closets or was piled in cowhide trunks under the care of Olivier le Dain, who also naturally looked after the king's razors, stocked in a case of red leather. Like most contemporary Frenchmen Louis remained entirely clean-shaven all his life, in contrast with such foreigners as Charles the Bold, who wore a thick mustache, and the bearded Germans and Scots, the more dandified English following the French fashion. But the barber had nothing to do with the royal underwear, which was washed and mended by women. Drinking and toilet vessels were kept in black leather cases, the monarch's private hunting horn in one of red leather. He loved, like the Northumbrian folk hero John Peel, to sound it in the early morning, amid the neighing of horses and the barking of hounds. His daggers were sheathed in white leather. The jewelry reposed in painted and gilded boxes. Sometimes he would play billiards or bowls with men he liked. But the chase was always his principal outdoor recreation. His library contained for the most part historical or medical works, little theology and still less of poetry, fiction or the long-winded scientific manuals of the day.

Such glimpses of Louis's private life are important for the recognition of a side of his character generally ignored by novelists like Scott and Hugo, of a melodramatic cast of mind. For their purposes, as for those of certain historians of similar outlook, it was inconvenient to mention that the "terrible" king, the human "spider," doted on faithful quadrupeds and pretty singing birds, on innocent ball games and the simple country people with whom he sat so long at table. Such relaxations do not seem to suit the deep political and commercial schemes and there can be no doubt that he prosecuted without much real sympathy for the men he intended to outwit.

The paradox was in fact uncommon among the more prosaic statesmen of his time. Louis, the greatest of them, appears almost a freak in the company of such people, excluding of course aesthetes like Lorenzo de' Medici and King René, in the French monarch's marked moral resemblance to an average northern European or North American citizen of much later times. He might have said, as they so often did before a pugnacious humanitarianism, in language at any rate, became fashionable in the bloodstained twentieth century: "The more I see of people the better I like dogs." Nowadays such remarks are made at the speaker's peril. In the fifteenth century also they tended to cause unpopularity and often, among keen diplomats and business-men, not to mention self-consciously Christian prelates, contemptuous mockery. But minds capable of deeper psychological insight are bound to query, on the well-documented evidence of Louis's lighter moments, the picture of him as basically a somber, remorseless tormentor of less-gifted persons.

That lurid image of brooding malevolence was drawn from the melancholy and snappishness that increased during his last four years, after his apoplectic stroke in 1479, rather than from his first fifty. In youth and middle age his rare outbursts of anger and pitiless severity, dwelt upon with such animosity by his political foes and later sensation-mongers, were generally justifiable by contemporary standards. They were really due more to the frustrations of his patriotic idealism than to any personal rancor. He did not wade, like a Stalin or Hitler, over the corpses of his victims to a throne. but simply struck down in-corrigible obstacles in his legitimate path to it.

He repeatedly pardoned men like Antoine de Chabannes, Duke Francis of Brittany and Count Jean V of Armagnac, who had offended him, one would have supposed, unforgivably. He moved with ex-traordinary reluctance to the punishment of clever traitors like Saint-Pol and Cardinal Balue. Even his most formidable rival, Charles the Bold, he would never, after the battle of Montlhéry, meet openly in arms. He tried to conciliate him again and again, always in vain, even after the humiliation of Péronne. He declined many tempting offers, such as that of the utterly unscrupulous Italian Campobasso, to have the Burgundian quietly ambushed and locked up or actually assassinated. Many rulers of that time who are given a far better reputation for justice than Louis XI by contemporary chroniclers and later historians would not have hesitated to resort to such violence in cases of equal menace to their personal safety or simply that of their dominions.

Mary's death in this year of 1482 had considerably heartened him while he himself was hanging on so grimly to life at Plessis. It had followed another fortunate demise, that of Count Charles II of Maine, old René's nephew, on December 11, 1481. Thereupon all the lands of the house of Anjou, including Maine, Bar and Provence, to say nothing of the claims to Naples and Jerusalem, passed to King Louis, who had bribed out of the way the only other possible competitor for their possession, the young Duke René of Lorraine, sharer in the victories of Morat and Nancy and son of the deceased King René's youngest daughter Yolande, sister of Jean of Calabria and Margaret of Anjou. Jean had died in 1471. The death of Margaret only about a month after that of Mary of Burgundy also relieved the king of France, though for the last six years she had been powerless to annoy him. The ex-queen of England had been living on a pension he had felt obliged, as her cousin, to allow her. She left a will in his favor, bequeathing to him her pack of hounds. "That's all I shall get out of her," he wrote characteristically to a correspondent. "But it's what I like best of all she had."

The rest of the Anjou inheritance now falling to the French crown greatly increased its wealth. Provence especially, with its fine harbors, only needed a new lease of life to regain its ancient mastery of the Mediterranean and the Atlantic so far as that ocean had been explored at this date. King Louis plunged with enthusiasm into the work of shipbuilding and the suppression of North African piracy. He sent two of the royal galleys to Alexandria, commending them to the protection of the sultan of Egypt. They would bring in their train, France hoped, many merchant vessels from the ports along her Mediterranean coast between Marseilles and Nice, with incalculable benefits to the commercial prosperity of the kingdom.

But the health of the sovereign himself had now been ominously deteriorating for nearly four years. A constitution by no means strong to begin with had suffered from incessant overwork and the repeated discomfort of journey after journey on military or administrative business ever since puberty. A naturally suspicious temperament, hardened by a series of frauds and follies committed by many of his most eminent associates, had been inflamed to continuous action by his one passion, that for the rehabilitation and rise to invincibility of France. This obsession practically forced him to labor almost alone.

He knew that if he relaxed for more than an hour or two in the hunting field the ground so painfully won over the previous period might be snatched from under his feet. He could not afford, like his father or King Edward IV, to bank on a personal popularity for the recovery of influence lost by self-indulgence. The Valois charm in his case, exercised always for an ulterior motive, had never been spontaneous, like that of even his worst ancestors. He was well aware that it could be relied on only for isolated victories, not for the winning of a general, permanent affection among his subjects. For he himself could not love them as individuals, but simply as the abstract token of a nation that absorbed the whole structure of his mind, its capacity for calculation and reflection, its conscience and its will.

It was only in 1482 that he definitely settled at Plessis. By then he could be sure that France at last existed more or less as he had so long wished, its citizens contented, its economy soundly based, its power respected far beyond its frontiers, its Church practically free of papal dictation and its unassuming dictator, himself, at least esteemed, like Philip the Good, for his skill in organization and diplomacy, if not adored, like Charlemagne, as an emperor, a conquering hero.

Yet no better army than that of Louis XI had been seen in Europe since Flavius Vegetius Renatus, the fourth-century Roman expert on military affairs, had written, "Let him who desires peace prepare for war." Vegetius had been wrong in his own time to concentrate upon the handling of the ancient infantry unit, the legion. For centuries, until the advent of the crossbow and gunpowder in the late Middle Ages, battles were to be decided by the shock power of cavalry. But Louis had been one of the first Europeans to see that, as even Crécy, Poitiers and Agincourt had proved, all fought before he was born, knights could no longer force a serious issue in warfare. The writings of Vegetius on the training and tactics of foot soldiers became the king's bible in his military studies. He found that the ancient Roman's maxims applied to siege operations, where horsemen were of little use, as much as to maneuvers in the open field. Since war in the fifteenth century had become largely a matter of capturing the greatly increased number of fortified settlements that had come into existence with the rise of nation-states, the king took care to make his officers acquainted with the manuscripts composed on this subject by Vegetius over a thousand years before.

For he was no longer fit himself, since 1478, when he had aimed cannon at the walls of Condé in Artois, to endure the rigors of a campaign. His first seizure had occurred in the following year, when he was fifty-six. Ever since then he had been afflicted with periodical breathlessness and migraine. As time went on he could only keep perfectly still when in a semirecumbent posture. This condition, followed by further more serious attacks of the same kind in March and September of 1481, gave rise, in so naturally restless a character, to increasing hypochondria. It was this feeling, as well as the certainty that his great work was more than half done, that sent him into the retirement of Plessis, the "spider's nest," from which, nevertheless, he continued to emerge occasionally in brief excursions.

In April 1482 he wrote to the abbot of St. Remi for a drop or two of the sacred oil supposed to have survived from the time of St. Remigius, bishop of Reims from 437 to 533, and to have been first used for the anointing of the kings of France in 496, when the Frankish sovereign Clovis was baptized by Remigius after a victory over the heathen Alemanni, an ancient German tribe. No one before

Louis XI had ever dared to apply for a sample of this holy fluid for a private purpose. The facts that he did so and actually received from the abbot a vessel alleged to contain some of the precious liquid prove the immense prestige and loyalty the king had by this time acquired. He kept the oil in his bedroom and perhaps believed for a time that it was doing him good.

Louis, at bottom a thorough skeptic, was incapable of true religious emotion. But he had no more reason than the majority of Frenchmen in his day to doubt that the world was supernaturally governed. He therefore employed the same methods to gain the favor of heaven as he had so successfully resorted to in the case of earthly magnates. He flattered the saints in paradise with costly gifts and approached them through their professional servants, the clergy. If one of the immortal residents above the mundane atmosphere did not respond as desired, the royal petitioner turned to another. On the whole he could consider that this policy had paid off, in spite of innumerable temporary frustrations by the way. A lot of important people who stood in his path, from Margaret of Scotland to Agnès Sorel, from Charles VII to Charles the Prince and from Duke Charles the Bold to Mary of Burgundy, had died suddenly through no contrivance of his own. Now there were no more personal obstacles to his ambition for France, except the sullen widower Maximilian, by this time generally despised and ineffective. The aging voluptuary Edward IV no longer counted. The French king had everyone in his pocket, he judged, both at home and abroad. Only this accursed bodily weakness frightened him.

By July he had switched from St. Remigius to St. Zenobius, an Italian about whom he did not know very much. But Lorenzo de' Medici, who knew and had everything, possessed a ring once worn by the saint. The Florentine statesman wrote that he would be glad to present this relic to his old friend Louis, together with any others the monarch fancied. The king, in accepting this gift with due grati- tude, characteristically demanded what the ring was supposed to do in what circumstances. If it didn't work on his particular disease, would Lorenzo kindly inquire in Italy what would do so. Lorenzo, with his usual politic good nature, complied with this request. Pope Sixtus IV sent the invalid a tiny piece of the skin of St. Anthony of Padua and the "communion cloth" of St. Peter, together with a rosary formerly owned by a monk named Jean of Ghent (d. 1419) whom Louis wished to have canonized for his correct prophecies of the king's birth and subsequent victories over the English. Even the sultan of Turkey, at the suggestion of Lorenzo, whom the Oriental ruler greatly admired, despatched to Plessis some objects of Christian interest still preserved at Constantinople.

The questions of the health and safety of Charles the dauphin, already rather a sickly child and peculiarly exposed to the machinations of his father's political enemies, a dwindling but not inconsiderable band, also began to worry Louis at this time. He planted the boy, now aged twelve, in the high castle of Amboise overlooking the Loire a few miles east of Tours, under the guardianship of Jean Bourré, also called du Plessis, a man close on seventy. This gentleman was instructed never to let young Charles out of his sight, never to go home for a holiday and never to let a visitor, even the old watchdog's brother, stay the night. For the anxious father feared not only infection by the plague but also violence, kidnaping or even murder. He had taken every precaution to prevent information about his own malady from leaking out. But he guessed correctly that sooner or later it would come to the knowledge of such objectionable people as the duke of Brittany and the son of the mad duke of Alençon, who had recently died at Chinon, where he had been imprisoned for high treason, an example of the mercy shown by the sovereign to such high-ranking traitors since the ill-advised execution of the duke of Nemours in 1477. Such conspirators, Louis believed, might well be already secretly busy all over the country.

The Norman physician and astrologer Pierre Choisnet was commanded to prepare a book of rules for Charles's conduct when he succeeded to the throne. The chief of these principles were those which had guided the present king himself, for instance the need for a monarch to live not for his own pleasure but for the common good and peace of his realm. He should never go to war except after consulting his subjects and even after obtaining their agreement should never venture to the field in person, like the rash sovereigns of the previous century, oblivious of the ruin that their deaths in battle might bring to their fellow countrymen. A French king should remember that he is divinely appointed and should therefore exercise the strictest piety and revere all priests.

Louis had himself on the whole stuck to this line of behavior. No sensible man could say that his reign, now drawing to a close, had been unsuccessful. He had consolidated the power and wealth of France, kept out greedy foreigners and maintained good relations with the Church, despite the misfortune of a feverishly ambitious and irascible pope in the Chair of St. Peter. England had been almost neutralized by the French display of power and forbearance in the matter of Burgundian intransigence. In Spain, again, Ferdinand and Isabella had been pleased by Louis's refusal of the pope's request to resurrect the claim of Anjou to Naples against the Aragonese dynasty. Nor had the king of France consented to interfere in Genoa, though again pressed by Sixtus to do so. "The Genoese, I am told," the monarch remarked pithily on this occasion, "will surrender to me rather than to Milan. Well, I for my part surrender them to the devil." He did not care for such inept politicians as the Genoese were proving to be at this date.

Unfortunately, after all this trouble had been taken to enable the dauphin to do even better when his time came, the boy grew up almost an imbecile. For nine years after his accession at the age of thirteen he left administration and policy to his prudent sister Anne, whom her father had grudgingly called "the least silly" of women, since females could not be expected to be more. But Charles VIII then rushed his splendid, hitherto steady kingdom into the mad adventure of the conquest of all Italy, as a steppingstone to the East, as if he were a new Alexander the Great. Ignominiously ejected by the Italians after a year of disgraceful debauchery in the peninsula, this worst possible successor to a parent who hated both brute force and brutish sensuality, though he didn't mind fraud on occasion, perished at the age of twenty-eight, almost certainly of the new disease of syphilis, which he had helped by his own example of sexual mania in Italy to spread all over the Continent.

The terrible unconscious irony of the father's loving dedication of Choisnet's book, edifyingly entitled *The Rosebush*, a plant symbolical of specifically Christian ideals, to his son, is worth quoting, both for the reason that Charles turned out later to be one of the most contemptible sovereigns who ever occupied the French throne and because this typically brief and lucid message is a good specimen, among very many others available, of the admirable prose style of Louis XI, as notable in old age as throughout his life. Of his contemporaries only Philippe de Commines could express himself better.

> Just as fragrant odors please lovers, so do virtuous maxims the wise. We, desiring that when thou comest, by God's grace, to govern and reign over this noble kingdom of France, thou shalt know and bear in thy heart what is suitable and necessary for so doing, send thee this *Rosebush*, concerned with the protection and defense of the common weal. Thus, when thou comest to man's estate, shalt thou each day take the scent of a rose and find therein more delight and consolation than in all the roses of nature, knowing also which of thy ancestors hath done best.

Louis would have made a good preacher in the manner of his day, which hardly changed in later times, at any rate until the less delicate, more lush rhetoric of the period of social revolution substituted a louder tone and a heavier punch for the sweet, gentle exhortations of the age of faith.

On September 21, 1482, the king, realizing at last that he had not long to live, paid a visit to his only son Charles at the castle of Amboise. Seated high in the great hall among assembled magnates and wearing his newly adopted sartorial splendor, the monarch in fact read to the dauphin, from a manuscript in the royal handwriting, a kind of farewell sermon. The Marshal of France, the archbishop of Narbonne, the governor of Auvergne and other soldiers, prelates, nobles, officials and lawyers listened gravely to what their beloved, mortally sick sovereign had to say. He spoke of the sad brevity of human life, the glory and religious devotion of France, increased by his own hand and those of his "true and loyal servants." He referred in solemn tones to the bliss of his ancestors in paradise. Then his voice hardened as he described in sterner language the "treachery of wicked lords and princes whose warring hath caused such pitiful bloodshed and desolation among my people." He was probably thinking chiefly of Duke Charles the Bold of Burgundy, but no doubt also of the earlier English invaders.

Next, with special emphasis, he admonished the dauphin to listen above all to those honorable and experienced counselors who had served his grandfather so faithfully. He acknowledged humbly, with admirable candor, that he had not himself done likewise when he succeeded Charles VII. He deeply regretted this shortcoming. But, as everyone knew, he had hastened to repent of it, reinstating many of the ministers and officials he had dismissed.

Then he paused, ordering his heir to state whether he were prepared to follow his royal parent's advice. The boy, naturally, whispered that he was so prepared. The king thereupon, in a deep voice, required him to take an oath to that effect. This was done. The earnestly phrased undertaking, duly registered by the lawyers present, has a hollow ring today. If Louis could have foreseen what was to happen in French history during the next dozen years, his heart would have broken there and then. But he could only note that the frail young prince appeared overawed, bewildered, on this impressive occasion. It was reasonable to hope that such a condition would not last long. But whatever the king's misgivings may have been he felt satisfied that he had done his duty to the end. The future lay in God's hands. And God would surely not permit all the good work brought to completion in the past, with so much anxious toil, to wither away.

Louis left Amboise that day for almost unbroken isolation at Plessis. The main reason for this retirement was his fear that the repeated attacks of prostration to which he was now subject would cause him to lose his former authority in company. Once those who attended him at official gatherings or even on informal occasions began to whisper behind their hands that the king seemed tired or to wonder why he had withdrawn from a public celebration, a council or a supper table so soon, the conspirators he suspected might be emboldened to make a dangerous move. That must not be allowed to happen. The only means of preventing it would be to increase the half-superstitious reverence for his person by receiving inevitable visitors in semidarkness, like a god in a temple, and forbidding access to anyone whose business he did not consider imperative. Commines saw to it that he was never troubled if it could possibly be helped.

But he was always ready, as he sat putting his multifarious papers in order, to admit the impudent medical tyrant Coictier, though that gentleman might be said to have a tomb-side rather than a bedside manner, with his perpetual reminders of his patient's mortality and the speaker's own demands for more and more privileges and favors. The monarch did not dare to refuse them. For he rightly supposed Coictier quite capable of poisoning him in a fit of fretful resentment.

Foreign ambassadors were reduced to despair. For Louis still would not delegate anyone to represent him. He would often wander about his alleged "spider's nest," which actually consisted of many small rooms in addition to his own sleeping and reception quarters. He would be thinking hard as he roamed about in this way, but less often about current affairs than those of the future, the present, so long as he lived, being secure enough, in his opinion.

At lighter moments he unpacked and rearranged his books on history and medicine, set up his billiard tables and bowling alleys, distributed his bird cages and introduced favorite dogs to their luxurious accommodations. But he spent a lot of time motionless, brooding or dozing in the firelight, as moods of vague hope and skeptical melancholy swept alternately over a mind once active exclusively in connection with practical projects. But for these he now had no energy left.

Applications for formal audiences were automatically rejected by his staff, at his express orders, no reason being given. Nor would he put up even intimate friends at the manor. He did eventually fortify it with an iron fence and four covered posts for his archers. But any ruler, or even local gentleman, who desired peace and quiet, would have done the same. The failure to be hospitable, however, so contrary to French monarchical traditions, was not forgiven by younger persons in good health who considered themselves entitled to admission to the royal presence. They started the "black legend," recounting how the

sinister Tristan l'Hermite seized and summarily executed prowlers outside the iron fence, how Queen Charlotte and her children were
never allowed at the manor, how Olivier le Dain and the lord of Lude
made a jest of helping themselves right and left to the king's private
property under his very nose, while he sat mumbling and concocting
murderous schemes over the fire in his bedchamber, shaking in his
slippers before the arrogant threats of the unspeakable Dr. Coictier.
For in the early days at Plessis, so it was reported, Louis had once,
with a flash of his old authoritative manner, warned the physician
to moderate his treasonable language, only to be silenced by the
cynical retort: "Send me to the block, then, as you've sent so many
others! But if you do you'll be dead yourself a week later!"

No doubt there were grains of truth in such tales. Invalids formerly
above the average in both mental and physical activity do not make
the best patients in the world and even tend to vindictive malice in
their relations with other people. But the stories were blown up to
ridiculous proportions by gossips interested in making a listener's hair
stand on end. Nor could the temptation to turn the king's last months
into a colorful melodrama be resisted by later chroniclers and even
professional historians who should have known better. The idea of a
wicked old "spider," poisonous to his final breath in the ominous twi-
light of a self-imposed solitude, contained every element required to
entertain a pitiless multitude fonder of thrilling fiction than dull fact.

Some of the ingredients in the real pattern of events at Plessis in
1482–1483 certainly remain rather mysterious. The nature of the organic
disability which had reduced Louis to something like immobility, bound
to slow up the business of his beloved kingdom, is not yet quite
clear. There is no doubt that he suffered from severe headaches, like
any other man much concerned with papers and books, and from
difficulty in breathing, also common in people who work a lot in
large, dusty libraries. The recurrent aphasia was more noticeable and
remarked upon. It appeared in all three of his cerebral congestions.
The suggestions of leprosy and syphilis lack foundation. In any case
true syphilis remained unknown in Europe until after his death. The
most likely cause of his decline seems to have been simply overwork,
affecting a precarious nervous system, inherited from a line of weak-
minded ancestors.

Although at this period he paid little attention to domestic administration, he sent plenty of despatches abroad, mostly about the
dauphin's matrimonial prospects. The children of the late Mary of
Burgundy had been seized by the ever turbulent citizens of Ghent, who
were keeping them in comfort but under close guard. The king had
long, for obvious political reasons, been plotting the marriage of the

infant Margaret to his son. Maximilian, on similar grounds, had resolutely opposed any such plan. But he now had little say in the matter,
since Ghent, in possession of the child's person, and stubbornly in revolt against the Austrian, favored the match.

A combined marriage contract and peace treaty to promote it was
signed at Arras on December 23, 1482, between the Ghent authorities
and the representatives of the king of France. It was ratified at Plessis
by the almost invisible monarch, who broke his rule of utter isolation
to receive the Flemish envoys in a darkened room. Seated on a
thronelike chair, he apologized to the deputation for not rising, then
took the oath with his left hand resting on the Bible, the right being
paralyzed. "Death was written on his face," the Flemings reported
afterwards, "though he was clad in ermine and velvet." The effect of
this treaty was to leave the archduke in control of the Netherlands,
the territory still so called today, i.e. the region north of Bruges and
Antwerp, but to deny him Flanders, Brabant, Liége, Namur, Luxembourg and of course Burgundy proper in eastern France. All these lands
were to come under the direct authority of the French crown. Louis's
lifelong ambition had therefore at long last been realized. Burgundy
as an independent power was dead. But its wealth, its moral energy
and its culture, the latter still superior at this date to that of its southern
neighbor, remained, however reluctantly at first, permanently at the
disposal of Paris. The great king who had fought Charles the Bold,
Maximilian of Austria and Edward of England to a standstill, though
far less with pike and gun than with paper and ink, to achieve this
result, could die happy.

The English, of course, was furious at the political defeat of their
best customer. But it was hopeless to think of retrieving the situation
by war, with their king now in mental, moral and physical decline,
though still only forty years old, their administration under his favorites, the Woodvilles, unpopular and an ominous dynastic crisis loom-
ing in the ambition of his surviving brother, Richard of Gloucester.
In fact, when the king of England at last died on April 9, 1483, his
little son Edward, aged twelve, was seized by Richard, lodged in the
Tower and a few months later, after the duke had proclaimed himself
King Richard III, murdered there with his younger brother. Louis himself lived just long enough to receive conciliatory messages from King
Richard and to understand, in all probability, that a long period of
freedom from the menace to France in that quarter was to ensue. He
had already isolated the allies of England one by one, from Brittany
to Aragon, and would certainly, if he had lived, have turned to his
usual expedient of encouraging trade between the two old enemies.

Edward had always eaten, drunk and fornicated far too much. His

constitution, like that of many physical giants, could not stand anything like the wear and tear that scarcely affected active men half
his size. A typical example of potentially heroic qualities ruined in
early middle age by indolence and excessive sensuality, the king of
England had been admirable for his military virtues, his patriotism
and his personal affability. He won many victories in the field, against
his fellow countrymen, during the baneful Wars of the Roses. But
after the final Yorkist triumph he recognized the need to concentrate
on the peaceful development of what was left of England. Like Louis,
with whom he never ceased to have a wildly oscillating love-hate relationship, he fascinated everyone he met face to face, carefully concealed his innate tendency to despotism and was not habitually cruel,
though sometimes ruthless.

Like Louis, too, he saw that only the encouragement of commerce
and industry could provide a sure foundation for the continuance of
his dynasty. Again, he had a distinct capacity for diplomatic intrigue
and was very fond of it. But he never approached the Frenchman's
genius for politics, lacking both the audacity and the powers of dissimulation, to say nothing of the clear, cool head, so evident in Louis.
The two men, who had so much to do with each other and so much
in common, nevertheless in other ways formed a perfect contrast. The
towering, handsome, boisterous Englishman, with his train of flashy
favorites both male and female, his lazy laugh and his magnificent
wardrobe, lost the game in the end to the little, skinny, rather un-
pleasant-looking, plainly dressed semi-invalid who confronted him on
bandy legs, cringing and slyly smiling, at Picquigny.

But Louis had not only the greater brain but the greater heart.
He would never have allowed, like Edward, his vision of national rehabilitation to be obscured by such self-seekers as the Nevilles and
Woodvilles, or by a treacherous brother, the duke of Clarence, so
similar in character to the worthless Prince Charles of France. The
ascetic French monarch contrived, in twenty years of incessant toil,
to bequeath to Europe a community that was to lead the Continent
in every facet of civilization for more than four hundred years. After
Edward's death, despite his Renaissance attributes, England had to
wait a century before emerging from medievalism.

In May 1483 the citizens of Ghent allowed the infant Margaret,
aged two years and ten months, to be transferred to Hesdin in the
Pas-de-Calais. On June 2 she was brought to Paris and on the twenty-
second, in the charge of Pierre de Beaujeu, a younger brother of the
duke of Bourbon and husband of the sensible and energetic Anne de
Valois, Louis's eldest daughter, then aged twenty-three, to Amboise.
There the little Burgundian was introduced to the thirteen-year-old

dauphin, already, it seems, precociously vicious. But he looked "graceful and proud, dressed in crimson satin over a doublet of cloth of gold, and riding a hackney," as he went to meet the baby born of Mary of Burgundy and Maximilian of Austria. Margaret was lifted from her litter and held up in the arms of Madame de Segre to be formally kissed by the boy prince. At the ceremony of betrothal in the Plessis chapel the children touched hands and said "Yes" to everything they were asked. But, fortunately for Margaret, they never married. After Louis's death changed political considerations caused Charles to marry Anne of Brittany when her father, Duke Francis, died in 1491. Margaret in 1497 married the Infante Juan of Castile and Aragon, was widowed a few months later and then in 1501 became the wife of Philibert II, duke of Savoy, and after his death in 1504 was appointed by Maximilian regent of the Netherlands and guardian of her nephew Charles, the future emperor Charles V. She retained the regency, which she held with much credit, until her death in 1530.

The king had not felt well enough to attend the betrothal upon which he had so long set his heart. He was represented by his chancellor. The dauphin, on conclusion of the rites, made a speech which he had learned by heart, thanking the people of France for their trouble and promising to be at their service all his life. He found a strange way of keeping this vow when he disgraced them by his idiotic invasion of Italy in 1494. The best service he ever did them was to die at twenty-eight.

But in 1483 these sad events still lay far in the future. The prevailing mood, just then, remained optimistic. The pope and most of the great nobles were now on good terms with Louis. As for the commercial outlook, on May 26 the chancellor had addressed an assembly of merchants at Tours in the king's name. He told them that in future all duties payable on goods, with the exception of customs imposed at the frontiers, would be abolished. Every French citizen, as was already the case in England and Italy, would be allowed to engage in trade without losing any privileges attaching to his social or official position. Merchants, furthermore, would now be responsible for their conduct to the local magistrates only, not to arbitrary interference by outsiders, however exalted. This enactment put an end to much former discrimination against traders by absentee landlords, whose families might not even belong to the territory affected.

Four days later the king suddenly again broke his rule of personal isolation to receive delegates from his "good towns," as he always called the French municipalities, whether in his private opinion they deserved the epithet or not. The audience took place, as had the meeting with the Flemish ambassadors at the end of the previous year, at Plessis. The monarch wore a long, fur-lined robe of crimson velvet and two scarlet caps, both of which he doffed in greeting to his subjects, disclosing without the least embarrassment a completely bald skull. He continued to keep the caps on his knees throughout the audience. But he ordered all others present to put on their hats, thus indicating that he regarded them as his "sons." For at this period and for long afterwards only the male children of a sovereign were entitled to remain covered in his presence.

He talked mainly about legal matters, saying that he meant to draw up a single code of law applicable to the whole country, with a view to preventing the endless wrangles in different courtrooms which had hitherto so impeded the course of French justice and opened the door to so much bribery, obstruction and other corrupt practices.

This scene, excitedly reported all over Europe, intimidated the king's enemies by suggesting that he had once more recovered all his old vigor and severity. It was now, too, that, in order to encourage this idea, he sent all over the Continent for every kind of animal to replenish his private collection. They included horses and dogs from Spain, Naples and Brittany, mules from Sicily, "little wolves" from North Africa and even moose and reindeer from Scandinavia. Louis, however, though fond of beasts and birds in a childish way, was no zoologist or breeder. He took no more interest in his menagerie than would a boy of nursery age. The new additions to it in 1483, the last year of his life, were clearly meant simply to enhance his royal prestige, and prove to foreigners, as well as to his own compatriots, that the rumors of his approaching end were all nonsense.

The deceased Edward's youngest brother, the duke of Gloucester, soon to assume the English crown as Richard III, was probably among those who pulled long faces at the news of the restored health of Louis XI. But Richard, destined to reign only two years, need not have worried. One of the French king's last official acts was to recommend his northern subjects to refrain from hostile moves directed across the Channel. He had expressed no satisfaction at the death of Edward, who had caused him so much anxiety. Louis, in fact could afford to be generous.

He had at last won over the dangerous Flemings, checked the rebellious Bretons and the rising ambitions of Castile. He had convinced the English that revival of their claims to French territory was not practicable, though he had tactfully left them their one beloved strongpoint of Calais, no longer politically important. He had maintained a steady friendship with the most reasonable Italian powers, Milan and Florence. Lorenzo de' Medici, the most eminent personality of the age, remained devoted to him. Medicean bankers had contributed largely to the new prosperity of France under Louis. The extremely difficult Pope Sixtus IV had finally, after many bitter quarrels, come to recognize the qualities of the monarch who had once threatened him with an ecumenical council. The king of France had even persuaded the latest sultan of Turkey, Bajazet II, from whom he had already received gifts, to preserve on his behalf the Christian relics and monuments at Constantinople.

In a word, Louis could die happy in the certainty that at long last most Frenchmen respected and many loved him, though he had for several years ceased to travel about regularly in France. And yet he did not want to die at this particular moment when, after enduring so much frustration and enmity, he had nothing more to fear from "wicked princes." At the suggestion of Lorenzo he sent for a famous Neapolitan hermit and ascetic, Francesco da Paola, founder of the Minim Friars, who lived under a rock in Calabria. The wise Florentine supposed, quite reasonably, that this simple soul might be able to teach the king how to live a few more years, since the invalid no longer trusted the varying bedside manners of his pompous doctors.

Francesco arrived at Plessis in a cart. When he diffidently entered the library the mighty sovereign fell on his knees before so much evident holiness. He begged his quiet visitor, as confirmed a recluse as himself, to pray for the extension of the life of a sick old man who still had so much to do in the office to which God had called him. The hermit did indeed promise to pray for him. But he added that the monarch's one hope lay in the mercy of heaven. No miracles could be expected from himself, he declared austerely. But Louis was sure that only a miracle could save him. He consulted Commines, who expressed a high opinion of the prudence and gentleness of the monk and advised that every step should be taken to make him comfortable, especially in the matter of diet. As he refused to eat meat or fish he was fed on lemons, oranges, pears and parsnips.

But the king's weakening mind was not content with the mere presence of this saintly vegetarian. Louis began, quite contrary to his former dealings with priests, to listen to Francesco's advice in political affairs, for instance in the matter of the previously Spanish territories held by France, the provinces now known as Roussillon and Cerdange. King Ferdinand V of Castile and Aragon, son of the great Juan II and about to lead Spain into its golden age of intervention in Europe, now that he had very nearly got rid of the Moors, seems to have pressed the Holy Man of Paola, by this time so notoriously influential with Louis, to arrange evacuation of the French conquests in question, east of the Pyrenees. But this proposal, or at any rate Francesco's hand in it, did not please the now Francophile Pope Sixtus IV. The pontiff, nervous of Spanish influence in Italy, sharply ordered the hermit to mind his own business. Louis continued to retain Roussillon and Cerdagne. They were, however, restored to Spain by his successor.

Perhaps Francesco was not quite so unworldly, so indifferent to the profits of diplomatic activity, as he appeared. But it is not necessary to suppose, with Sir Walter Scott in *Quentin Durward* (1827), that the man of lemons and parsnips was nothing more than an "ignorant, crack-brained peasant who, from laziness probably, had shut himself up in a cave." If this had been so, the former troglodyte would hardly have been allowed, after Louis's death, to live on at Plessis and die there in 1508 at the ripe old age of ninety-one. The truth probably is that Francesco's morals were at least superior to those of the king's other close associates at this time.

The miracle for which the afflicted monarch had hoped from the combined ministrations of the Holy Oil and the Holy Man of Paola did not occur. Nor did a visit from the young dauphin, to whom Louis repeated his advice of the previous year at Amboise, prevent another "stroke," which again rendered him speechless, on August 28. This time it fatally enfeebled him. When he could speak and move again, he had lost all his old dignity, so that his retainers, Commines noted sadly, treated him with scarcely veiled scorn. He did not seem to resent this behavior, though only a few days before he would have had those guilty of anything even approaching such an attitude, with the sole exception of the dreaded Coictier, severely punished and dismissed from his service.

The uncompromisingly realistic physician told his prostrate master rudely: "It is useless for you to put any faith in Francesco or that holy oil of yours or in anything else in this world. You are beyond help from earthly ministrations and had best turn to make your peace with God." "I do so," Louis answered humbly. "He will cure me. Perhaps," he added with what may have been a trace of his former caustic irony, "I am not so ill as you think."

But he did not really believe his own words. Calling for Pierre de Beaujeu, once his chancellor, now his son-in-law and Marshal of France, the king asked everyone else to leave the room. He then committed the government of the kingdom to the marshal until young Charles should be of age to assume it. They dying man laid down precise and explicit instructions on national policy. No attempt must be made to regain Calais or antagonize the English in any way. Peace must be safeguarded at all costs for at least five years, by which time he felt certain that France would seem invincible to the rest of Europe. For this reason Brittany too must be allowed the utmost latitude compatible with the broadest view of French interests. The word "peace," several times repeated, was the last that Beaujeu heard from the king's trembling lips before the royal seals were handed over to the newly appointed regent for transmission to the dauphin. The procession bearing these symbols of sovereignty was followed by the Royal Scottish Guard, the royal huntsmen and even the royal falcons.

Thus stripped of all former dignities and powers the monarch lay motionless and silent for a long time in his bed. At its foot Francesco and a group of priests stood muttering prayers for the dying. Once they heard the king murmur a last invocation to the Virgin: "*Ma bonne maîtresse, aidez-moi.*" Then, quite suddenly, he intoned the Latin text from Psalm LXXI which was inscribed on the wall of the bedchamber. "In thee, O Lord, do I set my trust. Let me never be put to confusion. I shall praise the mercy of my Lord for evermore." He never spoke again.

Louis XI died at eight o'clock in the evening of August 31, 1483. He was just sixty years old. The funeral service was held in St. Martin's Church at Tours. The corpse was buried, by the king's own wish, at the collegiate church of Cléry, where he had been made an honorary canon in 1471. The building stood close to the city of Orléans, was surrounded by meadows and vineyards and overlooked the valley of the Loire. That autumn, as if to mark the close of a glorious reign, the finest grapes yet harvested at Cléry were piled in vast numbers on the laborers' carts.

He was the contemporary prince, Philippe de Commines wrote, of whom most good and least evil could be said. This succinct verdict of course implied the rider "with justice," for malice had been busy with his reputation all his life and continues to be so today. Few commentators have been able to resist the romantic legend, started by Charles the Bold and reported for centuries, of the brooding, predatory "spider." It proliferated at once in the minds of the recklessly ambitious lords, such as Jean d'Armagnac, all of whom he outwitted. They despised and detested a king who looked and dressed, till his last months, like a back-street notary or peasant farmer, who yawned at pageants, cared nothing for dazzling ladies like Agnès Sorel and preferred dry accounts of treaties and the details of commerce to the epics of Charlemagne's time or the exquisite yearnings of love lyrics by Alain Chartier and Charles of Orléans.

In the opinion of the magnates of the fifteenth century a monarch, if he were neither handsome nor martial nor amorous, if he were no glamorous Edward IV or duke of Bourbon, must at least be as mild and accessible as the "*bon roi*" René of Anjou or even Charles VII. The other ruler whom everyone called "good," Philip of Burgundy, though he was no all-conquering soldier, could at any rate act like one.

As for diplomacy and business ability, in both of which fields Louis might be regarded as a supreme expert, Philip had put up a good show in the difficult years of the English dictation to France, both before and after the execution of Joan of Arc. He had left his duchy one of the richest and most respected, even on cultural grounds, in Europe. Above all, the Burgundian yielded to no one in his devotion to the twin chivalrous ideals in his time of love and war, then interpreted, in high society at least, as the courtship of every charming young woman in sight and the promotion of tournaments and vague projects for the conquest of the still dangerous infidels who held Jerusalem. But it was impossible to imagine Louis, at any period of his life, either embracing a famous beauty or presiding over knightly combats. As to the Holy Sepulcher, he told every pope who raised the question of its recovery that he had no time for such an enterprise while his Christian antagonists continued to give him such a lot of trouble.

This excuse was valid enough, obvious to anyone with more common sense that religious fervor in his mentality. But the pretext contributed to Louis's unpopularity with the French aristocracy, which would for the most part have liked nothing better than the transference of their military exploits to Syria rather than the incessant impoverishment of their estates by quarrels with their neighbors. Charles the Bold, however, did not fall into this category. He was bound, as a very conspicuous personification of a fifteenth-century warrior to meet head-on, for years on end, the most notable representative, King Louis, of a new era that tended, in the pursuit of power, to try negotiation before hard knocks. The splendor of Charles's presence, his incisive eloquence and wild daring in battle, masked a neurosis that in the end toppled over, according to his former chamberlain, Philippe de Commines, into first senseless cruelty and obstinacy and finally into madness. Yet even on the fatal fields of Grandson, Morat and Nancy he retained the admiration of many of his contemporaries. They were justified on the whole, after his death, in deciding to call him "the Bold" (*Le Téméraire*) instead of "the savage" or "the crazy," which he only became toward the end of his flamboyant career.

The temptation to turn Louis into the exact opposite of this glittering blusterer could not be withstood by most of the chroniclers of the day. They knew the king to be just as brave and resolute as his adversary. But the majority were Burgundians like Olivier de la Marche and Georges Chastelain or old-fashioned moralists like the Norman Thomas Basin, bishop of Lisieux (1412–1491). Basin could not accuse Louis of debauchery. But in those days eminent men who spent more than half their lives reading and writing in solitude were in general automatically suspected of wickedness unless known to be orthodox theologians.

Since their studies were carried on in secret, they must be dealing with the Devil and perpetrating merciless misdeeds. It was convenient for gentlemen discomfited by the king's cunning schemes to attribute their own failures to a supernatural source of unmitigated and invincible evil rather than to personal gullibility. Even so, the best of these historians and memorialists all acknowledged a certain cool charm and wit, as well as extraordinary firmness of purpose, in their bogeyman. The truly outstanding minds of the period, such men as Lorenzo de' Medici, Francesco Sforza, Juan II of Aragon, the earl of Warwick and Philippe de Commines, understood the king's greatness better. But they were not of course blind to his occasional mistakes, his sudden accesses of undue severity, his fundamental lack of ordinary moral scruple and his nervousness in old age, a mental degeneration caused entirely, however, by ill health.

It was from this last period, when physical decline made the previously acute and jovial Louis sometimes resemble a tyrannical old woman, that the idea of a satanic and ruthless despot, scheming both literally and metaphorically in the dark, took root. A modern student with no melodramatic obsessions, who notes the facts of the king's career and tries to estimate his character from them, can only record a series of peculiarities in which, as Commines maintained, the virtues substantially outweigh the shortcomings. A certain impulsive spontaneity led more often to good results, as during the siege of Paris by Charles the Bold and the meeting with Edward IV at Picquigny, than to bad, as in the temerity that landed a king of France in the Burgundian trap of Péronne. But this sometimes ill-judged precipitation was counterbalanced by the prodigious industry, alert intelligence and cool determination that built up a kingdom finally much more contented at home and deferred-to abroad than the strong duchy of Philip the Good.

The king's political imagination could be excessive, though never so extravagant as that of Philip's son, and his language at times as intemperate as the latter's. Louis's ambition never rested. But it never outran reason. His tricks in war and in negotiation, on the field of Montlhéry as in dealing with Margaret of Anjou, Edward of England and Maximilian of Austria and Flanders, could be compared with those of an incorrigible adventurer. But in the case of King Louis the adventure aimed not at any personal advantage but at the permanent establishment of the glory of his country in the sense of a civilized leadership of Western Europe. This inspiration kept his fertile invention within rational bounds. For the same reason his brain generally functioned calmly in desperate situations, if occasionally it worked, as at Liége, to the detriment of what might be considered his honor. This peculiarly

French idealism, found in several later rulers of that country, from Louis XIV to Charles de Gaulle, also rendered the recuperations of Louis XI after setbacks like his exile in Dauphiné and Burgundy, astonishingly decisive and rapid. Such resilience assured his ultimate victory.

He understood as well as Augustus Caesar the arts of dividing to govern. Like that emperor he never hesitated to embroil his adversaries, to defraud them, to reject pity or to exact vengeance when to be honest or indulgent would have imperiled the stability of his dominions, the essential preliminary condition of their historical permanence. Machiavelli was soon to erect this behavior, on purely logical grounds, into a necessity for a patriotic prince. That Italian statesman and author did not reach France until 1500. But at the court of Louis XII in that year the traditions of administration laid down by Louis XI had not been forgotten. It is certain that they contributed much to the foundations of a political philosophy still irrefutable in its argument if not in its morality.

French ethics in the fifteenth century were based ultimately on a theology providing for punishment or reward after death. They had been less affected, so far, by exclusively humanist considerations than in Italy. Consequently, they did not anywhere, except in the professional Church, attain a very high standard, least of all among politicians. King Louis's contemporaries, lay or ecclesiastical, hardly expected him to imitate his ancestor Saint Louis, an altogether exceptionally respectable sovereign for his day or any other. The chroniclers' righteous indignation in their judgment of their monarch's shifty eye and hard hand boiled up on mainly political grounds. For to most of them, Burgundians, Bretons or Normans, he remained a "foreigner." But even so they would have forgiven him if he had looked more like a model autocrat of the age. The undersized figure, with its thick torso and thin legs, the unfathomable, quizzical, green-gray gaze, pendulous nose and huge chin, suggested of themselves an eccentricity, secretiveness, prying disposition and grim obstinacy distasteful to those in search of a conventionally affable hero. The short doublets of coarse material, the extraordinary hats and the manners resembling a sly yokel's rather than those of a mighty sovereign of ancient lineage, offended a majority of his subjects in all classes. The churchmen acknowledged his punctilious observation of religious duties but looked in vain for true Christian piety. One prelate even dared to advise him to spend his money on poor mortals instead of on magnificent altarpieces and flattering addresses to the saints in heaven, which sounded unpleasantly like bribery for their favors in a secular occupation, especially when he hung images of the blessed on his clothing and stuck them in his peculiar headgear.

But popular kings like Charles VII and Edward IV, though they rivaled Louis as collectors of estates with a view to ensuring their territorial advantages over their wealthiest subjects, could not hold a candle
to him as administrators and organizers. Moreover, they constantly in-
terfered, as he very seldom did after the League of Public Weal revolt, in the management of existent institutions. His taxation exceeded
theirs. But it was not spent prodigally on court luxuries, like Philip's.
On the contrary, the expenditure of public funds was watched as closely
by Louis as by any modern treasury official. Yet he had inherited from
his father financial inflation and devaluation, a rocketing cost of living,
a scarcity of labor and its resultant high wage demands, together with a
chaos of newly rich and newly poor income groups involving all sorts
of exasperating social anomalies.

He studied this appallingly strained situation in detail. He provided
the remedies of increased industrial production, especially of silks at
Tours and Lyons and also of mines. He extended trade along improved
roads at home and in more and better ships overseas. But all these
measures, indispensable if ruined France were to survive the jealousies
of England, Burgundy, the Holy Roman Empire, Italy and Spain, cost
vast sums. The money could only be furnished by Frenchmen themselves. Naturally their grumbles, voiced by nobles, merchants and peasants alike, added to the monarch's unpopularity. For it was not miti-
gated by such lavish entertainments and conquests abroad as enabled,
for instance, even the most oppressive of Italian despots to draw cheers
and gaiety from their populations. But in the end all reasonable inhabitants of France had to admit that their "terrible" king had been
right to fleece them. From being the Cinderella of Europe this part
of it had risen to become, not only in a mercantile sense, its queen.

He had always intended this result, ever since he had first become conscious, in Languedoc, when he was sixteen, of the fatally weak character
of his father. Louis would have been pleased by the magniloquent
verdict, perhaps rather too unqualified, of the *Cambridge Modern History*: "Great he was in intellect and in tenacity of purpose, greater in
prosperity and even greater in misfortune. Whatsoever he did had its
determined end and that end was the greatness of France."

The first of modern historians, the German Leopold von Ranke
(1795–1886), an authority superior to any other of his day in this field,
wrote more soberly: "He was both generous in public and mean in
private life. His covetousness was leavened by a reckless devotion to his
ideals. His ineradicable suspicions, always on the alert, deeply pessi-
mistic, masked the optimism of a grand design, which he did not always work out in terms worthy of it."

Three centuries before Ranke the English chronicler Raphael Holinshed, from whom Shakespeare took the plots of *King Henry* VI and other historical plays, shed a more intimate light, which the dramatist did not use, on Louis XI, who is a cardboard figure in the work just mentioned*. "King Lewis was a man nothing precise in outward shows of honour, oftentimes having neither officers of arms, trumpet in his court, nor other royal appurtenances belonging to the part of a prince, which should be generous and replenished with pomp. . . . he caused a varlet or yeoman to be put in a coat armour of France, which for haste was made of a trumpet banner. . . ."

This incident, referring to an improvised embassy to Edward IV, has already been noted in these pages. But another Elizabethan Englishman, Francis Bacon, equated the French king with two monarchs whom that philosopher considered the best of the European sovereigns who lived into the early sixteenth century, Ferdinand V of Spain and Henry VII of England. Louis was certainly, often enough, more amusing than either of these two rather grave gentlemen. Like other rulers of the period he was fond of astrologers, reminding skeptics that such prophets were not invariably the numbskulls they mostly turned out to be. "Did you never hear," he would ask, "how one of them scored off the super-sophisticated tyrant Dionysius of Syracuse, a fellow somewhat like myself in some ways, except that he wrote tragedies? Well, Dionysius one day inquired of an astrologer who had failed to predict a certain disaster if he knew enough to tell when he personally, the astrologer naturally, not the king, would die. The wily stargazer guessed at once that if he set the date a long way ahead Dionysius, just to prove him a liar, would have him executed there and then. So he retorted, cool as a cucumber: 'Of course I know when I shall die, most mighty lord. It will be exactly twenty-four hours before you do.' Needless to say, the horoscope caster lived to a good old age."

On the other hand the king told one of the fraternity, who had unsuccessfully prophesied fine weather, that he was worse than any donkey. For whenever those much despised beasts scratch themselves and shake their ears everyone knows for certain that it is going to rain.

Like many men of outstanding capacity, lofty aims and solitary habits, King Louis XI preferred a jesting tone when discussing even serious matters. He generally meant what he said. But whether he did or not

---

* It is well known that the three parts of *King Henry* VI, written between 1590 and 1592 and owing much to playwrights other than Shakespeare, who was then in his later twenties, offer a telescoped and travestied version of history designed rather to please the riotous patriotism of the London mob under Queen Elizabeth than such serious students as even then existed of the political events of 1429–1471.—J.C.

it might well be useful later on to be able to dismiss his communications on any given occasion as frivolous. For if they succeeded in their purpose, which usually disconcerted somebody, that person would respect the king more than ever for so apparently casual a victory, while if they failed the adversary could always be laughed at for inability to see a joke. In a word, Louis outplayed, by and large, the wiseacres of his time in the game of practical politics. Lorenzo de' Medici was the only contemporary statesman who could have decisively won a round against him. But their respective ambitions never clashed. If they had, it is likely that each would have retreated, recognizing an invincible antagonist. As it was, they resembled each other too closely ever to think of quarreling.

The French sovereign, the only North European aristocrat of any political standing who saw clearly that the days of fighting noblemen as builders and rulers of nations were gone forever, may fairly be argued to have changed the whole face of the Continent's civilization by this one feat, bringing in its train the cultural revolution of the Renaissance, until his time only tentatively heralded among the artists and philosophers centered upon Florence. His methods of forcing his vision down the throats of the conservative establishment were sometimes deplorable. They included false promises, cynical betrayals, indifference to the suffering of others and the employment of scoundrels like Olivier le Dain, though never murderers, to gain ends that could not be acknowledged as his own without dishonor. People whom he instinctively disliked, the cowardly voluptuary Francis of Brittany for example, but especially women, from the harmless bluestocking Margaret Stuart, his first wife, to the brilliant Agnès Sorel and the vindictive Margaret of Anjou, the ultimately dethroned queen of England, he persecuted relentlessly, if with carefully calculated intervals of indulgence.

All these misdeeds were common form among the political leaders of fifteenth-century society as in modern times. It had been discovered long before the Christian era that it was impossible to govern or even influence men in the mass, with the best of intentions, by behaving with consistent frankness and generosity. Nor did the advent of Christian theory make any difference. The popes and prelates found themselves obliged to keep public order in the same way as secular princes. The priests talked more than the untonsured lords. As time went on they appeared less and less on the field of battle. But under Louis cardinals like Jean Balue and Giuliano della Rovere (who spent much time in France) could hardly be distinguished, except outwardly and audibly, from the dukes and counts in Burgundy or Armagnac who regularly dealt with them.

The object of all these people, however, almost without exception, was personal aggrandizement. They hoped, at bottom, simply to see themselves enriched, feared and flattered like so many petty tribal chiefs. Louis also aimed at this result, but only for the sake of the security and prosperity of France, an abstraction this essentially cold man truly loved, to the exclusion of any human being. For he did not even love himself. He merely believed, quite rightly, that his own intelligence alone, since he had repeatedly proved it superior to that of any of his compatriots, could build the unassailable glory of a land he considered unparalleled in the wealth of its natural resources and the audacity and ingenuity of its professional, mercantile and laboring inhabitants, once they were freed from the unconscionable turbulence and rapacity of the great families.

He achieved his purpose. His successor, the imbecile Charles VIII, could not disturb the foundations upon which Louis had erected a new France. Louis XII, for all his warmongering, like that of his predecessor, in Italy, really owed his title of "Father of the People" to the system that Louis XI had put into operation. It nearly enabled the next king of France, the attractive but unstable Francis I, to dispose of his most dangerous rival, the Emperor Charles V. Even the feeble French kings Henri II, Francis II and Charles IX, who followed Francis I, only failed to preserve their country's grandeur on account of a nonpolitical force, the Reformation, which Louis XI could not have anticipated. At last only Richelieu, who in many respects resembled Louis XI, could revive the "grand design" conceived by that monarch a century before and pave the way for the great climax of French civilization under Louis XIV.

The eleventh Louis, like the seventeenth-century cardinal, has suffered much posthumously from the malicious ingenuities of novelists, from Sir Walter Scott to Alfred Neumann, as Richelieu did in *The Three Musketeers* by the elder Alexandre Dumas (1802–1870) and quite recently in *The Devils of Loudun* by Aldous Huxley. The aims of both king and prelate were identical, their methods equally tortuous. Consequently, by an amusing irony, the crimes of which they have been so exuberantly accused by romantic authors are essentially similar to those often alleged by the culprits in question against their own political enemies. Again, the personal charm of both men arose from the ease with which they controlled, unlike most of their adversaries, their instinctive passions. This circumstance explains, through its purely intellectual basis, the failure of these two great patriots to attract outstanding women.

An impartial student of the reign and personality of Louis XI must conclude that the verdict of the *Cambridge Modern History* quoted above expressed the basic truth. Louis was a great man, though his intellect lacked the saving grace of cultural inspiration and any genuine warmth of temperament, for which he substituted the mask of a dry, sharp humor. But an iceberg, with its soaring pinnacles, occasionally gleaming surfaces and mysteriously deep foundations, may fascinate an observer as much as any charmingly sunlit landscape.

SELECT BIBLIOGRAPHY

Die Fürstinnen des Hauses Burgund-Österreich. E. J. H. von Münch. Leipzig, 1832.
Jacques Coeur et Charles VII. P. Clément. Paris, 1853.
History of Charles the Bold. J. F. Kirk. Philadelphia, 1864.
Le Roi René. R. A. Lecoy de la Marche. Paris, 1875.
Choix de Chroniques et Mémoires sur l'Histoire de France. Ed. J. A. C. Buchon. Paris, 1876.
Lettres de Louis XI. Ed. Vaessen. Paris, 1883–1909.
Louis XI. J. Zeller. Paris, 1884.
Lettres de Louis XI. Ed. F. Pasquier. Paris, 1895.
Louis Dauphin. F. Pasquier. Paris, 1895.
La Jeunesse de Louis XI. M. Thibault. Paris, 1907.
The Life of Louis XI. C. Hare. London, 1907.
Le Comte de Hollande. V. R. S. van Marle. The Hague, 1908.
Geschichte der Herzöge Burgunds. O. Cartellieri. Leipzig, 1910.
Maximilian the Dreamer. C. Hare. London, 1913.
Louis XI and Charles the Bold. A. C. P. Haggard. London, 1913.
Margaret of Scotland. L. A. Barbé. London, 1917.
The Life and Reign of Edward IV. C. L. Scofield. New York, 1923.
Mémoires de Philippe de Commynes. Ed. J. L. A. Calmette. Paris, 1924–1925.
Louis XI. O. W. Mosher. Toulouse, 1925.
Jacques Coeur. A. B. Kerr. New York, 1927.
Louis XI. P. Champion. Paris, 1927.
La Dauphine. P. Champion. Paris, 1927.
Un Financier Colonial. R. Bouvier. Paris, 1928.
Die Darstellung des Persönlichkeit Ludwigs XI. W. Dehne. Erlangen, 1929.
King Spider. D. B. Wyndham Lewis. London, 1930.
La Politica Italiana di Luigi XI. R. Cerioni. Milan, 1930.
La Dame de Beauté. P. Champion. Paris, 1931.
Louis XI. A de Montgon. Paris, 1936.
Louis XI. A. Bailly. Paris, 1936.
Le Roi Louis XI. P. Champion. Paris, 1936.
Louis XI. J. L. A. Calmette. Paris, 1936.
Le Grand Règne de Louis XI. J. L. A. Calmette. Paris, 1938.
Philippe le Bon. C. Gaspar et F. Lyna. Brussels, 1944.
Autour de Louis XI. J. L. A. Calmette. Paris, 1947.
Les Grands Ducs de Bourgogne. J. L. A. Calmette. Paris, 1949.
Jacques Coeur. H. de Man. Bern, 1950.
Gli Sforza. G. Nicodemi. Milan, 1951.

Die Ursprünge der Französich-Mailandischen Allianz von 1463. K. Bittmann. Wiesbaden, 1952.
Les Affaires de Jacques Coeur. J. Dauvet. Paris, 1952.
La Vie du Bon Roi René. J. Levron. Paris, 1933.
Philippe le Bon. P. Bonenfant. Brussels, 1955.
Histoire de Louis XI. T. Basin. Ed. A. C. P. Haggard. London, 1963.
Ludwig XI und Karl der Kühne. K. Bittmann. Göttingen, 1964.
Panorama des XIVe et XVe Siècles Français. A.-M. Schmidt. Paris, 1964.
The Waning of the Middle Ages. J. Huizinga. London, 1965.
The Ages of Plantagenet and Valois. K. A. Fowler. London, 1967.

Index

Abbeville, 64, 153
Accession, 136ff., 145ff., 284
Administration, 94, 257, 297
Adultery, 79, 84, 88
Africa, 168; North, 280, 291
Aggression, 174; excuse for, 219; papal, 248
Agincourt, battle of, 12, 13, 41, 42, 47, 140, 271, 281
Albi, 38, 41
Albret, Sire d', 41
Alexander of Bourbon, 61
Alfonso, King of Naples, 100–1, 175
Alfonso V, King of Portugal, 252
Alsace, 75, 77
Amadeus VIII, Duke of Savoy, 26, 100, 109, 110
Amadeus VIII, Pope, 73
Amadeus IX, Duke of Savoy, 26, 100
Ambassadors, 168–89, 177–78, 198–99, 234, 237, 249–50, 277, 286
Amiens, 64, 78, 153, 165
Anarchy, 53, 141, 173
Angers, 164; riots, 182
Angevin cause, 175
Anglo-Burgundian alliance, 13–14, 15, 32, 45, 61–62, 68, 156, 196, 198ff., 207ff., 216, 218ff., 230, 235, 273; Brittany, 183, 270
Anglo-French *entente cordiale*, 251–52
Anglophiles, 159, 160, 163, 181, 211, 239. *See under* name
Animals, 45–46, 63, 277, 291
Anjou, 69; house of, 175; inheritance, 279–80
Anne (daughter of Edward IV), 275
Anne (daughter of Louis XI), 130, 196, 284, 289; betrothal, 193
Anne of Brittany (wife of Charles VIII), 270, 290
Anne de France (daughter of Charolais), 160
Anne of Savoy, 100, 101, 109, 116, 117, 118
Anne of Warwick, 208
Aquitaine, English claims to, 196
Aragon, 68; France, 166–69, 171, 175; rebellion, 205–6
Aragon, King of, 164–67
Archelles, M. d', 106
Aristocracy, 37, 39, 42, 66, 105, 154, 249; affectations, 274; army, 52; arrogance, 40, 177; Burgundy, 129; characteristics, 42–46;

Charles VII, 54; Church, 179–80; diversions, 45–46; France, 53; Louis XI, 52–58, 119, 158–61, 179ff., 192, 295, 300; loyalties, 27, 29; monarchy, 30, 48, 63; power loss, 182–83; rebellion, 52ff., 107, 141, 177ff., 183, 239–40; as rulers, 217; women, 49–50
Aristotle, 48, 148
Armagnac, 12, 13, 45
Armor, 23, 33, 47
Army, 95; Charles the Bold, 224ff.; Charles VII, 52–53, 54, 55, 107–8, 141–42; development, 281; French, 12, 39, 253–54, 263–64, 270–72, 281; funds for, 150; "lance," 149–50; longbowmen, 271; Louis XI, 106, 172–73, 189–90, 193, 197, 200; Philip, 145, 149–50; size, 72, 150; Spanish, 168; Swiss, 74, 224–26, 229–31
Arthur, King, 42
Arts, 30–31; patronage, 48
Astrology, 264, 283, 299
Augustus, Emperor, 114, 297
Austria, 73, 95, 206, 225, 226, 236; England, 238, 239; France, 238
Authority, 267; administration of, 44–45; base, 106 (*see also* Government); Louis XI, 35–39, 63–64, 66, 286, 287; sovereign, 268
Autocracy, 66, 86, 134, 149, 241, 246–47, 261, 297; Louis XI, 142; Spain, 102
Avesnes, 145, 149, 150
Avignon, 267, 268

Bacon, Francis, 299
Bajazet II, Sultan, 292
Balance of power, 69, 112–13, 211–12
Balue, Cardinal Jean, 184, 198–99, 200, 214, 262, 279, 300; death, 265–66
Barcelona, 166, 168, 169, 174, 176; siege, 167
Basel, 73–75; assembly, 179
Basin, Thomas, 97, 112, 295
Bastard of Bourbon, 39, 40, 231, 232
Bastard of Orléans, 25, 54, 141. *See* Jean, Count of Dunois
Bastards, 181; royal, 112, 124
Beaujean, Pierre de, 293–94
Beaumont, Jean de, 125
Beauvais, 214–15